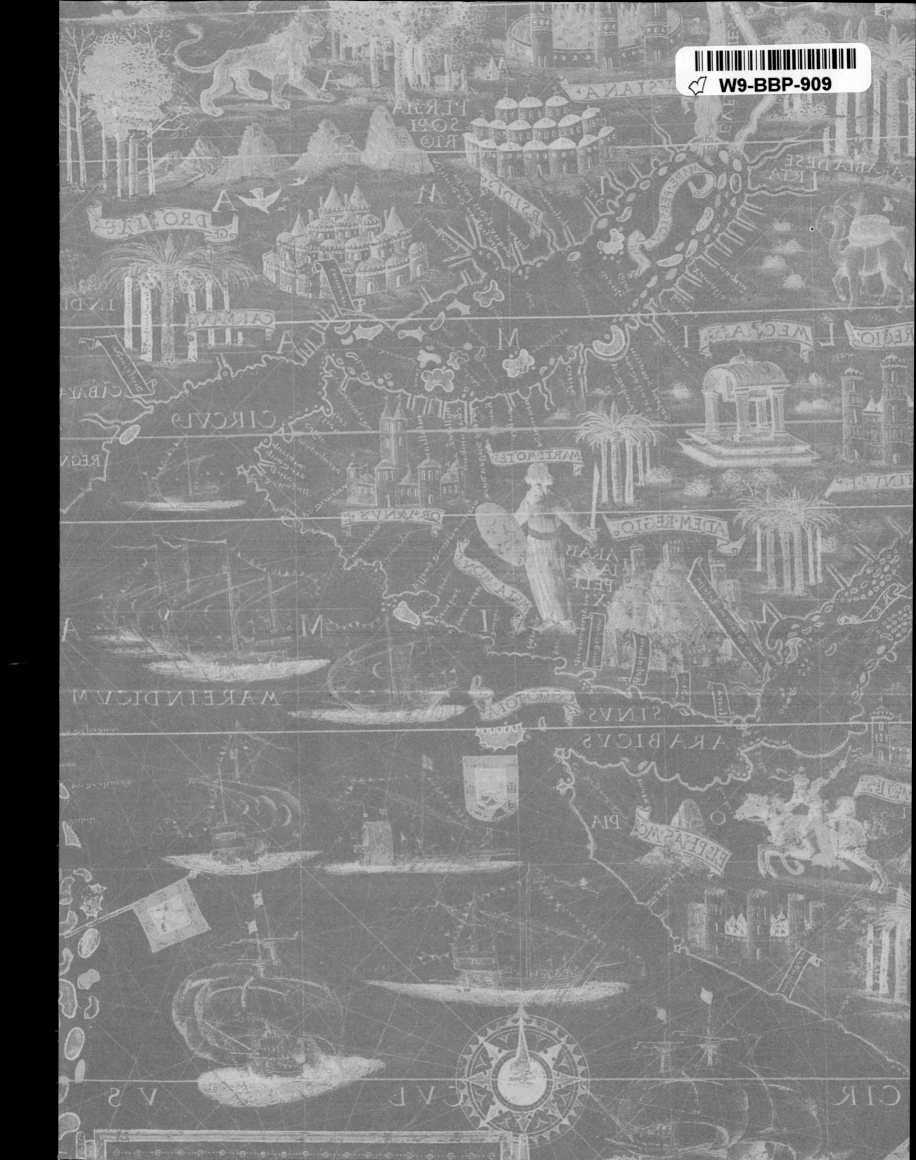

ATLAS OF EXPLORATION

SECOND EDITION

ATLAS OF EXPLORATION

FOREWORD BY JOHN HEMMING
DIRECTOR AND SECRETARY OF THE ROYAL GEOGRAPHICAL SOCIETY
(1975–1996)

SECOND EDITION

CONTENTS

Cartography Philip's

Contributors
EARLY EXPLORATION
Dr Mark Greengrass

ASIA
David Mountfield

AFRICA
Dorothy Middleton

CENTRAL AND SOUTH AMERICA
Sir John Ure

NORTH AMERICA
Dr Selma Huxley Barkham
Dr Alan G. Macpherson
James Steele

THE PACIFIC, AUSTRALIA, AND NEW ZEALAND
David Mountfield

THE ARCTIC
Dr Anita McConnell

THE ANTARCTIC
Ann Savours

OCEANOGRAPHY
Dr Anita McConnell

EXPLORATION TODAY
Shane Winser
Tim Furniss (Space Exploration)

Copyright © 1996, 2006, 2008 Philip's

Philip's, a division of
Octopus Publishing Group Limited,
2–4 Heron Quays, London E14 4JP
An Hachette Livre UK Company

Published in North America by
Oxford University Press, Inc.,
198 Madison Avenue,
New York, N.Y. 10016

www.oup.com/us/atlas

OXFORD
UNIVERSITY PRESS
Oxford is a registered trademark
of Oxford University Press

Library of Congress Cataloging-in-Publication Data available

ISBN 978–0–19–534318–2

Printing (last digit):
9 8 7 6 5 4 3 2 1

Printed in Hong Kong

Half-title page: Willem Barents's
expedition beset by ice in the
Arctic, 1596.

Opposite title page: Africa,
Arabia and India: extract from
the Miller Atlas of c.1519.

Opposite Foreword:
The Tibetan Plateau and
Mt Gungar in Northwest China.

FOREWORD

Humans are highly mobile creatures, migrating and traveling to every part of the world. In this we are not unique, for other creatures cover amazing distances and share our curiosity. What sets us apart is our ability to communicate our discoveries to others and to develop a collective awareness of the known world. In any society it is the adventurous people who set out to discover what lies beyond this known world who are the explorers.

Motives for exploration have changed over the centuries. Prehistoric people performed prodigious feats of discovery and movement, penetrating most of the habitable parts of the world as they followed the animals they hunted. They moved from Africa across Europe and Asia, reaching Australia about 50,000 years ago. From Siberia they migrated, about 14,000 years ago, across the Ice Age land bridge to Alaska, and then moved southward with astonishing speed, arriving at the southern tip of South America in barely 1000 years.

It was not, however, until the development of the earliest civilizations in the 4th millennium BC that people began to write about exploration. References to it can be found in Ancient Egyptian hieroglyphics, and many detailed accounts of explorers' journeys have survived from the civilizations of Classical Greece and Rome. Such accounts contributed to the enduring vision of the world created by the Greek geographer Ptolemy in the 2nd century AD which was to have an enormous impact on explorers in Europe. It would, for example, confirm Christopher Columbus in his belief that Asia could be reached by traveling westward across the Atlantic. Yet for almost a thousand years after the collapse of the Roman Empire in the 5th century AD, the finest explorers and cartographers were the Chinese and Arabs. Their maps outshone those of their counterparts in Europe, where the discoveries of ancient geographers were being suppressed by the Church.

For Europeans, the great age of exploration began in the 15th century AD when scholars rediscovered the works of Greek and Latin geographers. Remote lands began to be explored with the declared purpose of spreading Christianity, but the main motive was financial gain. The Portuguese made their way down the west coast of Africa and eventually around the Cape of Good Hope in search of a sea route to the spices of India. When four of Vasco da Gama's ships made the first return journey from India to Portugal in 1498, their cargo of pepper, ginger, cinnamon, and cloves was worth a fortune.

Such profit inspired Cabral's fleet of 13 ships that sailed from Lisbon in 1500 and accidentally discovered Brazil on its way to India. Similarly, Columbus set off westward across the Atlantic in the hope of reaching the rich empires of China and Japan. In later decades, it was the lure of gold that spurred on Cortés, Pizarro, and other conquerors in Mexico and Peru; and the search for a trade route to the Orient took Magellan around the tip of South America.

It was only in the 17th century that explorers started to venture forth for nobler motives. Some went purely for love of travel; others to satisfy scientific curiosity. James Cook, perhaps the greatest explorer of all, returned to England from his first circumnavigation in 1771. He had observed an eclipse of the sun on Tahiti, made brilliant charts of both islands of New Zealand, explored the fertile east coast of Australia and the Barrier Reef, and brought home a shipload of new botanical and zoological finds, but modestly wrote that "the discoveries made on this voyage are not great." On his second voyage, he sailed further south than any previous explorer and entered the Antarctic pack-ice. He laid to rest the notion of a habitable southern continent.

The 19th century saw a flowering of scientific exploration. All over the world, scientists tackled virgin fields of discovery. They began to classify plants, animals, and insects by the systems devised by the Swedish naturalist Carl Linné, and their investigations led inevitably to the elaboration of the theory of evolution by natural selection. Others explored in pursuit of archeology, geology, anthropology, ethnology, paleontology, or a host of other new natural sciences. The most famous explorers were the geographers who "filled in the blanks on the map," particularly in the mountains of central Asia, the deserts of central Australia, the approaches to the Poles, and the heart of Africa. Most of these great explorers were disinterested seekers after knowledge, but some acted on behalf of their governments as part of the colonial scramble for control over lands outside Europe, or were driven by thirst for fame or by national pride.

Today the main motive for exploration is the expansion of our knowledge and understanding of the world – something that is happening at an accelerating rate in every discipline all over the world. We are living in a golden age of scientific discovery, a time when vastly improved means of transport are opening every part of the earth, the oceans, and even space to people's eyes, and when more sophisticated instruments are enabling us to probe and analyse all the secrets of our planet.

Throughout history all great explorers, whatever their motives, have demonstrated bravery and endurance as they have ventured into the hidden recesses of our world, to the summits of almost all the major mountains, into labyrinths of cave passages, down raging white-water rivers, into the canopy of the rain forests, and amid fabulous reefs beneath the oceans. It is these qualities of bravery and endurance that excite our admiration for their achievements and make the accounts of their journeys featured in this atlas so immensely readable.

JOHN HEMMING

DIRECTOR AND SECRETARY OF THE ROYAL GEOGRAPHICAL SOCIETY (1975–1996)

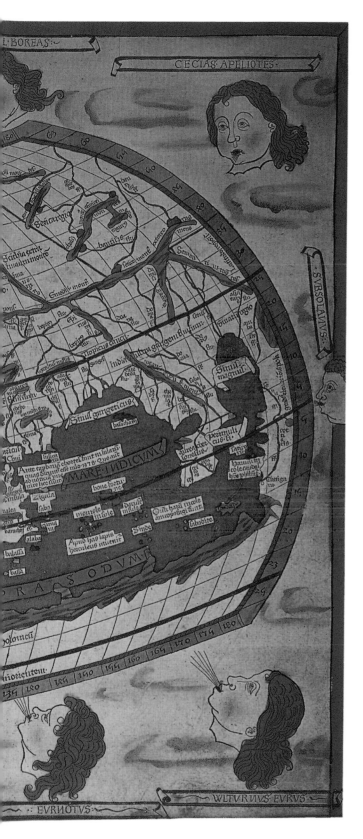

EARLY
EXPLORATION

The underlying theme of world history, from the formation of complex human societies to the present day, is the gradual evolution of one global civilization from what were once several distinctive, independent civilizations. The history of exploration has played an important part in this process, for its pioneers have pointed the way, albeit often unconsciously, toward the breaking down of barriers between civilizations in different continents of the world.

The earliest civilizations were to be found in the valleys of the rivers Tigris and Euphrates in Mesopotamia (Iraq), the Nile in Egypt and the Indus in modern Pakistan, where agriculture became more intensive in the 4th millennium BC and the dispersed human settlements of pastoral nomadism developed into more complex societies in what has been called "the urban revolution." There is evidence, in the form of pottery and metalwork, of contact between these early civilizations, and of the migration of people between them. However, it is only in the hieroglyphs of Egypt that archaeologists have found the first written references to exploration, and it is only in the later alphabetic languages, such as Greek and Latin, that detailed accounts of the journeys of explorers in Europe, Asia and Africa have been found. This section on early exploration is largely based on these written accounts.

Preserving the traditions of exploration in written form contributed to a civilization's vision of the world and reinforced its sense of identity. One of the most enduring of such mental pictures in the West was that created by the Greek geographer Ptolemy in the 2nd century AD. His famous *Guide to Geography* included information on how to construct maps and gazetteers for the lands of the major ancient civilizations in Europe, Africa, and Asia, with places accorded their latitude and longitude. As a guide to world geography, it left much to be desired, but it had an enormous impact on later generations in the West. Beautiful, late-medieval maps were based on Ptolemy's vision (such as the one opposite, which is a woodcut from a 1486 edition of his *Geography*), as was the world's first printed engraved atlas, used by Christopher Columbus to confirm his belief that Asia could readily be reached by traveling westward across the Atlantic.

The First Civilizations

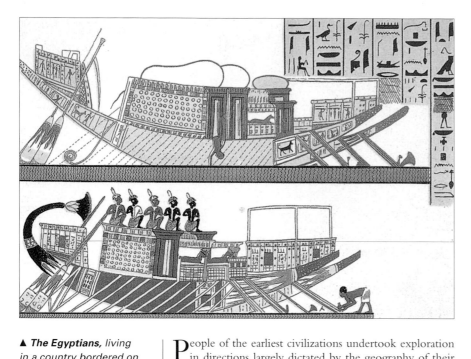

▲ **The Egyptians,** living in a country bordered on two sides by water and bisected by the Nile, used their maritime skills in the course of exploration. They built ships of cedarwood, which they probably imported from what is now the Lebanon.

People of the earliest civilizations undertook exploration in directions largely dictated by the geography of their immediate surroundings and the technology available to them. What, for example, was more inevitable than that Egyptians should explore up the Nile and travel along the western coastline of the Red Sea from Suez down to what is now Eritrea and Somalia? The river was central to their civilization, both in terms of its practical uses and its symbolic function – the Nile had almost the status of a deity – and the civilization had developed efficient sailing ships.

It was from the Nubian kingdoms of the upper Nile and the Horn of Africa that the products most highly valued by the Egyptians for use in their temples came – incense, ebony, panther skins, gold, ivory and, to a large extent also, slaves. Early exploration was partly motivated by the desire of the rulers to control supplies of these precious commodities.

Harkhuf

The Egyptian nobleman Harkhuf, who lived around 2300 BC, has some claim to be called "the first known explorer." He led several expeditions up the Nile, beyond the First Cataract to the land of Yam (southern Nubia).

Harkhuf's tomb at Elephantine (Aswan) carries an inscription in which he proudly recorded his explorations for posterity. He was sent by the king, he said, "to explore a road…" to Yam. After seven months he returned, "bringing all kinds of gifts," for which "he was greatly praised." From his third expedition he came back "with 300 asses, laden with incense, ebony, heknu, grain, panthers, ivory, throw-sticks and every good product. I was more excellent and vigilant than any count, companion, or caravan conductor who had been sent to Yam before."

On his last expedition, undertaken for the succeeding ruler, King Pyopi, he returned with "a dancing dwarf of the gods from the land of spirits." Its appearance created such interest that Harkhuf was instructed to escort the dwarf personally on the 500-mile (800-kilometer) journey down the Nile to Memphis because the king "desires to see this dwarf more than all the gifts of Sinai and of Punt."

Close by Harkhuf's tomb is that of another explorer of the same period, Pyopi-nakht. This "royal companion, ritual priest, leader of caravans, bringing the products of foreign lands to his lord," also recounted in his funerary inscription his exploits beyond the First Cataract into

Nubian territory. In this case, though, he had been sent to pacify or, if necessary, to subdue by force of arms, its dissident tribes and semisavage people. Another passage hints at the more extensive voyaging which he undertook down the coast of the Red Sea to recover "the body of his royal companion, the captain of ships, the caravan-leader, Anankht," who had been slain by Nubian tribesmen while building a ship for a voyage to Punt.

The Egyptian sources are not specific as to where exactly Punt (also known as Pwnt – "The Sacred") was. It must have been south of the great desert belt that stretches from the Persian Gulf across Arabia and northern Africa. Reputedly fertile, it was where the Egyptians found supplies of the precious myrrh and frankincense that they burnt in their temples and used both as a perfume and an embalming agent. So Punt should perhaps be equated with somewhere along the southern shore of the Gulf of Aden, or perhaps with the Somali coast of Africa.

Exploration under Queen Hatshepsut

The most remarkable evidence we have for the land of Punt, and for Egyptian exploration in general, comes from the huge mortuary temple for Queen Hatshepsut (reigned 1501–1479 BC), the only woman ever to rule the land of the pharaohs with the full title of queen. The monument still survives at Deir el-Bahri, across the River Nile from the modern city of Luxor. Although defaced by the vengeance of her brother after her death, as well as by the ravages of time, the magnificent pictorial frieze on the temple walls was doubtless intended by its patron as the best way to

▶ **The Great Wall of China** marked the northern boundary of the Chinese civilization. The first construction took place at the end of the 3rd century BC, although much of what can be seen today dates from the Ming dynasty (1368–1644). The wall is over 1400 miles (2240 kilometers) long, averages over 20 feet (6 meters) in height and has a central walkway nearly 13 feet (4 meters) wide.

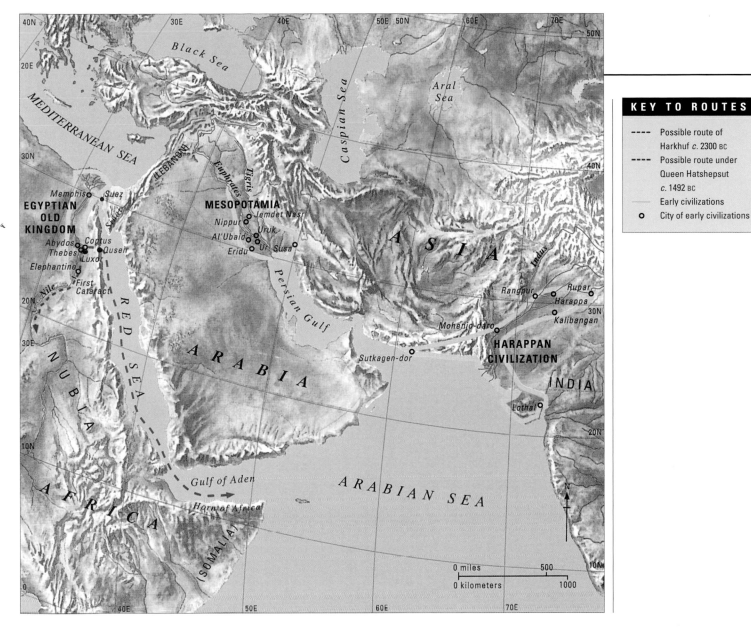

- - - - Possible route of
Harkhuf *c.* 2300 BC
- - - - Possible route under
Queen Hatshepsut
c. 1492 BC
——— Early civilizations
○ City of early civilizations

immortalize herself and the achievements of her reign. To us, it is the first dramatic record of exploration as a great human endeavor.

In a frieze consisting of ten pictorial scenes with accompanying hieroglyphic inscriptions, an expedition to the land of Punt, undertaken at her instigation in around 1492 BC, is recorded in great detail. The expedition would have involved crossing the 150 miles (250 kilometers) of desert from the Nile to the shores of the Red Sea and then rowing and sailing some 1500 miles (2500 kilometers) toward the Arabian Sea. The second scene records the arrival of the fleet in Punt, laden with merchandise for trading. A later scene in the frieze shows the fleet arriving back in Thebes. Some historians have surmised that this scene provides evidence for a Nile–Suez canal; for them, it is difficult to imagine the cargoes (which included myrrh trees in pots) being transported from the Red Sea to the Nile by caravan (a trek of some five days from Quseir on the Red Sea to Coptos on the Nile).

The mental boundaries of civilizations

Exploration was one of the ways in which ancient civilizations adapted in order to survive, but their capacity for adaptation should not be overestimated. These traditional societies had two distinct classes within them: a tiny, literate and controling elite, and an illiterate, servile majority who lay imprisoned within a parochial folk culture which separated village from village and region from region along the multiple divides of kinship, dialect, and attachment to the soil. As a consequence they did not welcome change,

▶ *The African chieftain of Punt is depicted in this detail from the frieze decorating the huge mortuary temple of Queen Hatshepsut. He is accompanied by his wife (whose size obviously made an impression on those who saw her).*

and explorers therefore tended not to be of humble origins. Even the literate minority must often have regarded exploration with some suspicion.

Each of the major civilizations developed profound concepts of its geographical and cultural limits. For the Egyptians, the First Cataract of the Nile was as important a mental divide between civilization and the unknown as it was a physical barrier. For the Persian Empire under Darius III, just as for the Greek troops of Alexander the Great, the Indus River in the 4th century BC formed a great mental, as well as natural, boundary. The Strait of Gibraltar became, for the Greeks, the Pillars of Hercules, marking the limits of the known and civilized world, beyond which not even Hercules had ventured. For the Chinese Empire, the equivalent geographical point was reached at the Jade Gates in the province of Xinjiang, where the Great Wall guarding the celestial kingdom, constructed in its primitive form for the first time by the Ch'in dynasty in around 221–206 BC, came to an end.

The Phoenicians and Greeks

In ancient literature, trade was generally despised, to be carried on, if possible, by "outsiders" to the established civilization. In the greatest trading sea of the ancient world, the Mediterranean, the outsiders were considered to be the Phoenicians and the Greeks. Their role in exploration was an exceptional one.

The Phoenicians

The first Phoenician trading colonies grew outward from the great Phoenician cities of the ancient world – above all, the mainland city of Tyre. In the 9th century BC, however, the Assyrians took the Phoenician cities one by one and the inhabitants were driven outward to found coastal colonies, generally as minority populations in previously existing civilizations. From here they traded the attractions of civilized living in return for raw materials, especially metals. This led them to establish colonies at Massalia (Marseilles) for the overland route for tin from northern Europe, at Gades (Cádiz) in Spain, close by rich copper deposits and on the coast of northern Africa – above all at Carthage (Tunis) – for gold, traded across the Sahara. But,

in a pattern to be repeated in the 15th century, it was logical for the Phoenicians to go directly to the source of supply. This is presumably the motive of Himilco, who was probably told to discover the so-called "Tin Islands" (the Isles of Scilly or St Michael's Mount) where tin was traded. The only surviving account of his voyage in the 5th century BC is in a book known as the *Ora Maritima of Avienus*, written about 800 years later. If that source is to be believed, Himilco took four months to reach the coast of Brittany, finding giant "sea monsters" and great beds of seaweed on the way.

Attempted circumnavigation of Africa

It is possible that an attempt to circumnavigate the coast of Africa was initiated, around the year 600 BC, by Necho, the reigning Pharaoh of Egypt, who issued a decree that a fleet should be equipped for such a voyage, using a Phoenician crew and captain. We only have the somewhat sceptical account of the Greek historian Herodotus to go on, and he had heard it from his countrymen on the Nile when he visited Naucratis. Herodotus recorded, with

KEY TO ROUTES

---- Approximate route of
Scylax 6th century BC

---- Approximate route of
Himilco 5th century BC

---- Approximate route of
Pytheas 340 BC

---- Approximate route of
Eudoxus 146 BC

o City BC

considerable scrupulousness, the accounts that he heard on his own travels in the 5th century BC and he is the most important source of reference for ancient exploration.

The Greeks

From the 7th century BC the Greeks colonized from the Aegean outward along and beyond the northern Mediterranean. Miletus, on the Aegean shore, was the base for expeditions through the Hellespont and Bosphorus to the Black Sea. Greek traders went far across the Black Sea to Georgia and the Caspian, possibly reaching deep into Russia as well. To the west they came up against Phoenician control of the Strait of Gibraltar. However, seizing the advantage created by a brief collapse in Carthaginian power in 340 BC, Pytheas of Massalia led an expedition on behalf of the trading community there through the strait and northward beyond the Breton coast to the British Isles and the sources of tin.

Pytheas was a geographer and accomplished astronomer who was not afraid of tackling complex problems. He had attempted to work out the position of true north, postulated the alternation of the tides with the phases of the moon and invented an accurate method of determining latitude with a calibrated sundial. Although the report of his celebrated voyage of reconnaissance no longer exists, a considerable amount is known about it from other sources.

He followed the route of Himilco to the west coast of Brittany and then proceeded to find the British Isles. His first view of Albion (Britain) was of Land's End in Belerium (Cornwall), where he found the natives "hospitable," "thanks to their trading contacts with foreign traders" and, sailing on round Britain, Pytheas noted the local customs of the inhabitants.

Marveling at the high seas "above Britain" he then set out on a six-day crossing to reach "Thule," which has subsequently been variously identified with Iceland, the Norwegian coast, the Faeroe Islands, and (most plausibly) the Shetlands. From there, he may have visited Ireland before returning to the continental coast in order to find the "Amber Island" and complete his assignment.

Like the Phoenicians, the Greeks were not above placing their skills in the service of great foreign rulers. Toward the end of the 6th century BC, Scylax, a Greek from Asia Minor, set out at the behest of Darius I, the Persian king, to investigate the course of the Indus River. He probably traveled through the Persian Empire and reached the Indus by way of the Kabul River, sailing down to its mouth on the Indian Ocean. He then sailed along the bleak Baluchistan coast, across the Gulf of Oman and along the southern coast of Arabia before returning by the Red Sea with good first-hand information about the Indian Ocean and colorful reports of strange one-eyed men to be found in India and men whose ears were fern-shaped and as big as baskets.

Eudoxus of Cyzicus

No exploration is without danger. The most enterprising and daring of the ancient explorers was the Greek Eudoxus of Cyzicus and his endeavors appear to have cost his life and those of his crew. Eudoxus was initially commissioned in c. 146 BC by Euergetes II, ruler of Egypt, to undertake a voyage to India. He was guided to India by an Indian pilot and returned with a cargo of spices and precious stones which were promptly seized as treasure trove under Ptolemaic law.

A second expedition took place, this time under the sponsorship of Cleopatra. Returning from India, however, Eudoxus's ship was driven ashore below Cape Guardafui (the Cape of Spices). The native inhabitants treated him well and it was here that he found, floating in the sea, the prow of a wooden ship with a horse carved on it. When he returned to Carthage, he learned that this was identical to the figureheads of ships to be found plying the Atlantic waters off Morocco and Cádiz. The flotsam was conclusive evidence of the sea route round the coast of Africa.

Eudoxus's last voyage was a rare example of a free-enterprise expedition in the ancient world. He had been forced to surrender his second Indian cargo to Cleopatra, so he built and equipped two further expeditions from his own resources, stocking them with gifts as well as colonizing tools. The first expedition ran aground off the coast of Morocco; the second expedition never returned.

▼ **Phoenician ships** underwent a technical revolution in design, with the long keel strengthened by a rope running fore and aft. This enabled the Phoenicians to build strong merchant ships out of cedarwood. These were equipped with a single rectangular sail, but also propeled by oar. For exploration, however, both the Phoenicians and the Greeks used their famous penteconters, which were small galleys, rowed by 50 men.

▲ *The Temple of Bacchus in Lebanon was just one of the many magnificent monuments built by the Greeks in the lands around the Mediterranean, which they explored and colonized from the 7th century BC.*

Alexander the Great

The empires of the ancient world were gradually pieced together around 500–300 BC. The most outstanding was that of Alexander the Great, whose conquests transformed the Greek world in the 4th century BC.

Alexander (who inherited the Macedonian throne at the age of 20 in 336 BC) had been Aristotle's pupil and

from him had acquired an appreciation of the value of knowledge as power. He understood the importance of scientific observation and he was well read in the Homeric legends, whose archaic voyages and conquests he aspired to emulate. Attached to his army were a number of geographers, astronomers, mathematicians, botanists, and engineers. Bematistae, or human pedometers, counted out the length of each day's march to assist the geographers in compiling their records.

His expeditions were concentrated into 11 years of military campaigning. Early in 334 BC he left the Macedonian capital, Pella, with up to 40,000 infantry and 5000 cavalry, marched through Asia Minor (Turkey) subduing local tribes and fought the Persian King Darius at the Battle of Issus. He then laid siege to the island fortress city of Tyre and captured the fleet of the Persian Empire.

Moving south, he met no further resistance except at Gaza. Instead, he was welcomed at the city of Memphis, where he was crowned pharaoh in November 332 BC. In the spring of 331 BC he founded the first of many cities, the sea port of Alexandria on the island of Pharos in the Nile delta. It would be a permanent reminder that Alexander had become the master of the Mediterranean. From there he and his troops marched for eight days through the desert to the shrine of Zeus Ammon in the Libyan desert, where he let it be known that "he had been told what his heart desired" by the Oracle.

In pursuit of the Persian king

The expedition into the unknown began with the defeat of Darius on the plains of the upper Tigris near Arbela. Darius became a fugitive, and the fabulous cities of the Persian

▶ **At Persepolis in Persia**
Alexander burned the royal palace – an act that has been interpreted as one of revenge for the burning of the Greek temples by the Persian King Xerxes 150 years previously. The Gates of Xerxes are one of the surviving edifices still to be found in Persepolis.

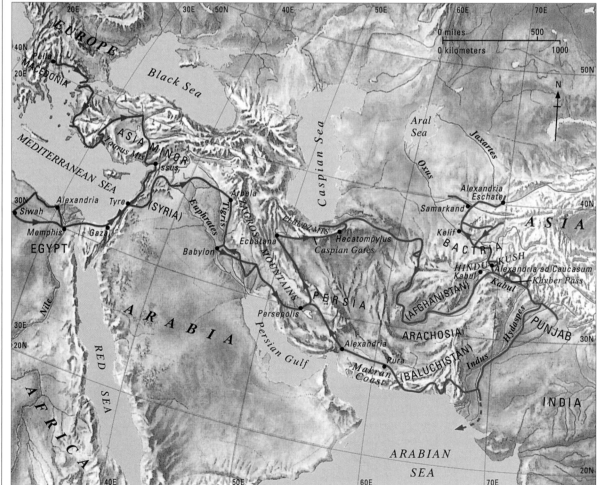

KEY TO ROUTES

— Alexander the Great
  334–323 BC

---- Nearchus 326–325 BC

Empire lay wide open to Alexander, who seated himself on Darius's throne. In January 330 BC, he continued his march to Persepolis, crossing the Zagros Mountains in southern Iran. When he arrived, he put Darius's palace to the torch and seized a vast treasure.

Alexander then chased Darius by forced marches northwest into the Persian (Iranian) mountains, following the caravan trails to Ecbatana (Hamadan), some 6000 feet (1800 meters) above sea level. By the time Alexander arrived, Darius had already made his way eastward to the Caspian Gates (now known as the Sirdar Pass), still the route which carries the main road connecting Tehran and Herat.

In the second half of July, Alexander finally caught up with Darius near Hecatompylus (Damghan) only to find him mortally wounded. Alexander waited for the main body of his army to catch up before descending through the dense forests of the north slopes of the Elburz Mountains to the shore of the Caspian Sea.

For the rest of the year, Alexander subdued native tribes and then, skirting the great Asian steppes, followed the watercourses and caravan trails through Arachosia (Kandahar) in pursuit of Darius's successor, Bessus. In the spring of 329 BC he took the army toward the Hindu Kush and founded another city – Alexandria ad Caucasum (so called because he believed himself to be in the Caucasus). There followed a brutal 17 days' march through the mountains into northern Afghanistan, crossing by the 11,400-foot (3475-meter) high Khawak Pass. Up to their waists in snow, suffering from frostbite and the effects of the high altitude, they lived off terebinth (the "turpentine tree") and the raw flesh of mules until they reached the valley of the Oxus River (Amudarya). The valley was mostly sandy desert and the river, over 1100 yards (1 kilometer) wide at Kelif, almost impossible to bridge. They eventually crossed it on rafts made from their leather tent covers stuffed with hay, finally captured Bessus in his native Bactria and despatched him to a singular and gruesome fate.

Alexander then followed what would become the Silk Road to Samarkand and marched on with his army into the steppes as far as the Jaxartes River (Syrdarya). Here, he founded another city, afterward known as Alexandria Eschate. Alexander probably believed that this river was the boundary separating Europe from Asia and that it flowed northward to the "Ocean." In the winter of 327 BC, 2000 of his men froze to death as they campaigned in the steppes north of the Hindu Kush.

The assault on India

In the spring Alexander and his men recrossed the Hindu Kush, probably through the 14,340-foot (4370-meter) high Kaoshan Pass, arriving in Alexandria ad Caucasum in about ten days. (It would take as long as that now.) Here, Alexander prepared for the assault on India, a subcontinent of which he knew little beyond the Indus River. Early in 326 BC, one arm of his army crossed through the Khyber Pass, while Alexander himself set off with a lighter force, following the Kabul River and marching through some of the wildest country in Asia.

Advancing now into the "Land of the Five Rivers" (the Punjab), he crossed the Hydaspes (Jhelum) when it was in full flood, and engaged in battle with a Punjab rajah in the middle of the monsoon season. Failing, however, to persuade his army to march beyond the Indus, a contingent of ships was built on the Hydaspes and the remainder of his army sailed down to the Arabian Sea. One portion of his army returned to the Persian Gulf by sea under the command of Nearchus; the remainder followed Alexander back by land, experiencing aching thirst in the desert of Baluchistan with its sandstorms and quicksands. He reckoned that the 60 days on the Makran coast had cost him the lives of 60,000 people and all their pack animals. Only when they finally struck inland to Pura, the capital of the province of Gedrosia in the former Persian Empire, did they know how far it was back home and that they were at last safe.

In the course of a decade, Alexander had traveled more than 20,000 miles (32,000 kilometers). He had founded more than 70 cities, and he and his commanders had added permanently to Greek geographical knowledge. They had also collected a vast amount of information about the plant life, the ethnography, and even the geology of the regions. In Bactria, for example, his troops unwittingly constructed an oil well when they set up his tent near the Oxus River. In southern Pakistan, they met natives who lived off fish, fed their flocks off fish meal, and lived in huts made from whale carcasses.

Alexander died in Babylon on June 10, 323 BC, at the age of 32. The story that he was poisoned is less likely to be true, however, than that the explorer's experiences (he had contracted dysentery in Bactria, and was wounded on the Indus) had worn him out. The vast empire he left behind him was quickly dismembered by his successors, but his remarkable achievements were to inspire others.

▲ *Alexander and Darius clashed at the Battle of Issus, after Darius had attempted to cut off Alexander's lines of communication to the rear. The narrow valleys of the Taurus Mountains were not, however, ideal terrain for Darius's large force, which was scattered and fled eastward.*

The Silk Road

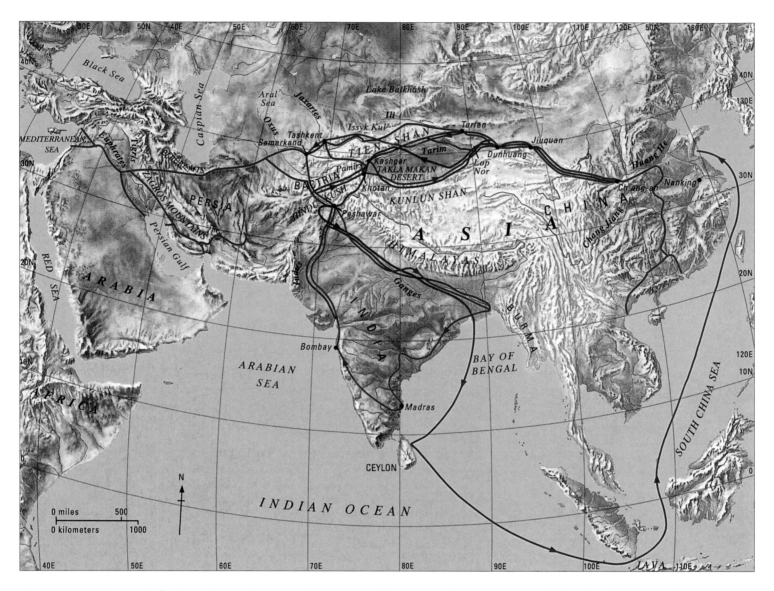

Two thousand years ago China and the West were held together by a thread. It was known as the Silk Road. Corals and pearls, amber and glass, woolens and linen were traded eastward from the stable civilizations of the Mediterranean, in return for lacquerware, spices (especially cinnamon) and, above all, silk from China.

The Greeks and Romans knew little of how the silk was made. It was produced, they surmised, by the mysterious "Seres" (the word derives from the Chinese for silk). Pliny, writing in around AD 70, thought that silk was a pale floss found growing on leaves. Pausanias, a century later, knew that it was spun by insects, but this view was not held universally until the eggs of silk worms were transported from India back to Byzantium by monks in the 6th century.

The Silk-Road trade was valuable. In around 100 BC, 12 caravan trains left China for the West each year and the taxes on them provided up to 30 percent of the Han dynasty's revenues. Pliny thought that these imports cost the Roman Empire a hundred million sesterces per annum.

The Silk Road was the central nervous system of all Asian landed exploration in the period before AD 1500. From the comparative safety of the Great Wall at Jiuquan, the caravans started their slow progress through what is now the Chinese province of Xinjiang. To lead a caravan through nomad country would have been dangerous at the best of times. In the centre of Xinjiang, however, lies the Takla Makan Desert, some 600 miles (1000 kilometers)

east to west and 250 miles (400 kilometers) north to south, a wilderness of pure sand, whose dunes reach to 300 feet (90 meters). This wasteland was shunned by explorers for centuries. Marco Polo referred to its "rumbling sands," while a Chinese historian said that "travelers find nothing to guide them but the bones of men and beasts and the droppings of camels."

To the north of the desert runs the mountain range of the Tien Shan and, to the south, that of the Kunlun Shan. Both had high rainfalls so that rivers flowed down toward the Takla Makan from north and south, creating a string of oases along the base of the mountain ranges. These oasis towns provided the stopping points for the vital 600 miles (1000 kilometers) or so of the Silk Road to Kashgar and the outer limits of the Persian Empire and its successors. When the steppes to the north were unsettled, traders could use the alternative southern route.

From Dunhuang, where the frescoed caves of the underground watercourses are decorated with Hindu figures over 1400 years old, the Bactrian camels were generally led on the northern route to Turfan. There, subterranean caves house some of the earliest and richest sources for Buddhist art. *En route*, dead cities, once oasis towns, are still visible in mud ruins of battlements and palaces. At Gaochang, for example, 4 miles (6 kilometers) of ramparts, 30 feet (9 meters) high in places, surround an eerie labyrinth of grid-plan streets and palace compounds.

The oasis towns were settled by a succession of nomadic peoples – Uzbeks, Kazaks, Kirgiz, and Uighur. They traded in horses, cloth, jade, spices, tea, and wood. At Kashgar, the great market town of the Silk Road, Persians, Afghans and Turks bartered their wares.

Exploration beyond the Silk Road

While the major civilizations were politically stable and the peoples of the steppes not restless, the possibilities for travel and discovery lay open from both east and west. This was the case particularly from *c.* 150 BC to *c.* AD 450. In about AD 120 a Greek merchant named Maes Titanius sent out agents to Kashgar to gain information about the Silk Road. This was the source for Ptolemy's fairly accurate descriptions of central Asia. From the east, the Han emperor Wu Ti despatched Chang Ch'ien, an emissary, to Bactria. The Huns, who seized him both on the way there and on the way back, kept him in captivity for over 20 years. In AD 97, a second ambassador named Kan Ying was sent by the Han emperors from China to Rome, but he too was captured before he reached his destination.

The Silk Road also provided oases of religious pluralism. Even now, frescoes and vast rock-carved buddhas, pagodas, Persian stupas, Islamic minarets and mosques stand in proximity with each other. In the first centuries of the Christian era, Buddhist monks and Nestorian Christians were amongst the most intrepid explorers. Their religion led them to explore very widely in south Asia, taking Buddhism to Burma, Ceylon and down the Malayan peninsula. One Chinese Buddhist monk, Fu-Hsien, known as "the Manifestation of the Faith," accompanied by three fellow monks, traveled by the southward side of the Takla Makan in 399. From there, he crossed into India through "mountains covered with snow both in winter and summer . . . they shelter also dragons which, if once provoked, spit out their poison."

Using the networks of Buddhist monasteries, Fu-Hsien spent 15 years traveling round India in search of Buddhist enlightenment and manuscripts. He returned via Ceylon and Java and ended with a hair-raisingly long voyage back to the Chinese mainland. Once back in Nanking, he wrote the *Fo-Kwe-Ki* (*Memoirs of the Buddha Dominions*), which gave details of his routes, the weather, and the names and sizes of towns he visited, as well as fascinating descriptions of the customs of the many different peoples he had encountered on his travels.

◄ **The traders** who met in the oasis towns of the Takla Makan Desert used camel trains led by Chinese drivers. The caravans (both people and animals) were accommodated in buildings constructed specifically for the purpose, known as caravanserai (shown in the background). From the Takla Makan, some traders traveled west through Persia to the eastern Mediterranean. Others turned south, crossing the Pamirs to the upper waters of the Oxus River and on into the Indian subcontinent.

Two hundred years later another monk, Hsüan-Tsang, determined to "travel in the countries of the west in order to question the wise men on the points that were troubling his mind." Riding an old horse, he left China in AD 629 and, the following spring, crossed the Tien Shan Range by a glacial pass. After traveling extensively in central Asia, visiting its Buddhist monasteries, he went south to India. Although he lost many manuscripts when he crossed the Indus River in around 643, as well as a collection of rare seeds, he eventually returned to Ch'ang-an in the spring of 645 where, on the emperor's orders, he was given a great welcome after his absence of 15 years. He brought back with him more than 700 religious manuscripts, statues of the Buddha, prayer-wheels and relics.

Hsüan-Tsang spent the rest of his life compiling the magnificent *Ta-T'ang-Si-Yu-Ki* (*Memoirs on Western Countries*), an official account of his travels, which was issued by the emperor T'ai T'ang. It was the most substantial record of China's neighbors produced under the auspices of its officialdom (many times longer than the Bible) before the 17th century.

▼ **Hsüan-Tsang** returned from his extensive travels accompanied by a train of pack horses, loaded with religious manuscripts and other precious objects. Dignitaries and chanting monks welcomed him home.

The Geography of the Ancients

The mental picture of the universe devised by the Greeks and Romans far outstripped their actual explorations of the Earth's surface. In their search for a full explanation of the world around them, they developed a geography based on their knowledge of Greek astronomy, mathematics (especially geometry), physics, astrology and, above all, philosophy.

Plato, writing in the first half of the 4th century BC, was the first philosopher to announce the concept of a round Earth located in the center of the universe with the celestial bodies in circular motions around it. Aristotle, who as a young man was associated with the Academy in Athens founded and led by Plato, provided crucial additional observations. These included the curved shadow cast by the Earth on the moon during a lunar eclipse, and the increase in height above the horizon of various stars as one traveled toward the north, which could only have occurred if the observer were traveling over the curved surface of a sphere. Strangely, he never noted the additional evidence in support of the concept of a round Earth much more commonly proposed by Europeans in later centuries, that of the disappearance of a ship below the horizon – hull first.

If the Earth were a circumference, how then was it divided up? Herodotus had thought that the surface of the Earth must be arranged neatly balanced around the Mediterranean: the Nile to the south matched by the Ister (Danube) River to the north and so on. Beyond the known world lay, so he believed, the surrounding "Ocean." One of Plato's contemporaries, Eudoxus of Cnidus, developed a more sophisticated theory of zones of climate based on their increasing slope (*klima*) away from the sun on a spherical surface.

This theory of Eudoxus was turned by Aristotle into the concept that the habitability of different regions of the Earth depended on their latitude. Knowing the intense heat experienced in the desert just south of the Mediterranean (indeed, the highest land temperature in the world has been recorded in Libya), Aristotle concluded that parts of the land mass close to the Equator, the torrid zone, were uninhabitable. The *ekumene*, the inhabited part of the Earth, was in the temperate zones. (Although there must be a southerly temperate zone, reasoned Aristotle, the Greeks would never reach it because of the intense heat of the torrid zone.)

The scholars of Alexandria

The mapping of the world by the Ancients reached its peak in the remarkable efforts of a generation of scholars in the world's first scientific research institute, the Museum and Library at Alexandria. Eratosthenes, the institute's librarian from 234 to 192 BC, made an astonishingly accurate calculation of the Earth's circumference as 250,000 stadia (25,000 miles/40,000 kilometers), which was, in fact, only half a percent out. He also wrote a book describing the inhabited Earth, in which he accepted the major divisions of the Earth's surface – Europe, Asia, Libya, and the five zones (one torrid, two temperate, two frigid) – and gave them mathematical boundaries in the form of irregularly spaced lines of longitude and latitude. In addition, he prepared a world map, an *orbis terrarum*, the first known atlas to use a grid pattern, basing his meridian on

▼ Abraham Ortelius produced his Theater of the World *in 1570. The mysterious* Terra Australis Incognita *– a huge southern continent taking up much of the southern hemisphere – is evidence of the influence of Ptolemy's* Geographia, *although much had subsequently been discovered about the lands to the west of the Atlantic Ocean.*

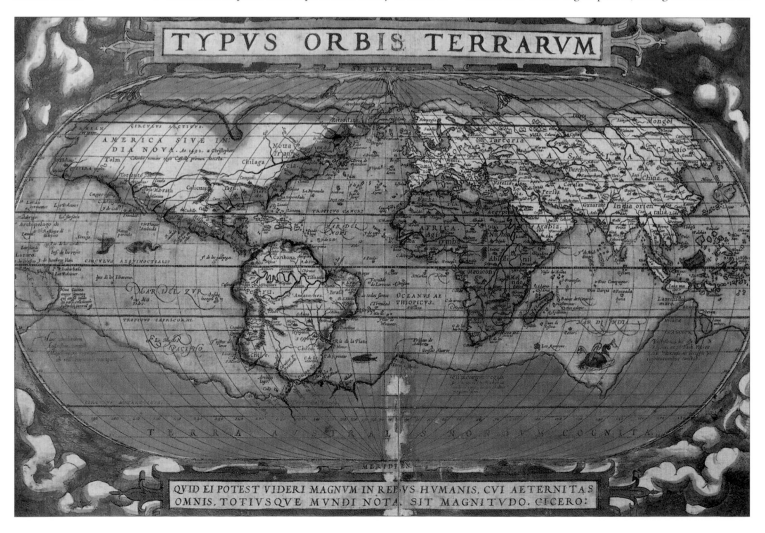

◀ **Strabo's** Geographia *was based mainly on the texts of earlier writers, but he is also known to have traveled widely: "Westward I have journeyed to the parts of Etruria [Italy] opposite Sardinia; toward the south from the Euxine [Black Sea] to the borders of Ethiopia."*

▶ **Ptolemy's writings** *were still considered authoritative by astronomers and geographers some 1300 years after his death. His model of the universe as revolving around the Earth fitted well with the ideology of the medieval Christian Church, which represented Earth as the dregs of the Universe, and the concentric rings of the planets as a graded scale of increasing perfection, leading to God.*

Alexandria and his prime latitude on a line through the Pillars of Hercules to Rhodes.

Eratosthenes's successor as librarian at Alexandria, Hipparchus, was the first to wrestle with the problem of how the curved surface of a sphere was to be represented on a flat surface. He devised two kinds of projections so that the distortion of the spherical surface on a map could be carried out mathematically. Both projections were only capable of producing a hemisphere, however. Either the central portion was too small in relation to the periphery, or the central portion was too large.

Strabo

Much of what is known about the ancient geographers comes from the Roman authority Strabo (*c.* 64 BC–AD 20). Most of the written record on geographical ideas in Ancient Greece and Rome has disappeared and has to be pieced together from surviving cross-references, but Strabo's great work on geography (the *Geographia*) remains almost intact. It was known in Christian Europe but it was never translated into Arabic. Only at the close of the Middle Ages did its alternative picture of the Indian Ocean as a sea rather than a lake begin to challenge the ascendancy of Ptolemy.

His research was conducted, inevitably, at Alexandria and he drew extensively on his predecessors. He accepted Aristotle's zones of habitability and his belief in the existence of an ocean surrounding the Earth's land mass. Unfortunately, he also accepted a calculation made by Posidonius, a few years earlier, that the Earth's circumference measured 18,000 miles (29,000 kilometers). Posidonius had arrived at this figure by using the height of the bright star *Canopus* above the horizon at Rhodes and Alexandria – which he assumed to be on the same latitude – and calculating the distance between the two places on the basis of the average sailing times for ships.

Strabo provided an inventory of the known world for the administrators of the Roman Empire, whose land surveys, military maps and coastal charts, to judge from surviving examples, were of a high technical proficiency. Upon such skills future exploration would rely.

Ptolemy

The greatest ancient geographer was Ptolemy (Claudius Ptolemaeus). Nothing is known of his life except that he worked at the library in Alexandria between AD 127 and 150. He was the author of the monumental work on classical astronomy – the *Almagest* – which long remained the standard reference work on the movements of celestial bodies. His concept of the universe agreed mainly with that of Aristotle. He conceived of the Earth as a stationary sphere, around which the celestial bodies moved in circular courses. Such was his influence that this became an article of faith in medieval Christendom.

After completing the *Almagest*, Ptolemy undertook to prepare a *Guide to Geography*. The intention was to produce the most accurate and precise map of the world that was humanly possible. Adopting a grid of latitude and longitude, Ptolemy's guide went on to detail in six volumes of tables the world's first geographical gazetteer, from which to revise the world map. The first and last volumes contained an invaluable discussion of map projections and then, finally, maps of different parts of the world based on the gazetteer.

Accurate measurement of space and time eluded Ptolemy. Latitude could only be determined approximately and there was no way of measuring longitude. So, the further he worked east from his prime meridian (a north–south line through the Canaries or the Madeira Islands) the more inaccurate he became. His problems were further compounded by his adoption of Posidonius's estimate of the Earth's circumference, rather than the more accurate one of Eratosthenes. It is not surprising that, on the basis of Ptolemy's calculations, Christopher Columbus was to estimate that Asia must lie very close to Europe in the west.

The more serious inaccuracy was a perceptual one. Ptolemy's maps showed the Indian Ocean as enclosed by land to the south – in effect turning it into a lake – a notion that had probably originated with a projection of Hipparchus. This *Terra Australis Incognita* appeared regularly thereafter on Islamic and European world maps, and was still being sought well into the 16th century.

The Roman Empire

The effects of the Roman Empire on the West's geographical perceptions may be measured by comparing the works of the Greek geographer Posidonius (c. 60 BC) with those of his counterpart from the 2nd century AD, Ptolemy. What had happened in the intervening years? It was not that the Romans had "discovered" lands unknown to the Greeks. But whereas the Greeks had known about these lands, the Romans actually *went* there: they marched them, measured them, mapped them.

The Romans conceived of their empire in terms of the model of world domination provided by Alexander the Great. Republican Rome minted coins with a globe on them with Alexander's motif of the scepter and palm and the inscription: *Terra marisque* (by land and sea). The beginning of Virgil's *Aeneid* recalls the prophecy supposedly made by Jupiter, that Rome would exercise an *imperium sine fine* (empire without end) over the world. The *Res gestae*, one of the documents to which Augustus put his name shortly before his death in AD 14, promised to have "submitted the world" to the dominion of Rome.

The Augustan age

The Augustan age (48 BC–AD 68) was a great period of Roman exploration, of which the most significant results

were to be found in four distinct areas of the empire: Nile Africa and the Middle East, North Africa and the Sahara, the Eastern Front of the empire and Persia, and the Danube and Northern Europe. In some cases, exploration was a by-product of attempts to settle political problems at the edge of the empire. The warring Nubian tribes of the Upper Nile and the activities of the Ethiopian queens, for example, were the reason for the expedition by Petronius in AD 29. In other (rarer) cases the purposes were more specifically those of reconnaissance. In AD 61–63 a detachment of Pretorian Guards marched up the Nile, perhaps with a future military expedition in mind. In Pliny's account, they reached far beyond the city of Merowe and, although they did not find the source of the Nile, they brought back specimens of African trade, such as ebony, and had clearly gone up the White Nile further than most, possibly any, of the Greek and Egyptian expeditions had done before. They would be the last Europeans to do so before the 1830s.

Not all the achievements of this period should be attributed to the servants of the empire, however. Some of them were the inevitable commercial results of the stability the empire created, which independent merchants were keen to exploit. It was, according to Strabo, in this period that trade between the Red Sea and the East increased considerably, with as many as 120 ships setting out in a single year. One resourceful Greek merchant named Hippalus decided to avoid the dangers of the pirates along the southern Arabian coast and made a direct passage to India. Around the same period a voyage of discovery was also undertaken by a freed slave who sailed directly across the Indian Ocean to the Deccan Kingdoms of southern India – the source of many of the products eagerly sought by the Red Sea traders.

Some of the Roman expeditions were undoubtedly among the most arduous and taxing imaginable. In 25–24 BC the Prefect of Egypt, Aelius Gallus, led an expedition into the Arabian Desert. Setting out from the Gulf of Suez with water supplies provided by camels, the expedition attained various oases settlements, each carefully recorded by Strabo, before meandering in the highlands of western Saudi Arabia, deceived by treacherous local guides. It may well have come quite close to the shores of the Gulf of Aden and the Aromatic Coast, the source for the precious spices of the Roman Empire. But in the end the tattered remnants of the expedition eventually reached the Red Sea and returned to Egypt. A similar, exhausting expedition led by Cornelius Balbus, the energetic pro-Consul of Africa, traveled over 900 miles (1600 kilometers) south of Tripoli into the Sahara Desert in 20 BC in search of the source for African gold. Each expedition, however, would provide information which would find its way into the geographical accounts of a Strabo, a Pliny, an Agrippa, or a Ptolemy.

Explorations in the east

On the Eastern Front, the conflict between a cautious consolidation of the empire and the possibilities of an adventurous extension to the Indus along the lines of Alexander the Great was most keenly felt. However, the Romans advanced cautiously, crossing the Taurus Mountains in around 78 BC, the Tigris River in 69 BC, and reaching the sources of the Tigris and Euphrates and the tablelands of Armenia shortly thereafter. Gradually, all the lands between the Black Sea and the Caspian Sea in the province of Asia were explored and the Euphrates River became a Roman border. As in the case of the Upper Nile, however, this did not preclude some expeditions from exploring the Caucasus Mountains. From their local contacts, the

Romans learnt how the inhabitants used toboggans and roller-skates in winter; and, more importantly, from the Parthians, something of Seres and the lands to the East.

Explorations in Europe

In Europe, the Romans never went beyond eastern Poland into Lithuania or Russia. But their exploration of the Ister (Danube) River mirrored that of the Nile, and one of the great achievements of the Augustan age was to identify the sources of the Ister. Roman occupation of Transylvania resulted in precise knowledge of the region, and roads were built south through the Transylvanian mountains to the Balkans. The great quest was for slaves and for amber; it was in search of a route for the latter that a financial procurator from Rome sent a horseman 500 miles (900 kilometers) through Moravia and Silesia to the Baltic coast. The man returned with sufficient amber to cover the studs of the safety-nets in the Roman amphitheater. Such contacts, and other naval expeditions to the mouth of the Elbe River and the Frisian coast, meant that the Romans were well informed on the Baltic coast as far east as Riga, and on the tribes of eastern Germany.

It was perhaps the settlement and occupation of Gaul, particularly its wooded and impenetrable Massif Central and the region between the Somme and the Rhine rivers, that most epitomized Roman exploration. If all the world had to be taxed, it also had to be accounted for, and this involved the precise surveying and measuring of the land surface. If the empire was to function, its roads had to be built and maintained, even over the most unpromising terrain. It was the Romans who took the Alps in their stride, creating the handsomely paved Little St Bernard Pass so that a large army could march more easily through the mountains without disaster.

▲ *The victories* of the Roman Emperor Trajan are celebrated in detailed relief carvings on a column in the Forum in Rome. Trajan spent much of his reign (AD 98–117) expanding and consolidating the Eastern Front of the Roman Empire, engaging in battles to establish Roman authority in the Balkan region, Persia (Iran), and Mesopotamia (Iraq).

Out of the North

Viking longships
Even to the modern eye, the Viking longships are impressive. The 9th-century Gokstad ship, recovered by a Norwegian excavation, is just over 76 feet (23.5 meters) long, clinker planked, with thin oak attached by a combination of lashings and small iron plates to 19 frames built up from a huge keel. An Atlantic crossing, made in 1893 in as little as 28 days from Bergen to Newfoundland in a replica of this ship, demonstrated how effective the design was. But the longship (*langskip*), was shallow, designed for coastal shipping and very different from the halfship (*hafskip*), which was shorter, broader in the beam, and much deeper in draught, resistant to high winds, capable of carrying cargo, and equipped with more elaborate sails.

A dragon's head was frequently to be found on the prow of these ships, as is shown in the two illustrations above.

In the period following the collapse of the Roman Empire in the 5th century AD, Europe became detached from its ancient heritage to such an extent that it is surprising that any sustained exploration emerged from it at all. Under pressure from the "Barbarians," who moved in from east of the Rhine and northeast of the Danube, Europe was ruled by a collection of kingdoms and principalities that ostensibly owed little to the classical civilizations of Greece and Rome. At the same time the advent of Christianity had powerful effects, both negative and positive, on travel and discovery. The negative influence was felt through profound changes to the West's "mental map," which owed much to Jewish notions of the Tabernacle as a microcosm for the universe. There was a growing belief that the Earth was flat, and Latin geographical sources were either ostracized or turned into fables.

Christian conversion, however, also provided the spur to exploration, particularly of the lands on the edge of Europe. The missions to England of Augustine in 597 and of Theodore and Hadrian in the 7th century, the one from Tarsus in Asia Minor (Turkey) and the other from North Africa, are evidence of a willingness to travel long distances for the faith. A Frankish pilgrim, Arculf, is especially well known because, on his return from the Levant in about 680, his ship was blown off course and he ended up on the remote Scottish island of Iona. He recounted his travels to the abbot of the famous Irish monastery there and, in due course, his account was given to King Aeldfrith of Northumbria, to be later carefully incorporated into Bede's *History*. The conversion of Ireland itself, which was undertaken by Palludius and St Patrick in the 5th century, led Irish monks to sail to many of the islands round the British Isles in search of solitude. The literature of the voyage, which was popular among the Celts, recalled recently abandoned pagan notions of a Paradise to the west, as well as Biblical concepts of a Jerusalem to the east which could be reached by those with faith.

Viking expansionism

Of all the activities of European explorers between about AD 400 and 1000, the expansion of the Scandinavian Vikings (also known as Norsemen) from the end of the 8th century onward was the most impressive. Like the barbarians from the steppes, the Vikings were driven by powerful and complex forces of land-hunger, rivalries, the lure of plunder and, eventually, the attractions of the settled life elsewhere. They turned eastward, settling in the coastal lands of the east Baltic, and then to western Russia around Lake Ladzhskoye. They evidently traded their way southward down the Dnieper and Volga so that, by the closing decades of the 9th century, they were in contact with the Bulgars and Khazars of Asia and their presence was felt south of the Caspian. It was not heroic exploration as the 19th century would have seen it, but much individual courage and determination was involved.

By the last decades of the 8th century it seems that all the necessary naval techniques had already been perfected by the Vikings in Scandinavian waters for them to begin their assault on the English and continental coasts and, from the 830s onward, incursions increased in intensity. Further expeditions from their new bases in western France took them southward round Gibraltar into the Mediterranean. Led by Bjorn Ironside, the son of a Danish king, and his notoriously slippery compatriot, Hastein, an expedition of 62 ships spent four years from *c.* 858 marauding off the coast of Spain and North Africa before showing their dragon-headed boats in the Balearics and putting ashore in southern France. They were eventually beaten off

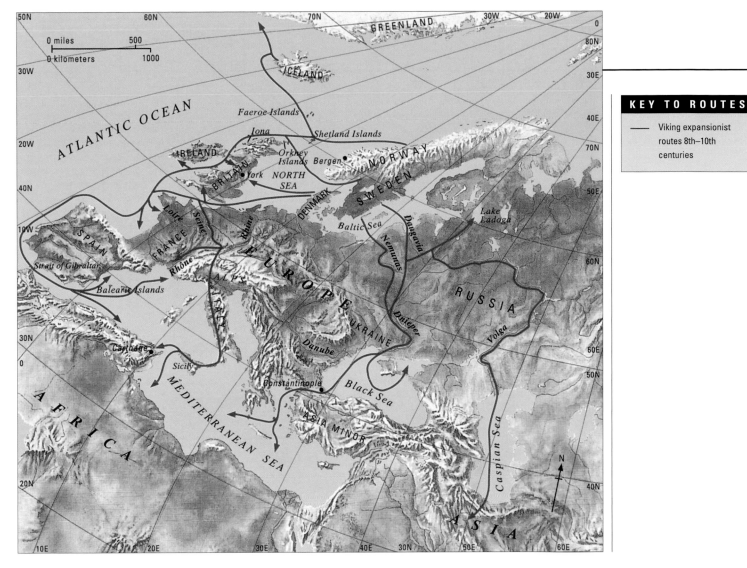

by a Moorish fleet, but a third of the original fleet returned to the mouth of the Loire in 962.

The most remarkable feats of exploration were those in the northern Atlantic. The Faeroes were settled from Norway early in the 9th century and this was followed two generations later by settlements in Iceland. Scandinavian sources from later on distinguished three separate voyages, each of which involved, by the most direct route, a journey of 1000 miles (1600 kilometers) from the Faeroes through difficult seas, navigating along the latitudes in ways which their sagas imply they took in their stride. The explorers mentioned in these breathtaking (and, at least according to the accounts, accidental) storm-ridden expeditions were a Swede (Gardar Svarvarsson) and two Norwegians (Naddod and Floki Vilgerdason). Floki was so disenchanted with the enforced winter spent watching livestock die for lack of hay that he christened it "Iceland." These voyages took place in the 860s and 870s and were soon followed by settlements.

Greenland was first visited by a European in *c.* 900 when a Norseman named Gunnbjörn was blown off course. But it was not until all the good land in Iceland had been taken up that the first attempt to settle Greenland was attempted in 978. That failed, but in the 980s Greenland became the home of fugitives from justice as the Viking states of Norway and England began to consolidate. One such exile was Eirik Thorvaldsson – better known as Eirik the Red, and a fugitive from first Norway, and then Iceland – who explored the land found by Gunnbjörn. It seemed to him to be an endless land mass, dominated by high mountains and glaciers. He called it Greenland to entice settlers to its shores.

The evidence suggests that the Norsemen made a good job of colonization, even in Greenland where the climate

was more extreme. Norse ships and navigational skills proved easily capable of meeting the severe demands of the North Atlantic, and there is convincing evidence that they reached the coast of Newfoundland (see pages 118–19). In their northern colonies there were seals and walruses to hunt, and grain could be grown because the global climate was favorable. The period 1000–1200 is known as "the little Climatic Optimum" to historical meteorologists and was a few degrees warmer than the years that followed, when subtle climatic change, as well as changing perspectives in Europe, brought this first, daring period of Europe's expansion to a close.

▲ *Eirik the Red described Greenland as dominated by high mountains and glaciers, although at the time the southeastern region was experiencing an unusually moderate climate. Settlers were able to grow certain vegetables – cabbages, for instance – and even some grain in the two or three months of summer.*

The Geographies of Islam

The end of the Ancient World in the centuries after the birth of Christ was marked by a change in the nature of religion. The religions of the ancient civilizations had taught their followers (mainly the literate elite) to accept the way the world was and their place in it, to avoid extremes, and to strive for uniformity and stability within an ordered view of the universe. Now, and partly because of the failure of those civilizations to encompass more than a limited degree of change, there appeared "transcendental" religions. Their distinctive features included the preaching of individual and universal salvation and an acceptance of change, instability and discontinuity in the name of religion. These were religions of exploration.

No event in world history between the death of Christ (and, with it, the foundation of the first great transcendental world religion, Christianity) and the European voyages of discovery was more significant than the rise of Islam. The mission of its founder, Muhammad (d. AD 632), was to unite the divided Arab peoples through a new religion. His message, obedience to the almighty power of God, initially aroused the opposition of conservative Arabs. Yet, within a century of the prophet's death, it had been carried across the Pyrenees to the west and to the outer confines of India to the east. By AD 750 Islam was the major civilization west of China.

The golden age of Islam

The "golden age of Islam" is generally associated with the dominance of the Abbasid Caliphate centered on Baghdad between the 8th and 10th centuries. It was a period of great commercial prosperity. Islamic gold and silver coins (dinar and drachma) circulated widely. Demands for foodstuffs, horses, wood, metals, and slaves led its merchants into contact with the civilizations of medieval Europe, India, and China as well as with the nomadic peoples of the Sahara Desert and the Asian steppes. This contact stimulated technical change and adaptation of all kinds.

Similar contact and adaptation also went on in the intellectual world. Greek, Roman, Persian, and Indian traditions all fed into Islam. But all knowledge was sacred and the mosque was both the religious and social center of the Islamic community and its center of learning. The only educational establishments outside the mosque were the hospitals (for medicine) and the observatories (for astronomy, astrology, and geography). The observatory as a scientific institution owed its birth to Islamic civilization, its typically domed roof replicating that of a mosque. Islamic cosmology was directly related to the principles of Islamic revelation and the teaching of the Prophet. Muslim studies in geography therefore viewed the Earth as an image of the spiritual world. This did not exclude, however, the most exact mathematical measurement of geographical coordinates. Islamic accuracy was assisted by the systematic use of the compass.

The geographies of Islam were truly impressive. They were descriptive and mathematical. Among the most significant in the golden age was *The Figures of the Earth,* attributed to Muhammad ibn Musa al-Khwarazmi. As Arab and Persian sailors made their way beyond the Indian Ocean to Java and toward China, there were descriptions of their discoveries. These discoveries were, in due course, integrated into the work of the great Islamic master of mathematical, descriptive and cultural geography, Abu Rayhan al-Biruni (973–1048). He was from Khorosan in central Asia, knew Turkish, Persian, Sanskrit, Hebrew and Syrian, and was in contact with all the great scholars of his day. His astronomical and geographical studies led him to advance the theory of the Earth's rotation about its axis and to speculate that

▶ **Al-Idrisi's map,** *which is accompanied by* The Book of Roger, *was on a vast scale, representing the world in 70 sections. The south is at the top.*

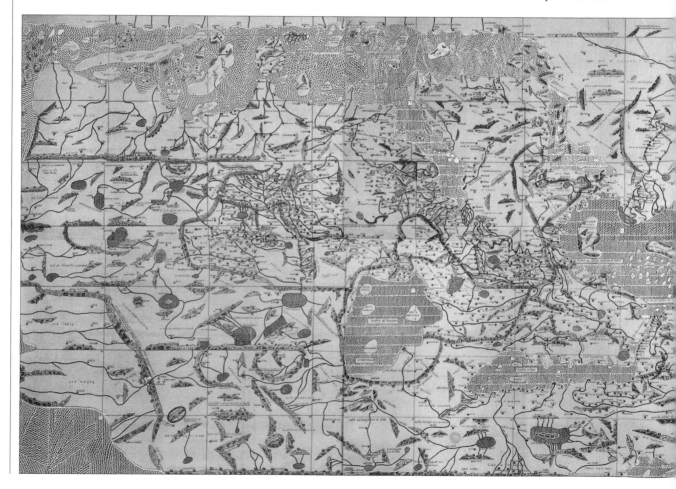

the valley of the Indus had once been a sea basin. His accurate calculations of the latitude and longitude of specific places were demonstrated in a mathematically based geography, the *Determination of the Coordinates of Cities*, designed to enable mosque builders to place their buildings on a precise alignment with Mecca. It was on the basis of such scholarship that cartographers such as Abu 'Abdullah al-Idrisi produced world maps.

'Abdullah al-Idrisi

Abu 'Abdullah ash Sharif al-Idrisi (1100–1165) was a Moroccan geographer who served at the court of Roger II, the Norman King of Sicily (reigned 1130–1154). Al-Idrisi studied in many mosques throughout the Arab world and had visited Asia Minor by the time he was 16 years of age. For his patron he wrote *The Book of Roger* and prepared a world map.

The work of al-Idrisi was based on Hellenistic and earlier Islamic sources, as well as first-hand information obtained by al-Idrisi from his own travels and reports made by emissaries who were despatched to specific areas. Thus, al-Idrisi was able to provide an account, for example, of the Wangara country on the Niger River, more than 650 years before it was visited by Mungo Park.

The map was on a vast scale, consisting of 70 sections formed by dividing the Earth north of the Equator into seven climatic zones of equal width. Each zone was divided into 10 equal parts along lines of longitude.

Al-Idrisi's map is highly detailed and beautifully executed. So, too, are the cartographic works of Pir Muhyi al-Din Ra, drawn in the 16th century, which contain maps of Africa and America of a standard unmatched anywhere in the world and which continue to astonish modern scholars by their accuracy.

▶ *The world picture* drawn by al-Idrisi (with the south at the top) corrected that of Ptolemy, made a thousand years earlier, which had represented the Indian Ocean as an enclosed lake and the Caspian Sea as merely a gulf of a larger sea. The coast of the Mediterranean is drawn in some detail, as is that of Arabia and Persia.

▼ *Islamic observatories* were centers of study for both astronomers and geographers. The science of geography relied, to a certain extent, on that of astronomy, and used observation of the sun and stars to establish positions of latitude.

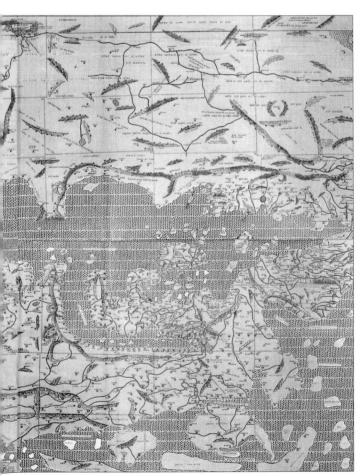

Islamic Travelers

▲ **Reaching Mecca** in time for the pilgrimage season in the Muslim lunar month of Dhu I-Hijja (November) was the predominant reason for the great caravans that set out from all quarters of the Islamic world. This 13th-century illustration shows musicians accompanying the travelers.

By the 12th century Arab cosmographers were producing encyclopedias of their knowledge of the Earth's surface. To this period belongs the incomparable Dictionary of the *Lands of Yaqut*, which is still an indispensable research tool for modern scholars. The work incorporated a great deal of local information, collected by extensive travel across the Islamic world, the *Dar al-Islam*. Islam obliged every male Muslim (save the poor, the enslaved, or the insane) to undertake the *hajj* or pilgrimage to the holy places of Mecca and Medina at least once in his lifetime. Islamic travel was also encouraged by the *rihla*, the elaborate study tours of the great mosques and teaching centers by its scholars. One of the five sacred pillars of Islam was to share one's material well-being with others, including travelers, and the foundation of almshouses for wayfarers across the length and breadth of the Islamic world served to make it the first tourist civilization.

Ibn Battuta

By the beginning of the 14th century the terrible destruction caused by the Mongol invasions of east European and Asian lands had long since come to an end; in its place was stability created by Mongol rule, the "Pax Mongolica," which provided the right conditions for travel across the Eurasian steppe heartlands. The most remarkable of the travelers of that period – and of any age before the advent of steamships and railroads – was Ibn Abdullah Ibn Battuta (his name means "Duckling's son"). Ibn Battuta was born in Tangier in 1304 into a family of judges and, having received the traditional education of a lawyer, he decided to undertake a pilgrimage to Mecca. He turned it into a

lifetime of travel, covering about 75,000 miles (120,000 kilometers) across the length and breadth of the Muslim-influenced world.

Setting out in 1325 eastward across the Maghrib, Ibn Battuta made his way to the Nile and to the great cities of Islam – Alexandria (where he visited the great lighthouse and studied its distinctive law school), Cairo (with its impressive hospital) and, in due course, Damascus and Basra. He stayed in colleges, picking up an impressive array of scholarly diplomas on the way. In Alexandria he visited the first of a sequence of Sufi holy men, who predicted his life of travel and urged him to visit the other great Sufi mystics. In Jerusalem, he was presented with a *khirqa*, a Sufi cloak worn by disciples as a sign of their dedication to a life of seeking for God and of self-denial. It was doubtless his dedication to the former, as well as the attraction of the latter, that drove him onward; he vowed never to travel the same road twice in his life, save when visiting Mecca.

Ibn Battuta certainly trusted to his luck when traveling. His first long sea voyage was to Somalia and the coast of what is now Tanzania, where he described the difficult relations between the Muslim-Arab traders and the "pagan" Africans whom they enslaved. His return journey took him to Ormuz (Hormuz), across the Persian Gulf and back through Arabia to Mecca in 1330. Hearing of the generosity of the Sultan of Delhi toward scholars, he then set out for India, taking the Silk Road route across the steppes via "the land of the Turks" in Anatolia. His expectations of the Sultan of Delhi were initially not misplaced and Ibn Battuta found himself courted – even being appointed a grand *qadi* (judge) of Delhi.

But the Sultan of Delhi was notoriously unpredictable and Ibn Battuta only avoided disgrace by undertaking an opportune embassy to China. On his way from Delhi, his caravan was beset by marauders and he was lucky to escape with his life. On the Malabar Coast he became embroiled in local wars and was shipwrecked near Calicut. He chose to go to the Maldive islands, and visited Bengal ("a hell crammed with good things"). Deciding to resume his mission to China he sailed for Sumatra, where the local Muslim sultan gave him a new ship in which he made his way to the great Chinese port of Ch'uan-chou (Quanzhou).

Travels in China

There are difficulties with his very summary account of his travels in China and perhaps his claim to have reached Peking (Beijing) was exaggerated. The culture shock of stepping outside the Dar al-Islam was too much for him: "China was beautiful, but it did not please me. On the contrary I was greatly troubled thinking about the way paganism dominated this country. Whenever I went out of my lodgings, I saw many blameworthy things. That disturbed me so much that I stayed indoors most of the time and only went out when necessary." His greatest pleasure was meeting a fellow Moroccan, a young scholar named al-Bushri, who had also left home to travel to the east in the company of an uncle.

Returning to Tangier in 1349, Ibn Battuta embarked on a final journey, north to Granada and south across the Sahara Desert to the Niger River and Timbuktu. From 1354 until his death in 1370 he fulfilled the request of the local sultan and dictated his remarkable book, known as the *Travels*. The work provides extensive geographical and topographical information, and invaluable historical, religious and ethnographic detail. It has become one of the outstanding medieval sources for world history and a travelog admired by all explorers and travelers.

◀ *Arab dhows,* such as the
replica shown here, sailed
from the Red Sea ports
across to the west coast
of India at least as long ago
as the 1st century BC.

KEY TO ROUTES

—— Ibn Battuta 1325–27
—— Ibn Battuta 1328–30
—— Ibn Battuta 1330–46
—— Ibn Battuta 1349–54

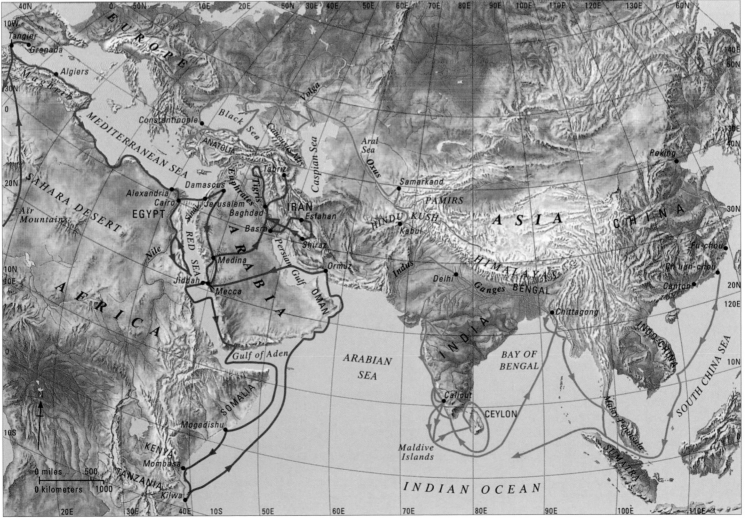

European Discovery of Asia

Europe was unique among the medieval civilizations of Eurasia in that it was left comparatively undisturbed by the Mongol invasions. The Mongols were responsible for the last, and most violent, assault of nomadic steppe peoples upon the civilized world of Eurasia, and their effects in China, the Middle East, and India were profound. By contrast, although there was a brutal incursion into Poland and Hungary in 1240, the Mongols made no effort to occupy or annex eastern Europe. As a result, Europe's leaders persisted in believing that they might gain the assistance of the Mongol khans in their fight to drive back their greater enemies – the Muslims – against whom they crusaded in the Holy Land between the end of the 11th and the end of the 13th centuries.

Journeys to the Mongol court

After the church council of Lyon in 1245, Innocent IV despatched two Franciscan friars – Giovanni da Pian del Carpini and Benedict of Poland – as ambassadors to the Mongol court. Giovanni, who was from near Perugia in Italy, had been one of the early associates of Francis of Assisi and had played a leading role in the establishment of the Franciscan order. Its vow of strict poverty, coupled with its evangelical aspirations, made Franciscans (like Buddhist monks) well suited to the challenges of travel in remote lands. With Benedict as his interpreter, he journeyed through Poland and Russia to Mongolia and, two years later, returned to report on his journey in his *History of the Mongols*. He was the first European since 900 to be on record as having traveled east of Baghdad and returned to tell the tale. His largely sympathetic description of the lifestyle and customs of the Mongols contradicted many of the beliefs then held about them. Much of his account was incorporated into the widely read medieval encyclopedia, the *Speculum Historiale* of Vincent of Beauvais, and provides historians today with one of the fundamental accounts of the Mongol people.

Many others followed Giovanni in the course of the later 13th century. Among the more notable were André of Longjumeau in France, who was despatched in 1249, and Guillaume of Rubruquis in Flanders (William of Rubruck), who left in 1253. Both were sent by the great crusader, King Louis IX of France. A man claiming to represent the Great Khan had come before the king, then on

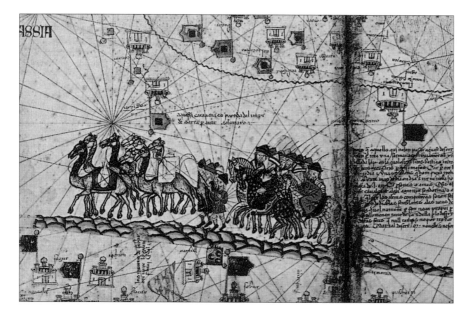

▲ *The journeys* of men such as Giovanni del Carpini and William of Rubruck did much to increase European knowledge of Mongol culture. In subsequent years trade routes with China, which had been severed by the movements of the Mongol armies, were re-established. This illustration from a 14th-century Catalan manuscript depicts European merchants traveling along the "Silk Road."

Prester John
The myth that Christian Europe had a mighty ally to the East in their battle against the Muslim Saracens was something people wanted to believe was true. In about 1165 a letter was sent to the Pope purporting to come from Prester John, but whose true authorship has never been finally determined. The letter was taken as confirmation of Prester John's existence, and missionaries were sent to look for him.

A legend like this found great credence among the crusading armies of the 13th century. There were reports that a Prester John figure (sometimes called King David) would destroy the Saracens from the East. Pope Honorius III was so convinced that King David was on the move westward that he passed the good news on to England and France. Prester John was to act as a beacon to explorers and it is a sign of Europe's greater knowledge of Asia that, from around the 1330s, the search for the land of Prester John changed its focus, first from Asia to Ethiopia and then further south to central Africa.

his way to the Seventh Crusade. The Great Khan, he said, was eager for an alliance against Islam. The khan, following the example of his mother, had reputedly converted to Christianity. It was expected that all the leading Tatars would emulate him.

André of Longjumeau

André of Longjumeau's task was to make an alliance with the Mongols and to assist in their Christian conversion. He failed on both counts. After a remarkable overland journey, he reached the court of the Great Khan at Qaraqorum to find that the khan had died, the empire was in the hands of his mother, and that she was certainly no Christian. She dismissed him with an insolent missive to his sovereign.

The return overland journey back lasted over a year. Despite his disappointments, he recounted hopeful reports that the khan's grandfather had converted to Christianity after a vision in which God had promised him dominion over Prester John (the mythical Christian potentate of Asia). He also brought cheering news of a Mongol chief whom he reported to be a Christian.

William of Rubruck

Louis IX was in the Holy Land when he received André of Longjumeau's optimistic account. With him was William of Rubruck, who also knew some Arabic and to whom Louis now gave a Bible, a small sum for expenses, and commendatory letters. In the company of a dipsomaniac friar and two servants, William left Constantinople in May 1253. He crossed the Black Sea to the Crimea and then went overland across the Don River, finally arriving at the court of the Great Khan Mangu on December 27, 1253.

William stayed at the court until winter was over, but he made little progress with the khan and mistrusted the Nestorian Christians in the court entourage whom he regarded as heretics. He did, however, carry a letter back to Louis IX, returning to Cyprus by mid-June 1255, although by then the king was back in France. He also wrote up his travels for the king, describing the Don and the Volga rivers, and explaining that the Caspian Sea was a lake. He showed a keen interest in ethnology, and much of his account was embodied in the 13th-century encyclopedia of his fellow Franciscan, Roger Bacon.

Changing perceptions of the world

The reasons for this European interest in travel in the 13th century are not hard to find. First, there was, in the 12th century, a tremendous acquisition and transmission of knowledge and ideas and the beginnings of Europe's recovery of its classical heritage. Through Christianized Arabs and Jews in Spain, Sicily and the crusading kingdoms, fresh translations of Greek, Syriac and Arabic manuscripts in Latin became available, thus transforming every branch of knowledge and science and Europe's perception of the wider world. At the same time, Europe was transformed by the formation of a more urban and politically sophisticated society, which created a demand for education and the beginnings of a literate laity.

The second reason for this new urge to travel was that the Crusades took Europeans to the southern end of the old trade routes across central Asia at a time when Mongolian power was at its greatest. It was in 1264 that Kublai Khan took up residence at Peking (Beijing) and established his summer retreat at Shangdu (Xanadu) in the hills northwest of the capital. Among his first visitors were the Polo brothers, Nicolò and Maffeo, who had left the Crimea four years previously.

The Journeys of Marco Polo

◄ **This map of the region** of the Imperial Palace at Shangdu (Xanadu) in China, is based on Marco Polo's account, including his comments about the area.

▼ **The young Marco Polo** (center) is depicted leaving Venice in the company of his father and uncle in an illuminated manuscript of the late 14th century.

▼ **Marco Polo's arrival** at Ormuz on his return journey is shown in this 14th-century illumination, according to which he brought back with him camels and an elephant.

Marco Polo surpassed all the other travelers of medieval Europe in his determination, his writings, and his influence. If his account is to be believed, his explorations through Asia lasted 24 years, during which he reached further than any of his predecessors, beyond Mongolia to China. He became a confidant of Kublai Khan and (by his own account, for it is not confirmed in Chinese sources) governor of a great Chinese city. He traversed the whole of China, all the way to the Pacific Ocean and perhaps went on as far south as Burma. He also states that he was sent on a mission to India. Most important, however, he returned to tell the tale which became, for generations of Europeans, the greatest travelog of their civilization.

His birthplace, Venice, was the center of commerce in the Mediterranean and increasingly, as a result of the Crusades, in the Levant and beyond too. Born in 1254,

Marco Polo was just 15 years old when his father Nicolò and his uncle Maffeo returned to Venice from their nine-year journey to the East. The family had trading offices in Constantinople and in the Crimea.

The travels of Nicolò and Maffeo

Marco Polo's book, *The Description of the World*, opens with an account of these earlier travels, which had taken his father and uncle to Surai and the court of Barka Khan, the son of Ghengis, who had bought their entire stock of jewels and made the journey worth their while. During their stay, however, a war broke out between Barka and the neighboring Khan of the Levant. The Polos took refuge at Bukhara, in the land of a neutral Tatar lordship. There they learnt the Tatar language and familiarized themselves with Tatar culture before journeying, on the encouragement of Tatar envoys, to the court of Kublai Khan at Shangdu (Xanadu) – a year's traveling.

Kublai, Khan of all the Tatars, had become Emperor of China. He proved a man of broad curiosity, eager to learn about Europe, and asked the two brothers to be his envoys to the Pope, requesting 100 missionaries to teach his people about Christianity and Western science. He also wanted some oil from the lamp at the Holy Sepulcher in Jerusalem. When Nicolò and Maffeo departed, they carried the Khan's Golden Tablet, his certificate of safe passage, and returned to Venice late in 1269.

Marco's great journey

In 1271, when the two men once more set out from Venice on their return journey to Kublai Khan, they took with them Nicolò's 17-year-old son Marco and two Dominicans, reluctantly accorded them by Pope Gregory X. Before they left the Mediterranean, the monks returned in panic, but the Polo family went on to Tabriz and Kerman and then, deciding against a sea voyage in the leaky ships they surveyed at Ormuz, traveled overland through the Persian Desert and Hindu Kush along the old Silk Road.

Polo's account of the "road to Cathay" is full of fascinating regional colors and textures, the record of a sharp-eyed merchant. In Badakhshan he noted the precious rubies and stones that were mined in the locality, and the

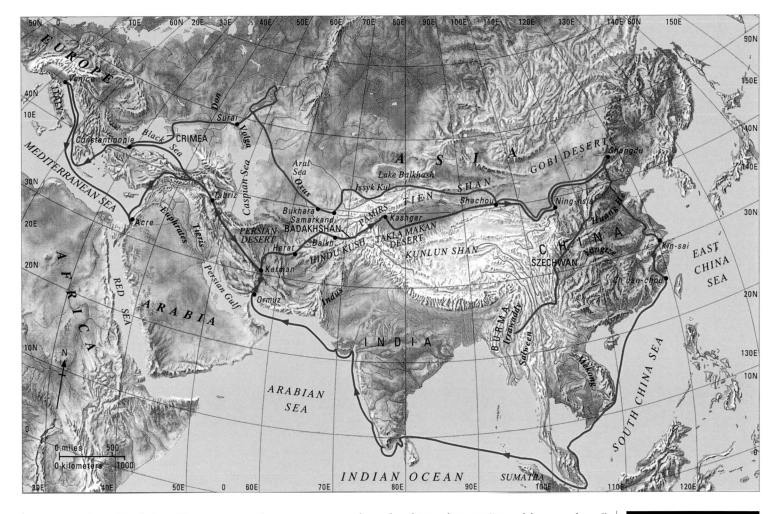

huge mountains with their sulfurous streams that were purported to cure ailments (and were successful, in Marco Polo's case). He remembered the excellent trout-fishing and that the "ladies of the nobility and gentry wear trousers ... there are some ladies who in one pair of trousers or breeches put anything up to a hundred ells of cotton cloth, folded in pleats. This is to give the impression that they have plump hips, because their menfolk delight in plumpness." Crossing the Pamirs and the Takla Makan Desert also left a deep impression on him.

At the court of Kublai Khan

Kublai Khan received the Venetians with honor. No better account re-creates for us the court of the khan. It describes the summer palace at Shangdu, to which the khan always retired for three months of the year. Marco Polo clearly knew its gilded halls and chambers and its 16 miles (25 kilometers) of enclosed parkland. He describes the khan hunting there, sometimes with a leopard perched on his horse behind the saddle, which he would unleash to catch a stag. Marco Polo's fascination with falconry and hunting may well have been one enthusiasm which he had been able to convey to and share with the khan. He also recognized the power of the court astrologers and describes how each year on August 28 the khan ceremonially left the summer palace on their instruction to return to Peking (Beijing), making a libation of the milk of some of his 10,000 snow-white mares as he did so in order to appease the gods.

The Venetians stayed 17 years, acquiring "great wealth in jewels and gold." Marco Polo's account gives details of a journey to "Tibet" (actually, what is now Szechwan); as always, there is a place to record the precious stones to be found there and also the gold and the falconry: "The people here ... have all their teeth of gold ... the men are all gentlemen, according to their notions. They have no occupation but warfare, the chase, and falconry. All the work is done by the women, and by other

men whom they have taken captive and keep as slaves." The cities of the rich Yangtze valley astounded even a cosmopolitan Venetian such as Marco Polo. He wrote: "At the end of three days you reach the noble and magnificent city of Kin-sai [Hangzhou], a name that signifies 'the Celestial City' and which it merits from its pre-eminence to all others in the world in point of grandeur and beauty, as well as from its abundant delights, which might lead an inhabitant to imagine himself in paradise.... According to common estimation, this city is one hundred miles in circuit. Its streets and canals are extensive and there are squares, or market places, [these] being necessarily proportionate in size to the prodigious concourse of people."

Return to Europe

Eventually the Polos returned home as escorts to a Tatar princess. After a dreadful sea voyage through the South China Sea to Sumatra and the Indian Ocean, they returned overland by way of Tabriz, finally reaching Venice in the winter of 1295. Then, three years later, in a sea battle off the Dalmatian coast with the Genoese, a "gentleman commander" of one of the Venetian galleys, one Marco Polo, was captured and brought back in chains to a prison in Genoa. His fellow prisoner, a writer of romances from Pisa called Rustichello, saw the literary potential of Polo's account and persuaded the Venetian to cooperate.

The resulting account was obviously embellished in places by Rustichello. The description of Marco Polo's first arrival at the court of Kublai Khan, for example, recalls the reception of young Tristan at Camelot, a familiar scene to a writer of medieval romance – indeed one already described by Rustichello himself. Yet Marco Polo recalled, before his death, that he had only told half the extraordinary things that had occurred to him in his amazing life, on the grounds that had he recounted the other half no one would have believed a word of it at all. In fact, there is now considerable discussion among scholars as to whether he even traveled further east than Persia.

China and the Outside World

When Marco Polo arrived in China in the latter part of the 13th century he was amazed by what he saw. China under the Yuan (Mongol) dynasty was a huge empire whose internal economy dwarfed that of Europe. Iron manufacture was around 125,000 tons a year (a level not reached in Europe before the 18th century). Salt production was on a prodigious scale: 30,000 tons a year in one province alone. Metal-casting techniques could make standardized military, agricultural and other equipment, and the administrative elite, the mandarins, could arrange delivery anywhere in the empire. A canal-based transportation system linked China's huge cities and markets in a vast internal communication network in which paper money and credit facilities were highly developed. The citizens of Suzhou, Nanjing, and Kin-sai could purchase paperback books from market stalls with paper money, eat rice from fine porcelain bowls, and wear garments of silk, woven to a standard that no European craftsman could match.

The mapping of China

Independent of any influence from the West, the Chinese mandarins – the scholar-bureaucrats on whom imperial government in China depended – had devised a grid pattern within which to represent the irregular surface of the Earth and their vast empire. Phei Hsui, appointed Minister of Works to the emperor in AD 267, had completed an 18-sheet map of China on a rectangular grid pattern using graduated divisions established by means of right-angle triangles. (The terms he used for his coordinates (*ching* and *wei*) also meant the warp and weft of cloth, which suggests that the origins for the grid pattern of Chinese maps lay in the silk on which they were painted.)

In AD 801, during the T'ang dynasty (618–907), the emperor's cartographer had completed a grid plan of the whole empire on a scale of 1 inch (2.5 centimeters) to 100 *li* (a *li* was about a third of a mile [half a kilometer]). The map measured some 30 feet (9 meters) long and 33 feet (10 meters)

high. Maps had become so popular that they were found even in the imperial bathrooms. These were maps of the "Middle Kingdom" (China) in which only China's immediate neighbors appeared, if any at all. China's links with the outside world had been limited mainly to the small numbers of merchants who traded beyond the Jade Gates and along the Silk Road. Then, under the Sung dynasty (960–1279), foreign trade had begun to expand outward.

Expansion of foreign trade

The Sung dynasty had actively stimulated foreign trade by the sale of licences and monopolies. Furthermore, the pace of technical innovation had considerably increased, and China's commercial and industrial development was so great that it seemed on the threshold of a mercantile, even an industrial, revolution. Just as Europe's industrial revolution was to result in the establishment of an overseas mercantile colonialism, so China seemed poised to go in the same direction centuries earlier.

Whereas under the T'ang only one port, Guangzhou, had been allowed to trade with foreigners, by the early 11th century there were seven others. A new emphasis was placed on boat-building, innovation in which was rewarded by the administration. The world's first paddle-boat was designed. Huge ocean-going junks, designed like fortresses, were sent into battle, equipped with cannon, rockets, and bombs of all descriptions. Explosive rockets, which would shoot across the surface of the water, were developed, along with submarine guns.

To these ports came Muslim merchants and, as the overland silk routes became impassable because of the Mongol invasions, so the sea routes to the Red Sea became increasingly important. By this means, silk, porcelain, tea, and spices reached the Arab world and, from there, Europe. The scale of this trade was considerable: nearly 10,000 pieces of broken Chinese porcelain have recently been found at Fustat near Cairo; similar sites have been discovered in Oman and along the Red Sea coast.

KEY TO ROUTES

—— Zheng Ho 1431–33
—— Subsidiary ships of Zheng Ho's expedition

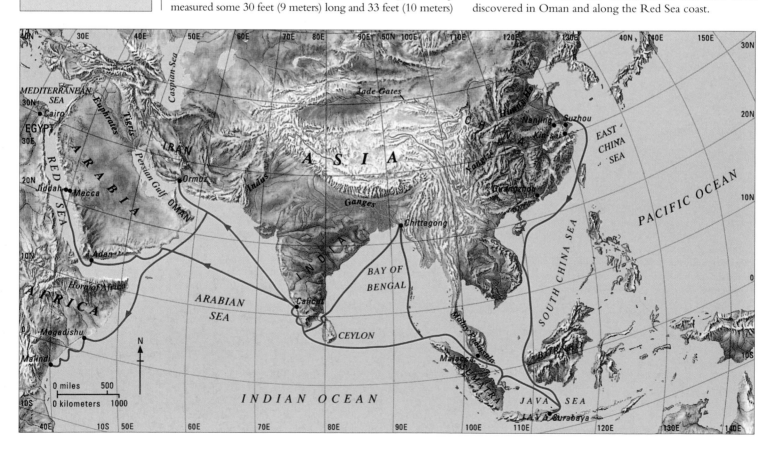

▲ **Under the Sung dynasty** (960–1279) China traded in ceramic goods with the Western world. This delicately glazed stoneware jar dates from that period.

▶ **Admiral Zheng Ho** returned from one of his voyages with a captive giraffe, which must have seemed a miraculous beast to the Chinese at that time.

Dissemination of technology

Not only trade goods reached the West via this route. Paper, printing, and gunpowder technology flowed westward, as did that of the magnetic compass. Another innovation, of eventual importance to Europe's overseas discoveries, was the stern-post rudder. Hitherto, European ocean-going ships had depended upon the use of an oar extending from the back of galleys. The stern-post rudder allowed for the construction of much larger vessels, whose direction could be more precisely determined.

The Sung dynasty finally fell to the Mongols, who extended the policies of maritime expansion adopted by the Sung and – particularly in the person of Kublai Khan, to whom Marco Polo claimed to have become a confidant – were eager to learn about the lands beyond their empire.

Admiral Zheng Ho

The swansong of Chinese maritime expansion took place in the early 15th century, in the early years of the Ming dynasty (1368–1644), with the expeditions of Admiral Zheng Ho. He came from the Muslim minority that had established itself in the trading communities of the Chinese coastal ports, was a king-maker, a diplomat, and also a great naval strategist. He was popularly known as the "Three-Jewelled Eunuch."

Between 1405 and 1433 Zheng Ho led seven armadas, consisting of up to 62 ships, carrying 40,000 soldiers, across the China Sea and Indian Ocean. His huge treasure ships were five times the size of those of the Portuguese. His two-fold purpose was to provide luxuries for the court and to collect tribute from Chinese overseas colonies.

The voyages of the ships in his fleet reached the east coast of Africa, Mecca, and the ports of India, Ceylon (Sri Lanka) and Sumatra. They may even have explored the coast of Australia, but most of the accounts of his voyages and charts were lost or, more probably, destroyed. He returned with many treasures – pepper, sapanwood (from which a red dye was produced), and exotic plants – as well as a selection of monarchs who had refused to kowtow, most notably the King of Ceylon.

◀ **This Chinese warship,** depicted in a 16th-century woodcut, is probably similar to the mighty treasure ships that sailed with Zheng Ho on his expeditions through the South China Sea and across the Indian Ocean.

Severing links with the West

The Ming emperors, with a background in rural China, distrusted the cosmopolitanism of their predecessors. Emperor Gaozong expressed this clearly: "China's territory produces all goods in abundance, so why should we buy useless trifles from abroad?" In 1433, and again in 1449 and 1452, imperial edicts prohibiting overseas trade and travel were issued. Any merchant caught attempting to engage in foreign trade was deemed a pirate and executed. Even learning foreign languages was forbidden, as was the teaching of Chinese to foreigners.

In this climate of distrust Zheng Ho's expeditions were no longer tolerated, and with his fall from grace in 1433 the Ming navy shrank to insignificance and China withdrew from the world.

Reconnaissance of Africa

The "Age of Reconnaissance," in which Europe discovered the rest of the world, was launched from one of the smallest of Europe's monarchies, Portugal. The capture in 1415 of the Moorish city of Ceuta in North Africa was followed by three-quarters of a century of patient, often difficult, exploration of the West African coast. Unlike Columbus's discovery of America, which would turn out to have been a bold stroke of undreamed-of significance, the Portuguese voyagers undertook a rational, progressive, even systematic, process of exploration, with clear political objectives, an evaluation of risk, and the expectation of reward. It was the prototype for modern exploration.

Prince Henry the Navigator

Portuguese exploration was directed by its monarchs and crown princes. According to Gomes Eanes da Zurara, the chronicler of Prince Henry the Navigator, who was the most renowned (but not the only) member of the royal house to plan and play a leading part in Portugal's reconnaissance, the Prince's aims were: "To discover what lay beyond the Canaries and Cape Bojador; to trade with any Christians who might dwell in the lands beyond; to discover the extent of the Mohammedan dominions; to find a Christian king who would help him to fight the Infidel; to spread the Christian faith; to fulfil the predictions of his horoscope, which bound him to engage in great and noble conquests and attempt the discovery of things that were hidden from other men; to find Guinea."

As Governor of Algarve, Prince Henry established a small school of navigation at Sagres. Here, and at the nearby port of Lagos, experiments in shipbuilding design produced a new type of ship, the caravel, which could withstand the high seas likely to be found on voyages of exploration. The first rewards of such voyages came in the form of the Atlantic islands. The Canaries had already been discovered – probably by Genoese sailors – in the 14th century. These, and the Azores and the Madeiras, were colonized from Portugal in the 1420s and 1430s, helping to dispel the prevailing fear of the Atlantic as a desolate and empty place, the "green sea of darkness." Even so, Prince Henry sent 15 expeditions southward between 1424 and 1434, and none of them would go further than Cape Bojador ("Bulging Cape") just south of the Canaries. Their fears may, even today, be understood.

Round Cape Bojador

Between Cape Draa and Cape Bojador the coast must have seemed dangerous, with heavy swells from the northwest around the Canaries, a stiff current and interminable surfy beaches. Even Henry's shield-bearer, a noble with crusading pretensions, failed at the first attempt to penetrate further than Cape Bojador. In 1433, however, he managed it, and brought back with him from the shoreline a flower, known in Portugal as St Mary's rose, to prove it.

Thereafter, the pace of Portuguese discoveries shifted into a higher gear. In 1441, Antão Gonçalves, Prince Henry's Chamberlain, and Nuno Tristão, also a member of his court, reached Cape Branco – a further 250 miles (400 kilometers) – where they took two natives captive. In 1444 Eanes brought back the first human cargo – 200 Africans to be sold as slaves in the market in Lagos. At the same time, the Portuguese monarchy bestowed on Henry a proportion of the royal profits from the enterprise and sole rights to grant licences to sail beyond Cape Bojador. The possibilities of the voyages became more apparent. Exploration was about to become exploitation.

Round Cape Verde

After Dinís Dias rounded Cape Verde, the western tip of Africa, in 1445, the prosperous Portuguese trade along the West African coast with the inland kingdom of Timbuktu soon occupied up to 26 caravels a year. By a succession of Papal decrees the Portuguese king was given permission to enslave all unbelievers, and to enjoy a monopoly in all matters, and in every place to which the Portuguese conquest had extended and might extend in the future.

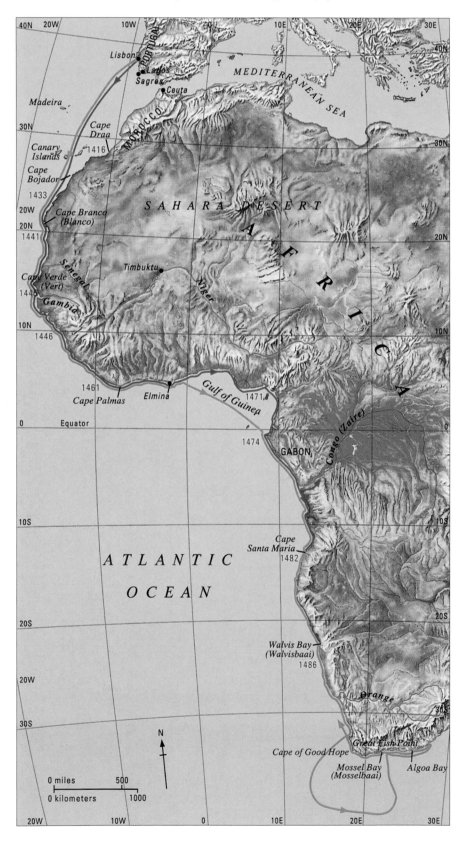

In 1460 Prince Henry died. His nephew, Afonso V, leased the monopoly of the Guinea trade in 1469 to Fernâo Gomes, a wealthy citizen from Lisbon, who committed himself in return to discover at least 100 leagues a year (about 300 miles [485 kilometers]) for each of the next five years. The contract resulted in an annual series of African discoveries, and by 1474 the Portuguese had crossed the Equator off the coast of Gabon.

In search of Prester John

When Gomes's contract expired, one was granted to Afonso's son, who became John II in 1481. The establishment of a fortress factory at Elmina increased Portuguese contacts with native Africans and taught them more about the inland African kingdoms. This revived the possibility of the existence of Prester John, the mythical leader of a powerful Christian, non-European people. By the 1480s attention was concentrated on Ethiopia. Every discovery of a river mouth on the west coast of Africa, such as when Cão explored the lower reaches of the Congo (Zaire), revived the possibility of a "western Nile," leading to Prester John's kingdom. By 1487 John II had organized a two-pronged strategy for finding the long-sought Christian ally. One expedition would go southeast overland, and another would go by sea around the African coast.

The overland expedition was a modest affair consisting of just two men: Pero de Covilhão and Afonso de Paiva (see page 38), which ended with Covilhão becoming a trusted councillor of the King of Ethiopia. The second expedition was more prestigious, and was carefully planned and organized. Under the command of Bartholomeu Dias, it comprised two caravels of 50 tons each and − an innovation − a store ship. With Dias went six Africans dressed in European clothes, to be deposited along the African coast to act as agents for the Portuguese and explain to the natives what products were required.

▲ The Portuguese carracks, with their characteristic stern towers, were merchant ships. Some exceeded 1000 tons. They were not ideal for exploration, but their huge size meant that sufficient stores and trading goods could be taken on long ocean journeys. The caravel, by contrast, was only 60–70 tons, about 70 feet (21 meters) in length, 25 feet (7.5 meters) abeam, and carried two or three lateen sails. "The best ships that sailed the seas," said the explorer Ca' da Mosto.

After landing the last of these mobile salesmen, the ships sailed into a gale. They ran before a northerly wind with close-reefed sails for 13 days and were driven away from the coast into open water. The crew gave themselves up for dead, but Dias turned east under full sail, and when no land was sighted after several days, turned north for about 450 miles (700 kilometers). Suddenly he viewed high mountains and on February 3, 1488, the ships anchored in Mossel Bay, about 230 miles (370 kilometers) east of what is now Cape Town. From here they followed the coast, running northeast another 300 miles (485 kilometers) to Algoa Bay and Great Fish Point.

Dias wanted to go on, but his crew would have none of it. Provisions were low and the supply ship had been left behind. Faced with a signed sworn testimony by all the captains, expressing their desire to return to Portugal, Dias agreed. But, as he passed the stone marker they had set up to record their achievement, Dias wrote that he did so "with as much sorrow and feeling as though he were taking his last leave of a son condemned to exile forever, recalling with what danger to his own person and to all his men they had come such a long distance with this sole aim, and then God would not grant it him to reach his goal." When his caravels came sailing into Lisbon harbor in December 1488, Christopher Columbus was among those who saw them arrive.

▲ Henry the Navigator (1394–1460), a Portuguese prince, established his court at Sagres on the southwest tip of Portugal, and encouraged the study and development of navigational techniques. Although he made no voyages of exploration himself, he sponsored many expeditions that extended Portuguese influence on the coast of West Africa, opening up commercial possibilities.

ARCTIC OCEAN

EUROPE

RUSSIA

SIBERIA

URAL MOUNTAINS

Lena

Yenisey

Ob

Volga

Amur

Irtysh

Lakes Baykal

ALTAI MOUNTAINS

MONGOLIAN PLATEAU

Black Sea

Constantinople
(Istanbul)

Aral
Sea

Syrdarya

Lake Balkhash

ASIA

GOBI DESERT

Peking
(Beijing)

Caspian Sea

Amudarya

TIEN SHAN

Tarim

MEDITERRANEAN
SEA

PERSIA

Huang

Jerusalem

Euphrates

Tigris

Baghdad

Esfahan

KUNLUN SHAN

ARABIA

Persian Gulf

Ormuz
(Hormuz)

TIBETAN
PLATEAU

Yangtze

C H

RED SEA

Mecca

Indus

Sutlej

HIMALAYA

Min-Jiang

Delhi

Agra

Yamuna

Ganges

Brahmaputra

I N D I A

Irrawaddy

Salween

Mekong

AFRICA

Bombay

DECCAN

ARABIAN SEA

BAY OF BENGAL

Goa

Calicut

CEYLON

Malacca

SO

SUMATRA

Area known of by Chinese in 1450

Area known of by Europeans in 1450

N

0 miles   500

0 kilometers   1000

INDIAN OCEAN

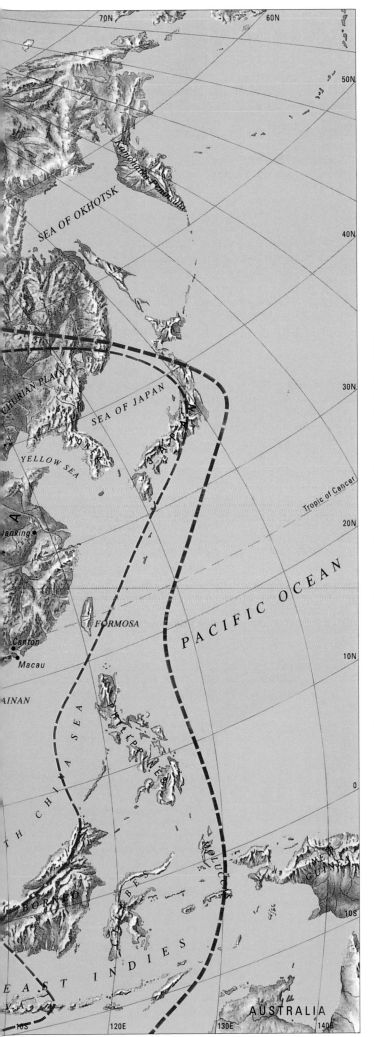

ASIA

S tretching over 17 million square miles (27 million square kilometers), Asia is the largest of the continents and the most densely
populated. It contains almost every type of landform and climate,
including the coldest, the hottest, and the wettest places in the
northern hemisphere. It has by far the biggest mountains, the widest
plateaus, the largest lakes and forests, and, except for the Sahara, the
most expansive deserts in the world.

Asia is also the home of the world's oldest civilizations. At least
one of these, China, maintained a remarkable cultural continuity and,
at the time the European age of discovery began, was in almost every
respect more advanced than the civilization of Europe. The Chinese
were also better equipped than the Europeans to undertake long-range
exploration, and many other Asian peoples were also long accustomed
to travel far beyond their own territories.

The continent was crisscrossed by ancient trade routes, and when
the Portuguese entered the Indian Ocean they found a vigorous
commercial network which had been in place for centuries. To speak
of pioneering European travelers in Asia as "explorers" is therefore
debatable. The story of the Europeans who attempted to make their
way to Mecca, a city visited annually by thousands of Muslims as a
matter of course, is an obvious example of the Eurocentric character
of "exploration."

Large areas that were relatively unknown did, however, exist in
Asia, and Europeans played a major role in exploring and mapping
them. In many cases they would have failed had they not been aided
and accompanied by Asians; nonetheless, the Europeans usually
provided the impetus.

Portuguese Pioneers

In 1487 Bartolomeu Dias set sail from Portugal with the intention of finding a sea route to the eastern coast of Africa, and from there to India. He rounded the Cape of Good Hope in 1488 but was forced to return to Lisbon shortly afterward (see page 35).

Another Portuguese mission set out for the East in 1487. It consisted of two men, Pedro de Covilhão, a courtier who had been a secret agent in Spain and North Africa and spoke fluent Spanish and Arabic, and Afonso de Paiva, born in the Canaries, also fluent in Arabic. The two men had been ordered to search for the route to India and to make contact with "Prester John," the legendary priest-king, whom an Ethiopian emissary to Portugal in 1452 had identified with the Negus of Ethiopia. Prester John, so the Portuguese hoped, would be a useful ally against the Muslims and in finding the route to India.

India and Prester John

Covilhão and Paiva arrived in Egypt posing as Berber merchants, with trade goods they had bought in Rhodes. They soon made contact with Arab merchants, familiar with the Indian trade, and accompanied some of them south through the Red Sea in a dhow. From Suakin near Port Sudan, Paiva set off inland in search of Prester John, while Covilhão boarded a pilgrims' ship sailing across the Indian

Ocean to the Malabar Coast. In India Covilhão visited the rich port of Calicut, noting the vigorous trade in spices, and sailed north to Goa. There he took another ship to Ormuz (Hormuz), at the entrance to the Persian Gulf, before embarking on the long voyage back to Sofala in Mozambique, the center of a gold trade. There, as well as hearing of Madagascar, he concluded from what local people told him that a sea passage existed between the Atlantic and Indian oceans (as Dias had discovered).

Covilhão had carried out his task with extraordinary success and had amassed much immensely valuable information. He headed back to a rendezvous with Paiva in Cairo, but Portuguese agents there told him that Paiva was dead. Covilhão, setting out to complete his partner's mission, gave the agents his papers to take back to Lisbon. He first went to Jiddah and from there may have visited the holy cities of Arabia. He arrived in Ethiopia in 1493, and he was still there, living in some comfort with an Ethiopian wife and on good terms with the Negus, when a Portuguese emissary arrived in the country in 1520. It has been assumed that Covilhão was prevented from leaving, but it is impossible to imagine a man of his resources being kept anywhere against his will for nearly 30 years.

Across the Indian Ocean

Unlike earlier exploratory voyages, the maritime expedition of Vasco da Gama in 1497 was "an armed commercial embassy": the Portuguese sought trade and were prepared to fight for it. After rounding the Cape, his ships called at the mercantile ports of East Africa, but were poorly received except at Malindi (in modern Kenya), where they were lucky enough to acquire a local pilot. He may have been Ahmed ibn Majid, a famous Gujerati navigator and author of a collection of charts and sailing instructions. In May 1498, ten months after leaving Portugal, the little fleet anchored off Calicut.

Muslim rule in one form or another had existed in Delhi for a long time, and Muslim sultanates extended as far south as Goa. Hindus ruled south of that, but on the coast (as in Africa) commercial affairs were largely controlled by Muslims. At Calicut, the Portuguese were well received by the Hindu ruler, but he was not prepared to antagonize the Arab traders to whom the arrival of the infidel Portuguese was highly objectionable. Vasco da Gama was unable to establish a trading station; his goods, being of the kind sold in West Africa, were unsuitable for the more sophisticated Indian market, and he experienced some difficulty in amassing a cargo of spices to take home to Lisbon.

The first part of the return voyage was extremely difficult; it took three months to cross the Indian Ocean against storms and headwinds, with many deaths from scurvy. In Lisbon, though the success of the voyage was limited, da Gama was well rewarded. His return prompted great celebrations and immediate preparations for another voyage, which departed in 1500 under Pedro Alvares Cabral.

The Portuguese had discovered that they could benefit most from the currents in the South Atlantic if they sailed far westward before turning back to the African coast. In doing this, Cabral accidentally reached Brazil in 1500. Less happily, he lost four of his 12 ships, one commanded by the veteran Bartolomeu Dias, in a storm. At Calicut Cabral found the reception still frosty, so he sailed south to Cochin, where he did good trade and established a factory. To the Arabs and Indians the Portuguese appeared as no more than a band of brigands, infidel sea rovers whose guns made them more than a minor nuisance. No one realized how big a threat they represented.

▼ *Portuguese buildings* in Goa serve as a reminder that in the 16th century the port became a major base for the Portuguese, enabling them to control trade to the west coast of India.

In the same year that Cabral sailed, an Italian, Lodovico de Varthema, set out for the East from Venice. After visiting Arabia disguised as an Arab (see page 50), he crossed the Indian Ocean to Diu on the coast of India, and then, via a detour to the Persian Gulf, traveled round India where he served with Portuguese forces. From here his travels took him to Bengal, Burma and the city of Malacca. It appears from his *Itinerary*, which was published on his return to Europe, that he may then have become the first European to reach the fabled Spice Islands (Moluccas).

The Portuguese Empire

The third Portuguese expedition to India, in 1502, was again commanded by Vasco da Gama, and bore even greater resemblance to a war fleet than his earlier journey. The Portuguese wanted the Eastern trade, but they had no chance of breaking into it by simple commercial competition. They could only take it by force. Their ships' guns made them invincible at sea: Vasco da Gama fought the first naval battle off the Malabar Coast, and Francisco d'Almeida, the first Governor-General of Portuguese India, provided further proof of Portuguese naval superiority by smashing an Arab-Gujerati fleet near Goa in 1509.

The amazingly rapid Portuguese conquest of the East was completed by Afonso d'Albuquerque, who succeeded Almeida in 1509. A brilliant strategist, Albuquerque possessed a degree of ambition, energy, and ability which prompted comparisons with Alexander the Great. He persuaded the Portuguese Government to build a powerful base at Goa, with fortified trading stations along the coasts protected by squadrons of warships. In less than five years Albuquerque advanced Portuguese power to the East Indies, capturing in 1511 the prosperous and strategically vital (though dangerous) city of Malacca, which commanded the strait between Malaya and Sumatra. This

◀ *Vasco da Gama* was a nobleman and soldier rather than a professional seaman. His expedition to India was well armed and appears to have been planned as a commercial enterprise rather than a voyage of discovery.

placed him in a powerful position *vis-à-vis* the local rulers, and Albuquerque kept court as if he himself were an oriental potentate.

His attempts to enforce Portuguese rule on the other side of the Indian Ocean were less successful. He bombarded Aden, the guardian of the Red Sea, in 1513. Though he failed to take it, his plans were of truly Alexandrian ambition. For instance, he hoped to dig a canal, with Ethiopian cooperation, which would divert the Nile away from Cairo, into the Red Sea. He was recalled to Lisbon in 1515, but died in Goa before setting sail.

KEY TO ROUTES
—— Covilhão 1487–89
—— Da Gama 1497–99
—— Varthema 1502–8
—— Almeida 1505–9
—— Albuquerque 1507–11

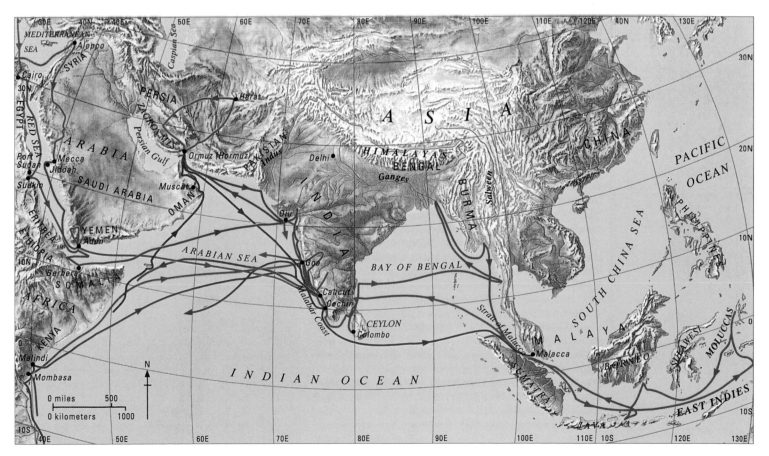

Missions to the Orient

▲ *In the 16th century many Jesuit missionaries traveled to Japan in the company of Portuguese merchants, who are depicted in this Japanese screen painting as having particularly big noses and voluminous trousers. The missionaries made many converts before the Japanese Government began its persecution of Christians in 1629.*

Goa, on the west coast of India, about 250 miles (400 kilometers) south of Bombay, belonged to the Muslim ruler of Bijapur. When the Portuguese Governor-General Afonso d'Albuquerque arrived there in 1510, it was a major market as well as the starting point for Muslim pilgrims to Mecca. After many of the Muslim inhabitants had been slaughtered, Goa, the first Portuguese territorial possession in Asia, became the capital of the Portuguese Empire in the East.

The arrival of the Jesuits

In Asia, as in America, Christian conquerors were swiftly followed by another group, Christian missionaries. Many Roman Catholic orders – Franciscans, Dominicans, Augustinians – were involved in missions, but by far the most enterprising were the Jesuits. They included men of remarkable intelligence and zeal, even, considering the times, of tolerance. It is hard to think of an institution, then or now, with such a high standard of individual intellect. Exploration was not their first priority, but Jesuit missionaries were specifically instructed to study the societies to which they were posted.

Francis Xavier

Among the first of the European missionaries to arrive at Goa was Francis Xavier, a disciple and friend of the founder of the Jesuit order, Ignatius Loyola. As the "Apostle to the Indies," Xavier set the high standards to which his successors aspired. A warm-hearted man and a traveler by inclination, he journeyed to Malacca in 1545 where he met a young Japanese, Yajiro, who had fled his country after being accused of a murder. (Although Japan was not entirely an unknown land, no European had visited it before 1542, when a Portuguese merchantman bound for Canton was shipwrecked on the island of Tane-ga-Shima, south of Kyushu.)

Xavier, convinced by Yajiro that Japan would be receptive to the Christian Gospel, sailed with him and two or three others to Kyushu in 1549. He is said to have made many converts but, perhaps more importantly, he fell in love with the Japanese: "the delight of my heart," he called them. Though he made no discoveries, he provided the first detailed, direct account of Japan by a European.

Xavier soon recognized the importance of Chinese influence in Japanese culture and, realizing that he could

not convert the Japanese unless the Chinese adopted Christianity first, he determined to go to China. He died, while still trying to gain entry, on an obscure offshore island in 1552.

The court of the Great Mughal

The court of the Mughal Emperor Akbar, at Fatehpur Sikri near Agra, was an obvious destination for the Jesuit missionaries based in Goa. Those who arrived at Akbar's court in 1580 anticipated a tough reception but found it better than expected. Akbar, instead of being a savage tyrant or an "oriental potentate," turned out to be an intelligent, industrious, courteous, and tolerant ruler. He appeared genuinely interested in the debates – "spirited" would be an understatement for these exchanges – that took place between Christian and Muslim holy men at his court. It is tempting, though probably incorrect, to think that Akbar derived some amusement from the contest: his suggestion that a Christian holding a Bible and a Muslim holding the Koran should simultaneously step into a fire to see who was consumed was declined by both sides.

Rhetorically the Jesuits may have had the best of it, as they were better informed about Islam than their opponents were about Christianity. Eventually, they also recorded a few conversions, including those of three nephews of the Emperor Jahangir, but these successes were few and short-lived. India had no need of yet another set of gurus, and from the reign of Shah Jehan (1627–58) the Mughal emperors became increasingly hostile. As elsewhere, however, the presence of the Jesuits in India furthered Europe's geographical knowledge about the region. One of the fathers, for example, decided that his time would be best occupied surveying the Ganges, and he eventually produced a detailed chart (almost 10 feet [3 meters] in length) of the river.

Father Ricci in China

Success in China looked even less likely. In 1557 the Portuguese had been granted a foothold at Macao as a reward for suppressing pirates, but early Jesuit missionaries were turned away. The chances of converting the Chinese to Christianity were probably less than the chances of the French, say, embracing Hinduism. Nevertheless, the China mission had success of a kind, largely due to the outstanding qualities of the Italian-born Matteo Ricci,

◄ *Three Jesuit missionaries* *arrived in Fatehpur Sikri in 1580 after receiving a request from Akbar that some learned fathers visit his court "with the chief* *books of the Law and the Gospel." He showed great interest in what they had to say but, to their disappointment, he did not convert to Christianity.*

▲ *Father Matteo Ricci, shown here with his first Chinese convert to Christianity, provided Europeans with unprecedented amounts of information on the geography and culture of China.*

who arrived in Macao in 1582. He saw that the only hope of being even tolerated in China was to adopt a highly conservative approach, seeking to adjust Christian doctrine to fit with Chinese ideas – tactics which, not surprisingly, drew criticism from his superiors. Ricci in effect became a mandarin himself, even regretting that he was not able to change the shape of his eyes and nose to make himself look more Chinese.

Ricci had been instructed to compile a description of China, and his success in comprehending the complex bureaucracy responsible for government, and his empathy with the mandarins, may be due to similarities in their training with that of the Jesuits. Besides producing a Mandarin–Portuguese dictionary and scouring Chinese literary classics for points of sympathy with Christianity, Ricci was also able to impress the Chinese with examples of European technology with which they were unfamiliar (one of his successors equipped the imperial army with artillery). He told the Chinese about the existence of the Americas, and he advanced human knowledge in several fields by synthesizing European and Chinese experience.

Ricci produced a Chinese version of a European world map, tactfully placing China in the center and adopting a projection that made it look larger than it is. He went on to produce his own world map, incorporating Chinese data and including a gazetteer, which was printed on 80 square feet (8 square meters) of silk and was probably the best world map available anywhere at the time. His eventual reward was an imperial summons to Peking (Beijing) – an extraordinary accolade – where he spent the last nine years of his life, dying in 1610.

Those who followed him maintained the high standards he had set, speaking perfect Mandarin and deploying extraordinary and various skills. Ferdinand Verbiest designed a new imperial observatory, and his successors embarked on a survey of China. Not completed until 1717, this survey resulted in a map, on 120 sheets of paper, that remained the best map of China until the late 19th century.

Beyond the Caspian Sea

As a result of the trade with Muscovy (Russia) set up by Richard Chancellor in 1553, the English harbored plans to find a northern route to Cathay (China) which would both outflank Islam and avoid infringing on the preserves of the Portuguese or Spanish. An expedition led by Anthony Jenkinson, a merchant with experience of the Near East, set sail for Archangel in 1557 and went from there to Moscow.

Tsar Ivan IV, not yet the tyrant associated with the name "Terrible," provided a safe conduct which took Jenkinson via Kazan and the Volga to Astrakhan, shortly before it was conquered by the Russians, on the north shore of the Caspian Sea. There he bought a ship to sail to the eastern shore. Progress among the Turkmen tribes was hazardous, but Jenkinson eventually reached Bukhara, the first Englishman to visit the city that was to claim the lives of many of his countrymen, but he concluded that farther progress was impracticable in view of the anarchic state of Turkestan. The old Silk Road was no longer functioning.

Jenkinson in Persia

It took Jenkinson over three dangerous years to get back to England, but he set off again in less than a year. This time he sailed south through the Caspian, discovering that, though an inland sea, it can be extremely stormy. Continuing on foot, Jenkinson and his companions came to the Persian province of Shirvan. The ruler Abdullah Khan was an impressive sight, adorned with gold, rubies, and pearls, and he entertained the visitors lavishly. Among other novel pleasures they learned to drink coffee.

After several luxurious weeks, they continued south to Qazvin, capital of Shah Tahmasp. The Persian ruler, a Muslim, was much less agreeable than Abdullah Khan: Jenkinson was thrown out of the palace, closely followed by a servant sent to purify the ground he had walked on. But Jenkinson, a man of admirable resilience, persisted and – through the intercession of Abdullah Khan – eventually received grudging permission to trade. He returned to England loaded with silks and other precious goods.

Fitch and Newbery

Efforts to follow up this promising beginning ended in failure. One man, Ralph Fitch, spent eight years (1583–91) wandering about southern Asia scouting for trade. He ranged as far as northern Siam (Thailand) and Malacca and gathered much information, though no hope of reopening Marco Polo's route to Cathay.

One of Fitch's companions was John Newbery, who in 1581 had tried a different approach from that pioneered by Jenkinson: via the Mediterranean, through Syria to the Euphrates and thence down to the Persian Gulf and Ormuz (Hormuz). Returning overland in disguise, via Persia to Constantinople, he presented a glowing report of commercial potential, but the long desert trek, among other hazards, was too much even for Elizabethan merchants.

Newbery accompanied Fitch and others to Ormuz in 1583, a venture aimed at establishing an English commercial presence in the East. They were captured by the Portuguese but escaped from captivity in Goa. Fitch continued east to Bengal, and in 1585 Newbery set out to meet him there. He never arrived, and his fate remains unknown. Fitch returned to England, where not everyone was pleased to see him as he had long been presumed dead and his property distributed in accordance with his will.

Ambassador to the shah

Despite the setbacks experienced by earlier travelers, Persia (Iran) was not entirely forgotten. Two brothers, Sir Anthony and Sir Robert Sherley, arrived in Qazvin in 1598. They were fortunate to find the throne occupied by Shah Abbas "the Great" – an infinitely more cultured man than Tahmasp – who had just returned from a victorious war against the Uzbeks and was in expansive mood. More importantly, he was interested in the Sherleys' proposal of an alliance against the Turks, his inveterate enemies.

KEY TO ROUTES

- Jenkinson 1557–64
- Newbery 1581–82
- Fitch 1583–91
- Sherley 1598–1600
- Herbert 1627–29

In suggesting that they could set up such an alliance with the Christian governments of Europe, the brothers were being over-optimistic. However, Shah Abbas sent Anthony back to Europe with just such a commission. He visited a number of cities without much result, though in Prague he impressed the Emperor Rudolph II sufficiently to be appointed to undertake a mission to North Africa.

His brother's failure to return left Sir Robert in a delicate position, but he began to enjoy life in Persia, marrying a princess of striking beauty and winning the shah's gratitude through his knowledge of military matters, especially gunnery. He too was appointed Persian ambassador-at-large in 1611 and, though no more successful in Europe than Anthony, he did at least return to Persia. He made a second visit some years later, and among the company who returned with him in 1627 was Sir Thomas Herbert. They came by sea to Ormuz, the Portuguese having been driven out a few years earlier by a combined Anglo-Persian operation.

Later travelers in Persia

Like Robert Sherley, who died in 1628, Herbert developed a strong affection for Persia and its people. Although his travels included few places that had not already been visited by Newbery or others, he did write marvelous descriptions of what he saw, including an account of the ruins of Persepolis.

Other visitors were less enthusiastic. The French jeweler Jean Chardin, who settled for a time in Esfahan after returning from India in the 1660s, found much to criticize. At about the same time the English doctor John Fryer complained about the climate and was scornful of the practice of ritual bathing – presumably he never had to explain the rite of baptism to the Persians.

The successors of Shah Abbas were less effective rulers, and the 18th century saw a long period of violence and disruption. The Persian trade, never very extensive and already in decline, petered out. Many years were to pass before the Europeans returned. In any case, the aims of the British had changed. The Portuguese era was over and, even before the Sherleys first arrived in Persia, Sir James Lancaster, having pioneered the route to India in 1591–92, had led the first fleet of the East India Company to the Indies.

◄ *Sir Robert Sherley*
(shown here in a portrait by Van Dyck) lived for many years in Persia and married a Circassian princess. Known as Lady Elizabeth (or Teresia) Sherley, she accompanied her husband on his diplomatic missions on behalf of the shah.

Jesuits in the Himalayas

▶ *Jesuit missionaries* made great efforts in the first half of the 17th century to spread Christianity throughout Asia. By the end of the century, however, their efforts had slackened, partly as a result of the initiative in overseas expansion passing from the Catholic to the Protestant countries of Europe.

By the 17th century the Portuguese had been largely displaced in the Far East by the Dutch and the English. They continued, however, to contribute to the European exploration of Asia.

Bento (Benedict) de Goes was a Jesuit at the court of Akbar, keen to investigate rumors of a lost Christian community beyond the Himalayas. The rumors may have stemmed from the Nestorian Christian communities in Asia and from garbled accounts of Tibetan Buddhism that suggested the lamas might be Christian priests. There was also a geographical problem still to be settled: was Marco Polo's Cathay the same country as China?

Goes set out from Agra on his extraordinarily dangerous journey in 1603. Disguised as a Muslim merchant, he traveled with an Armenian companion in a 500-strong caravan bound for Kabul. It took six months, and a further eight months passed before he was able to join another caravan across the Hindu Kush – passing out of Mughal dominions into lawless country. They went up the Oxus (Amudarya) Valley and over the Pamirs to Yarkand (Shache), surviving altitude sickness and several attacks by bandits. Goes was captured but escaped when his captors started fighting over his hat, which contained jewels.

After a diversion to Khotan (Hotan), they followed the northern branch of the old Silk Road to Karashahr (Yanqi). There they met travelers from Peking (Beijing) who were acquainted with the Jesuit mission and provided confirmation that Cathay and China were one and the same country. They continued on toward the East, past the Turfan (Turpan) Depression and across the Gobi Desert to the Great Wall at Suchou (Suzhou). Their journey had taken nearly three years.

Goes remained at Suchou for over a year. He was able to send a message to Matteo Ricci in Peking, but by the time a Chinese Christian brought Ricci's answer in 1607 Goes was dying.

▶ *Leh, capital of Ladakh,* is 11,500 feet (3500 meters) above sea level, on the southwestern edge of the Himalayas. Despite its remoteness, it was visited by a number of Jesuit missionaries.

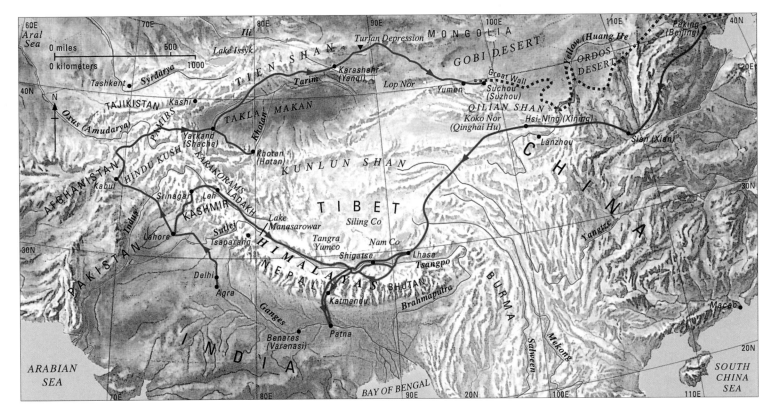

Across the Himalayas

Inspired by Goes, another Portuguese Jesuit, Antonio de Andrade, set out in 1624 to follow up the unconfirmed rumors of Christians in Tibet. He traveled as a Hindu with two Indian Christians, in a pilgrim caravan making for the famous though barely accessible Hindu shrine of Badrinath, northeast of Srinagar. From there, sometimes traveling with a single companion, he entered Tibet, thus becoming the first European to cross the Himalayas. The physical obstacles were enormous – they included crossing vast ravines on bridges made of frozen snow. At Tsaparang (Cha-pu-lan-tsung), capital of a small western Tibetan state, he succeeded in converting the ruler and was given permission to found a Christian mission.

Vain endeavors in Tibet

Christianity was naturally less popular with the lamas, and in 1630 a revolution put an end to the mission. Andrade, now the superior at Goa, sent Francisco de Azevado to Leh, capital of Ladakh, whose ruler now controlled Tsaparang. Azevado was 53 years old (few of the great Jesuit travelers were young men), but he succeeded in getting the Christian captives at Leh released and the mission restarted. It soon fizzled out again, however, in spite of the physical efforts of Azevado, who reported that he particularly disliked the bridges characteristic of Tibetan travel. They consisted of two horizontal ropes with loops suspended from them for the feet. He used to grab the ropes firmly in each hand and pray loudly.

A second Jesuit mission was founded in Tibet at Shigatse (Xigaze) by Fathers Cabral and Cacella in 1627. They made several extensive journeys in Tibet. Cacella died after an unsuccessful attempt to bring succor to his fellow Christians at Tsaparang. The mission at Shigatse, unpopular with the adherents of both the Panchen and Dalai Lamas, was closed down in 1631.

From Peking to Lhasa

The Portuguese still held Macao, but the maritime power and hostility of the Dutch meant that they were virtually blockaded. It was therefore all the more desirable to establish overland connections between China and India. The effort was led by an Austrian-born priest, John Grueber, a veteran of Middle Eastern travels who arrived in Peking in 1658. He set out in April 1661 with Albert d'Orville, a Chinese-speaking colleague who was also a capable surveyor. They traveled along the old caravan route to the Yellow River, crossing it twice to reach Sian (Xian) and Hsi-Ning (Xining), and then southwest through a desolate region of swamps, deserts, and mountain ranges. They reached Lhasa in October 1661, the first Europeans to visit the "forbidden city." No other European would reach Lhasa from China for nearly 200 years.

Grueber and Orville were not greatly enamored of the city, appalled by the dirt and shocked by such customs as letting loose a homicidal young man once a year so that those he murdered would obtain eternal happiness. Nevertheless, Grueber found many parallels between Tibetan Buddhism and Christianity.

They left Lhasa after about six weeks and crossed the Himalayas into Nepal – their exact route is uncertain. At Katmandu they found the king involved in war. They gave him a telescope which he focused on the enemy, receiving a nasty shock as the opposing troops seemed to have suddenly advanced.

The fathers entered India within a year of leaving Peking, traveling to Agra via Patna and the holy city of Benares (Varanasi). Orville died at Agra early in 1662, completely worn out by his travels, but the indestructible Grueber eventually returned to Rome after another challenging journey, with another colleague, from Agra to Ormuz (Hormuz).

Lahore to Lhasa

Although by the early 18th century the Jesuit missions in Tibet had long ceased to exist, another remarkable missionary, the Italian Ippolito Desideri, arrived in 1716. With his Portuguese companion Manuel Freyre he had traveled from Lahore to Kashmir in 1714 and, after recovering from snow blindness and other illnesses, reached Leh a year later. Their subsequent journey to Lhasa, via Lake Manasarowar and the valley of the Tsangpo River, was undertaken because Freyre insisted on returning by an easier – though much longer – route. He soon returned to India, but Desideri stayed on, learned the language, and wrote a book in Tibetan that was critical of Buddhism. It was with great disappointment that he obeyed an order to return to India in 1721. He did, however, make several more journeys, in the course of which he revisited Tibet, before leaving for Europe in 1727.

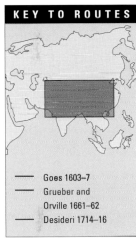

KEY TO ROUTES

——— Goes 1603–7
——— Grueber and Orville 1661–62
——— Desideri 1714–16

Advance of the Cossacks

▲ **The Cossack Timofeyevich Yermak** received a gift of armor from the Tsar of Russia for the part he played in the Russian conquest of Siberia. It was this armor which caused him to drown when he jumped into the Irtysh River in an effort to escape from a Tatar band.

In the 16th century Russia ended at the Urals, a boundary that had acquired more than physical significance. A few individuals did cross the mountains. Samoyed traders sold magnificent furs for trinkets to the powerful Russian frontier barons, the Stroganovs, but in 1578 the trade was abruptly cut off by the Tatars. Russia remained isolated from the vast country beyond the Urals.

The bleak expanse

Siberia, 5.3 million square miles (8.5 million square kilometers) in area, contains about ten percent of the world's land surface. It has no intimidating physical features such as high mountains, and its rivers provide an excellent communications network. It is possible to travel by boat over huge distances with only short portages between one system and the next. Nonetheless, Siberia poses severe problems for the traveler. Distances are immense and, above all, it is shockingly cold: many places record temperatures lower than those at the North Pole. Long-distance travel in winter, in a pre-industrial age, was almost impossible.

In 1578 a party of Cossacks, those free-ranging bands who were both mercenaries of and rebels against the tsar (sometimes at the same time), turned up on the Stroganov estates. They were led by a man of uncertain origin called Yermak, who agreed to lead an expedition into Siberia in exchange for subsidies. The Stroganovs hoped to restore the fur trade; no doubt they also wanted to get the Cossacks off their land.

The conquest of Siberia

Thus began a great epic, which has often been compared with the Spanish conquests in the Americas. Yermak's total force numbered about 800. Though no longer capable of threatening Moscow, the Tatars, led by Kuchum Khan, could still field some 30,000 horsemen. Otherwise the population of Siberia consisted of tribal peoples, some scarcely beyond the technology of the Stone Age. As in the Americas, the extraordinary speed of the Cossack conquest was due largely to guns – weapons far more effective than their actual damage potential when used against people who had no experience of them.

Starting out in July 1579, Yermak's men made slow progress and had to winter in the mountains. The following spring, discovering a new pass, they made rafts and descended into Siberia on tributaries that led eventually to the Tobol River, where they set up the next winter's camp. In customary Cossack fashion they terrorized and plundered the local people, though when they captured a Tatar chief, they loaded him with presents and sent him back bearing compliments to the khan.

That fooled nobody, and as they renewed their advance in 1581 the Cossacks ran into increasing opposition. Eventually Kuchum Khan lured them into battle. Legend relates how the Tatars placed a chain across the Irtysh River and waited in ambush as the Cossack boats approached. They realized too late that the boats were filled with dummies: Yermak's men were already ashore, attacking the Tatars in the rear. In the battle that followed the Tatars failed to make the most of their superiority in numbers and manoeuvrability, and they were overcome by Cossack fire power. Kuchum Khan vacated his capital, Iskir (now Tobolsk), which the Cossacks occupied.

Yet the Cossacks had won only a pyrrhic victory. Yermak was short of men and munitions; he was still outnumbered, but could not afford to retreat. He escaped from this predicament by a strategic master stroke. He sent his lieutenant, Ivan Koltse, to appeal to the tsar. Koltse took sledges piled high with valuable furs and traveled overland to Moscow in midwinter. Delighted with the news of the Cossacks' success, the tsar promised troops and, more importantly, transformed Yermak at a stroke from border raider into Russian empire builder.

Nevertheless, the Cossacks were hard pressed to last out until late summer 1584, when the reinforcements

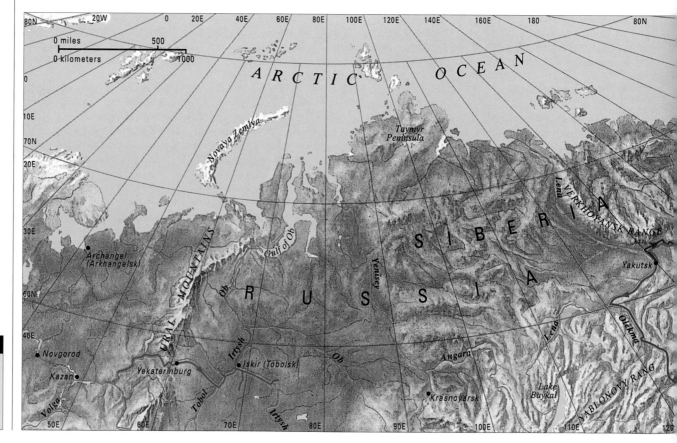

KEY TO ROUTES

——	Yermak 1581–82
——	Poyarkov 1643–46
——	Dezhnev 1643–49
——	Khabarov 1649–51

arrived. The following year, when campaigning resumed, Yermak was ambushed by a Tatar band. Forgetting that he was wearing armor, he jumped into the Irtysh in an effort to escape and sank like a stone.

Yermak's sucessors

With their leader dead, the Cossacks began to retreat to the Urals, but more reinforcements from Moscow restored their resolve. The Tatars, though still able to launch raids, were a spent force. Kuchum Khan was

eventually forced to flee south to the Nogai Tatars, who killed him.

The Cossacks advanced to the Ob River. The peaceable Samoyeds offered no opposition, and other tribes, who did fight back, were swept aside. The Cossacks expanded in numbers as news spread of the riches to be made from Siberian furs. Behind them came the tsar's officials and tax gatherers, and behind them arrived Russian settlers.

By 1628 the Cossacks were on the Lena River, and in 1632 they founded Yakutsk. From there they diverged: one group continued east and by 1639 reached the coast on the Sea of Okhotsk. Another group went to the north coast where, in 1648, Simon Dezhnev, a Russian government agent and one of the first Russian settlers on the Kolyma River, almost certainly sailed around the Chukchi Peninsula to the mouth of the Anadyr River. This was a remarkable feat which the Russian officers of the Great Northern Expedition were unable to repeat a century later.

A third group of Cossacks turned south, lured by tales of lush fields of grain (a rare crop in Siberia). The Cossacks were always exceedingly cruel, at least to the weak; faced with a more formidable foe, they normally opted for flight. If the accounts are true, the leaders of this push to the southeast carried that cruelty to revolting excess. Vasily Poyarkov reached the Amur River in 1643, subsequently following it to the sea. The local people, the Dagur (Mongolian village dwellers who today are almost extinct), did not provide enough food for the demanding Cossacks, so Poyarkov's men killed and ate them instead.

Poyarkov was followed a few years later by a larger band, armed with cannon and led by Yerofey Khabarov, who traveled a long way down the Amur River, slaughtering recalcitrant villagers *en route*. Whether the Cossacks knew it or not, these people were Chinese subjects, or so the Manchu considered, and in due course Chinese troops arrived. Although the Chinese were defeated, the Russians eventually pulled back from the Amur. The agreement was partly arbitrated by another group of Europeans who, in an altogether different manner, were also contributing to European knowledge of East Asia – the Jesuit missionaries based in China.

▲ *Yermak's river-borne advance* into Siberia combined Christian fervor with European firepower. The guns of his small band of followers secured victories over opposing forces who were only armed with bows and arrows.

The Great Northern Expedition

▶ **Peter the Great** was the moving force behind the first expedition of Vitus Bering to discover whether Asia and America were joined. His orders to Bering were: "Enquire where the American coast begins and go to some European colony; ask what the coast is, note it down and return."

By 1700 the Russians were established on the Pacific coast. In his new capital, St Petersburg, Peter the Great contemplated Siberian furs and encouraged the extension of Russian control of the Siberian peoples (even if, as in the case of the Koriaks, they were exterminated in the process). He was also intrigued by geographical questions. What were the mysterious islands legend said would be found east of Japan? Would it be possible to conduct trade with China from Kamchatka? Were Asia and North America joined together?

Siberia to Alaska

The last was the greatest, most intriguing question. Before 1720 Peter sent several men to reconnoiter in Kamchatka and the Kuril Islands, without clear result. In 1724 he planned a larger expedition, and to lead it he appointed a Danish officer in the Russian navy, Vitus Bering.

Peter died in January 1725, but Bering's expedition, approved by the Imperial Admiralty, went ahead. It took

Bering and his companions a year to reach Yakutsk, the last chance to acquire stores, and another year to reach the Sea of Okhotsk. They sailed to the Kamchatka Peninsula and crossed to the east coast on foot; Bering did not want to risk a voyage through uncharted waters around the south of the peninsula.

On the eastern coast they built a 60-foot (18-meter) boat, the *St Gabriel*, which in July 1728 put out into what is now known as the Bering Sea. Heading north, she reached 67°18′N, a point well to the north of the Bering Strait, but owing to persistent mist those on board had failed to observe the two continents on either hand.

There was little doubt the strait existed – in fact, the inhabitants of the Chukchi Peninsula had informed them of it – but Bering had no proof. After much disapproval in St Petersburg, he was told to try again, and this time he was appointed to lead a much bigger expedition. In the ensuing years Bering pursued his investigations in the North Pacific, which were to end with his death in 1741 on Bering Island (see page 160).

Under the command of Ivan Fyodorov with Michael Gvosdyov as cartographer, the *St Gabriel* had reached Alaska in 1732; Bering's deputy, Martin Spanberg, reached Japan from Kamchatka in 1738 and one of his subordinates skirted the unknown coast of Sakhalin in 1742.

The Siberian coast

Largely unconnected with all this, though still at first under Bering's overall leadership, a team of naval officers set out to map the entire northern coast of Siberia from Archangel to the Anadyr River, working mainly from boats.

This task, which began in 1733, was supposed to be completed in two years, but it was not finished after ten; it would have taken longer still but for an unusually mild year in 1737, when channels normally frozen became clear. In that year Lt Malgin completed the first section, from the White Sea to the Gulf of Ob, and Lt Ovzin the second, from the Ob River to the Yenisey. The next section, the Taymyr Peninsula, was tougher. Successive efforts to round it from the west failed. Another party approaching from the east also failed; its officers died in 1735, leaving the

KEY TO ROUTES

—— Bering 1725–30

—— Spanberg 1738–39

—— Great Northern
Expedition 1733–42

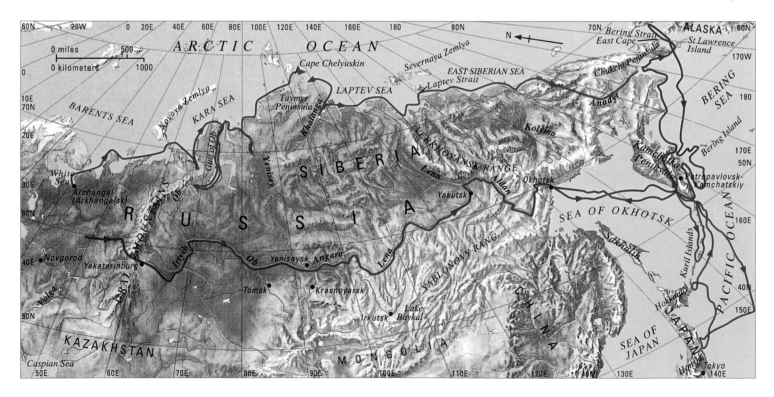

▶ **In 1741 Vitus Bering** and his men were forced to winter on the island later named after him, very close to their base in Kamchatka. Bering was among those who did not survive, dying of scurvy, a disease which claimed the lives of many oceanic explorers. Caused by a deficiency of vitamin C (due to a diet devoid of fresh fruit and vegetables), the symptoms include a loosening of the teeth in the gums, making it difficult to chew, and a general weakness that leaves the sufferer unable to stand, let alone walk.

▼ **The frozen northern coastline** created treacherous conditions for the surveyors, whether they were on foot or in boats.

pilot, Chelyuskin, to take charge. He set off to obtain orders from Bering in Yakutsk, nearly 1000 icy miles (1600 kilometers) away, but when he got there he found Bering had moved on.

The challenge of the Taymyr

Eventually a new commander, Khariton Laptev, was appointed to take over the attack on the Taymyr. His first effort in 1738 failed. The following year, having stockpiled food and received reinforcements, he tried again but was again forced back well short of what is today known as Cape Chelyuskin, the most northerly point of the Eurasian land mass. (There is strong evidence that local hunters had sailed around it earlier.) Laptev's party wintered in grim conditions on the Khatanga River. With the spring thaw he set out again, taking four weeks to fight his way down to the mouth of the river. His boat was then frozen in and carried out to sea by an unfriendly current. When water began to come in, Laptev and his companions were forced

to take to the ice. They spent a terrible night in the open and the following day set off for the coast, just visible 15 miles (25 kilometers) away. It was a two-day trek, but they made it safely and then – a stroke of luck – were able to retrieve most of their stores when the ice that gripped their boat drifted close to shore.

Understandably disillusioned with voyaging by sea, Laptev then decided to try to reach the cape overland. He divided his team into three and, between them, they carried out a fairly thorough survey of the peninsula, but the cape still eluded them. As its modern name proclaims, it was finally reached by the persevering Chelyuskin in May 1742, his eighth summer on the Siberian coast.

From the Lena to the Anadyr

In 1735, after the first party had been decimated by scurvy (only eight out of 44 survived), Bering had put Laptev's brother Dmitri in command of the last and longest section of the north coast, from the Lena to the Anadyr.

Although Simon Dezhnev had almost certainly sailed around the northeast cape nearly 100 years before (see page 47), his extraordinary voyage in a *kocha* (a primitive, flat-bottomed, open boat) was not known to participants in the Great Northern Expedition. Dmitri Laptev would have found it hard to believe. Like Chelyuskin earlier, he spent a great deal of time trying to get his orders clarified, and while he was doing so he missed the mild weather of 1737. In 1740 he worked his way some distance east of the Kolyma River, and in 1741, with 45 dog teams, he marched overland to the Anadyr River. His purpose was to sail from there around East Cape (Cape Dezhnev) back to the Kolyma, but no boats were available, and Laptev had perhaps had enough. He retraced his steps and returned from the Kolyma to St Petersburg.

The failure to repeat Dezhnev's achievement, and thus to confirm that Asia and America were separated by sea alone, marred the distinguished work of the Great Northern Expedition. But, in pleasant contrast with the Cossack conquest, it was one of the first great, centrally directed, long-sustained, national efforts in exploration to be conducted in a diligent, scientific manner.

Islam's Holy Cities

KEY TO ROUTES

— Varthema 1503
— Burckhardt 1812
— Burckhardt 1814–15

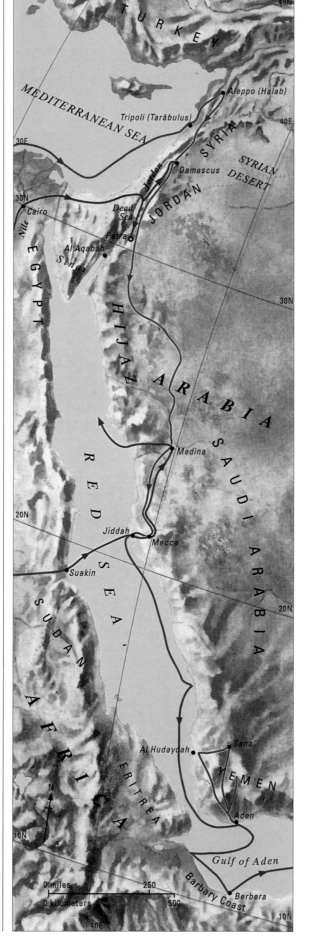

On the map Arabia is the part of Asia most accessible to western Europeans, yet it was one of the last regions that Europeans explored. The terrain is certainly inhospitable. Of the approximately 1 million square miles (2.5 million square kilometers) covered by the Arabian peninsula, only a small proportion near the coasts is cultivable. Inland it consists mainly of an arid plateau with a few short *wadis* (watercourses that are dry except immediately after rain) but no rivers, where the summer temperature can reach 130°F (55°C).

Nevertheless, Arabia was never entirely unknown in Europe from Roman times, and it had always been inhabited, even in remote parts. After the rise of Islam, however, it was barred to Christians. Any non-Muslim who wanted to visit the holy cities of Mecca and Medina – having heard them described by Muslims – had to do so in disguise. For some people the need for deception made the holy cities all the more alluring.

Infidels in Mecca

Pedro de Covilhão may have visited Mecca in 1492, during the European age of discovery; he was certainly at Jiddah and Aden. Otherwise Mecca's first European visitor was the Italian Ludovico de Varthema in 1503. Having somehow been enlisted in the guard provided by the Mamelukes for pilgrims from Syria, he spent three weeks in the city. He was the first non-Muslim to describe the Ka'aba, the central shrine of Islam.

Varthema left Mecca without incident, but in Aden his disguise was penetrated when, in a moment of panic, he forgot his Arabic. He was thrown into prison for three months but rescued, according to his own romantic account, by one of the Sultan's wives. Varthema subsequently traveled in the Yemen, which the Romans had known as Arabia Felix, before sailing on to India and the Spice Islands (the Moluccas).

The Governor-General of Portuguese India, Afonso d'Albuquerque, bombarded Aden in 1513 before sailing along the coast of Yemen where, according to legend, a Portuguese captain, Gregorio da Quadras, was shipwrecked and turned up later in Ormuz (Hormuz) on the Persian Gulf. If this account is true, da Quadras was by a long way the first European to cross Arabia – the next documented crossing was completed some 300 years later.

Although recorded visits by Europeans to the holy cities of Arabia are few, there is reason to believe that a considerable number occurred, albeit involuntarily. One such visitor was a Devon sailor, Joseph Pitts, captured off the Barbary coast by Muslim corsairs and sold into slavery. Forcibly converted to Islam, he accompanied his master on the *hajj* – the pilgrimage to Mecca that every Muslim is required to make at least once in their lifetime – in 1685.

Niebuhr and the Arabs

Arabia was the objective of one of the first truly scientific expeditions, sponsored by the King of Denmark in 1761. Six Scandinavian and German experts took part. After spending some time acclimatizing themselves in Egypt, they sailed with a pilgrim caravan to Jiddah and from there continued through the Red Sea to Yemen, taking observations, recording flora and fauna, collecting specimens. They suffered sore trials; malaria and exhaustion took a heavy toll. The remarkable Carsten Niebuhr, the self-taught surveyor on the expedition, was the only one of the six to survive, largely as a result of adopting local dress, food, and customs. After spending over a year recuperating in India, he returned to Denmark in 1767. The expedition had not covered any new ground, but it produced a clearer, more

accurate picture of Arabia. Equally important, it provided a great deal of information about the Arabs (greatly admired by Niebuhr), who had hitherto been regarded with extreme prejudice in Europe.

Niebuhr also recorded the rise of the fundamentalist Wahhabi sect. After a series of campaigns the Wahhabis captured Mecca in 1803, and the conflict extended into Jordan and Syria, making travel even more difficult. Notwithstanding the difficulties, Domingo Badia y Leblich, a Spanish convert to Islam, visited Mecca in 1807, traveling in some style with a swathe of attendants as Ali Bey al Abbasi, and later published an account of the city. He fixed the positions of Mecca and Medina with almost perfect accuracy, in spite of the theft of his chronometer near Mecca. He died preparing for a second visit in 1818. Two years later the German botanist Ulrich Seetzen, also fluent in Arabic, made the *hajj*. He was later murdered in the Yemen, and his account of his travels was lost.

Johann Ludwig Burckhardt

The Spaniard Badia was working for the French, the German Seetzen for Russia. Johann Ludwig Burckhardt was a Swiss working for the British, more specifically for the Royal Geographical Society. A paragon of accuracy and one of the most competent as well as learned explorers of the age, Burckhardt had spent years preparing for his travels. Like Niebuhr and, indeed, the majority of the best explorers, he adopted as far as possible the customs and to some extent even the beliefs of the societies he moved among. His knowledge of the Koran was so extensive that he produced learned commentaries on it and was able to carry off convincingly a disguise as a doctor of Islamic law. He also had the advantage of the patronage of Mehemet Ali, the powerful, Albanian-born ruler of Egypt who, having destroyed the ancient regime of the Mamelukes in Egypt, attacked the Wahhabis and drove them out of the holy cities.

After extensive travels in other parts, Burckhardt crossed the Red Sea from Egypt to Jiddah in 1814 and journeyed to Mecca, where he stayed for four months enjoying "perfect ease" and compiling his accurate and informative account of the city. Early in 1815 he moved on to Medina, where he continued his documentary work until he became sick – the power of quinine against malaria was not yet known – and decided to cut short his travels

and return to Cairo. He completed his substantial writings before dying in Cairo, still only 33 years old, in 1817. He left his valuable collection of manuscripts to Cambridge University, where he had studied.

After Burckhardt there was really little need for further reports on the holy cities, but that did not prevent Richard Burton, in the guise of a Pathan (a member of the Pashto-speaking people in Afghanistan and northwest Pakistan), from entering Mecca as a pilgrim in 1853. Burton was certainly an intrepid traveler. His trip to Mecca brought him fame – not to be underestimated as a motive for explorers – although today he is chiefly remembered for his later travels in East Africa and his search for the source of the Nile (see pages 72–73). Personal idiosyncrasies apart, he could not add much to Burckhardt's account, and his plan to expand his travels by traversing Arabia had to be abandoned because of fierce fighting in the interior.

The Arabian Desert

▶ **Bertram Thomas** crossed the "Empty Quarter" in 1930–31, with a large and well-prepared expedition. He had a stroke of luck – it rained – which helped provide grazing for his animals. Thomas also found the desert less empty of people than was supposed, stumbling upon one hitherto unknown group of desert dwellers.

In 1819 Captain George Sadlier, a British officer despatched from Bombay, arrived near Bahrain to make contact with Ibrahim Ali (son of the Egyptian ruler Mehemet Ali), who was commanding operations against the fundamentalist Wahhabi sect. He hoped to discuss combined operations against pirates in the Persian Gulf. Finding that Ibrahim had already withdrawn westward, Sadlier resolved to follow him. However, he did not catch up with Ali until near Medina. It was pointless to return the way he had come, so he continued to Yanbu on the Red Sea, thus becoming the first Englishman, and possibly the first European, to cross Arabia.

The Hadramawt and the Nafud

The British were becoming steadily more involved in the whole region. In the 1830s Lt James Wellsted, a naval officer on the lookout for sites for coaling stations, pushed into the Hadramawt, the mountainous area in southern Arabia. There he discovered the remains of an ancient city dating back over 2000 years ago, when the Hadrami kingdom thrived on the incense trade.

The first European to cross the Nafud (Red) Desert in the north was a Swede-Finn, G. A. Wallin, who was employed by the Egyptian Government in the 1840s and traveled as an Arab. On a second trip he arrived at Al Muwaylih, near the Gulf of Aqabah, in 1848 and then crossed the mountains of the northern Hijāz to Tayma and Hā'il, where he had stayed before. His journey took him through mostly unmapped country, but as he carried no scientific instruments bar a compass he was unable to carry out precision surveys.

Individualists and "tourists"

The first European to follow Wallin to Hā'il was William Palgrave, a considerable scholar as well as a Jesuit priest and a spy for the French emperor. He traveled as a Syrian physician with a genuinely Syrian companion. From Hā'il they went to Riyadh, whence, after a short and decidedly tense stay, they moved on to Al Qatif on the Gulf, having thus crossed Arabia from west to east. A few doubts were cast on the truth of Palgrave's account, presumably as a result of his ornate literary style and his enigmatic remark about leaving "much untold" – the latter no doubt forming the subject of secret despatches to Louis Napoleon.

A self-conscious literary style is also associated with travelers in Arabia, notably Charles M. Doughty, who is regarded by some as the greatest European explorer of Arabia and certainly as the author of the finest book on the subject, *Travels in Arabia Deserta*. Notwithstanding his insistence that style – in his case a mixture of Chaucer, the Elizabethans, and Arabic influence though in the end recognizably Victorian – was more important than content, he was a scholar and a most acute observer. As Wilfred Thesiger was to do in the 20th century, Doughty admired the Bedouin and deplored the corrupting influence of towns and "civilization."

Doughty entered Arabia in 1876 with a *hajj* caravan from Syria but, south of Tayma, deserted it and wandered off by himself. He did not pretend to be anything other than a Christian and was largely dependent for support on the nomadic groups which he followed. That he survived for 21 months was a miracle.

A number of other travelers contributed to the growing knowledge of central Arabia. Carlo Guarmani, a Syrian-Italian horse dealer, visited Al Jawf and other places on two occasions in his search for good stock during the 1860s. The Alsace-born Arabist Charles Huber crossed the Nafud in 1878 but was later murdered by his guides. More improbable visitors, tourists almost, in the same year were Wilfred Scawen Blunt and his wife Lady Anne, prominent figures in upper-class English literary circles. They traveled under the protection of a local sheikh; he was looking for a wife, they were looking for stallions for their stud.

After the British took over Aden in 1839 there were more British visitors to southern Arabia, though the Hadramawt clung on to its secrets. The fertile valley of the Wadi Hadramawt was not known to Europeans until the German archaeologist Leo Hirsch visited it in the 1890s. Endemic tribal hostilities made travel hazardous until 1937, when the British political agent W. H. Ingrams effected "Ingrams's Peace." People like the Dutch official P. van der Meulen and the British traveler Freya Stark put the finishing touches to the exploration of the region.

The last barrier

The northern deserts of Arabia were also well known by the 1920s, thanks to contributions from people such as

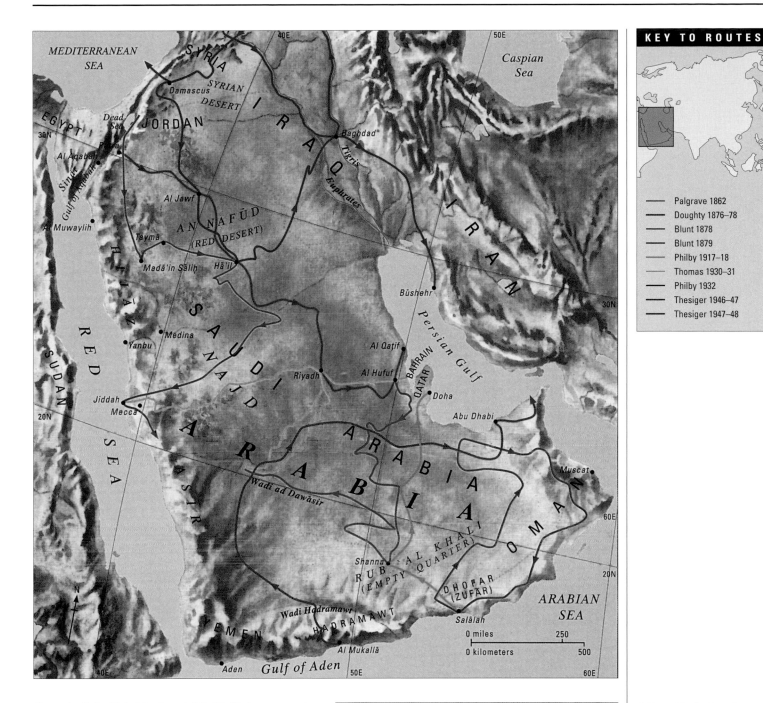

KEY TO ROUTES

Palgrave 1862
Doughty 1876–78
Blunt 1878
Blunt 1879
Philby 1917–18
Thomas 1930–31
Philby 1932
Thesiger 1946–47
Thesiger 1947–48

Gertrude Bell, Alois Musil, and W. H. Shakespeare, who was killed in a Saudi battle.

The largest, most forbidding region of Arabia, the Rub 'al Khali ("Empty Quarter"), which covers an area of about 250,000 square miles (650,000 square kilometers), was the last to be traversed. In 1930–31 Bertram Thomas, minister of the Sultan of Muscat, crossed it from Dhofar (Zufar) in the south to Qatar on the Gulf. H. St John Philby, a Muslim convert long resident in Arabia, repeated Thomas's achievement two years later, crossing the northern part of the Rub 'al Khali. He was unable to continue south to Dhofar, as intended, but he found lakes formed in craters made by meteoric impact in the middle of the Empty Quarter.

Last of the great Arabian travelers was Wilfred Thesiger, another of those intelligent, slightly mystical, socially discontented individuals who find some kind of fulfilment in the desert. He crossed the Rub 'al Khali twice in 1946–48, and his *Arabian Sands* remains a fine record of a society that even then was on the verge of extinction.

◄ *Freya Stark* – traveler, writer, geographer, historian, and archeologist – was particularly drawn to the desert. She wrote: "I never imagined that my first sight of the desert would come as such a shock of beauty and enslave me right away."

Central Asia

During the 19th century European explorers tended to congregate in south-central Asia, in the region between Persia and western China. Topographically this is the most complex region on Earth – a jumble of vast mountain ranges interspersed with high (though not necessarily flat) plateaus and deserts. Other complications played a part, notably political ones, for this was the era of the "Great Game," the time when the Russian and British empires approached, touched, and threatened to clash like the subterranean collisions that threw up the Himalayas. The activities of many of the travelers in this region were more or less secret at the time, and their aims are still not always clear today, their priorities questionable.

The wandering vet

William Moorcroft is a case in point. He arrived in India as a vet working for the East India Company (over which the British Government had taken some control in 1784) and was interested in improving animal stocks. His later travels may also have had a political purpose, but the extent to which he was a British agent remains uncertain.

He set off in 1812 with a young Anglo-Indian officer, Hyder Jung Hearsey. Their journey brought them across the Himalayas, into western Tibet, in search of the goat whose wool was used to make Kashmir shawls and jumpers. On the way back they explored Lake Manasarowar, once a place of Hindu pilgrimage and popularly believed to be the source of the Ganges, Indus, Brahmaputra, and other great rivers: the only one Moorcroft could locate was the Sutlej.

Moorcroft undertook a second, much longer journey in 1819–25, on which he became the first European to travel from India to Bukhara. After two years in Tibet, where he became involved in machinations to combat Russian influence, he stayed in Xinjiang and Kashmir. Here he signed a treaty beneficial to his employers before crossing the Hindu Kush. It appears that he and his British companion mysteriously died in or near Bukhara in 1825, although the French Lazarite missionary Abbé Huc was to insist that Moorcroft was living in Lhasa some years later.

The Russian advance

The Russian push into central Asia only seriously got under way in 1825. It was preceded, however, by Russian officers, usually trained surveyors, performing similar tasks to those of Moorcroft and his successors. Among the latter were Alexander Burney and James Gerard, who followed Moorcroft to Bukhara, and James Wood, who found the source of the Oxus (Amudarya) in 1838.

The Russians reached the Aral Sea a few years later, and exploration of its shores revealed the hitherto unknown outlet of the Jaxartes (Syrdarya). By 1860 Russian expeditions had ventured much further. Some were led by scientists like Semenov, who explored the Tien Shan; others were governed by strategic considerations.

International travelers

In spite of the difficulties (political rather than geographical), numerous travelers from other Western nations entered central Asia in the mid 19th century. An American,

▼ *George Hayward, shown here posing in the dress of a district chief in 1870, was an assertive character. Ironically, he was murdered while exploring in the Pamirs later that year, possibly because he had given offence to just such a chief.*

▶ *Moorcroft and Hearsey disguised themselves as fakirs – the latter apparently more successfully than the former – for their journey through the Himalayas (painted here by Hearsey).*

Charles Masson, became the greatest non-Asian explorer of Afghanistan. Three German brothers, the Schlagintweits, carried out scientific expeditions in the 1850s, first in India and the Himalayas then further afield, becoming the first Europeans to cross the awesome Kunlun Range between Tibet and Xinjiang. The flamboyant Hungarian Arminius Vambéry wrote a colorful account of his travels, but his writings have been shown to contain a substantial element of fiction.

Botanists such as the Frenchman Victor Jacquemont and the Austrian Carl von Hugel traveled in Kashmir and the Himalayas, looking for new flora. Godfrey Vigne moved north of Kashmir in the 1830s to the Karakorams and was the first to describe the Nanga Parbat massif in the western Himalayas. Some people doubted his account of a huge glacier system in the Karakorams on the grounds that glaciers would not exist so near the tropics.

Imperial agents

A rebellion against the Chinese in Xinjiang, which seemed likely to offer another opportunity for the Russians to extend their hegemony, prompted two British expeditions in 1868. The leaders, Robert Shaw and George Hayward, regarded each other as an interloper. Hayward was a notoriously rough-and-ready explorer, but he was also easily diverted, and though he was first through the Karakorams, Shaw narrowly beat him to become the first Briton in Yarkand (Shache). Both were then imprisoned by the rebel leader Yakub Beg in Kashgar, where one of the Schlagintweits had been executed. The British explorers, however, were released after a few months.

Hayward's later journeys took him into the Pamirs, which the British hoped would provide a barrier against the Russians. He was murdered by a local chief in 1870.

◄ *These Tibetan musicians, playing Ida-man (kettledrums) and a sor-na (shawm), were painted by Hyder Jung Hearsey during his 1812 expedition.*

His work was continued by Shaw, in company with military experts, who came to the unwelcome conclusion that Russian forces could easily negotiate the passes through the Pamirs.

The most persevering of the British explorers was Ney Elias, a truly remarkable traveler who made seven or eight treks through central Asia, the longest of which, begun in 1872, extended to nearly 5000 miles (8000 kilometers). He crossed the Gobi Desert and the Altai Mountains between China and Mongolia, rode over 2000 miles (3200 kilometers) across Siberia in a horse-drawn sleigh, camping out – in midwinter – at night, until he arrived at Nizhniy Novgorod. From there he returned to England by train.

In later years Elias explored the passes in the Pamir mountains and in 1885–86 he became the first Englishman to succeed in crossing them.

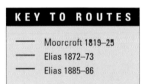

KEY TO ROUTES

— Moorcroft 1819–25
— Elias 1872–73
— Elias 1885–86

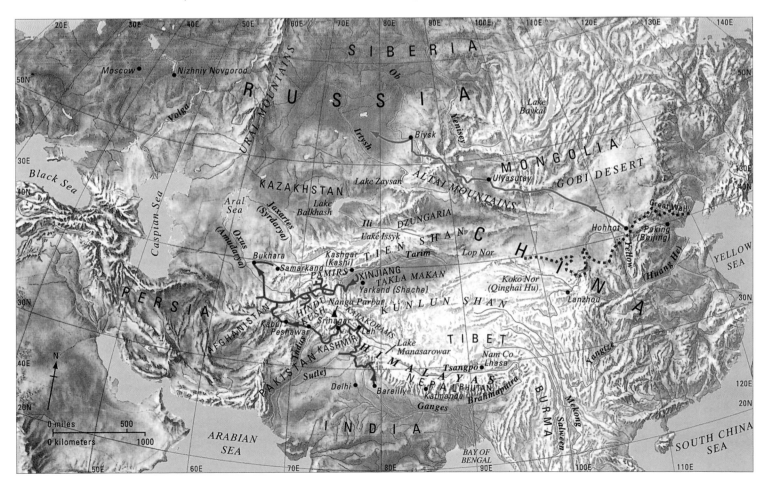

Roads to Lhasa

The last Capuchins (who had replaced the Jesuits in Tibet) left the country in the 1740s, and for the next 30 years Tibet was free of any European presence. In India, meanwhile, the British East India Company was increasing its influence to such an extent that it virtually controlled most of the country. An astute and ambitious Governor, Warren Hastings, launched two probes into the still virtually unknown land beyond the Himalayas. The British were, as always, interested in trade, but also in discovering what influence the Chinese had in Tibet. They were also simply curious.

British emissaries

Hastings's first emissary was a young Scot, George Bogle. On reaching the border in 1774, he was strongly urged to turn back, but he persevered, entering into correspondence with the Panchen Lama at Shigatse (Xigaze), who eventually invited him to visit. The two men got on well, though Bogle confessed himself frightened by the intense curiosity of the people on the streets. He observed their customs with mixed feelings, noting (like many other Europeans) the Tibetans' lack of interest in washing. He persuaded his Tibetan servant to wash with soap, and the man seemed quite pleased with the result, but his friends laughed at him and he did not repeat the experiment.

Bogle waited for nearly a year at the grand monastery of Tasilhumpo, near Shigatse, while his proposal for a trade agreement, approved by the Panchen Lama, was considered in Lhasa. The final response was negative, no doubt on Chinese advice. Disappointed, Bogle returned to India, with (to the consternation of his family) a pretty young cousin of the Panchen Lama as his wife. Governor Hastings's second emissary was Lt Samuel Turner who attended the incarnation of the new Panchen Lama at Shigatse in 1783 – a baby of 18 months.

British relations with Tibet might have turned out differently if Warren Hastings had still been Governor in 1792, when the Tibetans appealed to the British for help against an invasion from Nepal. The new Governor, Cornwallis, having lost an army in North America, was unwilling to embark on risky military ventures in Tibet. Accordingly, the Tibetans turned to the Chinese, who drove out the invaders and urged closure of the border with Nepal and India. This measure proved very effective: the passes being few and closed in winter. They were patrolled by Chinese and Tibetan guards and, though local traders and pilgrims could gain admission, Europeans were kept out.

One of the few who got through was the brilliant but eccentric Thomas Manning, who posed as a Chinese doctor. He could speak the language, but his disguise seems to have been otherwise thin; nevertheless, he reached Lhasa in December 1811. He was impressed by the Potala (the palace of the Dalai Lama), but the city – "begrimed with smut and dirt ... mean and gloomy" and infested with diseased dogs – was no Shangri La in Manning's view. His account is amusing but not very valuable; it is largely concerned with the unsatisfactory character of his servant or his persecution by the Chinese officials in Lhasa. The latter succeeded in having him expelled in April 1812.

The Abbé Huc

The next Europeans to reach Lhasa were also not without eccentricities. They were Evarist Huc and Joseph Gabet, French Lazarite missionaries who, following Jesuit predecessors such as Orville and Grueber, entered Tibet from the north. Their book *Travels in Tartary, Thibet, and China* (the English translation was by William Hazlitt, who did nothing to tone it down) suffered a similar fate to Marco Polo's *Travels*: a rollicking story, uninhibited by false

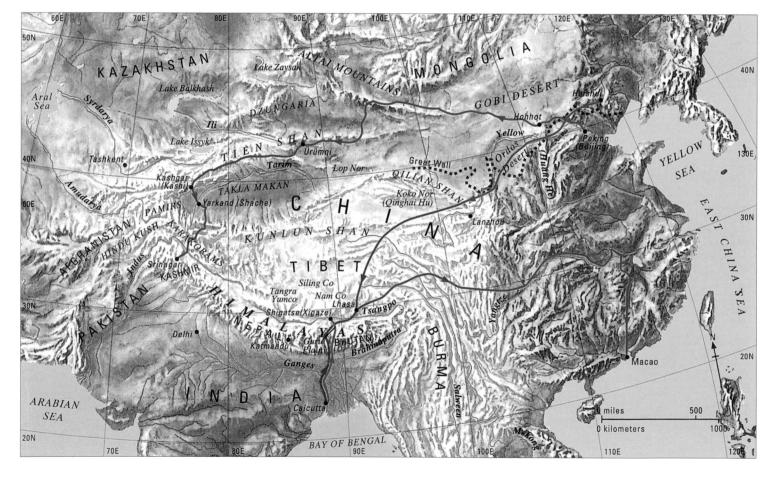

modesty or undue scepticism, it was regarded by some as thoroughly misleading, particularly in its account of the life of Mongolian nomads. The Russian explorer Przhevalsky was one critic.

Huc and Gabet, in the guise of Buddhist monks, started from Heishui north of Peking (Beijing) in 1844, passing through Mongolia before turning south into Tibet. At a monastery on the Tibetan Plateau they reported among other wonders the existence of a miraculous "Tree of Ten Thousand Images," whose leaves and bark were inscribed with the written characters of a prayer. Reaching Lhasa in a Chinese caravan of 2000 men, they perceived a more attractive picture than Manning and were delighted with the "marvelous variety of physiognomies, costumes and languages" in the streets. But they lasted an even shorter time, being forced to leave after less than two months in March 1846.

They had a tough journey north with a Tibetan escort across the high, icy plateau – the Abbé Huc memorably describes sliding down a glacier at great speed – until they reached the upper Yangtze. They arrived in Macao in October 1846.

The Younghusband expedition

The British became increasingly obsessed by Tibet, this attractively out-of-this-world country to the north. Crisis loomed when they learned that a Russian agent, a Mongolian and former Buddhist monk, had managed to establish himself in Lhasa and had acquired powerful influence over the Dalai Lama. Political and economic motives – the British insistence on free trade – combined to provoke the Younghusband expedition of 1903.

Francis Younghusband, a soldier with mystical leanings, was born in India and had gained a great reputation as an explorer. In the 1880s he traveled from Peking to India, crossing the Gobi Desert, visiting Kashgar and Yarkand (Shache), and crossing the Karakorams by the lofty Muztag Pass, not used for years and never before by Europeans. From India he made several treks to the northwest before he was appointed to lead what was supposed to be a diplo-

▲ *The Potala*, the palace of the Dalai Lama in Lhasa, greatly impressed all early travelers to Lhasa. However, opinions differed as to the attractiveness of the surrounding streets.

◀ *Francis Younghusband* was an English soldier on whom the Karakoram and Pamir mountains, which he explored in the 1880s and 1890s, had a mystical effect. In later years he was to found an organization concerned with uniting all religions.

matic mission to Lhasa, though he was accompanied by 300 sepoys and more than 1000 soldiers.

On the Guru Plain, 150 miles (240 kilometers) southwest of Lhasa, the mission was blocked by a considerable Tibetan force. Neither side wished to open fire first; neither would give way. Then a chance shot led to general firing and, muskets being no match for machine guns, the slaughter of the Tibetans ensued: "a terrible and ghastly business" Younghusband admitted. The Dalai Lama fled, and his Regent was forced to concede British demands. However, as the British could not possibly garrison Tibet, in 1907 they concluded a treaty in which they handed over Tibetan sovereignty to China.

The Surveyors

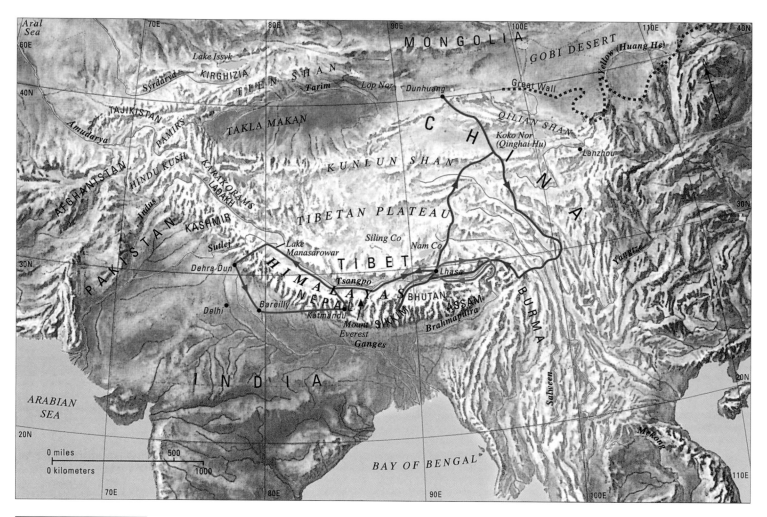

KEY TO ROUTES

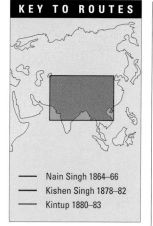

— Nain Singh 1864–66

— Kishen Singh 1878–82

— Kintup 1880–83

One of the greatest achievements of British rule in India was the "Great Trigonometrical Survey," begun in 1802, which involved the surveying and mapping of the whole Indian Empire. The surveyors, measuring their angles and distances in often highly unhelpful conditions, were themselves explorers; apart from topographical phenomena, they came upon several remote ethnic groups hitherto unknown outside their own area. Their work remains largely anonymous, although one head of the service gave his name to Mount Everest.

The British interest in Tibet, given an added edge by suspected Russian intentions, had been frustrated by the closing of the border in 1792, which excluded Europeans although Asian merchants and pilgrims were admitted. In the early 1860s Captain Montgomerie of the Survey, who had surveyed much of Kashmir while himself under hostile surveillance by the Maharajah, suggested training men drawn from the local population, who would have a better chance of entering Tibet unopposed.

The first "Pundit"

Montgomerie's secret agents, for that is what they were, were mainly ex-teachers, some of whom had family links in Tibet. They underwent up to a year's training, learning to walk with a consistent stride while counting their paces with the aid of Buddhist prayer beads, thus enabling them to measure distance. As record-keeping would be difficult, they were told to memorize their notes, though they also had slips of paper, plus a compass, concealed in prayer wheels. Thermometers were hidden in hollow walking sticks, sextants in a hidden compartment inside a medicine chest or strongbox.

Several of these men performed astonishing feats, notably the first of them, Nain Singh, whose code name ("the Pundit") came to be adopted for the whole group.

Nain Singh set out in 1864 to survey the route to Lhasa. Disguised as a horse dealer from Kashmir, he traveled through Nepal with his cousin Mani Singh, but at the Tibetan border a suspicious official turned them back. Nain Singh made another attempt on his own, this time posing as a dealer in spices from Ladakh, with a false pigtail pinned inside his cap. He was allowed in as long as he promised not to leave the caravan with which he was traveling. Unfortunately that caravan was not going to Lhasa. Where the roads parted, Nain Singh feigned illness and fell out, later joining another caravan on the road to Lhasa. Independent travel was out of the question as the country was infested with bandits, an even worse danger than the appalling roads or the dizzying bridges and fragile ferries across thunderous rivers.

Fearful of being recognized when he reached Lhasa, he stayed indoors, creeping out at night with his sextant to take sightings from the roof (his location of Lhasa was correct to the nearest minute). Although not a Buddhist himself, he was a little afraid of the penetrative mental powers of the Panchen and Dalai Lamas, both of whom he met. He was relieved when they turned out to be children.

Returning via Lake Manasarowar, Nain Singh encountered more trouble at the border, but he found another, unguarded route into Nepal and arrived at the Survey's station at Dehra Dun about 130 miles (200 kilometers) northeast of Delhi after an absence of 21 months.

The following year he was off again, this time to investigate the source of the Indus and the rumored Tibetan

goldfields – a clue that there was more to the work of the Pundits than simple surveying. He was unmasked by a chieftain on the upper Indus, who identified Nain Singh and his companions with such precision that the work of a double agent must be suspected. However, nothing adverse came of this, and the goldfields – at a height of 16,000 feet (5000 meters) – were duly reached.

Kishen Singh

Nain Singh had all the qualities required of a great explorer, but the longest and most remarkable journey of all was undertaken by one of his successors, Kishen Singh, who began his fourth journey for the Survey in 1878. Proceeding to Lhasa, he joined a Mongolian caravan and crossed the high Tibetan Plateau – surviving attack by bandits – to the fringes of the Gobi Desert. Enterprisingly, he chose to return via a different route, which took him over 700 miles (1100 kilometers) east of Lhasa, though his hope of reaching Assam was thwarted. Having long been given up for dead, he arrived home after more than four years with his clothes in rags but his sextant, carefully wrapped in felt, still safe in its hidden compartment. His calculation of his own position was out by less than 10 miles (16 kilometers), a staggering performance after a journey of some 3000 miles (4800 kilometers), during which he took many sightings in secret and measured distance by his own pace.

The question of the Brahmaputra

Perhaps the most gallant, certainly the most poignant, of the Pundits' stories concerns the search for the source of the Brahmaputra. This mighty river emerges from the Himalayas in Assam and flows westward before turning south toward the Bay of Bengal. It was known that on the other side of the Himalayas a great river, the Tsangpo, ran roughly parallel but flowing east. Was it connected with the Brahmaputra, as stated by the Tibetans?

The plan, drawn up in 1880, was simple. A pundit named Kintup was to descend the Tsangpo as far as possible and throw in some tagged logs. On the other side of the Himalayas, observers would keep watch for the logs on the Brahmaputra.

All went far from well. Kintup entered Tibet posing as bondsman to a Mongolian lama who, once over the border, sold him to a Tibetan official, pocketed the cash and disappeared. After six months Kintup escaped. Pursued, he took refuge in a monastery, but the lamas concluded a deal with his former owner, and he became their servant instead. A few months later he asked to visit a distant shrine but, once out, he made for the Tsangpo. He cut 50 logs, tagged them, and hid them in a cave.

A year behind schedule, he returned to the monastery and, after a decent interval, asked permission to visit Lhasa. From there he sent a message to his chief at the Survey advising him when to start watching for logs on the Brahmaputra. He returned to the monastery and performed his humble tasks there for several more months before applying to go on yet another pilgrimage. This time the lamas, impressed by his devotion, gave him his freedom. He hastened to the Tsangpo, retrieved his logs, and threw them into the river.

In due course, no doubt, they came tumbling through the Himalayas and down the Brahmaputra, but they did so unnoticed. When Kintup returned to India, he learned that his message from Lhasa had never been delivered. There were no observers on the banks of the Brahmaputra.

▲ *The Panmah glacier* in the Karakorams was painted by Colonel H. H. Godwin-Austen, who led a topographical survey of the region in the 1850s.

▲ *Nain Singh* had all the qualities required of a great explorer – resourcefulness, determination, and patience. He adopted several disguises in the course of his work, and during a journey to Lhasa obtained a temporary job in his old profession of teacher in order to obtain enough money to continue his travels.

◄ *Kintup* – code name K. P. – showed enormous determination in his efforts to demonstrate that the Tsangpo and Brahmaputra were the same river. This photograph was taken in 1913, some 30 years after his return from Tibet to India.

Peaks and Plateaus

▲ *Sven Hedin* was driven by an urge to "conquer Asia" and "tread paths where no European had set foot" as a result of his early travels in the Near East when he was a young diplomat in Persia.

▼ *The Mongolian Plateau* was crossed by Nikolai Przhevalsky four times in the 1870s. In the southwest he discovered a species of wild horse to which his name has been attached.

The German Alexander Humboldt, one of the greatest explorers of any age, is generally remembered for the years, 1799–1804, that he spent in South America (see pages 106–7). However, he also explored central Asia, undertaking in 1829, at the age of 60, to investigate the region on behalf of the Russian tsar. He traveled east across Siberia to the Altai Mountains and Dzungaria, areas that were later explored by Peter Semenov and others, but as he never wrote an account of his expedition it has been largely forgotten.

Przhevalsky in Mongolia

Without doubt the greatest Russian-born explorer of Asia was Nikolai Przhevalsky, whose travels between 1870 and 1885 encompassed a huge area in Mongolia, western China, and northern Tibet. Przhevalsky was a soldier whose journeys were subsidized, though not generously, by the Russian Government. A keen hunter, he was also an excellent naturalist. As a surveyor he was not always perfect: his location of Lop Nor was out by some margin.

Although there were no really substantial new geographical discoveries to be made, Przhevalsky vastly increased knowledge of central Asia. He was the first to make sense of the mountain systems north of Tibet. Very determined, he was not easily diverted from his objectives by physical difficulties or by human opponents, such as the bandits who stole his camels or the Chinese peasant who set a mastiff on his amiable dog, Faust. (Przhevalsky shot the mastiff on the grounds that "if you let them kill your dog one day, they may try to kill you the next.")

On his first journey through central Asia, in 1870–73, Przhevalsky and his two companions crossed Mongolia in a highly uncomfortable Chinese cart, via the town of Urga (Ulan Bator). They followed the caravan trail across part of the Gobi Desert until they came to the Great Wall at Kalgan (Zhangjiakou). Thence they rode on horseback to Peking (Beijing), where they acquired a small caravan (seven camels) and returned to Kalgan, before moving off westward to the Ordos Desert and Yinchuan.

They followed the Yellow River (Huang He) through the desert, in "the silence of the tomb" for 300 miles (480 kilometers), then passed through still grimmer desert and mountains. They were making for the great lake Koko Nor (Qinghai Hu), 10,500 feet (3200 meters) above sea level, but were forced to turn back through lack of stores and money when still three or four weeks' journey away. After a rough journey back they recuperated in Kalgan before setting out once more. They finally succeeded in reaching the mysterious, dark blue expanse of Koko Nor in October 1872, thus accomplishing "the dream" of Przhevalsky's life. From the shores of the lake they journeyed south to the Yangtze before lack of money and supplies forced them to turn back.

Przhevalsky never reached another objective, Lhasa, though not for want of trying. Once he had to turn back when his camels died on the Tibetan Plateau; another time, less than 150 miles (240 kilometers) away, he was blocked by Tibetan guards – he did not have Younghusband's firepower. On that attempt, in 1879–80, he made a remarkable return journey, traveling south of Koko Nor and then due north across the full extent of the Gobi Desert to the Russian border. Przhevalsky died in the Tien Shan mountains preparing for another expedition in 1888.

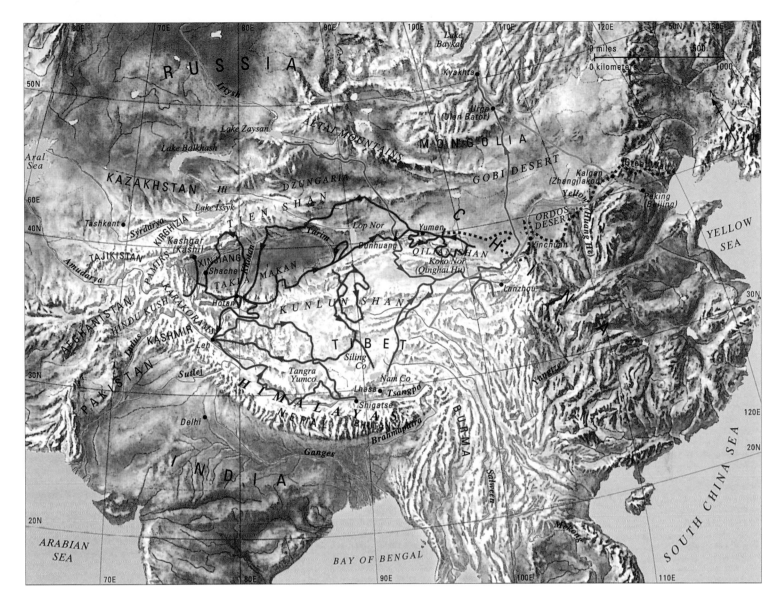

The adventurer

For toughness and determination Przhevalsky could be compared with the Swede Sven Hedin, the last of the old explorer-adventurers. He covered immense distances. Between 1894 and 1897, he calculated, he walked and rode further than the distance between the Poles. On his expedition of 1893–94 he traveled to Tashkent and, accompanied by Khirgiz tribesmen, crossed the Pamirs in midwinter – "only a step separated me from the stars." Next he set off into the Takla Makan Desert, a silent, shadeless graveyard of vast mounds of sand, where extreme heat made him forget the icy mountains. Things soon went seriously wrong when the party – four men, eight camels, and some sheep – ran out of water, apparently having miscalculated the position of the Khotan (Hotan) River.

This episode, as described by Hedin, has become a classic explorer's tale. Two of the men and all the animals died. Attempts to drink the blood of the sheep had failed because it coagulated too quickly. Hedin was left with one man, Kasim, who had taken an unfair share of the last of the water. They staggered around, at one point realizing that the tracks they came to were their own: they had gone round in a circle. Kasim collapsed in the sand, Hedin pressed on a few yards further, and finally stumbled on the Khotan. Unfortunately it was dry. At his last gasp, he heard a splash, saw a waterfowl rise, and found a surviving pool.

That experience did not prevent him recrossing the Takla Makan not long after, where, investigating some wooden posts in the sand, he discovered the remains of a town dating from the earliest days of the old Silk Road. He later discovered several more, but not being an archaeologist, he left their investigation to others.

In 1900–1 he made two attempts to reach Lhasa, but both failed because the Tibetans forced him to turn back. On his last individual expedition, starting from Leh in 1906, he explored the valley of the Tsangpo River and visited the monastery of Tasilhumpo, over a century after George Bogle (see page 56). But Hedin's most valuable work was as head of a large-scale Sino-Swedish scientific expedition which conducted numerous programs and experiments at stations between the Caspian Sea and the Great Wall in 1928–34.

The archaeologist

Hedin's contemporary Marc Aurel Stein, though his travels were no less extensive, was a totally different character. Of Hungarian origin, an intellectual, and a thorough "orientalist" before that term gained unfavorable overtones, he was employed by the Education Service in India, but had no difficulty in gaining official permission for his endless journeys.

In the years 1897–1927 he crisscrossed the region between the Hindu Kush and the Gobi Desert, where he once discovered his own footprints, dating from three years previously. A map of his journeys looks, in the words of the travel-writer Eric Newby, like the "footsteps of a demented centipede." More tactful though no less vigorous than Hedin, he was essentially an explorer of cultures. His greatest coup was his visit in 1907 to a famous place of pilgrimage, the "Caves of the Thousand Buddhas" at Dunhuang near the western end of the Gobi, from whose keeper he extracted, for a small fee, marvelous manuscripts and scroll paintings. Like Hedin, Stein is regarded in China as no better than a bandit.

KEY TO ROUTES

Przhevalsky 1870–73
Przhevalsky 1879–80
Hedin 1901–2
Hedin 1906–8
Stein 1906–8

Southeast Asia

Although civilizations like that of Annam or Java had flourished in Southeast Asia and long-distance maritime voyaging had begun there many centuries ago, little was known of these developments outside the region. The commercial voyages of the Portuguese and their successors in the 16th and 17th centuries began to open windows, but it was not until the 19th century, spurred on by colonialism or scientific enquiry, that the rich and diverse lands of Southeast Asia were explored by Europeans – with the essential assistance, of course, of some at least of their ethnically diverse inhabitants.

A naturalist in the Indies

Scientific endeavor is perhaps best represented by an indefatigable English naturalist, Alfred Wallace, who had already spent four years in Amazonia (see pages 108–9), before he arrived in Singapore in 1854. During the following eight years he traveled among the islands of the Malay or Indonesian Archipelago, from Malaya to New Guinea, collecting hundreds of specimens. He arrived at the theory of evolution by a process of natural selection independently of Darwin; he is also remembered for identifying the "Wallace Line," which marks the division between Asian and Australian types of fauna, and shows that the western and eastern islands of the archipelago once formed parts of separate continents.

Indochina

French political involvement in Indochina dated from 1787, when, following the work of French missionaries, a treaty was signed with the King of Annam giving the French two footholds on the coast. The king's successors after 1820 resented French influence, and the persecution of Christians led to direct intervention, with the capture of Tourane (Da Nang) in 1862 and Saigon a few months later. By a treaty of 1862, three provinces of Cochin China (south Vietnam) were ceded, and in the following year Cambodia became a French protectorate.

The Mekong Expedition

The expedition to explore the Mekong River was urged on the French Governor by a 24-year-old naval officer, Marie Joseph François Garnier. In view of Garnier's youth, command was given to Captain Doudart de Lagrée, the chief representative and virtual ruler at the court of King Norodom of Cambodia. Garnier's notion, a reasonable though incorrect hypothesis, was that the Mekong might provide a route through the length of the peninsula into the Chinese province of Yunnan, part of which was in rebel hands at the time. The aims of the expedition were frankly imperialist and commercial; scientific enquiry was a secondary consideration. However, Lagrée and his men were to traverse some 5400 miles (8700 kilometers), two-thirds of it through unmapped country. Garnier himself was to be responsible for most of the observations.

Before embarking on the expedition proper, Lagrée led a diversion to the famous ruins of Angkor, which had been little known until they were visited by the French explorer Henri Mouhot in 1861.

The journey up the Mekong began in July 1866. Five of the six members of the expedition – excluding a few soldiers, later sent back for bad behavior – were naval officers, two being qualified physicians. They traveled in a well-armed gunboat, but on reaching the rapids at Kratie prudently changed to Cambodian dugouts, hauled along by men with hooked poles. The tumultuous Khong Falls on the Laotian border destroyed any lingering hopes of steam navigation on the Mekong.

KEY TO ROUTES

— Wallace 1854–62 (with dates that places were visited)

— Lagrée and Garnier 1866–68

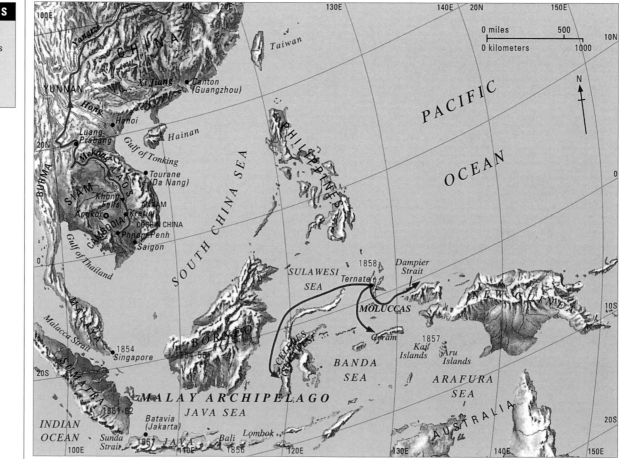

◄ **Banteay Sei,** whose chief entrance is shown here surrounded by jungle vegetation, is some 20 miles (30 kilometers) from the main ruins of Angkor Wat – a vast temple complex dating from the 12th century. Doudart de Lagrée was the first European to provide a detailed and accurate description of the ruins.

The Frenchmen experienced all the discomforts of 19th-century European travelers in a tropical forest. Besides heat, damp, and disease, the lesser fauna such as mosquitoes and leeches plagued them cruelly. Garnier memorably describes landing on an island to take sightings and finding it so infested with leeches that he was forced to climb a tree to escape them.

There were compensations, however. For one thing, the peaceable Buddhists of Cambodia and Laos were hospitable and eager to help. At Luang Prabang, the royal capital of Laos, the local ruler himself contributed to a memorial the French erected to Mouhot, who had died there. Local people brought in samples of flora, supposing all Frenchmen to be keen naturalists like Mouhot.

Some of these little, semi-independent states were highly attractive; Garnier marked down one as an ideal health station for convalescent colonial officials. At several places Lagrée was excited to discover further remains of the ancient Khmer civilization.

A disappointing outcome

The expedition reached Luang Prabang, in April 1867, but not far beyond it Lagrée decided to forsake the Mekong altogether. In the Laotian highlands the river had become comparatively shallow, no longer the great artery it was further south.

The expedition set out overland for the Chinese border, making slow and haphazard progress because every local chieftain, curious to see a European, demanded a ceremonial visit, which frequently required a diversion of several days. The remote mountain people of northern Laos were no less interesting to the Europeans, but the expedition, seriously behind schedule, had almost exhausted its cash and trade goods, and was increasingly reliant on local hospitality.

In October 1867 they finally reached the Chinese border, but in very poor shape. Lagrée soon died, and Garnier took over command. Any hope of establishing friendly relations with the Panthay rebels of Yunnan (Muslims who at that time maintained an independent state in the west of the province) had to be abandoned when the Frenchmen were attacked by a xenophobic mob. They escaped and made their way overland to the Yangtze, descending the river to Shanghai and from there going by sea to Saigon in what is now Vietnam.

From an official point of view the results of the expedition were disappointing, but a great deal of knowledge concerning what was soon to become French Indochina had been gained. Because the Mekong had failed to prove an Asian version of the Mississippi, Garnier shifted his enthusiastic commendations to the Hong (Rouge or Red) River, flowing from central Yunnan to the Gulf of Tonking via Hanoi. Garnier died at Hanoi in 1873 in a scuffle with Black Flags (Chinese mercenaries) shortly after capturing the city – still only 34 years old.

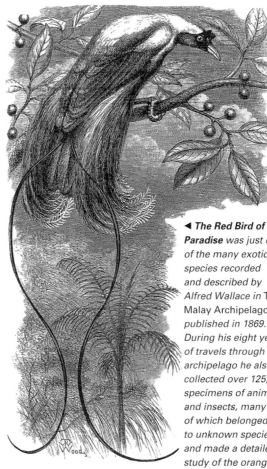

◄ **The Red Bird of Paradise** was just one of the many exotic species recorded and described by Alfred Wallace in The Malay Archipelago, published in 1869. During his eight years of travels through the archipelago he also collected over 125,000 specimens of animals and insects, many of which belonged to unknown species, and made a detailed study of the orang-utan in Borneo.

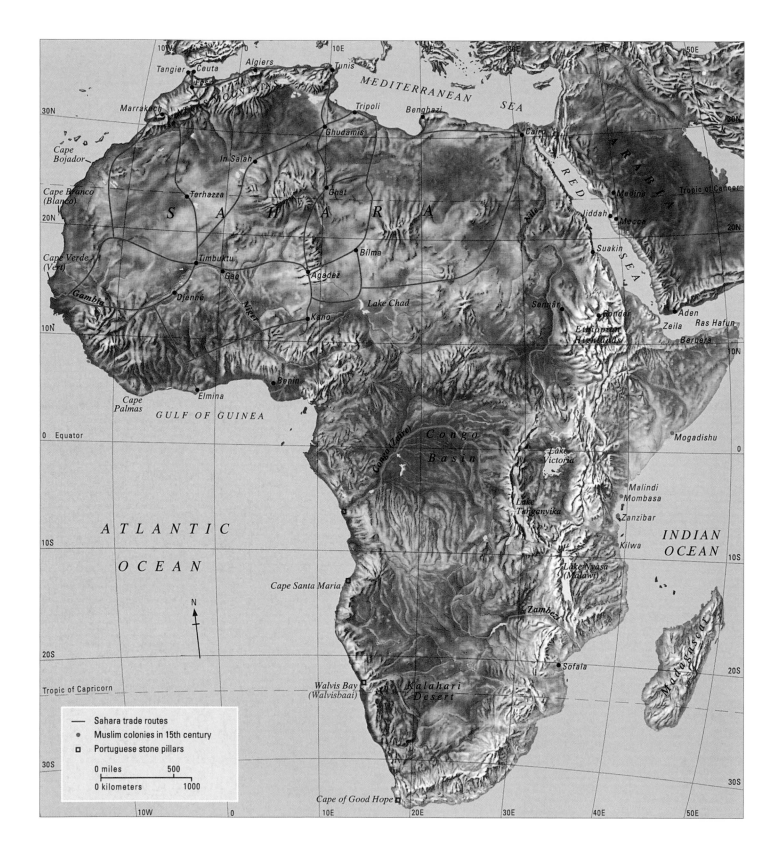

MEDITERRANEAN SEA

Tangier Ceuta Algiers Tunis
Marrakech Tripoli Benghazi Cairo
Cape Bojador
Ghudamis
In Salah Ghat
Cape Branco (Blanco) Terhazza Tropic of Cancer
Medina
Jiddah Mecca
Cape Verde (Vert) Timbuktu Bilma Suakin
Gambia Gao Agadez
Djenné Niger Lake Chad Sennâr Gondar Aden
Kano Ethiopian Zeila Ras Hafun
Highlands Berbera

Benin
Cape Palmas Elmina
GULF OF GUINEA

Equator Congo (Zaïre) Lake Victoria Mogadishu
Congo Basin Malindi
Mombasa
Lake Zanzibar
Tanganyika
Kilwa

ATLANTIC INDIAN
OCEAN OCEAN

Lake Nyasa (Malawi)
Cape Santa Maria
Zambezi
N
Madagascar
Sofala

Walvis Bay (Walvisbaai) Kalahari
Desert

Tropic of Capricorn

——— Sahara trade routes
•   Muslim colonies in 15th century
□   Portuguese stone pillars

0 miles   500
0 kilometers   1000

Cape of Good Hope

AFRICA

Embracing one-fifth of the world's land mass, Africa is seamed with rivers which cascade from wide tablelands to flow east into the Indian Ocean and west into the Atlantic, is pitted with great lakes, and has snow-capped mountains standing on the Equator. Its systematic exploration by Europeans began in real earnest with the foundation in Britain, in 1788, of the Association for Promoting the Discovery of the Interior Parts of Africa. However, this does not mean that it was not explored by people from outside Africa in earlier times. Between the 5th century BC and the 1st century AD both the Greeks and the Romans explored the Nile, and between the 7th and the 12th centuries Arab invasions provided opportunities for exploration for a remarkable series of scholars and travelers in North and East Africa.

The Portuguese voyages of the 15th century along the African coast did much to establish the shape and extent of the continent. The capture of Ceuta, in present-day Morocco, in 1415, gave Portugal access to the African mainland, revealed something of the geography of the northwest, and suggested possibilities of trade, especially in the gold which had been coming for centuries across the Sahara from the West African coast. By 1435 Portuguese seamen had rounded Cape Bojador, hitherto their furthest point from home; by the 1470s they were in the Gulf of Guinea and in contact with what came to be called the Gold Coast (now Ghana). On the western coast they erected stone pillars engraved with the royal arms of Portugal as a claim to sovereignty.

In 1482 Diogo Cão reached Cape Santa Maria in modern Angola, after sailing up the Congo (Zaire) River to what would be called the Livingstone Falls. Six years later Bartholomeu Dias rounded the Cape of Good Hope, but lacking adequate provisions he was forced to return to Portugal without having explored the eastern coast. It would be another ten years before this was achieved by a European.

Europeans in East Africa

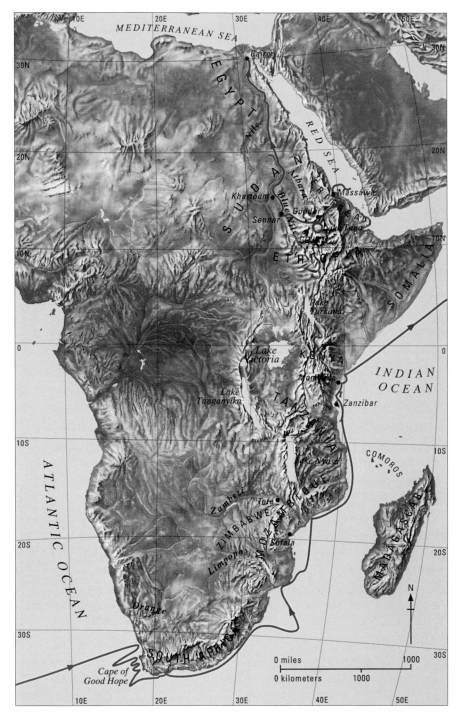

▼ **James Bruce** was not the first European to reach the source of the Blue Nile at which, in this engraving based on a romantic painting by R. M. Paye, he is shown drinking the health of George III. However, it was an achievement for which he is remembered to this day.

In 1498 Vasco da Gama established the sea route to India by sailing up the east coast of Africa to Mombasa and then across the Indian Ocean to Calicut on the Malabar coast. As this route became established, there were landings on the eastern mainland of Africa. In 1605 a settlement was founded at Sofala, and two years later a firm foothold was gained in Mozambique. By the middle of the 17th century an avenue for trade was being pursued up the Zambezi River as far as Tete. Jesuit missionaries and peaceful traders began to find their way inland as far as the borders of present-day Zimbabwe.

The Portuguese mission

The first Portuguese voyages to Africa had been planned by Prince Henry "the Navigator" with more in mind than the extension of commerce. Both he and his successors also sought the extension of Christendom and the over-throw of Islam. By traveling east they hoped to find the empire of Prester John, the priest-king who was a potent legend in medieval and early modern times. He was said to preside, somewhere in Asia or Africa, over a kingdom where wealth and virtue were universal and where he himself enjoyed eternal youth. By the time the Portuguese voyages were under way, the legend had become associated with the remote but not unknown Christian realm of Abyssinia (as Ethiopia was then generally called).

The Portuguese began to make contact with Abyssinia following da Gama's voyage to India and in 1520 despatched an embassy which was to make the country better known through the writings of its chaplain, Francisco Alvarez. During the following century Jesuit missionaries came to Abyssinia intent on converting the emperor and his subjects from their practice of Coptic rites to those of Rome. By the time the mission was expelled in 1633, the missionaries had to a certain extent explored the land. Among them were Pedro Paez, who visited the source of the Blue Nile in Gojam in 1613, and Jerônimo Lobo, who followed him a few years later.

James Bruce and Abyssinia

A century on, the fashion for exploration, inspired by the spirit of the Age of Enlightenment, began to take hold in the West, and a true explorer was ready to brave the unknown in Africa. James Bruce of Kinnaird was the son of an old Scottish family. He acquired a taste for travel when in Spain and Portugal on business, and in 1768 he set out to seek the source of the Nile. Conceiving this to be in Abyssinia, he made his way to Massawa on the Red Sea coast (in modern Eritrea) and some time in 1770 arrived in Gonder and settled himself, with remarkable success, in the imperial court. He was accompanied – though he never mentioned the fact in his subsequent book – by Luigi Balugani, the Italian draughtsman who remained with him throughout his later travels.

Bruce spent three years at the court, making himself useful as a doctor and popular as a sportsman, but he was hampered from pursuing his quest by the civil war then raging. The young emperor was under the dominance of one of Abyssinia's war lords, Ras Michael, who was engaged in a ferocious power struggle with his rival Fasi. Bruce managed to hold his own in a dangerous atmosphere by virtue of several advantages: he was a big man of powerful physique, he spoke Arabic, he was a fine rider, a good shot, and something of a swordsman.

Fortune played into his hands when he found on his arrival that there was a smallpox epidemic. By his confident bearing he succeeded in calming the fears of three important ladies at the court – the Iteghe (or dowager empress) and her daughters, one of whom was the wife of Ras Michael. Bruce fumigated the palace chambers "with incense and myrrh ... washed them with warm water and vinegar, and adhered strictly to the rules which my worthy and skilful friend, Doctor Russel, had given me in Aleppo," adding "the more scrupulous and particular, the more the confidence of the ladies increased." Fortunately for Bruce, Ras Michael's son survived the disease.

Bruce's finest hour

At last Bruce was allowed to join Ras Michael's troops in a campaign that brought him within reach of his goal and in November 1770 he found himself at the spring south of Lake Tana from which the Blue Nile rises. For the rest of his life his attainment of what he always regarded as the source of the main Nile was to remain his finest hour, though it is hardly to Bruce's credit that he dismissed the Jesuits who had preceded him as "liars."

He came next to Sennar in the Sudan, where he was asked to attend the king's harem – an alarming experience described by Bruce in a passage which might have come out of *Gulliver's Travels*. "Although all acquaintance with the fair sex has hitherto been much to my advantage," he did not enjoy being forced to strip to the waist in order that his white skin might be marveled at. Moving on from Sennar, he traveled to Cairo and from there home.

Bruce was not, however, as warmly received as he had expected; his awkward manner and confused way of telling stories did not go down well in society. Fanny Burney was chiefly impressed by his bulk – she thought him "the tallest man you ever saw – *gratis*." Dr Johnson, the translator of Le Grand's French version of Lobo's *Travels*, passed the ambiguous judgement that the Scottish explorer was "neither abounding nor deficient in sense; I did not perceive any superiority of understanding."

When James Bruce published an account of his travels in 1790, the handsome five-volume work, illustrated by his companion, the talented Balugani, was greeted with expressions of incredulity, although time has proved it to have been an extremely fair and well-observed account of the people and customs of Ethiopia. James Bruce died in retirement at Kinnaird.

▲ *The coastline of East Africa, Madagascar and the Middle East was broadly known to European navigators by the mid-16th century, as represented in this map of 1558 by Diego Homem.*

▶ *For most of the 18th century the relationship between Europe and Africa was dominated by the slave trade. The voracious demand for slaves could only be satisfied by raiding, and this gave rise to fierce wars in the interior. The slave traders guarded their territory jealously against rivals and actively discouraged explorers from venturing into the areas they regarded as their reserves. As a consequence, explorers' knowledge of the African interior developed far more slowly than their knowledge of the coastline.*

The Mystery of the Niger

▲ **Mungo Park** *described this bridge over one of the tributaries of the upper Senegal River, as being "carried away every year by the swelling of the river in the rainy season."*

The founder of the British Association for Promoting the Discovery of the Interior Parts of Africa, Sir Joseph Banks, corresponded with James Bruce on plans to sponsor individual travelers. On June 18, 1788, 12 members of the Saturday Club in London met for dinner and sketched out their plans. There was plenty to "discover" in the interior of Africa, plenty of blanks on the map, but it was debatable which of these should first receive attention.

Records of the Association note that "the southern extremity of the African peninsula may perhaps be justly considered as explored," and eastern Africa had been pretty fully reported on by Bruce. North and west seemed to offer a more promising field for investigation, so Banks and his friends looked to the Sahara and beyond for the solution of the mystery of the Niger.

First ventures

The middle reaches of the Niger were known by hearsay to be located in the vicinity of Timbuktu. The river was a magnet for the romantic explorer, just as El Dorado had been in the past, and as Lhasa would be in the future, its legend linked with the gold trade of the Moors across the Sahara. It was not known where the river rose, which way it flowed (Leo Africanus some 200 years earlier thought westward) or how it ended.

Some geographers tried to link it with the Nile, some with Lake Chad, some even with the Congo (Zaire) River. Captain J. K. Tuckey, leading a naval expedition in

1816, was instructed to make his way up the Congo (Zaire) River to ascertain whether it was connected with the Niger. Like Diogo Cão in 1482, he was stopped by the great falls 100 miles (160 kilometers) upstream.

The Association's first ventures to put the Niger on the map were abortive. Simon Lucas, attempting to take the southern route from Tripoli, found his way barred by warring tribes. John Ledyard, a widely traveled American who had sailed with Cook on the third Pacific voyage, died in Cairo while preparing for a journey westward. Daniel Houghton set off from the Gambia and reached the Niger, only to die on his way back in 1790.

Johann Ludwig Burckhardt

The Swiss Johann Ludwig Burckhardt was thwarted by illness. He was the most scholarly of the travelers to be employed by the Association and spent three years in Syria learning Arabic before taking the road. He arrived in Cairo in 1812 (after visiting Petra on the way), to find that no caravan traveling in the direction of Timbuktu was expected. Unwilling to remain idle, Burckhardt turned south into Nubia, where he was the first European in modern times to see the temples of Abu Simbel; then, disguised as a pilgrim, he traveled to Mecca. Back in Cairo he fell ill and died of dysentery before he could embark on his journey into the desert. His records of what he had experienced in five years of travel were published by the Association in five volumes between 1819 and 1830.

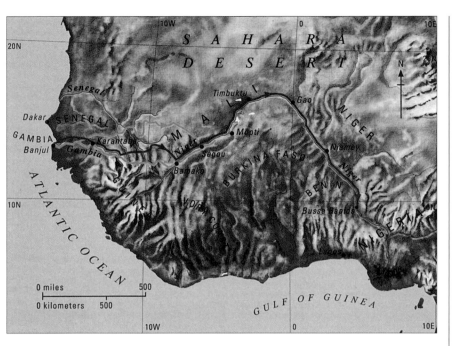

▲ *Mungo Park* *is one of the most famous names in the annals of African exploration. A Scotsman and farmer's son, he arrived in West Africa at the age of 24, determined to find fame and fortune. He was greatly helped in his travels by his talent for learning languages.*

KEY TO ROUTES

—— Park 1795–97
—— Park 1805–06

◄ *On Park's first expedition he was held prisoner for several weeks by Muslim Moors at a camp composed of "a great number of dirty-looking tents." Here he had to withstand, without retaliating, insults and ill treatment before at last being allowed to leave (minus most of his possessions). He wrote afterward that "never did any period of my life pass away so heavily."*

Mungo Park's travels

The great name in the Association's history is that of Mungo Park, the Scottish doctor. A ship's surgeon, with a taste for travel, his interest in botany had brought him to the notice of Sir Joseph Banks. In 1796 he set out from Karantaba on the Gambia River, modestly equipped with "a few changes of linen, an umbrella, a pocket sextant, a magnetic compass and a thermometer; two fowling pieces and two pairs of pistols." He wore a large hat in which he kept his papers.

Park was traveling through the country ruled by successive chiefs in the conglomeration of states bordering the Niger. To the north the Muslim Moors operated the trade routes. These people were uniformly aggressive and obstructive, especially the Tuareg, the famous "veiled men of the desert," who were to put up such continuous and fierce opposition to any strangers attempting to enter their territory. The pagan negroes in the southerly part of Park's route were more kindly, especially the women, who fed and sheltered him. He records that some of them composed a song of which the refrain was "Oh, pity the white man, no mother has he!"

After terrible hardships and robbed of nearly all he possessed, he reached the Niger at Ségou in modern Mali on July 20, 1796. There he "saw with infinite pleasure the great object of my mission: the long sought-for and majestic Niger, glistening in the morning sun, as broad as the Thames at Westminster, and floating slowly to the eastward." Having run out of provisions, he then had to return.

In 1805 the British Government, taking up the running from Banks and the Association, sent Park back to the Niger in command of a quasi-military expedition made up to a total of 45, with a rabble of ill-disciplined soldiery. The venture was a disaster, the death toll almost total. With great difficulty Park secured a boat downstream from Timbuktu in which to navigate the river, but he lost his life in the Bussa Rapids, either by drowning or in a fight with unfriendly tribesmen on the bank.

Navigation of the Niger

In 1822 an expedition backed by the British Government, and officered by Hugh Clapperton, Dixon Denham, and Walter Oudney, set out from Tripoli. This venture was concerned as much with the pioneering of commercial openings as with exploration, but it did locate Lake Chad and provide useful information from the states of Sokoto and Borno in modern northern Nigeria. The results were promising enough from the trading point of view for Clapperton to be sent back to Africa in 1825, accompanied by his manservant Richard Lander.

Clapperton and Lander

Explorers are on the whole an unlikeable lot, jealous of their own fame and ruthless in overcoming both material and human obstacles. Richard Lander, however, is one of the most engaging travelers ever to set foot on the African continent. The almost illiterate son of a Cornish innkeeper, he was cheerful and affectionate, and had a mania for travel.

He carried a bugle with him on which he played appropriate homely airs – "Over the hills and far away" – as he and Clapperton set off on their second mission. As Clapperton lay dying at Sokoto, the furthest point of their journey, Lander recited to cheer him a "little poem 'My native Highland home' " (Clapperton was a Scot). When the end came "I flung myself on the bed of death and prayed Heaven would in mercy take my life." Fortunately, Heaven turned a deaf ear, and Lander returned to England with his master's papers and his own pertinent comments.

The Lander brothers

Lander was sent again to Africa in 1830, accompanied by his brother John (to whom His Majesty's Government paid no salary), with rather casual instructions from the Colonial Office to follow the Niger. They landed at Badagri (an evil haunt of slave dealers), dressed strangely in scarlet tunics, full Turkish trousers, and straw hats bigger than umbrellas, causing much amusement to the local people.

The simple Cornish brothers were to succeed where the more sophisticated Mungo Park had failed. In the face of every possible setback they sailed down the Niger from Bussa, south of Timbuktu, not far beyond where Park lost his life. John Lander graphically describes the river banks: "They were embellished with mighty trees and elegant shrubs, which were clad in thick and luxuriant foliage, some of lively green, and others of darker hue." The brothers noted as they went the great confluence of the Benue with the Niger, and emerged at the delta, thus establishing the course of the river.

They were shabbily treated by the Government on their return, Richard receiving £100 reward, John nothing; private enterprise did better in that the publisher John Murray paid £1000 for their book. Richard was the first traveler to be honored by the newly founded (later Royal) Geographical Society of London, receiving 50 guineas. He died on a subsequent expedition designed to open up trade in the Niger delta and upstream, and launched as a result of his and his brother's earlier success.

▼ *Heinrich Barth* made this sketch of Kano, which he visited after having learned of its existence from a Hausa slave. He spent a month there early in 1851 and became extremely knowledgeable about the city and its environs.

▶ *The Lander brothers* at Badagri, in their idiosyncratic costumes: "So unusual a dress might well cause the people to laugh heartily ... but the more modest of the females, unwilling to give us any uneasiness, turned aside to conceal the titter from which they were quite unable to refrain."

◄ **Sandstorms,** such as this one painted by J. S. Lyon in the Libyan Desert in 1820, were among the hazards faced by Barth and his companions on their journey south from Tripoli to Lake Chad. According to James Bruce, the best way of dealing with a sandstorm was to lie flat on one's face until it had blown itself out.

KEY TO ROUTES

— Clapperton, Denham,
 and Oudney 1822–25
— Clapperton and
 Richard Lander 1825–27
— Lander brothers 1830
— Barth 1850–55

The "white man's grave"

The Landers' epic journey proved the Niger to be navigable into the interior of Africa at a time when the abolition of the slave trade was encouraging the pursuit of legitimate trade and of Christian missions. Expeditions, both privately and officially sponsored, followed after the journey of Richard and John Lander to the Niger's delta, but the death toll from fever on the river, which came to be known as the "white man's grave," was so heavy that progress came to a halt. Eventually, with improvements in medical knowledge and better observance of hygiene, it became possible to pursue the Niger adventure.

Much was due to Dr William Baikie, who first sailed up the river in 1854, and from 1857 to 1864 was in charge of a government trading settlement at Lokoja at the confluence of the Niger and Benue. Baikie was a true pioneer, proving the efficacy of quinine against malaria and moreover adjusting himself to local conditions and mastering local tongues. He translated the Book of Genesis into Hausa and compiled a grammar of the Fuldi language. He adopted the comfortable local dress of a long cotton shirt and baggy trousers, and lived with a black mistress who bore him several children. It is sad to relate that, although he avoided the deadly local fever by dosing himself regularly with quinine, he died of dysentery.

Heinrich Barth: a scholarly explorer

Neither the commercial nor the anti-slavery lobbies were to remain satisfied with a foothold on the Niger at Lokoja. What Clapperton had reported of the states of Borno and Sokoto along the south bank of the river suggested a promising field for trade. The philanthropists, on the other hand, felt that penetration of these lands would provide a chance to destroy the slave trade at one of its sources. An expedition was officially sanctioned by the British Government in 1849, to be led by James Richardson of the Anti-Slavery Society accompanied by a geographer and a geologist to study the lie of the land.

The geographer chosen was Heinrich Barth, a well-recommended young German from Berlin, who was to prove himself one of Africa's most successful explorers. Barth was a master of Arabic and had all the painstaking thoroughness associated with German scholarship. The expedition's route was south from Tripoli across the Sahara to Lake Chad.

Richardson and later Overweg (the geologist) died at an early stage, but Barth was not discouraged. He traveled on alone, covering a distance of some 10,000 miles (16,000 kilometers) over a period of five years, with pitifully little cash from a parsimonious British Government and often in danger as a Christian in a Muslim country.

Barth thoroughly examined Lake Chad and, striking south, explored the upper waters of the Benue, which he proved to have no connection with the lake. Later on he traveled west to Timbuktu, before returning to England in 1855. His meticulous observations were incorporated in five volumes, but they were not written in the lively style expected by Victorian readers, who showed far more interest in other explorers' accounts. Barth received the Patron's Medal from the Royal Geographical Society and various other honors, but he died feeling that his achievements had not been fully recognized.

The Nile Quest

▲ **Richard Burton** was
painted by Lord Leighton
in 1876. The scar made
by a Somali spear in 1855 is
visible on his cheek. Burton
was both an outstanding
swordsman and a fine
oriental scholar. He was
not, however, a man who
could stand correction.
As Speke put it, he was
"one of those men who
never can be wrong."

Once the mystery that had cloaked the Niger for so long had largely been dissipated, travelers began to look for another legendary goal, the source or sources of the Nile. In 1839 and 1841 the Viceroy of Egypt, Mehemet Ali, launched two expeditions with the purpose of achieving economic expansion southward into the Sudan. They reached the navigable head of the Nile at a place called Gondokoro near modern Juba, leaving only the rapids south of Gondokoro between the travelers and the Nile sources. Adventurers and traders then began to move southward, raiding the land for ivory and slaves. In their detestable way they contributed to geographical knowledge by blazing trails through unknown country and sometimes allowing explorers to tag along with them and to share their protection.

Paths of the Arab traders

In the 1840s a new direction was given to the search for the sources of the Nile by missionaries working inland from Mombasa on the east coast on behalf of the Church Missionary Society. Ludwig Krapf, Johann Rebmann, and Johann Erhardt made some important journeys and collected information from the Arab traders operating inland from the east coast. There were, they learned, great lakes and huge mountains. Krapf and Rebmann saw these mountains for themselves, apparently covered in snow – an astonishing sight in Equatorial Africa.

The Paris Geographical Society awarded the men a medal, but the British geographers lagged behind, ridiculing the idea at first. The mountains were, in fact, Mount Kilimanjaro and Mount Kenya, and although they do not form part of the Nile system, it was the report of their existence that set others thinking about the possibility of an approach to the Nile from the east coast.

Burton and Speke: explorers at odds

Two men whose names will always be associated with the Nile first came together in 1854: Richard Burton and John Hanning Speke, both British Indian Army officers. Burton had recently accomplished his spectacular journey to Mecca and was keen to travel in Africa. Speke's enthusiasm was big game hunting; his preoccupation with finding the source of the Nile was to develop later. In 1856 the British Royal Geographical Society (RGS) invited Burton to lead an expedition in search of the Nile sources from the east coast of Africa. Instructions were based largely on the reports of the Mombasa missionaries, and reference was made to a map drawn by Erhardt of a vast inland sea which was to resolve itself eventually into Lake Victoria, Lake Albert, and Lake Tanganyika.

Like many African travelers, Burton and Speke started off in Zanzibar, the base of the Arab ivory and slave traders, where the Indian bankers had their depots and where porters congregated for hire. They set off on 16 June 1857 from Bagamoyo, not knowing at this stage whether they were likely to find one lake, or two, or three. The RGS told them to explore first "the Nyasa" (the Swahili word for lake) and then to turn north to investigate possible mountains which might give rise to the White Nile.

The two men made their way west to Lake Tanganyika, which ranks as Burton's "discovery," but arrived there too ill and with stores too depleted to explore the lake. Burton's legs were paralysed. Speke was almost blind from ophthalmia, and he had gone deaf owing to a beetle penetrating his ear. It was impossible to hire a boat to take them to the north end of the lake, where a river was reported as running either out of or into the lake. In the first case it might be the Nile, in the second case it could not be. It was not until Livingstone and Stanley visited the northern tip of Lake Tanganyika in 1872 that the Ruzizi was finally identified as an inflowing stream.

Back at Tabora, both somewhat recovered, Speke took an opportunity to visit a lake to the north, of which he had heard from the Arabs. His immediate claim that this lake, which he had no hesitation in naming "Victoria," was the source of the Nile was no more than an inspired guess, and it was to be many years before this was confirmed by further exploration. Burton, according to Speke, "snubbed" him "most unpleasantly" and thus began the famous quarrel between Burton and Speke over whether Lake Tanganyika or Lake Victoria was the source of the Nile.

Speke and Grant

The argument could only be resolved by the collection of more information. In 1860 the RGS sent Speke back to Africa with James Augustus Grant, a more congenial companion than the brilliant, eccentric Burton. The two men worked their way up the western side of Lake Victoria into Buganda – the first European visitors to this Bantu kingdom – of which Speke has left historians an interesting account. His description of how he measured the vital statistics of some of the royal ladies sent a delicious shiver of horror down Victorian spines.

After five months in Buganda, subject to the whims of the Kabaka Mtesa, Speke was allowed to make a quick dash to the northern end of the lake, where he identified the Nile flowing over what he called the Ripon Falls. Together with Grant he then followed the river downstream into Bunyoro, but since time was pressing and supplies were running short they had to cut across country to Gondokoro, where they hoped to find boats to take them down the Nile to Khartoum. Here, to their amazement, they encountered an old friend, Samuel Baker.

African followers
The porters recruited by Burton and Speke in Zanzibar were among the many Africans who made exploration of the continent possible. Without them no long expedition could have taken place in East Africa, where the prevalence of the tsetse fly prevented the use of pack animals.

A work force of 350 or more could be needed, making it essential to recruit loyal captains and headmen with organizational skills. Such men also played an important part in negotiations with local chiefs, for most spoke Swahili and mission education had taught them some English.

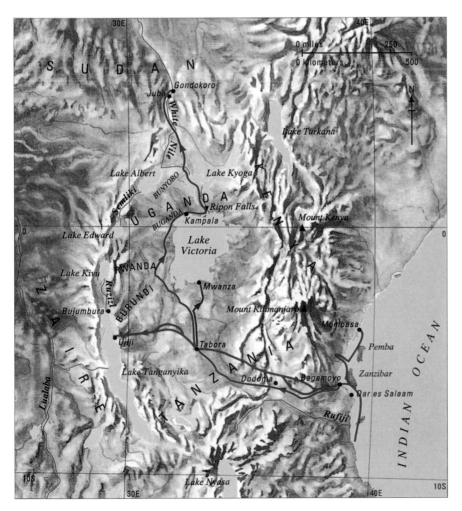

◀ *John Hanning Speke*
was, in contrast to Burton,
reserved and aloof in his
manner, a poor linguist,
uninterested in scholarly
pursuits, and a devoted
big game hunter.

▲ *James Augustus Grant,*
Speke's companion in the
search for the source of
the Nile, was a modest,
unassuming Scot, whose
loyalty to Speke never
wavered.

KEY TO ROUTES

— Burton and Speke
1857–58

— Speke 1858

— Speke and Grant
1860–63

The Bakers and the Nile

Samuel White Baker was a wealthy sportsman who had spent a roving life, having no necessity to earn a regular living. He and his brother founded and for a time managed a farm in the highlands of Ceylon (Sri Lanka), a ploy which left them plenty of time for big game hunting. On their return to England Sam's wife died, leaving him temporarily at a loss with four little daughters to care for.

Entrusting the children to a sister, Baker left England and went off to the Balkans to hunt wild boar. Idly wandering one day into the market place at the Turkish garrison town of Vidin (in modern Bulgaria), he found an auction of slaves in progress. On impulse he bid for a beautiful girl who was one of a crowd of Hungarian refugees being put up for sale and was to become his wife Florence.

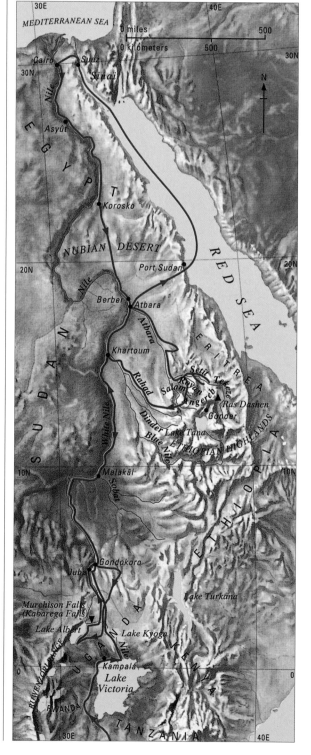

Search for the source

Together Sam and Florence went off to Africa to search for the source of the Nile. They started off up the Nile from Cairo in April 1861, disembarking at Korosko, where the river takes its great bend to the west, and here they mounted camels for an exhausting ride across the Nubian Desert. At Berber Baker made his plans to study what he called "the great drains of Abyssinia" – the Atbara, Setit (Tekeze), Royan, Salam, Angereb, Rahad, and Dinder rivers, and the Blue Nile itself, pouring down from the highlands to swell the yearly flood of the White Nile.

The Bakers made a pretty thorough survey of the rivers in these foothills of Ethiopia. They had learned Arabic and could converse with the local people, and they made several interesting visits to chiefs.

Exactly a year after they had set off from Berber, the Bakers arrived in Khartoum, ready to begin the real expedition up the main course of the White Nile. Their arrival at Gondokoro coincided with Speke's marching in from the south with Grant. Baker was disappointed to hear that Speke had "discovered" the source of the Nile in Lake Victoria. "Does not one leaf of the laurel remain for me?" he asked. Speke reassured him that, though he had virtually settled that Lake Victoria was the main source, there was another lake to the west which probably formed part of the Nile system.

With some instructions and a map from Speke and Grant, the Bakers set off across country to find this lake. The distance from Gondokoro to the northern end of Lake Albert is no more than 180 miles (290 kilometers) in a straight line, but due to various misfortunes and at the whim of their "guide," an ivory and slave trader, the Bakers were forced to travel a rather more circuitous route. Their porters mutinied, they were obliged to ride on oxen when the horses died, and they were afflicted by fever. Sam and Florence, however, made the best of things, making friends with the local people and even, on one protracted stay, planting vegetables to vary their diet.

Baker was one of the few African explorers who made jokes and could bring a comic scene to life. On one occasion he had himself carried toward a local encampment attired in a full dress Highland suit; on another he had a tweed suit ready so as to accentuate his likeness to Speke and so inspire confidence in the locals.

A goal attained

All difficulties at last overcome, they reached the lake on March 4, 1864. "The glory of our prize burst suddenly upon me!" wrote Baker. "There, like a sea of quicksilver, lay far beneath the grand expanse of water … I felt too serious to vent my feelings in vain cheers for victory and I sincerely thanked God for having guided and supported us through all dangers to the good end … I called this great lake 'the Albert Nyanza'."

To reach the lake they had crossed Speke's Nile west of its exit from Lake Victoria and had come to Lake Albert near the southern end. Owing to the mist which for most of the year hangs over the Ruwenzori Range, it seemed to Baker that a huge lake stretched far to the south, and he saw no mountains.

The Bakers skirted the eastern shore of the lake by boat and at the northern end found a river flowing into the lake, and almost immediately south out of it. The inflowing current they assumed (rightly) to be the Nile, which they had already crossed higher up on its way from east to west, but Florence insisted that they should make sure.

On their way upstream they were stopped by the great falls which Baker named Murchison – today a National

Park and a popular tourist resort. The Bakers then landed on the north bank and made their way back to Gondokoro, thence to Khartoum and Cairo, where they arrived in the summer of 1865. They left a stretch of the Nile between the two lakes unexplored and the dimensions of Lake Albert still in doubt.

The continuing dispute

Meanwhile, Speke and Grant sailed down the river with "Speke's Faithfuls," the 18 porters who had stood by them all the way from Zanzibar – some 4000 miles (6500 kilometers). Speke cabled home "The Nile is settled," and he and Grant returned to a hero's welcome in London. But the Nile was not settled. There were the inevitable gaps in Speke's account, and the fact that he had gone alone to the source told against him.

Burton was hostile as ever, and the row between the two men spread. In the interests of geographical truth Burton and Speke were invited to address the British Association for the Advancement of Science in September 1864. But on the appointed day Speke died in a shooting accident, news of which was brought to the hall where a large company was assembled to hear the two men discuss their differences. The gap in the program was hastily filled by a talk from Burton on the customs of Dahomey, and one from David Livingstone, who had just returned from his Zambezi Expedition. It was an obvious move to ask Britain's foremost African explorer to undertake a further expedition to locate the Nile source.

▲ *Samuel Baker* painted *this picture of himself being chased by an elephant – one occasion on which the hunter became the hunted.*

Florence Baker possessed a "share of *sangfroid* admirably adapted for African travel ... [and] was not a *screamer,*" Baker (pictured left) wrote, and later declared that he owed "my success and my life" to her. She first comes into focus at Baker's camp on the border of Abyssinia and Sudan in 1862, which was decorated with "many charms and indescribable little comforts that could only be effected by a lady's hand." It was rougher going at Gondokoro, rendezvous of the ivory and slave traders who were devastating the countryside. There Florence helped to quell an incipient mutiny among their men, and to persuade the least hostile of the traders to let them acccompany him into the interior. Surviving heat stroke and a virulent fever, Florence was finally able to reach Lake Albert and drink of the waters of the Nile.

David Livingstone

▲ *In 1850 Livingstone* took
his family with him on his
second expedition to Lake
Ngami. He is shown here
in the foreground with one
of his children. "Wagon
traveling," he wrote,
"is a prolonged system of
picnicking, excellent for the
health and agreeable to
those who ... delight in
being in the open air."

▲ *The steam launch* the
Ma Robert *(named after
Mrs Livingstone), caused
endless problems on the
Zambezi Expedition.*

▼ *This photograph* of
*Livingstone and his (now
motherless) daughter Anna
Mary was taken on his return
from the Zambezi in 1864.*

David Livingstone (1813–73) had originally come to the
notice of the Royal Geographical Society in 1849
when he had been the first European to cross the Kalahari
and to stand on the shore of Lake Ngami (now the Ngami
depression). He was born near Glasgow, into a family of
straitened means, strict living, and religious fervor. Largely
self-educated, he qualified as a doctor and was accepted for
service with the London Missionary Society, a Protestant
interdenominational body with interests in southern Africa.

He arrived at the Cape in 1841 on the way to
Kuruman (in Bechuanaland, now Botswana), some 1000
miles (1600 kilometers) to the north – to the station built
by the veteran missionary Robert Moffat, whose daughter
Livingstone was to marry in 1845. The young couple
were perpetually on the move, building three successive
mission stations in an effort to establish themselves beyond
territory constantly in dispute between Boer farmers and
the local people.

Missionary expeditions

In 1849 Livingstone undertook his first expedition to Lake
Ngami, together with William Cotton Oswell, a wealthy
big game hunter who paid all expenses and was to become
a lifelong friend. In 1850 Livingstone again visited Ngami,
taking his wife and four children with him. In 1851 the
same party reached the Cuando and Zambezi rivers,
beyond which lay a "blank on the map." The region
contains a vast watershed, abounding in streams, swamps,
rivers, and seasonal floods, from which the Zambezi River
flows south and east to the Indian Ocean, and the Congo
(Zaire) River flows north and west to the Atlantic.

Livingstone's understanding of the nature of the ground
he was to traverse, his careful notes and well-designed
maps, have placed him in the front rank of geographers. It
is often claimed that others – the Hungarian László Magyar,
for instance, and the Portuguese Candido – reached the
source of the Zambezi and crossed the continent before
him, but it was Livingstone who recorded the geography
and gave it to the world. His 1851 journey convinced him
that only by prospecting further north could he find sites
for mission stations out of the range of Boer harassment.
He sent his wife and family off to England and prepared
himself for his great adventure.

Across Africa

Collecting supplies in Cape Town, Livingstone set out alone
for the homelands of the Makolo, and Sekeletu, their chief,
between the Cuando and Zambezi rivers. He traveled west
with a handpicked group of African companions – not hired
porters – to prospect an avenue of trade with the coast
which might be the means of combating the slave trade that
was beginning to penetrate inland. Returning disappointed,
he made his way down the Zambezi River and visited
the great falls of "Mosi-oa-tunya," or "the smoke that
thunders," which Livingstone called "Victoria."

Livingstone returned to England in 1856, convinced
that his purpose in life must be to fight the slave trade, and
that the best way of doing this was to encourage "industrial
pursuits" and the cultivation of land by the African people,
thus giving them goods (other than human beings) to trade
in. He spent most of his time in England drumming up the
support of the British people.

The Zambezi Expedition

In 1858 Livingstone led an expedition to Africa, sponsored by the British Government and by the RGS. His aim was to open up the Zambezi as a highway into the interior. But he had six colleagues all wanting directions and encouragement, and he needed to establish relations with the Portuguese authorities who controlled the Zambezi River some way beyond Tete. Livingstone had neither the gift for handling colleagues and subordinates (nor the wish to acquire it), and he detested the Portuguese.

The Zambezi Expedition, which had taken such a hold on Livingstone's imagination, was also ill-conceived from a practical point of view. Livingstone allowed himself to assume that the river was navigable as far upstream as the Victoria Falls, yet on his way downstream in 1856 he had cut across country between Zumbo and Tete, and so had never reconnoitered the part of the river which contains the steep fall of the Kebrabasa (Cabora Bassa) Gorge. The river was impassable at this point, and the energies of the expedition were diverted to the ascent of the Shire River into Lake Nyasa (Malawi).

Many things went wrong: the steam launch from which much was expected gave endless trouble; the Universities Mission, led by Bishop Mackenzie, failed to establish itself on the Shire River; Mary Livingstone died of fever. Not even the ascent of the Shire and the geographical information gained on the lake could redeem the Zambezi Expedition, which was recalled in 1864.

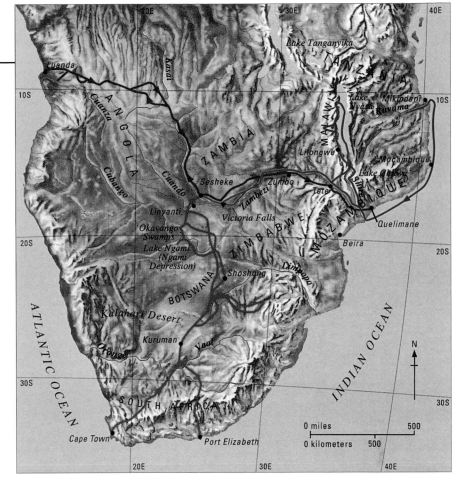

Thomas Baines

One of the members of the Zambezi Expedition was Thomas Baines (1820–75), an artist from King's Lynn, Norfolk, who first came to Africa in 1848 and is perhaps our chief witness of what southern Africa looked like in the middle years of the 19th century. His appointment to Livingstone's expedition was a disaster, since he was treated most unjustly by the great man, who never withdrew false charges made against the artist. Baines survived, however, as did the splendid pictures which were the best things to come out of a mismanaged expedition. His fine painting of the Victoria Falls was done on a later visit to the Zambezi River with James Chapman in 1861.

Further Exploration of the Nile

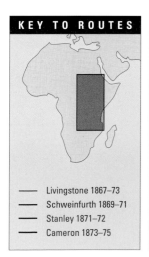

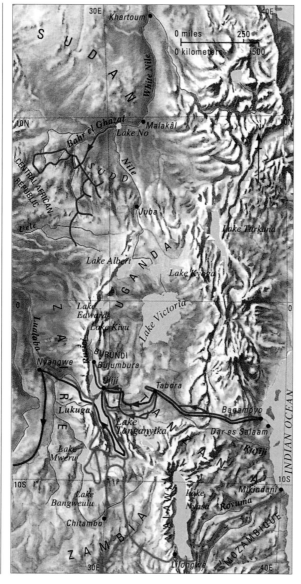

▲ **In describing his famous meeting** with Livingstone, Stanley explained that he uttered his, by now immortal, words through want of anything better to say: "I would have run to him, only I was a coward in the presence of such a mob – would have embraced him, only, he being an Englishman, I did not know how he would receive me; so I did what cowardice and false pride suggested was the best thing – walked deliberately to him, took off my hat, and said 'Dr Livingstone, I presume?'"

KEY TO ROUTES

— Livingstone 1867–73
— Schweinfurth 1869–71
— Stanley 1871–72
— Cameron 1873–75

South of Khartoum the Nile is choked by rotting vegetation or *sudd*, which comes from the swamps of the Bahr el Ghazal and Lake No. It was into this unhealthy channel that the adventurous young Dutchwoman Alexandrine Tinné determined to penetrate when cruising up the Nile in the 1860s. She was accompanied by her mother and aunt, and a domestic staff which included lady's maids. They were well provisioned in the only steamer available for hire at Khartoum, arousing the envy of Sam Baker and offending his sense of propriety – "A young lady alone among the Dinka tribe! … They are naked as the day they were born!" The Tinné party was serious, however, penetrating a long way up the Bahr el Ghazal in 1863 into desolate country where several of them died, including Tinné's mother. Tinné herself was to meet an even sadder fate, for she was murdered in an expedition across the Sahara in 1869.

Georg Schweinfurth

Some years later, between 1869 and 1871, the Bahr el Ghazal, with its many affluents, was more thoroughly explored by the genial German botanist Georg Schweinfurth. He was primarily in search of plants and other natural specimens, but he also brought back useful geographical information. He made his way on foot into the dense Zaire forest, where he was the first European to meet with the pygmy Akka people. He was the first European, too, to stand on the bank of the Uele River. He realized that it formed no part of the Nile system, instead linking it with the Chari and Lake Chad. In fact it belongs to the Congo (Zaire) system.

Livingstone's last journey

Back in England, Livingstone and his close friend Sir Roderick Murchison worked out a scheme for finding the sources of the Nile, centering on Lake Tanganyika as the most likely origin. Livingstone was to make his way by the Rovuma River, which was not in Portuguese territory, and then to Lake Nyasa and so north to Lake Tanganyika.

The expedition left in 1867, only modestly equipped, but it was not thought that an experienced traveler like Livingstone need be away long. In the event he spent six years on his last journey, drifting here and there in the wake of the Arab caravans which traded round Ujiji on Lake Tanganyika, isolated in an Africa ever more demoralized by the slave trade and swept by disease. His powers, moral and physical, began to fail him, supplies ran out, communications with Zanzibar were cut, and his porters mutinied.

"Dr Livingstone, I presume?"

When Henry Stanley broke through from Zanzibar to Ujiji in late 1871 with supplies and home news, he found a tired and broken man. Livingstone revived in Stanley's bracing company, and together they visited the northern end of Lake Tanganyika and ascertained that the Ruzizi flowed into and not out of the lake, which could not therefore be connected with the Nile. Livingstone became ever more convinced that the Lualaba River – in truth the Congo (Zaire) – to the west of Tanganyika was a headwater of the Nile, and that somewhere at its source were the four fountains from which Herodotus had claimed the great river rose. Yet, he doubted. "I am oppressed," he wrote, "by the apprehension that it may, after all, turn out that I have been following the Congo, and who would risk being put into a cannibal pot and converted into a black man for it?" Yet he would not take Stanley's advice to return to England to restore his health, but was determined to trudge on until he found the Nile fountains.

Livingstone died early in May 1873 on the shores of Lake Bangweulu, a whole 10°S of the Equator (where the Nile sources lie). Chuma and Susi, Livingstone's devoted African captain and headman, buried his heart and internal organs beside a tree, on which they carved his name and the date. Then with other members of the expedition they carried their master's body (suitably prepared to prevent decomposition) and his precious journals 1400 miles (2250 kilometers) to the coast, so that he might rest among his own people. His body was taken home to England to a hero's welcome and buried in Westminster Abbey.

Stanley's successful relief of Livingstone in 1871 was not well received by the mandarins of the geographical establishment in London, who considered this Yankee

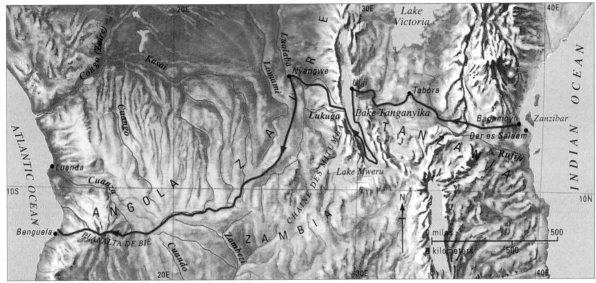

▲ *In* Missionary Travels
Livingstone described an incident involving a canoe and a hippopotamus robbed of her young.

KEY TO ROUTES

—— Cameron 1873–75

journalist to be trespassing on their territory. Moreover, Stanley had returned to Zanzibar at the precise moment that an official search expedition arrived from England. The would-be searchers melted away in discomfiture, to be replaced by one of the most vigorous and successful of the Victorian explorers.

Verney Lovett Cameron

Verney Lovett Cameron, an officer in the Royal Navy, had developed a hearty loathing of the slave trade during service in the anti-slavery squadron off the East African coast; he was also a dedicated explorer. He persuaded the Royal Geographical Society that it was worth proceeding into the interior, to see if Livingstone was still in need, and on March 28, 1873, he set off from Bagamoyo on the old trade route to Tabora. There he met Susi and Chuma with their master's body. Cameron resolved to go on to Ujiji to rescue any remaining possessions and papers of Livingstone's.

Having arrived at the explorer's old camp, he decided to continue westward to the Lualaba and perhaps the Congo (Zaire). He first made a thorough survey of Lake Tanganyika, identifying 96 inflowing streams as well as the only outlet from the lake – a channel leading to the Lukuga River and thence to the Lualaba. Marching on from the lake, Cameron became convinced that the Lualaba could have no connection with the Nile, but probably flowed on to become the Congo (Zaire). Unable to secure river transport at the Arab camp of Nyangwe, he abandoned any further search in that direction and turned south. He arrived at the Atlantic coast north of Benguela in Angola on November 7, 1875, the first European to make an east–west crossing of Africa.

▼ Livingstone's funeral *was held in Westminster Abbey in April 1874 – nearly a year after his death. His* faithful companions, Susi and Chuma, made the journey to England, but were too late for the funeral.

Henry Morton Stanley

Henry Morton Stanley (1841–1904) was keen to exploit Africa's resources for the sake of European entrepreneurs and for the good of the local people. He never became popular with the Establishment, but was accepted and even admired for his drive and efficiency.

He was born illegitimately at Denbigh in North Wales and at the age of five was consigned to the St Asaph Workhouse where he received a fair education. He ran away to sea and led a roving life in America, eventually finding his true vocation as a reporter. He worked as a war correspondent for the *New York Herald*, and was commissioned by them to "find Livingstone."

Stanley's relief of Livingstone in 1871 changed his life; he conceived a devotion for the older man and at the same time learned the rudiments of exploration techniques. On hearing of his hero's death in 1873, he decided to follow up Livingstone's researches on the Congo (Zaire) and Nile river systems, and at the same time to

examine the findings of Speke, Burton, and Baker. It was a grandiose project, funded by the *New York Herald* and London's *Daily Telegraph*.

Expedition to the Congo and Nile

On November 17, 1874, a well-equipped caravan marched out of Bagamoyo. Over 350 strong, it included just three Europeans and was led by the experienced Manua Sera as chief captain. The route was by Lake Victoria, where Stanley visited the kingdom of Buganda, "discovered" by Speke and Grant in 1862. The *Lady Alice*, a boat carried by the expedition in sections and named after Stanley's American fiancée (who married someone else in his absence), was launched and the lake explored, confirming Speke's estimate of its extent and importance. There were some rough encounters with the lake people, for which Stanley was to be severely criticized, especially for his actions at Bumbiri, where casualties were inflicted on the local population.

Stanley then headed south for Lake Tanganyika, noting Lake Edward on the way. His circumnavigation of Tanganyika finally proved that it had no connection with the Nile, its only outlet (as Cameron had observed) being the Lukuga River, which in turn drains into the Lualaba River. He then set himself to examine Livingstone's theories on the Lualaba, and from Nyangwe, the Arab trading post on the river which had been Livingstone's and Cameron's furthest point north, embarked on one of the worst journeys in the history of exploration.

With the aid of 22 canoes as well as the *Lady Alice*, Stanley was to prove that the Lualaba River (which he called the Livingstone) was in truth the Congo (Zaire), flowing north and then west and southwest in a great arc across the Equator and down impassable cataracts to the sea. Initially he was faced with the turbulent white water of the Stanley Falls (Chutes Boyoma), where the boats had to be constantly pulled out of the water. By the time they reached the foot of the Falls, Stanley and his men had fought 24 battles against the forest people, and there were eight more to come against warriors in war canoes.

The Falls behind them, they embarked on the 1000 miles (1600 kilometers) of the Upper Congo (Zaire) waterway. However, the worst hazard was still to come – the 220 miles (350 kilometers) of the Livingstone Falls, with its 32 murderous cataracts, during which the river descends just under 900 feet (300 meters). Here, Frank Pocock,

▶ **Stanley** posed for this photograph in London, after returning from his successful expedition to find Livingstone. At his side is Kalulu, the African child "given" to him by an Arab trader. Kalulu drowned in a canoeing accident in 1877, on the expedition down the Congo (Zaire) River.

KEY TO ROUTES

—— Stanley 1874–77
—— Stanley 1887–89

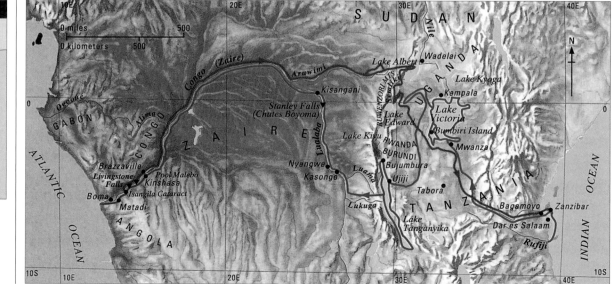

◀ **Zaidi,** one of Stanley's boat captains, became trapped on a rock above the Stanley Falls after his canoe had capsized. During the attempted rescue, the two men in the canoe also became trapped on the rock. All three were forced to spend the night there above "half a mile of Falls and Rapids and great whirlpools, and waves rising like hills in the middle of the terrible stream," before being rescued in the morning.

Stanley's only remaining European companion, and by now a close friend, was drowned. The exhausted band left the *Lady Alice* to rot on the bank above the Isangila Cataract and staggered on. They managed to send a message to Boma at the mouth of the river, which brought help in the form of four friendly European traders and plentiful refreshment.

Of the 350 who had marched so bravely out of Bagamoyo three years before, only 114 reached the sea at Boma, having proved once and for all that there is no connection between the Nile and the rivers to the south.

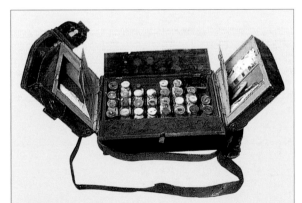

Medical supplies
Malaria and dysentery were among the many dangers faced by African travelers, but their efforts to combat these diseases were somewhat haphazard. Quinine was found to be effective at preventing malaria, but many explorers relied on their own preparations (such as "Livingstone's rousers," fearsome homemade pills) and improvization (such as a charge of gunpowder in warm water as an emetic) to keep them going.

On his return from finding Livingstone in 1871 Stanley, in consultation with the pharmaceutical firm of Burroughs and Wellcome, designed a medicine chest containing "all the medicines required for my black men as well as for my white men, beautifully prepared and in most elegant fashion." The chest included purgatives, emetics and disinfectant, as well as quinine, packed in glass phials which were screwed down to prevent deteriorioation.

The aftermath
Stanley emerged from the Congo (Zaire) expedition eager to interest the British Government in the development of this huge and fertile region. Rebuffed by the cautious Conservative administration, he was more than ready to respond to the advances of the Belgian King Leopold, who had been quick to see in the Congo (Zaire) basin the empire he sought. In July 1879 Stanley was back at the river mouth, with instructions from the Belgians to build a railroad up the side of the Falls and to launch steamers on the Pool Malebo, from where the river was navigable for 1000 miles (1600 kilometers) upstream.

Leopold was only just in time, barely ahead of France in the person of Count Pierre Savorgnan de Brazza. De Brazza had in fact come through Gabon and up the Ogooue River in 1878 while Stanley was circumnavigating Lake Victoria, and could have reached the Congo (Zaire) and claimed it all for France. But by failing to branch into the Alima River, the Frenchman came out on the right bank of the Congo (Zaire) in Pool Malebo and found the other man was in control of the region. Brazzaville, capital of today's Congo, therefore stands on one side of the Pool, with Kinshasa (as Leopoldville is now called) on the other.

Emin Pasha Relief Expedition
Stanley was to return to the Congo (Zaire) on the Emin Pasha Relief Expedition (1887–89), the aim of which was to rescue the German botanist Dr Emin, who was stranded at Wadelai near Lake Albert. He was the one surviving provincial officer in Egypt's short-lived empire in southern Sudan (hence the title "Pasha") which had been destroyed by the Madhist uprising of 1881.

For reasons never fully explained Stanley chose to come up the Congo (Zaire) from the west coast rather than by the better-known and shorter road from the east. Having left the river at the Aruwimi confluence, the expedition struggled for five months through dense, dangerous and unexplored forest until they reached open upland country and the western shore of Lake Albert. On the homeward lap, eastward to the coast, they became the first travelers to see the full expanse of the Ruwenzori Mountains. They traced their way round the mountains, up the Semliki River to Lake Edward, from where the water flows into Lake Albert. Thus was the whole geography of the Nile sources at last laid down on the map.

The Central Lakes

▶ *Joseph Thomson had*
a high regard for his men,
who included Chuma ("full
of anecdote, fun and jollity")
and Makatubu ("a capital
fellow, full of life and
energy").

In 1877 the Royal Geographical Society launched the African Exploration Fund with the aim of following up routes to the central lakes of Africa which its own explorers had already traversed. An expedition was sent out in 1878, under the leadership of the cartographer Keith Johnston, on a route from Dar es Salaam to Lake Nyasa (Malawi) and Lake Tanganyika.

When Johnston died at an early stage of the journey, his 20-year-old second-in-command, Joseph Thomson, took over. Thomson was only too aware of his inexperience and keenly felt his inadequacy: should he simply turn back, he asked himself. But he concluded, "I felt I must go forward, whatever might be my destiny. Was I not the countryman of Bruce, Park, Clapperton, Grant, Livingstone and Cameron?" (Thomson was a Scot and thus belonged to a nation which contributed much to the history of exploration in Africa.)

Joseph Thomson

Joseph Thomson is one of the most attractive figures among African explorers. Informal and full of fun, he was a prudent traveler, taking as his motto: "He who goes slowly, goes safely; he who goes safely goes far." Where other travelers challenged an unfriendly crowd with guns, Thomson charmed them with parlor tricks – removing and replacing his two false teeth with magical words and gestures, or frothing fruit salts in water. He prided himself on accomplishing notable journeys with no bloodshed.

Thanks to his unfailing cheerful humor, Thomson was on good terms with his men. He declared early on that there would be no corporal punishment, and that all misdemeanors would be paid for by fines. This, however, did not please the porters, who much preferred swift, painful chastisement to loss of pay.

Safari to the lakes

Thomson led his safari successfully to the north end of Lake Nyasa (Malawi) and achieved a useful exploration of Lake Tanganyika. In 1882–83 he was put in command of a more ambitious journey through modern Kenya, from Mombasa to the northern end of Lake Victoria, through the territory of the reputedly hostile Masai. This was an area well known to ivory traders; it had been skirted by the Mombasa missionaries Krapf and Rebmann in the 1840s, but not penetrated to any purpose by explorers.

Taking a route from the coast to Mount Kilimanjaro, Thomson then struck north along the line of the Rift Valley, that geological phenomenon which runs from Lake Nyasa (Malawi) in the south up to the Dead Sea. He was the first traveler from the outside world to assess the nature and importance of this impressive feature.

His outward route crossed today's Amboseli National Park, from where he made a diversion to Mount Kenya, "discovering" Thomson's Falls (Nyahururu) and catching the first sight of the gazelle called "Thomson's" in his honor. Eventually he turned west past Lake Baringo and journeyed to the shore of Lake Victoria just south of the present Kenya–Uganda border; he returned home by crossing what was to become Tsavo National Park.

Later, Thomson traveled in North and West Africa. He also worked for the British South Africa Company and was instrumental in negotiating with local potentates political, trading, and mining rights in what is now Zambia. The work proved damaging to his constitution, however, and despite a period of recuperation in South Africa, he died back in England at an early age.

His last words are said to have been: "If I were strong enough to put on my clothes and walk 100 yards, I would go back to Africa yet."

KEY TO ROUTES

—— Thomson 1879–80
—— Thomson 1882–83

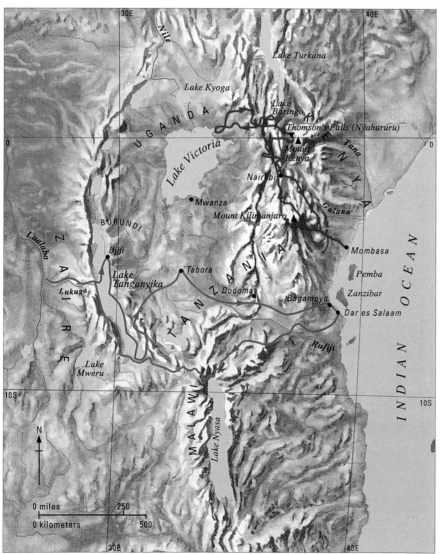

Great moments

Joseph Thomson has left us a picture of the country around Mount Kilimanjaro before the hunters and poachers came:

"There, toward the base of Kilimanjaro, are three great herds of buffalo slowly and leisurely moving up from the lower grazing-grounds to the shelter of the forest for their daily snooze and rumination in its gloomy depths. Farther out on the plains enormous numbers of the harmless but fierce-looking wildebeest continue their grazing, some erratic members of the herd gamboling and galloping about with waving tail and strange, uncouth movements. Mixed with these are to be seen companies of that loveliest of all game, the zebra, conspicuous in their beautiful striped skin .... But these are not all. Look! Down in that grassy bottom there are several specimens of the great, unwieldy rhinoceros, with horns stuck on their noses in a most offensive and pugnacious manner. Over that ridge a troop of ostriches are scudding away out of reach of danger, defying pursuit, and too wary for the stalker. See how numerous are the herds of hartebeest, and notice the graceful pallah springing into midair with great bounds as if in pure enjoyment of existence. There also among the tall reeds near the marsh you perceive the dignified waterbuck, in twos and threes, leisurely cropping the dewy grass. The warthog, disturbed at his morning's feast, clears off in a beeline with tail erect, and with a steady military trot truly comical. These do not exhaust the list, for there are many other species of game. Turn in whatever direction you please, they are to be seen in astonishing numbers, and so rarely hunted, that unconcernedly they stand and stare at us, within gunshot."

Joseph Thomson: *Through Masai Land* (3rd edition, 1885)

The Desert

▲ *René Caillié was the first European to see Timbuktu – and return to tell the tale.*

While British explorers mapped much of Central Africa, German, and especially French, names predominate in the European exploration of the desert country north of the Niger and its border states. It was a Frenchman who succeeded in being the first to reach Timbuktu and to survive. In 1824 the Geographical Society of Paris offered a prize of 10,000 francs to the first traveler to accomplish this feat, and in 1827 the young Frenchman René Caillié set out on a lone journey. From humble origins, poorly educated and with scarce resources, he was nevertheless determined to explore Africa. For some years he had worked in France and in Sierra Leone at menial jobs, until he had saved 2000 francs from his wages. "This treasure," he thought, "seemed to be sufficient to carry me all over the world" – but he did not want the world, only Timbuktu, the "forbidden city."

He arrived in Tripoli in May 1825 ready to set out, but found himself caught up in the toils of local bureaucracy. He fell in love with the daughter of the British Consul, who agreed to their marrying – on condition that the marriage was not consummated until Laing's return.

Laing finally set off on July 15, 1825, accompanied by his West Indian servant "honest Jack le Bore" and two West African boat builders – he was hoping to leave Timbuktu by river. The party was attacked by Tuareg tribesmen, and Laing was left severely wounded while his three companions were killed. Laing struggled on to Timbuktu, but was murdered on his way home by fanatical Muslims; his journals were never recovered. His bride waited two years for the news of his death to filter through.

Duveyrier: dreamer of a Utopian future

The travels of Heinrich Barth in the 1850s (see page 71) proved an inspiration to a younger generation of would-be travelers, not least to Henri Duveyrier, a devoted Saint-Simonist. One of the tenets of this complex philosophy, sometimes defined as an early kind of socialism, was to advocate friendly cooperation between nations.

Young Duveyrier saw opportunities for such cooperation with the peoples of North Africa. After a short visit to Algeria in 1857 he was convinced that the vigorous and aggressive Tuareg would be ideal trading partners for the French. In 1859, at the tender age of 19, he set out on his famous journey among the Tuareg of northern Algeria. Despite official disapproval of the idealistic teenager let loose in what was regarded as an area of delicate equilibrium, the young man accomplished important research. However, his dream of a Utopian future with French and Tuareg in partnership within the French empire was shattered in later years, with the massacre in 1889 of Colonel Paul Flatters's survey team and military escort in Tuareg country. Duveyrier committed suicide in 1892.

The German geographers

Of the three German geographers to make their mark in Barth's wake, Georg Schweinfurth is perhaps best known for his journey in the watery wastes of the Bahr el Ghazal and into the forests of the Nile–Zaire (Congo) divide in 1869 (see page 78). Accompanying Gerhard Rohlfs, he also covered a large, unexplored area of the Libyan Desert.

Gerhard Rohlfs came to Africa as a young man with the Foreign Legion, learning Arabic and becoming familiar with desert conditions at their most harsh. A sturdy walker, he made numerous excursions into the North African desert during the 1860s, most importantly a traverse in 1865–67 from Tripoli to Lagos by way of Borno and the Niger River. In 1873 he led an expedition on a 36-day march to Siwa Oasis and in 1878–79 penetrated as far as the Oases of Kufru. By the time of his death, Rohlfs had become an undisputed authority on North Africa.

Gustav Nachtigal was a trained doctor and served for some years as military surgeon in Algiers and Tunis. Alexandrine Tinné met him in the course of her fatal bid to cross the Sahara in 1869 (see page 78) and described him as "discreet, unassuming, and honest." Nachtigal was appointed by the King of Prussia to lead a mission to the Sultan of Borno in 1869. He then continued eastward on one of the outstanding journeys of the time, much of it through unexplored and hostile territory, passing through Darfur and arriving on the Nile just south of Khartoum five years later. His account of his travels, *Sahara und Sudan*, was the basis for his reputation as one of the great explorers of Africa. He was later responsible for the annexation of Togo and Cameroon to the German flag.

▲ *Caillié drew this view of Timbuktu in 1828, but although Heinrich Barth, looking out over the rooftops some 25 years later, considered Caillié to have depicted the individual dwellings well, he felt that "in his representation the whole town seems to consist of scattered and quite isolated houses, while, in reality, the streets are entirely shut in, as the dwellings form continuous and uninterrupted rows."*

Caillié's journey to Timbuktu

The usual approach to Timbuktu was via an established route running southwest from Tripoli. Caillié, however, set off in April 1827 from the neighborhood of the Konkoure River on the coast of modern Guinea. He traveled disguised as a Muslim, explaining his poor Arabic by pretending that he was an Egyptian Arab taken as a slave to Europe in childhood and now returning home. He kept his notes folded into a Koran, logging his journey while pretending to study Holy Writ, and concealed his pallid European face by wrapping himself in a rug.

Having overcome a severe attack of scurvy, he reached Timbuktu in April 1828. Though he "experienced an indescribable satisfaction" on attaining his goal, he was disappointed to find a city composed of "ill-looking houses built of mud" and no gold roofs or pavements. He returned via the hazardous 1000-mile (1600-kilometer) desert journey north through Morocco with a caravan bound for Fez.

Alexander Gordon Laing

Caillié, alone and with no backing, was lucky; Alexander Gordon Laing, a British Army officer and an experienced traveler, government-sponsored, was consistently unlucky.

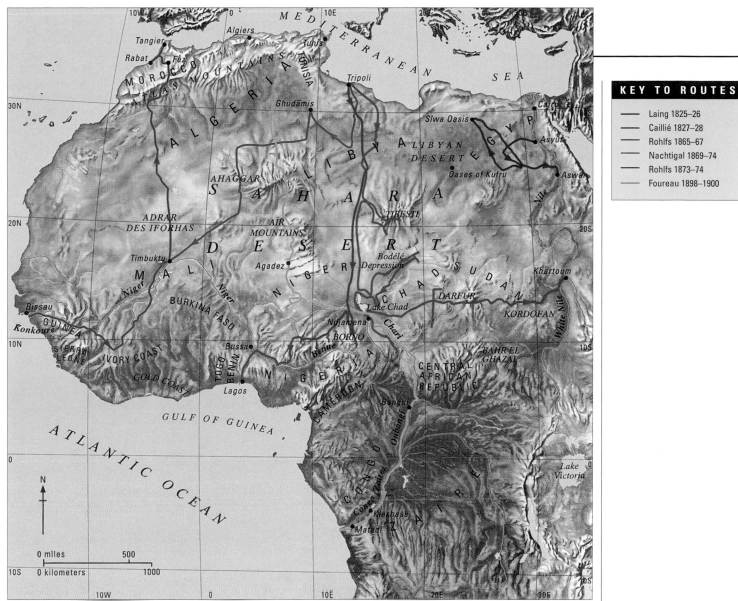

——	Laing 1825–26
——	Caillié 1827–28
——	Rohlfs 1865–67
——	Nachtigal 1869–74
——	Rohlfs 1873–74
——	Foureau 1898–1900

Further French exploration

The colonial period accelerated the work of explorers in the Sahara. They included the Frenchman Louis-Gustave Binger, who first came to West Africa on military duty, but proved himself more than a simple pioneer in the interests of his country. In 1887 he embarked on the three-year journey on which he did more than any traveler of his time to open up the country in the great bend of the Niger River. In 1892 he undertook to draw the boundary between the British Gold Coast and the French Ivory Coast, of which latter territory he became Governor in 1893.

The commanding position France achieved in the great expansionist years in North Africa was undoubtedly thanks to Fernand Foureau. Despite sustained opposition from the powerful Tuareg he managed to carry out surveys deep into the desert and finally succeeded in overcoming local opposition. This was achieved by a military escort commanded by Major Lamy, which advanced into the modern Republic of Chad, returning by way of the Congo (Zaire).

The Vicomte de Foucauld, posted to Morocco in the French army, traveled disguised as a Jewish rabbi into dangerous country, and his *Reconnaissance au Maroc* established him as a Saharan authority. More important, it brought him under that spell which the desert sometimes casts on travelers and led him to become a priest of the Trappist order. He lived the rest of his life in hermit-like seclusion among the Tuareg of the Hoggar in Algeria. He was murdered by raiders in 1916, leaving behind him a reputation not only for outstanding saintliness but also for penetrating scholarship.

◄ *The nomadic Tuareg fiercely opposed any strangers entering their territory and were feared by many explorers of the Sahara.*

Southern Africa

In southern Africa there were no geographical riddles to be solved, and no such towering figure as Livingstone or Mungo Park dominates the scene. Here was wide, open country, at first only briefly penetrated here and there by the Portuguese from Mozambique. The Cape victualing station founded by the Dutch East India Company in 1652 developed rapidly into a thriving colony in need of more land. Hence the early journeys into the interior, such as the "Great Trek" of 1834, were by farmers searching for pasture. At the same time, official expeditions were launched from the colony to buy cattle from the Hottentot people (pastoral farmers of mixed Bushman and Hamitic descent), and to investigate rumors of gold and copper in the interior. In 1777 Colonel R. J. Gordon, a Hollander of Scottish extraction traveling independently in southern Africa, reached the Orange River.

The naturalists

Among the first European visitors were the naturalists, in search of the abounding beauty of southern Africa's plant and animal life. The Swede Carl Thunberg, "Father of Cape Botany" and a pupil of Linnaeus, went plant-hunting with his compatriot Anders Sparrman. They swam rivers together and slid down precipitous rocks in search of rare specimens. Later, Thunberg joined Francis Masson, an undergardener at the Royal Gardens at Kew in England, who was sent to South Africa by King George III in order to collect plants. Between 1772 and 1774 Masson made three journeys and was sent again to the Cape in 1786, when he collected a further 117 plants and bulbs and identified rare specimens of *Erica* and *Protea*. Linnaeus named the genus *Massonia* after him.

William Burchell is another famous name in the South Africa story. During his travels in 1811–12 he produced more than 500 drawings and sketches of men, animals, birds, plants and scenery, and collected numerous natural history specimens.

The missionaries

The missionaries were not far behind the naturalists. By the end of the 18th century the London Missionary Society had established itself in southern Africa, and in 1813 the Reverend John Campbell traveled as far north as Bechuanaland (Botswana) to look for possible mission sites; in 1821 the famous missionary Robert Moffat and his wife Mary established a mission at Kuruman.

The hunters and traders

A less sympathetic group was soon to arrive – the big-game hunters, crazy for sport and for trophies. In their pursuit of elephants, rhinoceros, and of anything else that moved, Cornwallis Harris, Roualeyn Gordon Cumming and their like made known great tracts of land. By contrast, William Cotton Oswell, though sometimes described as the "Nimrod of Africa," took an intelligent interest in

the country, financing and to a large extent managing Livingstone's early journeys.

Traders soon came to vie with the sporting gentlemen in shooting elephants for ivory to provide capital for businesses in the interior. One of the most enterprising of these was James Chapman, whose ambition to carry trade to the Zambezi resulted in the road to the Victoria Falls. By the 1850s southern Africa had become a land of opportunity for settlers, traders, and missionaries alike, often at odds with each other and with the local people.

Francis Galton and Charles Andersson

In August 1850 Francis Galton, a wealthy young man who was to make his name as an amateur scientist and inventor, landed at Walvis Bay on the coast of southwest Africa. Together with his Anglo-Swedish assistant Charles John Andersson, he wanted to follow Livingstone's trail to Lake Ngami (now the Ngami Depression) but, finding the road north from the Cape blocked by disputes between Boer settlers and the local Bantu, he decided on an approach from the west across what is now Namibia.

They journeyed from the coast up the Swakop River, planning to use as their base a string of German missions, which operated under constant threat from the hostile

▶ **One hundred years** after Francis Masson's journeys to South Africa, Marianne North visited the country on her self-imposed task of painting the world's tropical flora. This South African View with Cabbage Plant comes from the African section which she was able to add to the North Gallery at Kew Gardens in west London.

▼ **The first crossing** by a European of the Orange River (other than at its seaward end) was made by the Reverend William Anderson, on an expedition northward from the Cape seeking to establish a mission.

KEY TO ROUTES	
——	Gordon 1777–78
——	Campbell 1813
——	Moffat 1820
——	Galton and Andersson 1850–52
——	Andersson 1853–54
——	Andersson 1857–58

Hottentot tribes south of the river and sometimes from the unpredictable Damaras to the north. Galton arrived at Otjimbingwe to hear that the Hottentots were behaving very aggressively. He decided to tackle the powerful Hottentot chief Jan Jonker Afrikaner so that he might continue his exploration unhindered.

Like Baker in Central Africa some years later, Galton had come equipped with a fancy dress in which to astonish the locals: "I had packed my red hunting coat, jackboots, and cords, and rode in my hunting cap; it was a costume unknown in these parts and … even Ceylon (my ox) caught the excitement and snuffled like a warhorse." As Galton put it: "Conceive the effect" on Jonker. By dint of threats of vengeance on the part of the Cape Colony Government (and partly no doubt owing to Galton's strong personality and extraordinary appearance), Jonker and his marauding friends promised to keep the peace – an undertaking which lasted out Galton's time.

The journey north

Instead of making their way to Lake Ngami, Galton and Andersson headed north into hitherto unknown Ovamboland, but they were thwarted through lack of a guide from reaching the Cunene River and perhaps crossing into Angola. Much of the experience Galton acquired on the journey was incorporated in his *Art of Travel*, a handbook for explorers which ran into eight editions before the end of the 19th century.

Galton returned to England in January 1852, but Andersson stayed on, setting up a store at Otjimbingwe and becoming deeply involved in the tribal politics of the region as champion of the Damara people. In 1853 he succeeded in reaching Lake Ngami after a trek through Bechuanaland (Botswana) to the western end of what was then open water. He worked his way along the northern coast to the entry of the Taokhe River. Local difficulties prevented him from looking for the Okavango (Cubango) River, which he was to reach on a later expedition in search of the Cunene River. He died on his last attempt to reach the Cunene, and his exhaustive *Birds of Damaraland* was published posthumously.

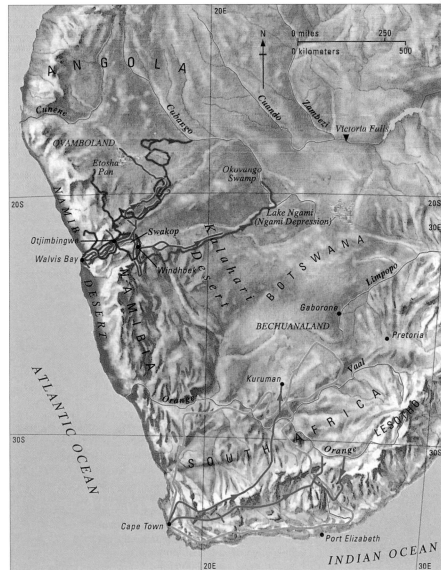

The "Scramble" and its Aftermath

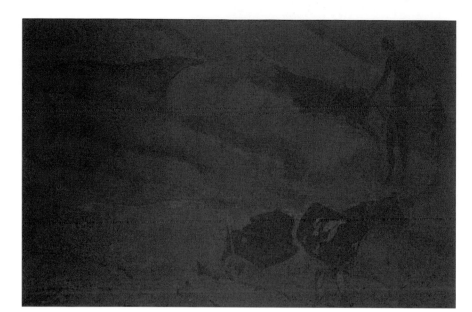

▲ *The Tassili n'Ajjer rock paintings* in the Central Sahara are believed to date from between 6000 and 1500 BC, and were uncovered by Henri Lhote in the 1950s. This one depicts a woman and child with a herd of cattle.

The Berlin Conference, called by Bismarck of Germany and in session from November 1884 to February 1885, may be taken as marking the end of the primary exploration of Africa. Its purpose was chiefly to regulate and even to check the speed with which Europe was laying claim to Africa, but the movement had gone too far to be halted, and by the end of the century journeys were being taken increasingly for political rather than geographical reasons. The Belgian King Leopold at Pool Malebo, on the left bank of the Congo (Zaire), and France in the person of de Brazza on the right bank had set the pattern for what was to be called the "Scramble."

The ambitions and rivalries of the powers did, however, sometimes give rise to heroic exploits of the old pattern. Trying to forestall Britain on the upper Nile, the French captain Jean-Baptiste Marchand set out in 1897–98 to traverse the virtually unknown country of the Congo (Zaire)–Nile watershed, from Libreville in the west to Fashoda on the Nile 400 miles (650 kilometers) south of Khartoum. The steamer *Faidherbe* was carried in sections for part of the way, her boiler rolled along behind with the kegs of wine indispensable to a French expedition, all to be reassembled and launched on the hopeless swamp waters of the Bahr el Ghazal and Lake No. And in the end the exhausted party was recalled in face of British opposition.

Something of the old exploring spirit persisted, with Sir Harry Johnston, explorer, administrator and artist, leading a scientific expedition to Mount Kilimanjaro in 1884. During 1926–29 Colonel Robert Cheesman made valuable surveys of stretches of the Blue Nile in Ethiopia, and in 1933 Wilfred Thesiger was cutting his explorer's teeth on a daring lone excursion into the Danakil territory of the same country.

Post-war African travel

An interesting feature of African travel today is the fascination that the old routes still hold. In 1968 Colonel Blashford-Snell led an ambitious venture, manned and equipped by the armed services, on the descent of the Blue Nile, which Cheesman had only surveyed on foot. In 1974–75 Blashford-Snell followed Stanley on his passage of the Congo (Zaire) River, where his specially designed boats and trained crews encountered the same difficulties as had Stanley's locally built canoes manned by a hundred Zanzibari porters. In 1975 Christina Dodwell and a friend canoed down the Congo (Zaire) from Bangui to

Brazzaville, and as recently as 1985 the old pioneers were followed when Lorenzo and Mirella Ricciardi crossed Africa by boat in the wake of Livingstone and Stanley.

The deserts of northern Africa have been the object of intense interest, with the French being closely engaged in the site of their former colonial empire. Théodore Monod traveled a record 800 miles (1300 kilometers) in desert conditions in 1955, and Robert Capot-Rey's *Le Sahara français*, published in 1953, was one of the many studies made by him in the post-war years.

Scientific geography

Today the emphasis is on scientific geography, which has no political axes to grind, and is less interested than in the past in the exploration of mountains and the courses of rivers. A typical modern project was one sponsored by the Royal Geographical Society during 1968–70 to a region lying within the Rift Valley in Kenya, to the south and southwest of Lake Turkana. Under the leadership of Dr Michael Gwynn, 34 scientists plus a number of university students worked for three seasons on various aspects of this little-known semiarid region.

In 1983 the Kora Research Project, led by Dr Malcolm Coe and Richard Leakey, was set up to provide an ecological description of the Kora National Reserve for the Kenya Government.

▼ *Africa is a land of great contrasts.* Its terrain ranges from the Sahara Desert in the north (below), through the dense rain forests of Central Africa and the snow-capped peaks of East Africa (above), to the grasslands of the south.

▲ *The snow-capped peak* of Mount Kenya, right on the Equator, was first sighted by the German missionaries Krapf and Rebmann in the 1840s, but it was not climbed until 1899, when the geographer Halford Mackinder made his assault.

Mary Kingsley

Mary Henrietta Kingsley (1862–1900) was the forerunner of the anthropologists, many of them women, who have studied and recorded African life and customs in the 20th century. Her interests were primarily scientific, and after the death of her parents she decided to visit West Africa in 1893 to study nature in all its forms. She called it a quest for fish and fetish, returning with rare specimens of the former and valuable information about the latter. After her second journey in 1895 she returned to England with 65 varieties of fish, of which three were named after her as being new to science – as well as 18 reptiles.

Unwilling to "go to Africa in things you would be ashamed of at home," she traveled through bush and swamp in a long, tight-waisted skirt and high-necked blouse, armed with an umbrella, paying her way by trade in cloth, tobacco, and fish-hooks. Her travels in 1895 among the unpredictable Fang tribe in the interior of present-day Gabon were as noteworthy as her prowess as a navigator in the tangled creeks of the Niger delta. She died sadly young, nursing Boer prisoners during the South African war.

Tropic of Cancer

20N

Yucatán Peninsula

CUBA

HISPANIOLA

CARIBBEAN
SEA

NORTH

ATLANTIC

OCEAN

10N

Orinoco

G u i a n a   H i g h l a n d s

Equator 0

Quito

Galápagos Islands

Negro

A m a z o n
B a s i n

Amazon

Tumbes

Madeira

Cajamarca

Chan-Chan

Huánuco

10S

Pachacamac

Machu Picchu
Cuzco

B r a z i l i a n   H i g h l a n d s

Plateau of
Mato Grosso

São Francisco

PACIFIC

OCEAN

Arequipa

Lake Titicaca

Lake Poopó

20S

Tropic of Capricorn

100W

Tucuman

Paraná

SOUTH

30S

Santiago

ATLANTIC

OCEAN

40S

- - - Boundary of Aztec Empire
- - - Boundary of Mayan kingdoms
——— Main Inca roads
-·-·- Boundary of Inca Empire

P A T A G O N I A

N

0 miles   500
0 kilometers   1000

50S

Cape Horn

100W   90W   80W   70W   60W   50W   40W   30W   20W

30N   110W

Tropic of Cancer

20N

PACIFIC

10N

N

110W

CENTRAL AND SOUTH AMERICA

The southern tip of South America was first reached by humans at least 13,000 years ago, at a time when the climate was cooler and drier than today, and savannah-woodland rather than tropical rain forest extended through much of the Amazon basin. Their ancestors had migrated from Siberia to northwest America – across a bridge of land which existed at the time of the last Ice Age – and had then moved southward. As they had adapted to the various habitats of the American continent, they had established networks of paths which were to be developed and maintained to a level that greatly impressed the European explorers in the 16th century.

Of the 40 to 50 million people estimated to have been living in the Americas at the beginning of the 16th century, perhaps 17 million lived in Mexico and a further 15 million in the Andes. In Central America the Maya kingdoms had flourished for 600 years (AD 300–900), but it was the militaristic Aztec Empire of the Valley of Mexico (AD 1300–1519) which most impressed the Spanish *conquistadores* who came in search of gold. In the Peruvian Andes, the Inca Empire stretched 2900 miles (4300 kilometers) from north to south and may well have been the largest empire in the world at the time of first contact with the Europeans.

Each of these civilizations was politically integrated by a system of roads. In the Maya civilization of the tropical lowlands there were raised causeways up to 60 miles (100 kilometers) long, while in the Aztec Empire numerous roads converged on the capital of Tenochtitlán. Further south, the Inca road network of 25,000 miles (40,000 kilometers) extended from southern Colombia to central Chile. The Incas did not make maps, but a mapping tradition existed in the Aztec world. Surviving Aztec maps made for Europeans during their early years of conquest combine spatial information with history and depictions of monumental buildings.

Despite these maps and systems of roads, there is little evidence of direct contact between the civilizations of Central and South America. Exploration by both Aztecs and Incas appears to have reached its limit when the first Europeans marched into their lands at the beginning of the 16th century.

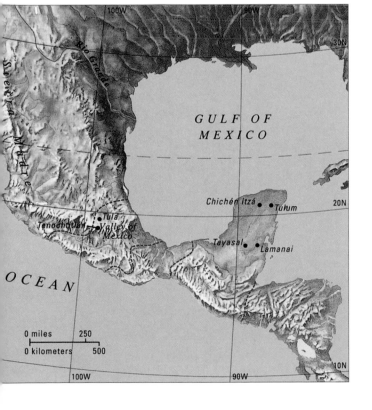

Columbus and the New World

▶ **No portrait of Columbus** is known to have been painted during his life. However, as the importance of his discoveries became apparent after his death, hundreds of portraits were produced, including this one by **Sebastiano del Piombo, which dates from the early 16th century.**

KEY TO ROUTES

—— Columbus 1492–93
—— Columbus 1493–96
—— Columbus 1498
—— Columbus 1502–04
—— Vespucci 1499–1500
—— Pinzón 1499–1500

Nordic explorers had reached North America long before the 15th century. However, the credit for the European discovery of the West Indies and Central America, as well as for opening up the New World to Europe, rests squarely with Christopher Columbus, or Cristóbal Colón as the Spanish called him. So too does the credit for persisting with a venture, in the face of hostility and ridicule, until he found a patron who would support and finance him.

Columbus's scheme

Born in the Italian port of Genoa in 1451, Columbus was aware of the excitements and possibilities of maritime exploration from an early age. He developed a knowledge of navigation and cartography, and sailed on a number of expeditions. Convinced (as were most of his more educated contemporaries) that the world was round, he became increasingly intrigued by the idea of sailing into the Atlantic beyond the Azores to reach the fabled lands described by Marco Polo – Cipangu (Japan) and Cathay (China). As yet nobody had any idea of the size of the oceans or of the existence of another continent between Europe and eastern Asia.

The natural sponsor for such an expedition appeared to be the Portuguese crown. It was from Portugal that the main thrust of exploration round the African coast had been launched in the early 15th century; and it was in a Portuguese ship that Columbus had already made a voyage to Guinea. But Columbus failed to convince the Portuguese crown that his scheme was viable. Next he tried France and then England for support. Finally he turned to Spain where the unified monarchs of Aragón and Castile – Ferdinand and Isabella – agreed to put up the money for an expedition of three ships and 120 men. They also agreed that Columbus should be hereditary viceroy of any lands he discovered.

Journey into the unknown

Columbus sailed in August 1492, his flagship being the *Santa Maria*, and put in at the Canary Islands to replenish stores. He then sailed due west for 33 days without seeing

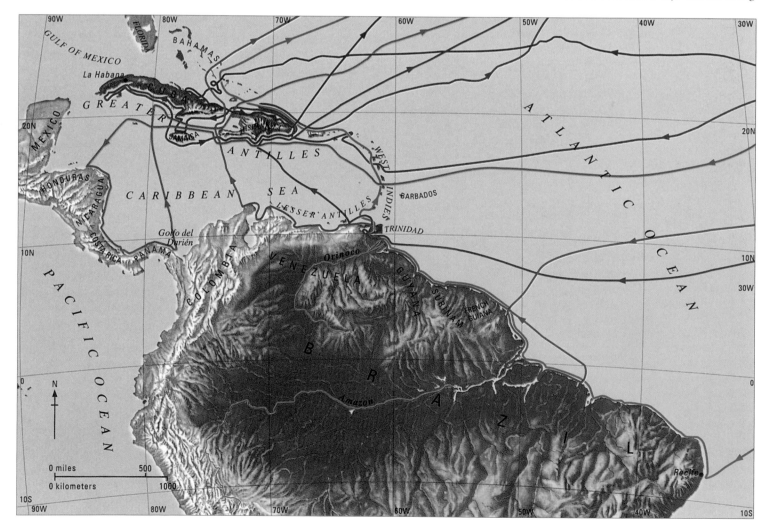

Columbus's flagship: the *Santa Maria*
This model from the Science Museum in London represents a merchantman as built in one of the Atlantic ports of Spain and Portugal during the 15th century, and it is as near as is known to the dimensions of Columbus's ship. The crew numbered around 40 and slept on the decks (hammocks were a native American invention only introduced to Europe after Columbus's voyage). The overall length of the ship would have been 100 feet (30 meters), and cooking would have been done over a firebox on deck.

land. At moments his little flotilla was nearly brought to a standstill by the entangled weed of the Sargasso Sea. At other times morale sank so low among the crew that he had to keep a second – false – log book, recording less progress than had been made so that his sailors did not know how far they were from home. But at last they were encouraged by seeing floating weed that could only have come from land, and by shore-loving Bosun birds.

When eventually they made their landfall it was in the Bahamas. From there they went on to Cuba and Hispaniola (now the Dominican Republic and Haiti) where they managed to barter for a few gold trinkets – such as nose-plugs – from the friendly natives. Having had the misfortune to ground and wreck his flagship on the coast of Hispaniola, Columbus decided to leave some of his crew behind to look for more gold while he returned to Spain to report to Ferdinand and Isabella. So uncertain was he of completing his return voyage safely that he wrote a brief account of his discoveries and put it overboard in a corked bottle. He hoped that if his ship went down, at least the bottle might reach Spain with news of his achievement.

East or West Indies?
Columbus made three more voyages to the West Indies, but always remained under the impression that he had reached the East Indies and was on the offshore islands of Cathay (China). He even despatched a mission to the Great Khan of the Moguls, because when the inhabitants of Cuba talked of gold at "Cubanacan" (in the interior of Cuba), he thought they were referring to "Kublai Khan."

Not everyone shared his geographical convictions, and it has been suggested that the alternative name of Antilles for his newly discovered islands may have indicated that some link was seen with the fabled Atlantic island of Atlantis. Be that as it might, the Spanish determined on rapid colonization, although Columbus himself proved less able as an administrator than as an explorer.

Ruling the new lands
The difficulty about colonization was that a title to the newly discovered lands had to be established. Only the Pope could authorize missionary work among the heathen, and this activity was the necessary justification for further exploration and settlement. Fortunately for Ferdinand and Isabella, Pope Alexander VI was himself a Spaniard and heavily indebted to them for military and political services elsewhere. The Pope therefore obliged by promulgating a series of bulls, notably the famous Inter Caetera, which postulated an imaginary north–south line in the Atlantic 300 leagues (about 900 miles/1450 kilometers) west of the Azores. The world was divided between the Iberian kingdoms, with Spain taking the hemisphere to the west and Portugal the lands to the east. Later, after representations from the King of Portugal, this line was moved further into the Atlantic – to 370 leagues (about 1100 miles/1700 kilometers) west of the Cape Verde Islands and consolidated into the Treaty of Tordesillas in 1494.

Mainland South America
With this mandate secured, the Spanish extended their explorations from the West Indies to the mainland. In Columbus's third expedition of 1498 he reached the mouth of the Orinoco, the largest river to have been discovered by any European at that date. The following year one of his captains, Vicente Yáñez Pinzón, explored even further south, sailing along the coasts of what is now the extreme north of Brazil and Guyana.

Also in 1499 Amerigo Vespucci, another Italian who had come to the New World via Seville, sailed with an expedition that reached the Gulf of Venezuela and the mouth of the Amazon. For a considerable time Amerigo Vespucci was indeed given the credit for discovering this newly found continental land mass and, by dint of his letters to the Medici family and the numerous maps and charts he made of the New World, this whole continent was given his name in perpetuity.

▲ *Columbus first reached Cuba in October 1492. He got the impression from the inhabitants that he might find gold if he ventured inland, but he was to be sorely disappointed.*

Explorers of the East Coast

Expeditions from Portugal as well as Spain had reached the coast of South America by the end of the 15th century. In their exploration of the sea routes around Africa, the Portuguese had found that, to take advantage of the currents in the south Atlantic, it was best to sail far westward before turning back to the African coast. While practising this manoeuver, Pedro Alvares Cabral struck land far out into the south Atlantic in 1500. He had in fact reached the coast of Brazil at a point just south of the present city of Salvador.

Cabral claimed the land for King Manuel of Portugal. He had every right to do so: it fell to the Portuguese side of the dividing line between Spain and Portugal sanctified by the Treaty of Tordesillas six years earlier. Indeed, there has always been some speculation as to whether the Portuguese anxiety to move the line further westward was not evidence that they already had some inkling of the existence of Brazil – or at least of some land mass jutting out into the south Atlantic. Be that as it may, Cabral sent home a ship with a valuable report and a few parrots – as an exotic and much prized gift – and continued his journey back across the Atlantic toward the Cape of Good Hope and other eastern discoveries.

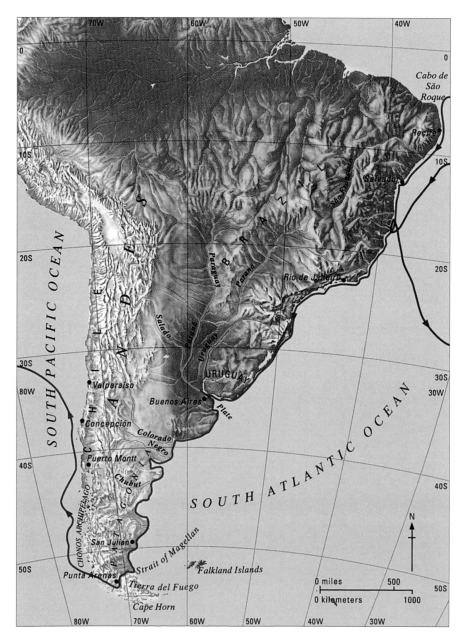

Settlement and slavery

The Portuguese remained preoccupied with the possibilities of lucrative trade with the East (Vasco da Gama had reached India in 1498) and with finding gold in West Africa (the "Gold Coast") rather than with exploiting or developing their South American discovery – "the Land of the True Cross," as Cabral had named it.

Soon, however, the qualities of the red dye-wood which grew so plentifully along this coast were found to be useful and profitable, and the country was renamed after this tree – Brazil. The native inhabitants also proved attractive, and Pedro Vaz de Caminha wrote to King Manuel: "There can easily be stamped upon [this people] whatever belief we wish to give them. And furthermore Our Lord gave them fine bodies and good faces ... one of the girls was all painted from head to foot with paint, and she was so well built and so rounded, and her lack of shame so charming, that many women of our own land seeing such attractions would be ashamed that theirs were not like hers."

Settlement followed discovery. Soon sugar was found to be a more profitable crop than timber, but sugar needed cheap labor, and the cheapest sort of labor was slave labor. The American Indians – Amerindians – were hunters by inclination, not laborers, and did not take kindly to toiling all day for white settlers. Some were captured or sold by warring tribes into slavery, but these were outnumbered by those who died (often of European diseases such as smallpox) or escaped.

To the Portuguese settlers the obvious answer seemed to be the importation of black slaves from their West African trading stations. The settlers also took mistresses among the natives, and so the mixed racial pattern of Brazil had begun in the earliest years of European settlement. But it was only along the coast that these settlements clustered; progress inland was daunting and difficult, not least because many of the major rivers (unlike those of West Africa) were attended by rapids and waterfalls relatively near the coast. The interior of South America remained a closed world.

Magellan's venture

When Ferdinand Magellan, a Portuguese who had served his country well in India and Morocco, was denied advancement in the nobility by King Manuel, he (like Columbus before him) turned to the Spanish crown. He offered to lead a maritime expedition to the Spice Islands (the East Indies) round the south of the American continent "without touching any sea or land of the King of Portugal."

The Spanish fitted out five ships for this venture, and Magellan set sail in September 1519. By the end of that year he was sailing down the east coast of South America toward Patagonia (now part of Argentina). Here the inhabitants appeared to the crews as giants, and it was decided to kidnap some to take home as curiosities. Antonio Pigafetta, a gentleman volunteer who became renowned for his account of the voyage, describes how they loaded two of "the giants" with gifts and then, when their hands were full, suggested that they might like to wear large iron bracelets on their ankles. It was the work of a moment to rivet them into their fetters.

The crews also persistently plotted against each other. After the first mutiny at San Julián in Patagonia, Magellan had the offending officers' heads cut off and their bodies quartered; others were marooned on the Patagonian coast. However, severe as these measures were, they were not to deter others later.

The search for the passage

One ship was lost on a reconnaissance during the winter, though the crew survived, and the remaining four resumed the voyage in October, soon entering the labyrinth of channels between the islands north of Cape Horn. Having penetrated deep into one channel, the sailors became convinced that there was no exit into another sea. However, Magellan persuaded them to press on by claiming that – in the words of his navigator, Pigafetta – "there was another straight (strait) going out" which he knew well "because he had seen it by a marine chart of the King of Portugal." This was sheer invention on Magellan's part, but the encouragement was enough. When the leading ships took refuge from a storm around a further headland they found the navigable waterways they had been searching for – now called the Strait of Magellan.

Magellan spent some time exploring among the intricate channels, and while he was doing so another of his ships, the *San Antonio*, mutinied and, deserting Magellan's fleet, made off for home. The Patagonian "giant" whom the mutineers had on board died of heatstroke when the ship reached warmer climes. Meanwhile, the other Patagonian kidnap victim with Magellan was faring much better, showing signs of conversion to Christianity and being christened Paul by his captors.

The sailing and charting was continued by Magellan and his remaining ships. They were able to work for long hours as even in October the night is only dark at that latitude for three hours – a fact which astonished the crew.

On November 20, 1520, Magellan and his ship finally broke out of the channels into the ocean beyond. Their first impression had been of a smooth and sunny ocean which they consequently named the Pacific. However, the journey which followed was full of fresh hazards, the chief among which was the ocean's sheer size. Magellan himself was to be among the men who died – killed in a skirmish in the Philippines (see pages 150–51). Only 18 of the original crews of 243 reached home to tell the tale, three years after they set out. The New World had proved, after all, to provide a sea route to the East Indies; a southwest passage was less intractable than a northwest one.

▲ *Lopo Homen's map* of Brazil (1519) illustrates the rich flora and fauna as well as documenting the Portuguese claim with national flags.

▼ *Magellan assembled his* fleet at Seville, which in the 16th century was Spain's richest and most populous city, and a major center of exploration.

Cortés Conquers Mexico

In the first years of the 16th century rumors began to filter through to the Spanish in Cuba and Hispaniola of a more developed and richer indigenous civilization to the west of these islands and to the north of the Isthmus of Panama.

These rumors were confirmed by reports from the modest expeditions that nosed along the coasts of Yucatán and the Gulf of Mexico in 1517 and 1518. The following year the Spanish Governor of Cuba, Diego Velázquez, fitted out a more ambitious expedition to Mexico and appointed his secretary, Hernán Cortés, who was also a shareholder in the enterprise, as its commander. The Spanish lust for gold and adventure was as great as ever, and Cortés had little difficulty in attracting 600 volunteers to sail with him.

Cortés was the son of a noble Spanish family from Extremadura, one of the poorest and climatically harshest regions of Spain. After studying at Salamanca University he had decided to seek his fortune in the New World. Soon after he had left Cuba on his expedition to Mexico he renounced his allegiance to the Governor and determined to make the expedition, and whatever conquests it might achieve, wholly his own.

He landed first at Tabasco and, on the strength of information he gleaned there, sailed on to the port that is now Veracruz. There he spent four months preparing to march inland and confront the power of the Aztec Empire. So that there should be no turning back, he burned his boats on the shore – all except one, which he despatched back to Spain to explain why he had declared direct allegiance to the crown rather than to Velázquez.

The route to the Aztecs

Cortés led his band of soldiers of fortune on the rough, steep route from the tropical coastal forests of Veracruz to the high plateau of central Mexico. He chose his route to maximize his chances of gaining supporters and, in doing so, was obliged to cross some of the most difficult mountain passes in the country. This policy paid off: after some initial resistance the independent city state of Tlaxcala, which had been regularly subjected to slaving raids by the Aztecs, formed an alliance with Cortés. It was then clear that the Aztec capital of Tenochtitlán in the high valley called Mexico, the center of Aztec power and the treasure house of the empire, must be Cortés's objective.

At this point Cortés received an embassy from Montezuma, the Aztec king, who wished to dissuade him from advancing further into the kingdom. To this end Montezuma sent him valuable gifts, but these had the opposite effect from that intended: far from buying off the Spaniards from a further advance, they incited them to press on in the expectation of more such golden artifacts. Cortés also sent some of the gifts back to the King of Spain – the formidable Emperor Charles V – to persuade him to endorse Cortés's own independent command.

Penetration of the Aztec capital

Undeterred by threats or gifts, Cortés continued his march on Tenochtitlán. He succeeded in convincing Montezuma

▼ *In the final attack* led by Cortés on Tenochtitlán, more than 15,000 Mexicans died in a single day. The city's capture by the Spaniards signaled the collapse of the Aztec Empire.

that his purposes were friendly, and the Aztec army then escorted the Spanish force across the causeway into their cherished capital and lodged them in a palace in the very center. The fearless demeanor of the *conquistadores*, their dazzling armor, and their awe-inspiring horses all combined to bemuse Montezuma and his subjects. Cortés's native allies remained on the shores of the lake outside the city, and Montezuma himself occupied an equivocal position as part guest and part hostage of the Spaniards. For a while an uneasy calm prevailed.

It was unfortunate that Cortés had to leave his little army at this moment. This was because the Governor of Cuba, learning of Cortés's repudiation of his control, had sent another Spanish captain, Narváez, to arrest him and bring him back to Cuba. Cortés decided to confront Narváez at the coast and did this so successfully that Narváez's men decided to join with Cortés and return with him to Tenochtitlán.

In Cortés's absence the fragile relationship between the *conquistadores* and the Aztecs had become strained to break-ing point. His lieutenant, Pedro de Alvarado, had allowed the Spaniards to indulge in some looting and destruction, and sporadic fighting had broken out. Cortés was able to re-enter Tenochtitlán but, having done so, found himself and his whole force trapped within the palace. The Aztecs had rejected the authority of Montezuma, whom they considered now to be a tool of the *conquistadores*. When at Cortés's insistence Montezuma tried to reason with his own people, they stoned him and he was mortally wounded. The Spaniards no longer had any effective hostage and, isolated in the midst of the Aztec horde, their position had become desperate.

Surrender of Tenochtitlán

It was then that Cortés showed his mettle. Gathering his band around him, he fought his way out of the palace and the city across the broken causeways by night. A third of his men fell in the fighting, and almost all the treasure,

▲ *This plan of the Aztec capital*, Tenochtitlán, is *attributed to Cortés (left) and was first published in 1524. It shows the palace in the* center of the city and the causeways over the surrounding lake.

baggage and spare weapons were lost. But Cortés was reunited with his allies from Tlaxcala and determined on a counteroffensive. He returned to besiege the Aztecs in Tenochtitlán: he cut off the food and fresh water, built boats from which to bombard the island fortress, threw up new causeways, and waited while the diseases the Aztecs had contracted from the Spaniards – notably smallpox – took their toll. By 1521 the city had surrendered, and the Kingdom of Mexico was at the feet of Cortés. The looting then started in earnest. The Spaniards combed the fallen city for gold, and tortured prisoners to reveal where more was hidden. They turned on each other, and even on Cortés himself, with accusations of secreting treasure for personal gain. When the haul of gold proved disappointing, Cortés tried to console his followers with grants of land.

Further exploration

As soon as he could, Cortés turned his energies once more to exploration, leading expeditions to the Pacific coast of Mexico and even despatching ships into that ocean. He sent other commanders into the Mayan region of Guatemala. As so often happened with the Spaniards, rival commanders fell out with each other. In 1524 one of Cortés's commanders, moving southward, clashed with one of the Spanish commanders from the Isthmus moving northward. Once more, Cortés's presence restored good order and unity.

Eventually he himself returned to Spain to report on his conquests and his administration to Charles V. The emperor received him affably enough and made him Marquis of Oaxaca (in Mexico), but Charles V did not feel comfortable with his overmighty subject and gave Cortés no real authority. The greatest of the *conquistadores* retired to die as a private citizen in his native Spain.

▲ *Aztec sculptures, such as the wind god Ehecatl, had a grotesqueness which was highly symbolic and reflected complex religious beliefs.*

Pizarro and Orellana

The exploits of Cortés in Mexico were to inspire the discovery and conquest of another ancient civilization in the New World – that of the Incas of Peru. After Vasco Núñez de Balboa had reached the Pacific Ocean and claimed it for the Spanish crown in 1513, he set up the port of Panama, from which expeditions started to sail in both directions along the Pacific coast. One of the main objectives was to find whether there was any channel through the Panama Isthmus; another was to establish whether there was any truth in persistent rumors that a kingdom of immense wealth lay to the south. Among those who heeded the rumors was Francisco Pizarro, who was authorized by the Governor of Panama to take an expedition in search of this unknown kingdom – the empire of the Incas.

Seizure of the Inca

After two unsuccessful attempts to find the Incas, Pizarro finally landed at Tumbes in northern Peru, in 1532, with 177 men, of whom 67 were cavalry. He marched inland, encountering friendly envoys and gaining confirmation of

the mineral riches of the country, but he then faced crossing the Andes to meet the Inca, Atahualpa. The horses and men shivered and slithered on the precarious mountain ledges along which their route lay. True to his protestations of friendship, the Inca had not defended the passes, although some of these had man-made fortifications at strategic points.

Having crossed the Cordillera, the Spaniards advanced directly on Cajamarca where the Inca and his vast army were waiting to receive the small Spanish contingent. Fearing that they might, after all, have walked into a trap, Pizarro devised a daring and treacherous plot to seize the Inca himself. He enticed Atahualpa to pay him a visit in the main square of Cajamarca, which was lined by long, low buildings on three sides. Each building had some 20 openings on to the open space in the middle; the cavalry was therefore able to sit mounted and concealed, ready to charge out at a given signal. On arriving at the square with an unarmed retinue, Atahualpa was approached by Pizarro's chaplain, a Dominican friar, who then made a fairly peremptory attempt to explain Christianity. When

KEY TO ROUTES

— Cabot 1526
— Francisco Pizarro 1532
— Almagro 1535–37
— Orellana 1540
— Gonzalo Pizarro 1540–42
— Valdivia 1541–47

Atahualpa – not surprisingly – declined to be instantly converted and rejected the proffered Bible, the friar returned to Pizarro calling, "I absolve you."

With cries of "Santiago" Pizarro and his men set about slaughtering the Inca's retinue to the accompaniment of artillery and musket fire. Total panic ensued: it was a massacre, not a battle, in which more than 2000 – possibly as many as 10,000 – of the Inca's retainers were cut down.

The greed of the Spaniards

Once the Inca was taken prisoner, Pizarro was able to consolidate his hold on Cajamarca. The *conquistadores* soon realized that Atahualpa had a high ransom value. To secure his release the Inca offered to fill a whole room with gold and silver, and precious artifacts started pouring in from all over his kingdom.

Rumors then spread among the Spaniards that the Inca was using the messengers who brought in the gold to rally military support for his rescue. Pizarro set up a hasty parody of a trial, in which the charges against Atahualpa included that "he was guilty of idolatry and adulterous practices, indulging openly in plurality of wives." The Inca was predictably condemned to death. The Spanish Emperor Charles V strongly disapproved when he heard of the Inca's judicial murder, but the Spaniards went on to found their own capital on the coast at Lima.

Further conquest and exploration

Diego de Almagro, one of Pizarro's companions (later to become one of his enemies), set out in 1535 to explore further south and became the first European to reach Chile. The extremes of cold endured in the Andes were followed by the extreme heat of the Atacama Desert. The discovery of Chile was to be consolidated by Pedro de Valdivia, who in 1541 founded the city of Santiago in one of the most beautiful and fertile valleys of South America. Further south, Valdivia found colonization was harder. He had various encounters with the Indians, but did not press his conquests too far south; nor did he go eastward across the Andes into what is now Argentina. The area of Patagonia had been explored two decades earlier, in part by Sebastian Cabot who (despite his Venetian birth) was also operating with a Spanish commission. Cabot explored the River Plate (named after the silver he found there) and the Paraná and Paraguay rivers.

Orellana navigates the Amazon

In 1540 a group of *conquistadores*, under the leadership of Gonzalo Pizarro (the brother of Francisco Pizarro), marched from Quito in modern Ecuador eastward, out of the land of the Incas and into the cinnamon forests, where they came on a wide river with roaring waterfalls: the Napo. Here the decision was taken to send Francisco de Orellana ahead down the river, in a brigantine which took many weeks to construct, to find food with which to reprovision the whole expedition.

After three days Orellana reached an even wider river. As there was still no food to be had and the natives were hostile, he pressed on. By the time he had found supplies it seemed virtually impossible to return to Pizarro's main party. At least, it seemed easier and more exciting to go on downstream on a mighty and unknown river which, he realized, must eventually reach the Atlantic and hence the sea route to home.

Fighting off the hostile Indians on the shore, Orellana made his way some 3000 miles (4750 kilometers) down the world's mightiest river, which he named Amazon after the ancient legend of warrior women. He sailed up to the

◄ *Francisco Pizarro* was a man of remarkable courage and ruthless determination who was nearly 60 years old when he set out with fewer than 180 men to conquer the empire of the Incas.

West Indies and eventually returned to Spain, where his discoveries were considered sufficiently remarkable to outweigh the dubious ethics of his having abandoned his comrades. He was granted a commission to conquer and colonize the region he had discovered, but died on the return journey to the Amazon.

Gonzalo Pizarro and his men, stranded on the banks of the Napo, waited for weeks for Orellana's return with news and food. Eventually they reluctantly followed the river bank to look for him, taking two months to reach the junction with the larger river to which Orellana had been borne by the swift current in less than three days. They found the half-demented figure of one of their comrades who had been abandoned to his fate by Orellana when he objected to the plan to press on down the river.

They retraced their steps to Quito, living off the jungle and anything they could seize from Indian settlements, eating insects, snakes, and their own leather belts. When they reached Quito in June 1542 – two years after they had set out – they had shrunk from a party of 350 to a mere 80 survivors. The Amazon River had become known to Europeans, but at a terrible price.

◄ *In a parody of a trial* the Inca Atahualpa was condemned to be burned at the stake. The only mercy Pizarro showed to him was to commute the sentence, according to some accounts, to garrotting. This woodcut from an early Peruvian codex shows him being beheaded. Whatever the form of execution, it marked the beginning of the total conquest of Peru by the Spaniards.

The Search for El Dorado

▲ *An engraving by de Bry, dating from the end of the 16th century, depicts an Indian prince being coated in gold dust. According to* the legend of El Dorado, the prince was then floated on a raft to the middle of Lake Guatavita where he threw a pile of gold into the water.

KEY TO ROUTES

— Balboa 1512
— Benalcázar 1533–39
— Quesada 1536–37
— Federmann 1536–39
— Raleigh 1595
— Raleigh 1617

Although the early *conquistadores* did much harm to the Amerindians, this was not the intention of the Spanish crown. As early as 1503 Queen Isabella issued an order forbidding cruel treatment of the Amerindians – but with the important exception of "a certain people called Cannibals." The royal decree went on to say that "If the said Cannibals continue to resist, and do not wish to admit and receive to their lands the Captains and men who may be on such voyages by my orders, nor to hear them in order to be taught our Sacred Catholic Faith … they may be captured and taken to be sold."

The region inland from Cartagena was designated "Cannibal country" in this decree, so there were no inhibitions on the Spanish *conquistadores* who first entered the territory which is now Colombia. Settlements were established on the coast in the first decades of the 16th century, largely to facilitate raiding parties to open up the interior.

Vasco Núñez de Balboa (who was to claim the Pacific for the Spanish crown in 1513) led one such expedition in 1512. His particular objective was to contact an Indian chief called Dabeiba, apparently a collecting agent for gold in the region. Indeed, the precious metal was so plentiful that the whole mainland was then officially designated Castilla del Oro.

Encouraged by the examples of Cortés and Pizarro, gold fever reached its height in the 1530s, with three separate expeditions – under Jiménez de Quesada, Federmann (a German), and Benalcázar – meeting together to establish a settlement on the site of the present city of Bogotá and then to explore and exploit the surrounding countryside. These commanders, unlike their contemporaries further south in Peru, avoided falling out between themselves and concentrated on despoiling the natives.

The gilded man

As the commanders collected more and more gold, and captured increasing numbers of Indians, one story began to recur: it concerned a gilded man – "El Dorado" – and the curious rites which took place at an inland lake called Guatavita, near Bogotá. These rites revolved around the initiation of a new ruler, who would be floated out on the water on a raft of rushes, with his principal subject chiefs and a great pile of gold and emeralds. The prince was then, according to Juan Rodríguez Freyle writing much later in 1636, "stripped to his skin, and anointed with a sticky earth on which they placed gold dust so that he was com-

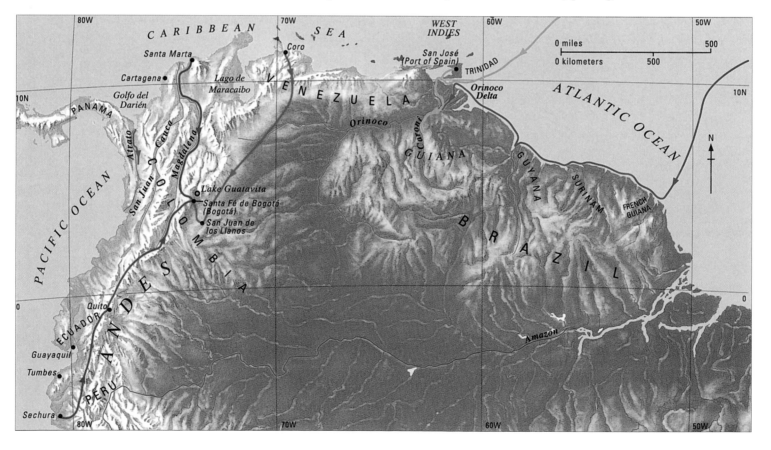

pletely covered with this metal ... when they reached the center of the lagoon ... the gilded Indian made his offering, throwing out all the pile of gold into the middle of the lake, and the chiefs who accompanied him did the same."

This is one version of the origin of the El Dorado legend, although the term was later to be attached to a mythical city of gold rather than to a man. The practical point that emerged from the story of the Indian prince and his raft was that the floor of Lake Guatavita was lined with golden artifacts and precious stones. As corroboration, some gold ornaments were washed up on the fringes of the lake.

▲ *This illustration from the Codex Köler shows* the conquistadores *on Federmann's expedition marching to Seville.*

▶ *Sir Walter Raleigh was accompanied by his son Wat on an expedition up the Orinoco. The boy was killed in a Spanish ambush.*

The lake of gold

Minds immediately turned toward draining the lagoon. First one of Quesada's captains and then his brother attempted the task. The latter waited until the dry season of 1545 and then organized a chain gang with gourds instead of buckets. They lowered the level of the water by 10 feet (3 meters) and salvaged some 4000 gold coins.

Forty years later a rich Spanish merchant – Antonio de Sepúlveda – employed some 8000 Indians to cut a V-shaped notch in the rim of the lake through which the water drained out. This time the level of the water was lowered by 65 feet (20 meters) before the cut fell in, killing many of the Indians and causing the scheme to be abandoned. Twelve thousand pesos had been salvaged and "Sepúlveda's cut," as it was known, is visible to this day.

Numerous other attempts followed. At the beginning of the 19th century, one of Simón Bolívar's friends developed a plan to siphon the water out of the lake. At the end of the same century a public company wanted to drain out the water through a tunnel. This company finally exposed the bed of the lake, only to find a surface of mud and slime, more than 3 feet (1 meter) deep, which could not be walked upon. By the following day the sun had baked the mud so hard that it could not be penetrated by picks or shovels. By the time drilling equipment had been procured, the baked mud had blocked the tunnel and the lagoon had refilled with water. A few items were found and later sold at Christie's in London, but the secret gold hoard of the Indians (if it ever existed) eluded the Spanish *conquistadores* and still eludes treasure seekers today.

Sir Walter Raleigh and the Orinoco

The sight of Spanish coffers filling with gold from the New World was a continual provocation to the sea captains of Elizabethan England. In 1595 Sir Walter Raleigh set sail for Guiana to attempt to find El Dorado – this time seeking the fabled golden city in the forests beyond the Orinoco River.

Raleigh lost two of his ships on the Atlantic crossing but eventually landed in Trinidad. There he attacked the Spanish settlement at San José (now St Joseph, near Port of Spain) and captured its Governor, Antonio de Berrío, who warned him against the hazards of the Orinoco. Undeterred, he and his depleted crew canoed upriver for some 500 miles (800 kilometers), continually losing themselves in the maze of interlocking streams. When the rains came, Raleigh recorded "our hearts were cold to behold the great rage and increase of the Orinoco," and conditions forced him to turn back.

Raleigh had collected samples of what he imagined were gold-bearing ore and rocks which "exceeded any diamond in beauty"; but he had not accumulated any substantial treasure in bullion or precious stones. Instead, he came back with an ecstatic account of the beauties of the flora and fauna of the tropical rain forests. He wrote a glowing account of "a country that hath still her maidenhood." Elizabeth I, who had backed the voyage financially as well as morally in the hope of rich gains, was unimpressed and declined to allow Raleigh to colonize the region.

Raleigh nonetheless maintained his enchantment with Guiana even during his years in disgrace and imprisonment under James I. In 1617 he sailed there again to make a last desperate attempt to find his El Dorado. The king was so fearful of offending the Spaniards (who claimed sovereignty over the whole region) that he gave details of Raleigh's plans to the Spanish ambassador. Raleigh was ambushed and his son, Wat, killed; he returned disgraced to face the wrath of the king and ultimately execution.

▼ *Greed for the gold used in Inca ornaments attracted many Spanish explorers to the area around the present city of Bogotá in Colombia.*

Missionaries and *Bandeirantes*

In the 16th century the spread of the Gospel was often little more than a pretext for the exploration of South and Central America. The real motive was the greed for gold, with slaves providing labor for mining precious metals. But in the 17th and 18th centuries missionaries took over the main thrust of exploration, genuinely intent on converting and protecting the Indians. In Brazil, *bandeirantes* (armed marauders collected into bands known as *bandeiras*) were equally intent on rounding up Indians as slave labor for mines, plantations, and farms. Inevitably these two groups came into conflict.

The Pope and the Spanish and Portuguese crowns had prohibited the enslaving of Indians from the earliest days of European settlement in South America. But there were loopholes: Indians captured in a righteous war could be retained as slave labor; so could Indians captured by one tribe from another and sold to European settlers as an alternative to being massacred. Any raiding party could claim to be involved in a "righteous war."

While the Spanish crown was fairly fastidious about trying to keep its settlers to the rules, the Portuguese crown had a less tight grip on the administration of its overseas possessions. Cases of settlers being excommunicated and handed over for punishment to the Inquisition – officially the penalty for slave trading in American Indians – were almost unknown.

The greatest center for the *bandeirantes* was São Paulo in southern Brazil, from where large bands would set out into the interior of Brazil or Paraguay for extended expeditions. Skirmishes, disease, and hunger all took their toll. Sometimes whole expeditions disappeared without trace, either because they had attempted to cross too arduous a natural obstacle or because they had tackled an Indian tribe stronger than themselves.

The *bandeirantes* seldom systematically mapped the terrain they traversed, nor did they accurately record any discoveries they made. But they effectively opened up the interior of the continent.

The Jesuit communities

The most effective force ranged against the *bandeirantes* was the Society of Jesus – the Jesuits, who had landed in Brazil as early as 1549 to convert the heathen. They penetrated deep into the forests and swamps, into the savannahs and mountains. At first their efforts appeared to help the settlers: they preached peace and made cannibalistic and belligerent tribes more docile. But when the Jesuits realized that even the Indians they had converted to Christianity were not immune from the attentions of the slave raiders, they began to collect their converts into communities which could be protected by the authority of the Church and, if need be, by organized self-defense.

The earliest of these communities, known as *reducciones*, was established in 1608. The Jesuits built huge stone mission churches, cultivated and distributed crops, clothed the Indians, and educated the Indians in the scriptures. They converted local dances and traditions into more seemly Christian rituals, and taught arts and handicrafts. However, the *reducciones* were not always safe from predatory attacks by the Portuguese *bandeirantes*.

In 1629 bands from São Paulo sacked five such *reducciones* in Paraguay, burning churches and Indians indiscriminately. They drove off huge numbers for a march to the slave markets on the coast – a journey that claimed as many fatalities as any slave ship bringing negro slaves from Africa. Some 30,000 Indian souls were lost to the Jesuits in this way in the following years. A massive exodus was organized by Father Montoya and Father Macedo to lead 12,000 surviving Indian converts down the Paraná River to safer havens. Their rafts were smashed in the rapids, but they continued on foot through the forests, singing hymns to keep their spirits up. They finally returned to the Jesuit heartlands in Paraguay, southern Brazil, and an area of Argentina still called Misiones.

Further north, in the mouth of the Amazon, the huge island of Marajó – approximately the same size as Switzerland – defied all incursions by settlers. The "Nheengaiba" tribes simply disappeared into their marshes and harassed any intruder with a withering fire of arrows. The island withstood the Portuguese until, in 1658, the Jesuit Father Antonio Vieira sent Indian converts there to spread his message of peace. Some 40,000 Indians promptly accepted both the emissaries and the faith.

Father Samuel Fritz

The most memorable of all the Jesuit missionaries was Father Samuel Fritz, a Bohemian who began his work in the forests around the headwaters of the Amazon in 1686. Alone by canoe he covered a region of some 1000 miles (1600 kilometers) of river, establishing over 50 Christian

▼ *Diego Homen's map* of Portuguese possessions in South America was drawn in the 16th century, at a time when Europeans were more interested in acquiring gold and slaves than in spreading the Gospel.

▶ *The missionaries* built huge stone churches deep in the forest. Around the churches they created reducciones, *communities which might defend themselves against the bandeirantes and in which discipline tempered with paternalism was the order of the day.*

◀ **Among the many perils** *faced by missionaries in their exploration of the forests were rapids and waterfalls, in which rafts or canoes were often smashed.*

KEY TO ROUTES

—— Fritz from 1686

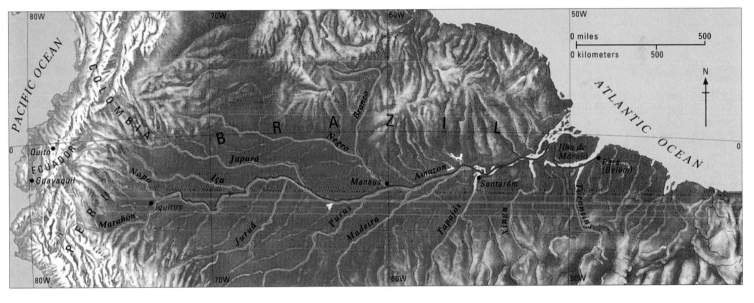

settlements of Omagua and Yurimagua Indians. Inevitably he succumbed to exhaustion and fever: he recorded (in a document known as the Évora manuscript and only discovered in 1902) how he had lain sick in a Yurimagua village while the flood waters rose all around him. He was too immobile to be able to quench his thirst, enduring not only sleeplessness but "the grunting of the crocodiles that were roving around the village, beasts of horrible deformity … the rats made their way into my dwelling place, and [were] so hungry, that they gnawed even my spoon and my plate and the haft of my knife."

Eventually he was evacuated by other missionaries to Pará (now Belém) at the mouth of the Amazon. But because he had been proselytizing in territory disputed between the Spanish and the Portuguese, the latter viewed him with suspicion and kept him under house arrest for 18 months while they consulted Lisbon about what they should do with him.

Finally allowed to go back to his own domain, several thousands of miles upstream, Fritz charted the course of the river as best he could with the primitive instruments available to him. (When La Condamine, with much improved navigational gear, passed that way half a century later he was impressed by Fritz's efforts.)

Fritz spent the years until his death at the age of 70 in 1723 protecting his protégés against the incursions of slave raiders. He, too, had to organize an exodus – this time to the Andean watershed. When his body was stripped for burial, he was found to be unusually afflicted by bites, and it was revealed that this gentle priest, who had combated for so long the violence of the Portuguese, had never killed an insect.

The Jesuits' foes

Although the Carmelites, the Mercedarians, the Franciscans, and others had been active in the 17th and 18th centuries, the Jesuits were the most effective and powerful. But in South America, as in Europe, they also attracted the most jealousy and hostility.

When the Marquis of Pombal, the effective ruler of Portugal in the mid-18th century, started persecuting the Jesuits in Portugal, he had little hesitation about extending his persecution to the New World. In 1756 he stripped the order of its temporal powers and two years later decreed that they should be expelled from Brazil. The colonial administrators carried out his command with alacrity and much brutality, and as a result one of the great forces for exploring the continent was lost.

Academics on the Amazon

▶ *Isabella Godin is remembered as one of the great survivors of the Amazon. She struggled on alone through the forest for many days after all her companions had either died or deserted her.*

Until the 18th century the discovery of South America had mostly been carried out by Italians, Spanish, and Portuguese, with some major contributions by Englishmen such as Sir Walter Raleigh and Germans such as Father Fritz. Now it was the turn of a Frenchman.

In the early years of the 18th century the French Academy of Sciences heatedly argued over the precise shape of the world. Isaac Newton had maintained that it was not a perfect sphere, instead bulging at the Equator and flattened toward the poles. The French scientific world tended toward the contrary position: the globe was elongated at the poles and attenuated in the middle.

To resolve the controversy the Academy sent one expedition to the Equator and another to the polar regions, each to measure the precise length of a degree of latitude. Leading the equatorial expedition to Quito was an aristocrat called Charles-Marie de la Condamine, a former soldier turned mathematician, cartographer, and naturalist.

La Condamine's expedition

La Condamine set out in 1735 with a small group of French companions. The Spanish crown only agreed to this unprecedented foreign intrusion on its preserve as a favor to Louis XV of France, but the Frenchmen were still treated with grave suspicion. They were taking careful measurements and using scientific instruments, which suggested gold prospecting to the local authorities.

La Condamine had to waste eight months on a special journey to Lima to get the Spanish viceroy's support for his researches. To make matters worse, one of the French party, a Dr Senièrgues, was lynched by a hostile crowd in the bullring; another went mad after the botanical specimens representing five years' sweltering work were destroyed by a careless servant; another died of fever; the expedition's draughtsman was killed in a fall from a ladder. To cap it all, they heard that the polar expedition had returned from Lapland with conclusive evidence that Newton's theory was correct and the French one wrong.

Despite this bad news, La Condamine's scientific curiosity was not yet satisfied. Instead of returning home he crossed the Andes and followed the whole course of the Amazon River to the Atlantic, as Orellana had done two centuries earlier. He was the first trained scientist, equipped with instruments for observation and charting, to navigate these tortuous waters. Some of the higher tributaries were particularly arduous: he had to cross and recross the Chuchunga River more than 20 times in a single day. Further downstream, a balsawood raft proved the best conveyance. La Condamine concluded: "A canoe on such

KEY TO ROUTES

— La Condamine 1743
— Isabella Godin 1749

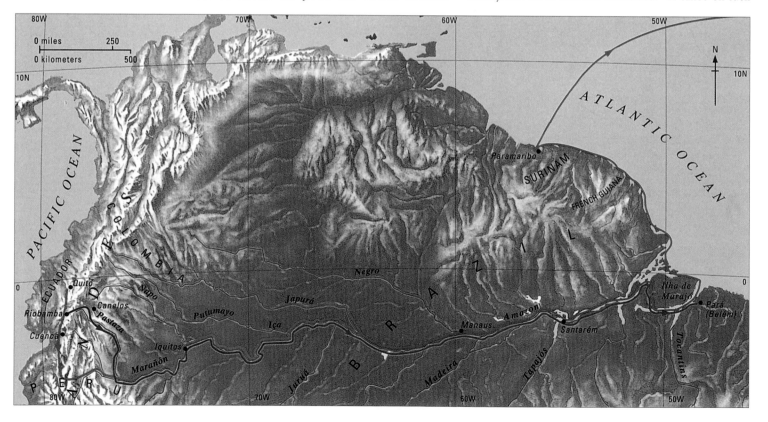

A Dutch expedition through Brazil in the 1630s included a naturalist and a number of painters. Together they produced over 100 pictures of native peoples, flora and fauna, among them the fig and the anteater.

an occasion would be dashed into a thousand pieces ... but the beams of the raft being neither nailed nor dovetailed together, the flexibility of the lianas, by which they are fastened, have the effect of a spring."

Extending the knowledge of the world

While negotiating these hazards, La Condamine was continually gathering information. He plumbed the depth of the river regularly and measured its width. He kept compass and watch always to hand in daylight hours and charted twists in the river. He corrected Father Fritz's more primitive findings. He gauged the force of the stream and recorded details of the flora and fauna of the river. He was particularly intrigued by encounters with electric eels which, he found, could give such a severe shock when touched even with a stick that they inflicted "a painful numbness in the arm" and could "lay one prostrate." He was also the first to codify in a systematic way the miraculous qualities of latex.

Owing to the devastation of disease and slavers the Indians were far less of a danger to La Condamine than they had been to Orellana. But he nonetheless formed a poor opinion of them: "Voracious gluttons ... pusillanimous and timid in the extreme, unless transported by drunkenness ... notwithstanding there are at present no man eaters along the banks of the Marañón, there yet exist inland tribes of Americans who eat their prisoners."

Eventually La Condamine reached the city of Pará (now Belém) at the mouth of the Amazon and from there took ship to French Guiana, where he had to wait a further five months for a passage to France. He returned home in February 1745 after ten years of South American travels.

Some of the information he had gleaned, such as

about the shape of the Earth, had been partially overtaken. Other information, for instance that there were no poisonous snakes on the Amazon, was plainly erroneous. But these misconceptions were far outweighed by the massive contribution he had made to Europe's knowledge of the world beyond its own frontiers. His work was to contribute to the establishment of the meter – originally defined as one ten-millionth of the distance from the Pole to the Equator – as the world's most widely used unit of measuring length. La Condamine had paved the way for the scientific explorers of the following century.

An Amazon survivor

When La Condamine returned home down the length of the Amazon, one of his scientific colleagues, Jean Godin des Odonais, and his wife Isabella resolved to do the same. Due to Mme Godin's frequent pregnancies Jean then decided to go ahead on his own, but in 1749 his wife set off to join him. She was accompanied by her two brothers, a young nephew, three Frenchmen including a doctor, three maid servants, an African slave, and 31 Indian paddlers and porters. The party safely reached Canelos, where a well-stocked canoe was expected. But Canelos was deserted, following a smallpox epidemic, and all Mme Godin's Indians fled into the forests.

Should they press on or turn back? Mme Godin, calculating that it was only 12 days downstream to her rendezvous, had a light canoe built, and the depleted party drifted downriver. Their only skilled paddler drowned, and eventually the frail craft capsized. The rest of the party swam ashore with what they could salvage of their food.

The able-bodied men righted the canoe and decided to sail, unencumbered by passengers, to fetch help. Mme Godin and her family waited 25 days on the river bank, tried and failed to make a raft, then set out on foot. Unable to follow the tangled river bank, they tried to cut out the curves by striking through the jungle, but soon lost their way in the dank forests.

Starving and tired, all but Mme Godin died. Leaving seven bodies behind her, she stumbled on alone, eating insects and roots where she could. After nine days she refound the river, and two Indians in a canoe picked her up. She survived to be reunited with her husband and to become a legendary warning to Amazonian travelers.

▲ *Rivers* invariably provided the only possible route through the Amazon forest. When Isabella Godin's party left the river they soon became hopelessly lost and died of starvation.

Baron von Humboldt

▲ *Humboldt's enquiring mind* resulted in his contributing to many disciplines – anthropology, zoology, and medicine among others. Despite the risks he took during his travels, he lived to be 90.

▲ *Humboldt and Bonpland,* shown here on the bank of the River Orinoco, traveled in canoes that were swamped frequently in the turbulent and alligator-infested waters. But equally there were dangers in the thick tropical vegetation on land. Humboldt's dog – a sizable mastiff – was eaten by a jaguar.

In five years of intensive travels in South and Central America and the Caribbean, Baron von Humboldt was to contribute more to the sum of human knowledge than the French scientist La Condamine had done in ten. One reason for this was that during the years between the travels of La Condamine and Humboldt, Europe had made great advances in scientific knowledge. But perhaps an even more powerful reason was to be found in Humboldt's own personality: seldom has any man combined such intellectual curiosity about every aspect of life with such a tough physique and such an adventurous spirit. In a lifetime which extended from an acquaintance with Frederick the Great of Prussia to a friendship with Sir Walter Scott, he was rightly considered the last truly Renaissance Man.

Humboldt's accomplishments

Humboldt arrived in Venezuela in 1799. From then until 1803 his passion for exploration and knowledge was to take him to Cuba, Colombia, Ecuador, Peru, and Mexico. Together with his invariable companion Aimée Bonpland, he traversed the watershed between the Orinoco and Amazon river systems by means of the unique River Casiquiare. He found this river, often referred to as a canal, to be a fast-flowing branch of the Orinoco, discharging into the River Negro and thence into the Amazon. The myth of "a river that flowed both ways" was exploded. But in his quest for the truth, Humboldt had nearly lost his life in the hazardous waters.

Humboldt's curiosity led him into other dangers. He experimented with curare, the poison which the Indians used on their arrows, drinking it to prove that it was only lethal when injected into the bloodstream. He also drank the juice of the cow tree, until one of his companions started vomiting balls of rubber. He persuaded the unfortunate Bonpland to hold one end of an electric eel while he held the other, and they received alternate shocks of anything up to 600 volts. He calmly measured the atmospherical electricity during an earthquake that sent everyone else scurrying for safety. All these and many other painful experiences were dispassionately recorded and analyzed for the benefit of his successors.

It was when he got into the mountains around Quito, in Ecuador, however, that Humboldt took most risks. He climbed various volcanoes and then determined to make an assault on the 20,560-foot (6267-meter) summit of Chimborazo, believing it to be the world's highest mountain. Conditions were against him. At the snow line his guides deserted him. A little higher a mist descended, making it impossible for them to see the way forward or back. He suffered acutely from mountain sickness. Then the track narrowed into a knife-edge with a 1000-foot (300-meter) precipice on one side and an ice-slope of over 30 degrees on the other and, to cap it all, a hail storm hit them. Only with the greatest reluctance and at a height of over 19,000 feet (5800 meters) – the highest ever to have been reached by any man at that date – did Humboldt turn back.

A scientist and philosopher

Humboldt was not only a recorder of scientific data and an adventurer, he was also a philosopher. His observations on the problems of the region have stood the test of time. He denounced slavery and forced labor wherever he encountered them, objecting to humans being used as pack animals and "described in the same terms as would be employed in speaking of a horse or mule." He was – more predictably – revolted by cannibalistic practices, but understanding toward a missionary who had found himself unable to punish "an Indian who, a few years before, had eaten one of his wives, after having taken her to his canuco (hut), and fattened her by good feeding."

He wrote rationally about "the warlike republic of women without husbands" which had given the name to the Amazon River. He praised the mission stations for their compassionate work among the Indians, but he deplored the excessive discipline of some establishments.

Humboldt's heritage

Humboldt is principally remembered in the context of South America today on account of the cold ocean current running up the west coast which bears his name. It was characteristic of him that he recognized the connection between the coldness of the water, the warmth of the air, and the lack of rain on the coast of the Atacama Desert. However, on his return to Europe, via the United States, he was lionized as no explorer/scientist has been before or since. He was compared with Napoleon, whom he met, as one of the great figures of a heroic age, and with Goethe, whom he also met, as one of the great thinkers of his time.

▲ **Mount Chimborazo**, viewed here from the Tapia plateau, denied the indefatigable Humboldt his goal of reaching the summit. (The alpinist Edward Whymper finally scaled the peak nearly 80 years later.)

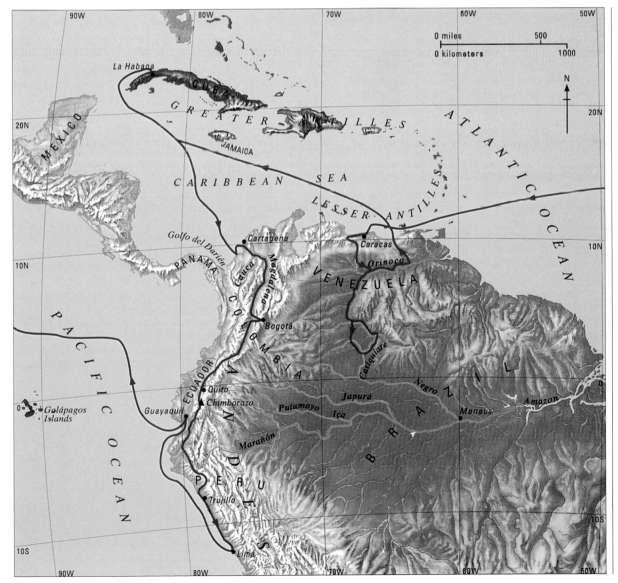

Navigators and Naturalists

▲ **Nineteenth-century naturalists** such as Bates, Wallace, and Spruce spent many years of their lives exploring the upper tributaries of the Amazon by canoe with native paddlers.

Throughout the second half of the 18th century the coastline of South America was being systematically charted and surveyed, a process in which the British navy played a large part. Commodore George Anson had made his celebrated voyage around South America – and on around the world – in 1740–44. He had lost four of his seven ships by the time he landed at the uninhabited islands of the Juan Fernández group (where Selkirk had been marooned 40 years earlier) for refitting.

The crew of one of the lost ships, the *Wager*, had been shipwrecked among the islands off the southern Chilean coast. They included John Byron, whose account of their explorations and adventures is a classic seafarers' tale (and was used by his grandson, Lord Byron, in his description of the storm and wreck in *Don Juan*). In 1764, undeterred by his experiences, Byron made a voyage to the Falkland Islands and to parts of Tierra del Fuego.

Further British and Spanish expeditions

At the end of the same decade Captain James Cook, spurning the shelter of the Strait of Magellan, rounded Cape Horn in the *Endeavour* before going on to Australia and New Zealand. Cook was an outstanding navigator but had a wider scientific curiosity and enlisted for his voyage two astronomers and the distinguished botanist Joseph Banks.

In terms of comprehensively surveying the South American coast, Cook was surpassed by Alessandro Malaspina. This Italian nobleman sailed around these coasts in the service of Spain between 1789 and 1794, collecting both scientific information and secret political intelligence. Unfortunately for him, his political views were so radical that he was imprisoned on his return and only released after the intervention of Napoleon.

The British navy continued its preoccupation with charting South American waters well into the 19th century.

HMS *Adventure* and HMS *Beagle* sailed in 1826, their captains being instructed "to avail yourself of every opportunity of collecting and preserving specimens of such objects of natural history as may be new, rare or interesting."

Lieutenant Robert Fitzroy, who took over command of the *Beagle* after her original captain committed suicide, also led the *Beagle*'s subsequent, even more ambitious, survey voyage between 1831 and 1836. Like Cook, Fitzroy also recruited a naturalist in the person of Charles Darwin, whose deductions from the voyage were to make it one of the most memorable in the annals of discovery (see pages 110–11).

The activities of British naval officers were not confined to the high seas. Some of the most daring journeys and most graphic accounts of travel in the High Andes were the work of officers such as Captain Basil Hall (1820–22) and Lieutenant Charles Brand (1827).

Scientific expeditions on land

As the 19th century progressed, there was increasing emphasis on scientific expeditions on land. Two Bavarians, the zoologist Johann Baptist von Spix and the botanist Philip von Martius, came to Brazil in 1817 with the Archduchess Leopoldina, who arrived to marry the future emperor Dom Pedro. Spix was to study the aboriginal inhabitants and the climate as well as the fauna, Martius the climate, soil, and flora. They explored the rich gold–mining valleys around Ouro Preto in the south of Brazil, then moved up to the Amazon basin where Martius nearly died in a canoe capsize. They returned to Bavaria in 1820, having sent home 85 species of mammals, 350 of birds, 130 of amphibians, 116 of fish, 2700 of insects, and 6500 of plants.

Much less scientific and reliable was the flamboyant English naturalist Charles Waterton, who wandered in the Guianas between 1812 and 1824. He fished for alligators with shark hooks; he rode on the back of a giant cayman, seizing its front legs "as a bridle"; he wrestled with a boa constrictor, securing its jaws with his braces. Nothing, one feels, was lost in the telling.

The American William H. Edwards spent eight months on the Amazon in 1846, a region which he dramatically described as one where "the mightiest of rivers rolls majestically through primeval forests of boundless extent ... where gold has tempted, and Amazonian women repulsed, the unprincipled adventurer; and where Jesuit missionaries, and luckless traders, have fallen victims to cannibal Indians and epicurean anacondas."

Charting nature's riches

Alfred Russell Wallace and Henry Walter Bates set off together for the Amazon in 1848 and were soon joined by another British naturalist, Richard Spruce. Between them the three men spent 32 years on the Amazon and its tributaries. Wallace – like Darwin – developed ideas on evolution. Bates alone collected over 14,000 different species of insects of which 8000 were new to science. Spruce sent back over 30,000 plant specimens to most of the leading natural history museums and universities of Europe. He also mapped much of the 10,000 miles (16,000 kilometers) of river and stream which he navigated by

Anson 1740–44
Byron 1764
Cook 1768–69
Malaspina 1789–94

coberta (a covered canoe). Moreover, he classified 21 vocabularies of Amazonian Indian languages.

While collecting all this material, the naturalists survived repeated bouts of malaria and dysentery, and had frequent narrow escapes from the more aggressive varieties of natives and wildlife. Bates's canoe was attacked one night by an anaconda, which hammered a hole in the chicken coop on board with its head and then ate a couple of hens. Wallace almost stumbled over a black jaguar on one occasion, and Spruce awoke in his hammock with a fever to hear his bearers plotting to kill him and make off with his "trade goods" – the stock of mirrors, beads, and trinkets which he took for barter purposes.

They did not allow these hazards to interfere with the regular routine of field research and the maintenance of Victorian standards of dress and self-discipline. They drank their "sundowners" of *cachaça* at dusk while the Indians washed their "forest suits" and laid out their butterfly nets and ammonia bottles.

At the same time they were also struggling financially. Bates's agent gave him four pence a specimen and took 20 percent commission on the deal, which meant that after 20 months of work Bates's total profit was £27. Spruce saw the whole of his meager savings disappear after 12 years' work when the Guayaquil bank, with which he had deposited it, failed. Wallace lost all his collections from six years' effort when the ship in which he was returning to England caught fire and sank. There were times when their funds from home did not arrive, and they were reduced to borrowing to survive at all. Their subsequent books give a vivid picture of those practical difficulties of life as well as of the dramatic risks.

On their return to England they were recognized for the work they had done: Bates became the first paid secretary of the Royal Geographical Society in London as well as a fellow of the Royal Society. Wallace went on to work in Southeast Asia (see page 62), whence he corresponded with Darwin about his own independent ideas on evolution.

Darwin and the *Beagle*

In 1831 Captain Robert Fitzroy set sail in HMS *Beagle* on a voyage, for the British Admiralty, to continue charting the coasts of South America and "to carry a chain of chronometrical measurements round the world." He took with him Charles Darwin, a 22-year-old naturalist who had never been abroad and was never to go again. Darwin was full of enthusiasm to explore the Andes, the pampas, and the virtually unknown offshore islands: the Falklands, Tierra del Fuego, and the Galápagos.

Darwin's explorations on land (for it had been agreed with Fitzroy before they left that he should be able to leave

KEY TO ROUTES

— Darwin/*Beagle* 1831–36

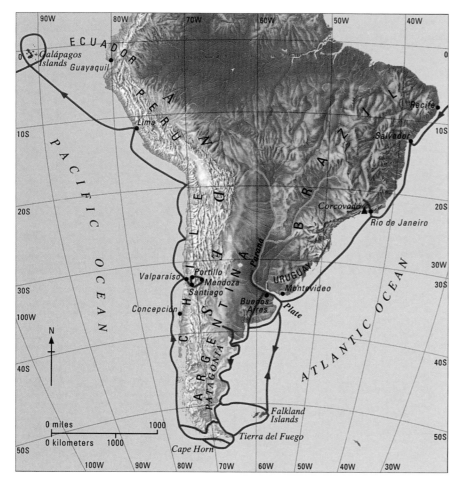

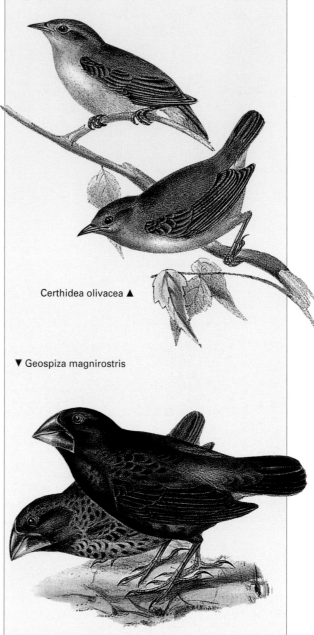

Certhidea olivacea ▲

▼ Geospiza magnirostris

▶ **Charles Darwin** *was 22 years old when he was offered the post of naturalist on HMS* Beagle. *The observations that he made during the voyage were the main inspiration behind his theory of evolution by natural selection, one of the great theories in the history of science, first published in his book* On the Origin of Species by Means of Natural Selection *(1859).*

Galápagos finches

Darwin was amazed by the number of different species of finch on the Galápagos Islands, and the variety of their beaks. On one island the birds had developed beaks suitable for feeding on fruits and flowers; on another they had thick strong beaks for cracking nuts and seeds; on yet another the beaks were smaller to make it easier to catch insects. It was clear that the birds had evolved these different beaks in response to the different types of food that were available on the islands. Darwin went on to conclude that they had been able to develop in this way because they were the first birds to make the journey from the mainland to the islands, and so had not had any competitors for food and water. The woodpecker-type of finch, for example, had been able to evolve because there was no mainland woodpecker already established on the Galápagos. Isolation had led to the development of new species.

◄ *Darwin* was immediately impressed and intrigued by the birds of the tropical forests, such as the Toco toucan (*Ramphastus toco*), when he explored the area around Salvador on the Brazilian coast in 1832.

► *When the* **Beagle** visited the Falkland Islands in February 1833, Darwin recorded great numbers of foxes (*Canis antarcticus*) which were fearless enough to harass the men in the party that went ashore.

the ship for lengthy periods) included many adventures. He climbed Corcovado at Rio de Janeiro. He explored in small boats and on land among the channels of Tierra del Fuego, nearly getting stranded on one occasion. He set off with gauchos on horseback across the Argentine pampas. He hunted ostriches in Patagonia and shot a condor in Chile. He traversed the Andes, where he suffered mountain sickness in the high passes between Portillo and Mendoza; he rode a giant tortoise in the Galápagos and "found it a very wobbly seat."

While participating in all these innocent adventures, Darwin was keenly observing and taking notes all the time. His studies at Cambridge had extended to geology and entomology as well as natural history. He amassed a large collection of insects in Rio and an even larger collection of fossils in Patagonia. Indeed, he commented that "we may conclude that the whole area of the pampas is one wide sepulcher of ... extinct giant quadrupeds." He became convinced that the Andes had been below the waters of the ocean and had been thrust upward. This conclusion owed much to the sea fossils he found high in the mountains and to his noting the frailty of the Earth's shell during a particularly severe earthquake at Concepción in Chile.

The seeds of an idea

It was in the Galápagos Islands, however, that Darwin experienced the first inklings of his later theories about the process of natural selection and the common origin of species. He was impressed by the variety of wildlife, and when he looked at his many specimens he was struck by the fact that the majority belonged to species which, while resembling other species in South America, were unique to the islands.

He also discovered that the species differed from island to island, although many were only 50 to 60 miles (80 to 90 kilometers) apart. These differences, he deduced, could only have developed in an environment where creatures were without predators or competitors for food and water, and so could gradually evolve in ways best suited to local conditions. This led him to question the accepted current belief in the creation of unchangeable species as described in the Book of Genesis. As he wrote in his journal, "In July opened first notebook on Transmutation of Species. Had been greatly struck from about the month of previous March on character of South American fossils, and species on Galápagos Archipelago. These facts (especially the latter) origin of all my views."

All this collecting and theorizing placed a considerable strain on Captain Fitzroy, whose cabin Darwin shared. The decks of the *Beagle* became littered with bones, rocks, plants, skins of birds, and even rotting fish and fungi.

Worse than the disconcerting clutter was the extemely disconcerting talk. Fitzroy was a devout Christian and a fundamentalist: he sincerely believed every word of the Bible to be the literal truth. Darwin had himself been intended for a career in the Church, but now he was beginning to doubt. Could the Creation possibly have taken place as late as 4004 BC (the date confidently expounded by the Church)? Could the flood really have covered the Earth and Noah's Ark rescued all the surviving species? And could the heavens and the Earth, and all that dwelt therein, conceivably have been created in seven days? Fitzroy, who was already deeply disappointed at his inability to implant a missionary in Tierra del Fuego, began to feel he was harboring a religious subversive in the person of Darwin.

It took many years for Darwin to digest and record all the results of what turned out to be a five-year voyage. When eventually he published his *On the Origin of Species by Means of Natural Selection* in 1859, it was followed the next year by a public debate in Oxford in which Darwin's supporters argued the issues with Dr Wilberforce and other leading clerics. The meeting was interrupted by an elderly gray-haired man who denounced Darwin and all his works: he was Vice-Admiral Robert Fitzroy, late of HMS *Beagle*.

▼ *The* **Beagle***'s artist,* Conrad Martens, painted this watercolor of native people visiting the Beagle off the coast of Tierra del Fuego.

The High Andes

▲ **Edward Whymper** climbed most of the outstanding peaks of Ecuador, but he was most proud of his discoveries about ways of avoiding mountain sickness.

Edward Whymper, who had become Europe's most celebrated alpinist in 1865 by reaching the summit of the Matterhorn, arrived at Guayaquil in Ecuador in 1879 to explore the Andes. His particular interest was the problem of mountain sickness, which appeared to afflict mountaineers worse in South America than at comparable heights in Europe.

Whymper's ascents

On his arrival Whymper left directly for Chimborazo, the peak which had so narrowly defeated Baron von Humboldt nearly 80 years earlier. Traveling through this unsettled country, Whymper subsequently wrote in his *Travels Amongst the Great Andes of the Equator* that he believed in "adopting a policy of non-intervention in all that did not concern us … trusting more to our wits than to our credentials, and believing that a jest may conquer where force will fail, that a *bon-mot* is often better than a passport."

By the time Whymper had reached his second camp on the mountain, the altitude was indeed affecting him and his companions far worse than it had in the Alps. Despite feeling feverish and suffering severe headaches, they continued to scale the western summit, only to find that it was lower than the eastern one. They crossed the intervening plateau and conquered the true summit of Chimborazo, finally returning to camp in pitch darkness.

Whymper next turned his attention to the volcano of Cotopaxi. As they ascended the slope, the party found that volcanic ash was penetrating their clothing, ears, eyes, and nostrils. They camped as near the steaming mouth of the volcano as they dared, but found that the rubber sheet of their tent floor was melting on lava at a temperature of

▲ **Edward Whymper** captioned this illustration of his mountain camp in the Andes as his "bedroom" and his "kitchen."

▶ **In the course of his expeditions** to find the lost Inca cities, Hiram Bingham had to cross several rope bridges over deep gorges.

110°F (43°C). Whymper crawled to the rim of the volcano at night and looked at the glowing molten mass below.

He climbed most of the other outstanding peaks of Ecuador, discovered unknown glaciers, took measurements of heights, and collected rare mountain plants, butterflies, and even earthworms. But he saw his most important achievement in the area of his original interest – mountain sickness. He established that this was related to atmospheric pressure – the barometer had dropped to 14 inches (35 centimeters) on the summit of Chimborazo – and made recommendations to aid future climbers.

Bingham's discovery of Machu Picchu

The Andes had a very different appeal for Hiram Bingham, a young American lecturer in Latin American history at Yale University, with a particular interest in the Incas. Following Pizarro's brutal conquest of the Incas in 1532, the Spaniards had installed Manco as a puppet ruler. He, however, had led an unsuccessful rising against the Spaniards in 1537 and then fled to the western watershed of the upper Urubamba River, where he had established the cities of Vilcabamba and Vitcos.

Eventually the Spaniards had succeeded in invading Vilcabamba, and Manco's youngest and only surviving son, Tupac Amaru, had been carried off to Cuzco and beheaded. The Inca civilization had finally come to an end.

In 1908 Bingham and a friend set out to explore the Inca fastnesses on muleback, hoping to find the lost Inca cities of Vilcabamba and Vitcos. After four days' ride from Cuzco, the terrain became more difficult, with the trail sometimes being so steep that they were forced to crawl on hands and knees. They cut through dense undergrowth and bamboo thickets, and eventually found an impressive Inca ruin – but not Vilcabamba or Vitcos.

Bingham returned in 1911 with a larger expedition from Yale. From the Urubamba Valley he was guided to the top of one of the neighboring mountains, where he was rewarded with "an unexpected sight, a great flight of beautifully constructed stone-faced terraces, perhaps a hundred of them, each hundreds of feet long and ten feet high . . . suddenly I found myself confronted with the walls of ruined houses built of the finest quality of Inca stone work . . . hiding in bamboo thickets and tangled vines, appeared here and there walls of white granite ashlars carefully cut and exquisitely fitted together." The ruins were overshadowed by a towering sugar-loaf peak called by the locals Huayna Picchu, and the name Machu Picchu was promptly given to the ruins themselves. Bingham was convinced that he had found the lost Inca capital of Vilcabamba.

Bingham was determined to find Vitcos as well, which had been originally described as having close by it "a temple of the sun and inside it a white stone above a spring of water." He was taken to sites with smaller white rocks, sites with larger non-white rocks, and other rocks that overlooked caves rather than springs – the whole Urubamba Valley seemed to be riddled with Inca sites.

Bingham persevered. He knew that Vitcos was reputed to have wonderful views and ornate buildings. Eventually, on a high ridge, he found just such a set of Inca ruins, with "the lintels of the doors being of marble and elaborately cut." He was at once convinced that this place, called

Rosaspata, was Vitcos. When his Indian guides led him to a gigantic white granite boulder above a dark mysterious pool and ornamented with Inca carvings amid the ruins of a temple, Bingham was sure that this was the sacred spot he sought. Its position so close to the ruins confirmed the identity of Vitcos.

Bingham returned to the Urubamba Valley the following year, where his associates cleared the vegetation from the terraces of Machu Picchu while he continued to explore for fresh sites. He never repeated his extraordinary luck of the previous year, but he did go on to find other Inca remains, notably at Espíritu Pampa.

The last Inca capital

Another American explorer, Gene Savoy, returned to Espíritu Pampa in 1964 and 1965, and found that it was far more extensive than Bingham had realized. It had to be this site, and not Machu Picchu, which was the last, lost capital of the Incas. The location was correct, and it was at the right altitude (much lower and warmer than Machu Picchu). The ruined buildings fitted more closely to contemporary descriptions, and its sheer size suggested a capital. Lastly – and most macabrely – its position close to a navigable stretch of the river would have made it possible for Pizarro to have floated down it a sinister message in 1539 (as he was reputed to have done): the body of Manco's murdered wife, Cura Ocllo, in a basket.

The last capital of the Incas had been found, but exploration in the forests and gulleys around the Urubamba still continues. The hazards that beset Bingham and his predecessors still persist, suggesting that the remaining mysteries of the Incas are not to be revealed to the faint-hearted.

▲ *Machu Picchu was almost certainly one of the last strongholds of the Incas in the mountains which, in the 16th century, the Spaniards found virtually impenetrable. Hiram Bingham mistakenly thought it was the lost city of Vilcabamba when he first saw it in 1911.*

Explorers in the 20th Century

▲ *In 1925 Colonel Fawcett, seen here at his camp in Mato Grosso, was intent on further exploration of the forest, despite having lost companions on previous expeditions to boa constrictors and piranhas. The horses could not be used in the dense terrain and had to be sent back at the outset of his final fatal journey.*

Percy Fawcett, a British army colonel, was a life-long explorer of the Mato Grosso region of Brazil and the tributaries of the Amazon, but he is best remembered for having disappeared there without trace in 1925.

Having undertaken mapping and frontier surveys on the Brazilian–Bolivian border, Fawcett became intrigued with the possibility of finding the ruined city of El Dorado in the Amazon jungle. He had read an 18th-century manuscript which described in detail a city of romantic riches with gold and silver artifacts, "great arches, so high that none could read the inscriptions on them," columns and statues – all awaiting discovery.

Fawcett set out in April 1925 on an expedition to explore the unknown forests between the center of Brazil and the east coast. He kept his precise route a secret, which made the Brazilian authorities suspect him of prospecting for oil on behalf of an international company. He was also known to be a mystic and a scientist, so some people thought he was seeking for hidden sources of solar energy.

There was no navigable river whose course Fawcett could follow, and the terrain was totally unsuited to pack animals, so his equipment was restricted to what he and his two companions (his 22-year-old son and his son's friend) could carry. At first he sent back a few messages, but then total silence descended. No one worried at first – after all, he had said he might be away for a year or two.

The search for Fawcett

Eventually, in 1928, an American press syndicate financed a rescue operation. This came back with some trinkets that might have belonged to Fawcett, and with reports that he and his companions had probably been killed by Indians on or near the Culuene River. According to other reports, a white man was supposedly held captive by Indians. A Swiss trapper claimed to have met an English colonel in the depths of Mato Grosso; an American missionary found a white child allegedly fathered by Fawcett's son.

A Brazilian anthropologist living with the Kalapalo tribe was regaled by a story – 25 years after the event – of how this tribe had been provoked by Fawcett and had clubbed him to death; they even handed over some bones which they claimed were Fawcett's. The bones were brought back to England, examined by experts, and found

not to be those of Fawcett – nor even of a European at all. To this day the precise circumstances of Fawcett's death are shrouded in mystery.

Following the course of the Amazon

Since the Second World War many young explorers have been drawn to South America, one of the last regions with access to the unknown, which – as Sir Walter Raleigh had said three centuries before – "hath still her maidenhood."

In 1950 a young Englishman called Sebastian Snow decided to travel from a point which he confidently claimed to be the source of the Amazon in the Peruvian Andes to its mouth at Belém some 3500 miles (5500 kilometers) away. As early as 1541, Francisco de Orellana had pursued the course of the river to the Atlantic Ocean. But what made Snow's trip remarkable was that he started so high up the river and intended to keep to the actual valley of the Marañón (the Amazon's principal source) for 500 miles (800 kilometers) before the river was reckoned to become navigable.

Snow took over nine months to accomplish the first 1250 miles (2000 kilometers) of the journey, either struggling along a trackless river bank or encountering repeated setbacks in canoes and rafts while negotiating the cataracts. (He could not swim and was therefore particularly vulnerable to capsizes.) Eventually he reached Belém, weakened by dysentery and malnutrition, but his spirit was to inspire followers.

Margaret Mee

From the mid-1950s to the late 1980s the botanist and explorer Margaret Mee – who only began her Amazonian travels at the age of 47 – undertook a series of canoe journeys up the more remote tributaries of the Amazon: the Arinos, the Içana, the Tefé, the Maués, the Araçá, and many others. She always had her sketchbook and easel with her to record in exquisite watercolors the exotic flowers of the rain forests. Her collection of paintings is now preserved at Kew Gardens in England.

KEY TO ROUTES

—— Fawcett 1925
—— Snow 1951–52
—— Hanbury-Tenison 1958
—— Hanbury-Tenison 1964–65

Crossing the continent

Later in the 1950s two Oxford undergraduates, Richard Mason and Robin Hanbury-Tenison, decided to take a jeep across South America at its widest point, from Recife on the Atlantic coast of Brazil to Lima on the Pacific coast of Peru. They knew there were few roads in the interior of Mato Grosso, but reckoned that they might find tracks between native villages. In this they were overoptimistic: having floated their jeep on a raft across the Araguaia River to the world's largest inland island of Bananal, they lurched through rough scrub country until the jeep's chassis broke decisively. Hanbury-Tenison continued alone through the country of the uncertain-tempered Karajá Indians to find help. Mason remained behind to guard the remnants of the jeep and their provisions.

After days of lonely travel on foot, swimming the rivers he encountered, Hanbury-Tenison returned with help. In the mended jeep the two men pressed on through the territory of the warrior Xavante tribe, passing the starting point of Colonel Fawcett's last journey. They skirted the swamps of the Pantanal, had their jeep towed by oxen through the Banadoz of Izozog in Bolivia, and eventually reached their destination. Richard Mason later returned with his friend John Hemming to find the unexplored Iriri River in the heart of Mato Grosso, but was brutally killed with arrows and clubs by a hitherto unknown tribe, the Kreen-Akrore.

Undeterred by Mason's death, Snow and Hanbury-Tenison returned yet again to South America in the 1960s. They set out in an inflatable rubber dinghy with two powerful outboard motors from the mouth of the River Orinoco in Venezuela to follow the Amazon river system to the mouth of the River Plate 6000 miles (9750 kilometers) away in Argentina. Snow became ill soon after the start of the journey and had to go home, leaving Hanbury-Tenison to complete an eight-month journey on his own. He arrived at Buenos Aires to be hailed as "El Intrépido."

▼ *Among the many indigenous peoples in the forests of Brazil are the Yanomamo. They have a reputation for warfare, and in some areas it is customary for the men to raid each other's villages, partly in order to kidnap women and children.*

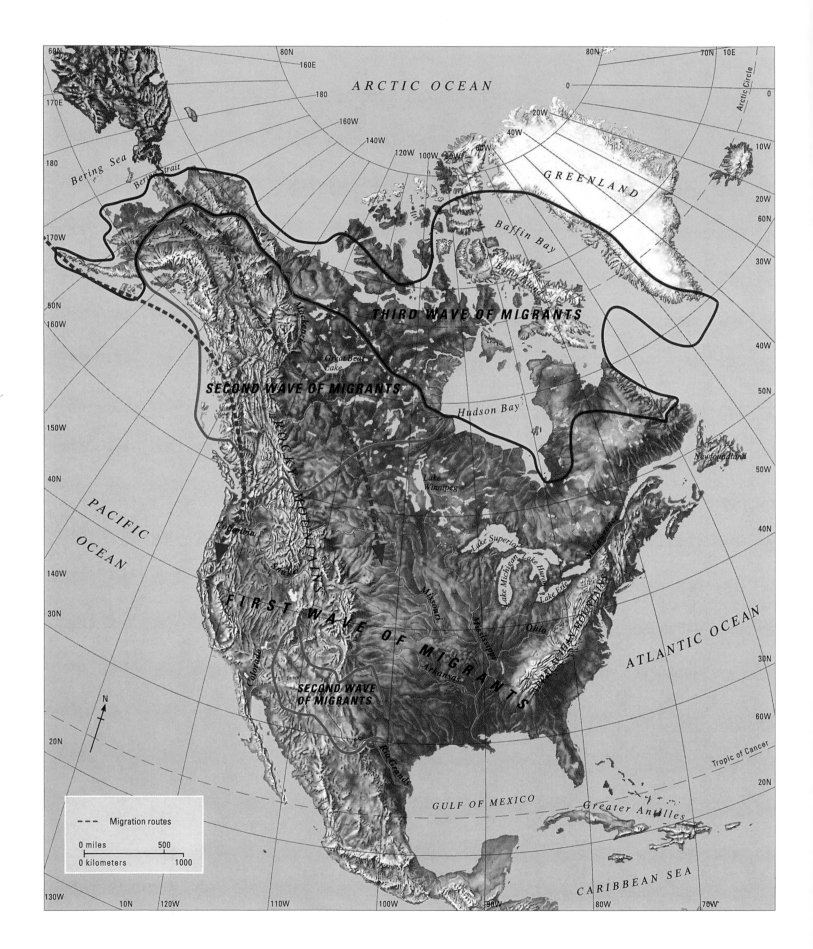

ARCTIC OCEAN

GREENLAND

Bering Sea

Bering Strait

Yukon

Baffin Bay

Baffin Island

THIRD WAVE OF MIGRANTS

Mackenzie

Great Bear Lake

SECOND WAVE OF MIGRANTS

Hudson Bay

Newfoundland

Lake Winnipeg

PACIFIC OCEAN

ROCKY MOUNTAINS

Columbia

Snake

Lake Superior

St. Lawrence

Lake Michigan Lake Huron

Lake Erie

FIRST WAVE OF MIGRANTS

Missouri

Mississippi

Ohio

APPALACHIAN MOUNTAINS

ATLANTIC OCEAN

Colorado

Arkansas

N

SECOND WAVE OF MIGRANTS

Rio Grande

Tropic of Cancer

GULF OF MEXICO

Greater Antilles

Migration routes

0 miles   500

0 kilometers   1000

CARIBBEAN SEA

Arctic Circle

NORTH
AMERICA

The first people to explore and settle in North America migrated east from Siberia across the Ice Age land bridge to Alaska – a bridge now submerged under the Bering Strait – about 14,000 years ago. From the northwest they migrated southward, passing either through the corridor which opened up east of the Rockies between two receding ice sheets, or along the Pacific west coast (any evidence of which is now submerged by up to 300 feet/100 meters of water).

The first wave of migrants progressed with astonishing speed, considering their initial lack of any traditional knowledge about the geography or ecology of the lands they were exploring, and it took barely 1000 years for the southern tip of South America to be reached. Their descendants are the contemporary speakers of over 500 different Amerind languages in the southern part of North America and in Central and South America. They were soon followed by a second wave of migrants whose descendants are speakers of languages in the Na-Dene group. The ancestors of the Inuit in the far north – speakers of the Eskimo-Aleut group of languages – migrated some time in the last 4000–8000 years into Alaska and northern Canada, and ultimately to Greenland.

Hunting, gathering, and fishing remained the basis of society in many areas up to the time of first contact with Europeans in the 16th century. The Europeans were to find that the American Indians had created networks of trails, which were often worn deep from use. Also evident was the existence of American Indian traditions of producing maps of the landscape. These were used by European pioneers exploring the continent, but were reportedly restricted to ephemeral materials – scratchings in the sand or the ashes of a fire, charcoal sketches on bark, or paintings on deerskin. A map of Virginia drawn in 1612 by John Smith, an English explorer, instructs the reader "that as far as you can see the little Crosses on rivers, mountaines, or other places have been discovered; the rest was had by information of the *savages*, and are set downe according to their instructions."

Norse Discoveries

▶ **Leif Eiríksson,** who sailed to North America in 1003, was described by The Greenlanders' Saga as "tall and strong and very impressive in appearance ... a shrewd man and always moderate in his behavior." This idealized picture contains a number of inaccuracies: no trading vessel, for example, carried shields over the gunwales while at sea.

In the late 9th and early 10th centuries AD Iceland was discovered and colonized by Norsemen of Viking background from Scandinavia and the British Isles. By about AD 900 they had discovered and explored the east coast of Greenland, but the successful colonization of the fjords of southwest Greenland by Icelanders from the West Quarter only began in 986, supplied thereafter by merchant ships from Iceland.

The Greenlanders' Saga, written in Iceland in the late 12th century, reports that the crew of a ship commanded by Bjarni Herjolfsson, sailing from the Eyrar in southwest Iceland to join the Greenland colony in 986, were the first Europeans to see and describe the coast of North America. They were storm-driven south of Greenland into a region of sea fogs – perhaps the banks of Newfoundland – and on regaining their bearings the crew did not immediately sail northeast to their intended destination. Instead they sailed north along an extensive western shore and made three landfalls which were described as "land covered with forest and low hills," "a flat country covered with woods" and "a land high, mountainous, and glaciered." These phrases represent the first European descriptions of North American shores.

The Vinland expeditions

After Bjarni Herjolfsson had made his discoveries it is recorded that at least two other landfalls on the North American coast were made, both probably related to attempts to reach the Greenland colony from Iceland. However, according to *The Greenlanders' Saga,* true exploration only began around 1003 when Leif Eiríksson sailed from the Eastern Settlement in Greenland to retrace Herjolfsson's discoveries in reverse order. In doing so, he named Herjolfsson's third landfall Helluland, and observed "no grass; hinterland all great glaciers; a single great slab of rock right up to the glaciers from the sea; land barren and useless." The second, which had "white sandy beaches shelving gently down to the sea" he named Markland. According to *Eirik the Red's Saga,* written in the late 12th century, there was also "an open harborless coast with long beaches and sands" – the Furdustrandir or "Marvelstrands"

– and a cape, Kjalarnes, succeeded southward by an indented coastline. Herjolfsson's third landfall was a north-pointing promontory with a grassy island offshore and a shallow bay to the west, to which Eiríksson gave the name of Vinland. Here he and his men built Leifsbúdir – Leif's Settlement – explored the locality, felled and seasoned timber, and overwintered. Leifsbúdir became the center of Eiríksson's land claim and the base for further exploration.

Two further expeditions from Greenland to Leifsbúdir, led respectively by Leif's brother Thorvald Eiríksson and by Thórfinn Thordarson, a merchant from Iceland, extended the area of exploration west, north, and southeast between 1005 and 1012. The most southerly point reached was a double fjord divided by a forest–covered headland, Krossanes, nominated as a second land claim. Both expeditions encountered native American peoples and became involved in hostilities in the course of their efforts to trade for furs and extract timber to supply the needs of the growing Greenland colony. Like all the other voyages of the late 10th and early 11th centuries, they were made in clinker-built, broadbeamed merchant ships which were very different from the Norse longships used for coastal navigation in Europe.

Norse settlement in Newfoundland

The only evidence of Norse settlement that has so far been discovered is on a raised beach above Épaves Bay near L'Anse aux Meadows, on the northern tip of Newfoundland. First excavated by the Norwegian scholars Helge and Anne Stine Ingstad in the early 1960s, and dating from about AD 1000, the site consists of three complexes of houses and outbuildings, with a charcoal- and slag-filled forge. These may be the remains of Leifsbúdir. If so, Vinland can be identified with northern Newfoundland, Markland with the southern coasts of Labrador and the North Shore of the Gulf of St Lawrence, the Furdustrandir and Kjalarnes with the long beaches on either side of Cape Porcupine, and Helluland with northern Labrador and the eastern shore of Baffin Island as far north as Cape Dyer. Krossanes may be the low headland that divides Canada

Bay into Chimney Bay and Bide Arm, partway down the eastern side of Newfoundland's Northern Peninsula.

Archeological evidence of the presence of the Norsemen in North America has also been found on Skraeling Island, off Ellesmere Island, in the form of fragments of chainmail armor, iron knife-blades and boat-rivets, copper fragments, woolen cloth, and a circular bone gaming piece.

Later attempts at exploration

The colony in Newfoundland was short-lived and Norse exploration of the North American coast seems to have been abandoned in the 11th century. In 1121 Eirík Gnúpsson, the Iceland-born "Greenlanders' bishop," made an exploratory voyage from Greenland "in search of Vinland," probably as part of his assessment of the material resources available to support the erection of a new diocese, but nothing is known of the outcome of this expedition. In 1347, according to the annals of Skalholt, a Greenland vessel, storm-driven from Markland, arrived in Iceland. This solitary record suggests that the Greenland Norse may have maintained occasional contact with southern Labrador, probably for purposes of cutting timber or fur-trading, rather than exploration. However, these visits appear to have been so few and far between that they left no imprint on the native peoples or the landscape.

In 1360 the surviving colony of Greenland Norse in the Eastern Settlement was visited by an English Minorite or Franciscan friar, a mathematician of Oxford and "a good astronomer," who "journeyed through the North, described all the places that he saw, and took the height [latitude] of them with his astrolabe, and put into writing all the wonders of those islands, and gave the King of England [Edward III] a book which he called *Inventio Fortunatae*, which began at ... latitude 54°, continuing to the Pole." If there is any truth in this account, it would appear that the Englishman made an exploratory survey of Baffin Bay and North American shores as far south as Cape Porcupine (54°N) in southern Labrador. He was undoubtedly assisted by the Greenland Norse.

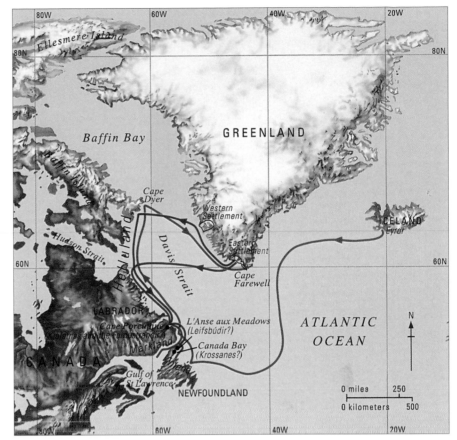

KEY TO ROUTES

— Bjarni Herjolfsson
— Leif Eiríksson
— Thorvald Eiríksson

Between 1350 and 1500 the Norse colony in Greenland declined and died, putting an end to the possibility of any further exploration of North America from a base in Greenland. It was only when, at the end of the 15th century, Europeans became determined to find a new westward route to China and the East Indies that the exploration of the vast lands on the western side of the Atlantic began in earnest.

◄ *Newfoundland* was explored by Norsemen at a time when the climate was several degrees warmer than it is today, but the natural vegetation was very similar. It was once thought that in the 11th century wild grapes grew in the area known as Vinland, but this idea has now been completely discredited.

Early Exploration of the East Coast

John Cabot's voyage to
America in 1497 (below) was
to have huge implications
for European fishermen
(opposite). His description

of the plentiful fish attracted
them in ever-increasing
numbers to the waters of
Newfoundland, particularly
from the 1520s onward.

▼ *Giovanni da Verrazzano*
charted the coastline
between Cape Fear and
Newfoundland in his search
for a passage to the Pacific
in 1524.

▼ *Ponce de León,* his health
broken by a two-year
campaign in Puerto Rico,
discovered Florida in 1513
during a futile search for
a "fountain of youth."

The first documented transatlantic voyage to have provided posterity with the name of a ship and an approximate date of the ship's arrival on the northeastern coast of North America is that of John Cabot's *Mathew,* which sailed west from England in May 1497. Exactly where the Genoese Cabot landed, toward the end of June, is uncertain, but according to a letter written by an English merchant, John Day, a few months after Cabot's return, he appears to have followed the coastline approximately between the northern tip of Newfoundland (the Strait of Belle Isle) and the southern coast of Cape Breton Island (the Strait of Canso).

John Cabot's achievements

This portion of the Atlantic seaboard of North America, a sailing distance of approximately 600–700 miles (1000–1150 kilometers) which the *Mathew* covered in about a month, was the eastern rim of the region known throughout most of the 16th century as "Terranova" or "Les Terres Neuves." Cabot was, of course, convinced that he had found the land of the Great Khan. However, whether or not his New Land really was part of China or of the coast that led toward Cipangu (Japan), or whether it was simply the "Island of Brasil" or some other island, a sufficiently convincing picture of the new "Londe and Iles" emerged from the various accounts of his 1497 voyage for the English King Henry VII to believe that the New Land existed, and to reward Cabot accordingly.

Even though Cabot had brought back no spices or precious stones on his first voyage, he had seen tall trees suitable for masts and signs of human habitation such as animal snares, a hearth, and a needle. Above all, he and his crew had been deeply impressed by an incredible quantity of fish of the sort called stockfish, that "in Iceland are dried in the open." Cabot's description of these fish soon reached Spain and Italy, and within a few years Terranova cod was having a sensational effect on the lives of many European fishermen, particularly, to begin with, the Portuguese, Bretons, and Normans.

Whatever illusions Cabot may have had, it is clear that practical fishermen can hardly have thought they were fishing off the shores of China or Japan. In Spain and Portugal part of the New Land was known in the early years of the 16th century as the "Tierra de los bacallaos"("The Codfish Land") and was placed on maps just to the southwest of the "Tierra del Labrador". It is also clear that a voyage to these new fishing grounds was not considered much more adventurous than a voyage to Ireland for Iberian mariners or a voyage to Iceland for English merchants. For instance, according to John Day's account, it had only taken 15 days for Cabot to return to England from the New Found Land. The extra distance on the outward voyage, of a month or more, was normally compensated for by excellent profits.

It was not long before Cabot's successful expedition had encouraged further exploratory travels, particularly by inhabitants of the Azores. These voyages, some under the patronage of the English King Henry VII and some under Portuguese auspices, gradually gave cartographers a set of place names for the coasts of the northwest Atlantic. Within a dozen years of Cabot's first voyage, the names of Gaspar and Miguel Corte Real, and of Johan Fernandez, who was known as the "Labrador" or Azorean landowner, were commemorated on maps as "Terra Corte Regalis" or "Tierra Nova de Cortereal" and the "Terra de Lavoradore."

It is not possible to distinguish accurately which of the Portuguese names that became part of the nomenclature of the Newfoundland coast were given, for instance, by the Corte Real brothers, and which were names that became permanently attached to capes, islands, and harbors because of fishermen's usage. Nevertheless, it is quite probable that religious names such as the Eleven Thousand Virgins, St Pedro or St Iria were given by explorers, whereas the small harbors on the Avalon Peninsula between Cape Spear (Cabo de Espera) and Cape Race (Cabo Raso) were almost certainly named by Portuguese fishermen. As they found it necessary to recognize and remember the outstanding physical features of a place, such as sandy beaches, waterfalls visible from the sea, or distinctive promontories, names were often copied from similar toponyms in Europe. Since it was the onshore cod fishing that first attacted European fishermen, familiarity with the harbors of southeast Newfoundland was achieved rapidly. Although mariners were well aware of the existence of the Grand Banks, it was not until the second half of the century that anyone wanted to fish in the open Atlantic, far away from wood and water.

Charting the coastline

From 1502 to 1524 all effective exploring and naming of the Atlantic coasts of Canada was accomplished by fishermen, while in 1513 Juan Ponce de León, the Spanish colonizer of Puerto Rico, discovered and named "La Florida." A series of men with royal approbation and support then started to fill in areas of the map that were still blank. Giovanni da Verrazzano, in 1524, and Esteban Gómez, in 1524–25, under French and Spanish auspices respectively, provided a long stretch of eastern America from Florida to Cape Breton with place names and a reasonably accurate coastline. Both men were seeking a strait or waterway that would lead to the western ocean. However, by the time they had finished their voyages, neither explorer thought there was any real break in the coastline and most navigators had begun to feel that the only hope of a passage through to the western ocean or Sea of China would be in the higher latitudes of the northern hemisphere. When, in 1525, Luis Vásquez de Ayllón put ashore at Cape Fear, in what is now South Carolina, and then followed the coast to Winyah Bay, he did so with the intention of establishing the colony of San Miguel de Gualdape. The colony did not survive beyond 1527.

John Rut

In 1527 John Rut started out with two ships belonging to King Henry VIII of England, the *Mary Guildford* and the *Samson*, and made a voyage which eventually took him from a point off the Labrador coast, at 53°N, south to Santo Domingo on the island of Hispaniola in the Caribbean. According to one of the Spanish witnesses who saw Rut's ship in the West Indies, this English expedition, like the less well-documented voyage of Sebastian Cabot in 1508–9, had attempted to find a strait through to Tartary, or the kingdom of the Great Khan, by following the northern fringes of the American continent, but "great islands of ice" had blocked their passage.

One of the important features of Rut's account is the information he provides about the number of ships fishing in Newfoundland waters. He wrote to Henry VIII that he had found, in the "Haven of St John" on August 3, 1527, 14 ships (11 Normans, one Breton, and two Portuguese) using the harbor, while a Spanish witness reported that Rut had seen a total of about 50 Spanish, French, and Portuguese ships along the coast of "Bacallaos." No other English ships were mentioned as fishing that year; only later did English fishermen develop a strong commercial interest in the Newfoundland fisheries.

Most fishermen who crossed the Atlantic were bound for the cod-fishing and the harbors with wide gravel beaches where the fish could be cured and dried. There were, however, a few ships from the Basque ports that were primarily concerned with capturing whales and sailed to the Grand Bay (the Strait of Belle Isle) through which immense numbers migrated annually. But before the Basque whaling industry had become firmly established in the 1540s, a French expedition was sent out by Francis I in 1534 which was to put a huge area to the west of Newfoundland on North American maps.

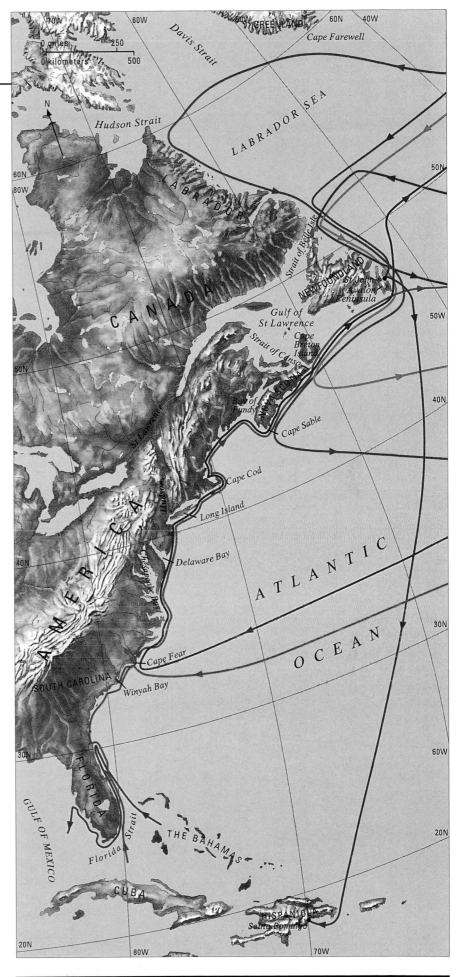

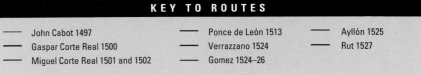

KEY TO ROUTES		
John Cabot 1497	Ponce de León 1513	Ayllón 1525
Gaspar Corte Real 1500	Verrazzano 1524	Rut 1527
Miguel Corte Real 1501 and 1502	Gomez 1524–26	

Penetration from the East Coast

— Cartier 1534
— Cartier 1535–36

▶ *Jacques Cartier's circumnavigation of the Gulf of St Lawrence in 1534, and his journey up the river the following year, did not immediately encourage European settlement but it revolutionized the cartography of the region.*

In April 1534 Jacques Cartier, commissioned by the King of France, set off with two small vessels and 61 men from St Malo in Brittany. On reaching the shores of North America, he sailed through the Strait of Belle Isle into what is now known as the Gulf of St Lawrence. He was the first recorded explorer to leave an account of this area, but he was definitely not the first man to name the harbors in the Strait of Belle Isle. On the southern shore of Labrador, between Chateau Bay and the St Paul River, he mentions eight names which were already in existence when he arrived. His great contribution to the geographical understanding of the North American continent did not begin until he was just to the west of the fishing station at the mouth of the St Paul River, then known as Brest.

Unlike the Portuguese names in southeastern Newfoundland, at least three of the southern Labrador names were transferred toponyms from the west coast of Brittany: Brest, Blanc Sablon, and Crozon (now called Middle Bay). Names from other parts of Brittany, familiar to fishermen, were also given to islands on the northern approaches to the incredible waterway which would allow transatlantic ships to sail nearly 900 miles (1450 kilometers) southwestward into the land that Cartier called New France. However, in the 1530s and 1540s neither cod-fishermen nor whalers had any desire to penetrate further into this waterway since their best fishing grounds were close to the east coast.

Cartier's achievements

At the time of Cartier's second voyage in 1535–36 when, with three ships and 110 men, he reached Hochelaga (Montreal) and wintered at Stadacona (near Quebec), no other explorer in North or South America had followed a waterway so far into the interior of a continental land mass. His Spanish contemporaries – men like Álvar Núñez Cabeza de Vaca and Hernando de Soto – were making strenuous attempts to penetrate into what is now the southern part of the United States, but the usefulness of the Mississippi as a waterway was not appreciated as rapidly as that of the St Lawrence (or the "River of Canada" as it was then called).

In 1542, the same year that Cartier returned to France after his last voyage, Jean Rotz had already depicted on one of the plates of his atlas the great gulf that Cartier had circumnavigated, and in the atlas of Guillaume Brouscon the following year, both a powerful St Lawrence River and a clear-cut Saguenay can be seen. But, by the time Cabeza

— Narváez/Vaca 1528–36
— Soto 1539–43

Hernando de Soto and his men arrived at the Mississippi after dealing ruthlessly with any opposition. Typical of Soto's behavior was the following episode: "Four Indians were taken, not one of whom would say anything ... the Governor (Soto) ordered one of them to be burned; and thereupon another said that two days' journey from there was a province called Cutifachique .... He set out for Cutifachique, capturing three Indians in the road who stated that the mistress of that country had already information of the Christians and was waiting for them in a town. It being discovered that the wish of the Caçica was to leave the Christians, if she could, giving them neither guides nor bearers because of the outrages committed upon the inhabitants ... the Governor ordered that she should be placed under guard and took her with him ... this brought us service in all the places that were passed, she ordering the Indians to come and take the loads from town to town."

de Vaca had completed his horrendous eight-year journey in 1536, it had become evident to Spanish explorers that without water transport the vast area between Florida and Mexico was going to present a very different set of difficulties from those of the St Lawrence Valley. Although Cartier and his men had wintered on land both in 1535–36 and in 1541–42, and had endured two terrible seasons of ice and snow, they had not abandoned their ships and were able to return to Europe after the ice thawed.

Spanish expeditions in Florida

Unlike the waterborne ventures of Juan Ponce de León in 1513 and Luis Vásquez de Ayllón in 1525–26 on the east coast of Florida and South Carolina, the large-scale expedition of Panfilo de Narváez and Álvar Núñez Cabeza de Vaca became totally detached from their original support vessels. Part of the expedition landed on the west coast of Florida near Tampa Bay in April 1528 and marched northward parallel with the coast. Five months later, after many hardships and Indian attacks, members of the expedition – having built five smaller ships on the Florida shore – managed to sail along the northern coast of the Gulf of Mexico until they reached the mouth of the Mississippi. Soon thereafter Narváez and four of the boats were lost, and only Cabeza de Vaca with a small party of men landed in November on the Texan coast near Matagorda Bay, where water transport ended.

Miraculously, Cabeza de Vaca and three companions managed to survive by becoming enslaved to Indian tribes. Passed from one tribe to another through northern Mexico, along the Rio Grande and across the Sierra Madre Occidental, the four men eventually reached the western sea. They were found by a Spanish slaving party and taken back to Mexico City, eight years after the expedition had commenced. When Cabeza de Vaca was brought before the Viceroy of New Spain, Antonio de Mendoza, he soon aroused a new interest in northward exploration.

Hernando de Soto

One more effort was made, however, to penetrate into the hinterland from Florida within little more than a decade after the first attempt by Narváez and Cabeza de Vaca. In 1539 Hernando de Soto landed near Tampa Bay with nine vessels, a large army of more than 600 men, and at least 2000 horses. Since he had accompanied Pizarro on the conquest of Peru, and had received from Charles V the title of "Governor of the island of Cuba and Adelantado of Florida," Soto had developed grandiose plans for bringing what would eventually be a large part of the southern United States under subjugation. Although he and his men crossed the Appalachians and marched through many little kingdoms which had remarkably prosperous farming economies, no gold was found.

Eventually, having traversed the Mississippi on rafts and wintered in the Arkansas valley near Little Rock, Soto returned eastward to the Mississippi where he died in May 1542. His second-in-command, Luis de Moscoso, had boats built in order to float down the Mississippi and along the shores of the Gulf. The army was reduced to almost 300 men by the time it finally arrived in the Mexican town of Pánuco (near Tampico) in September 1543, but as a result of the four-year expedition a large area of the southeastern part of the continent began to be shown on maps by Spanish cartographers.

The Spaniards in the Southwest

KEY TO ROUTES

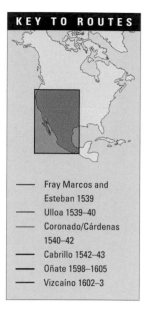

—— Fray Marcos and
    Esteban 1539
—— Ulloa 1539–40
—— Coronado/Cárdenas
    1540–42
—— Cabrillo 1542–43
—— Oñate 1598–1605
—— Vizcaíno 1602–3

Although the earliest known Spanish land expeditions in North America started from Florida, the most effective Spanish exploration of the continental hinterland was based on journeys northwestward from Mexico. Three years after Álvar Núñez Cabeza de Vaca had arrived in Mexico, in 1536, with fabulous legends of northern cities, Antonio de Mendoza, the first Viceroy of New Spain, made plans for an expedition that was to penetrate beyond the Gila River and the Rio Grande.

Fray Marcos and Esteban
In the spring of 1539 a Franciscan friar, Marcos de Niza, who had already been on expeditions in Peru, was sent by Mendoza as leader of a small exploratory party to find out about the rumored Seven Cities. The party included another Franciscan friar, Honoratus, and a number of Indians and slaves, including the African Esteban. One of the four known survivors from Cabeza de Vaca's expedition, Esteban was the only non-Indian member of Niza's party who already knew the country that lay between the Sierra Madre Occidental and the Gulf of

California. Fray Marcos sent him on ahead with Indian guides who were to act as relay runners in order to keep the two parts of the expedition in touch with each other.

Having passed Culiacán, Los Mochis and the River Mayo, Esteban's party started to head away from the coast toward the mountain passes between the Sonora and San Pedro rivers. Perhaps making up for the discomfort of some of his earlier journeys with Cabeza de Vaca, Esteban collected a harem of Indian women and developed an excessive sense of his own importance. Such behavior did not engender trust among the Zuni Indians, and they killed him – with the result that members of the second part of the expedition took fright. Although Fray Marcos certainly saw from a distance one of the many-storeyed villages that clung to the mountainside, he did not have time to pursue further investigations and he returned to Mexico City.

The expedition of Coronado
Far from discouraging Mendoza's interest in the north, the reports of Fray Marcos encouraged the organization of a much larger expedition under the leadership of the young Governor of Nueva Galicia, Francisco Vásquez de Coronado. In 1540, with a force of about 250 cavalrymen and several hundred Indian servants, Coronado followed almost the same route as that of Esteban and Fray Marcos until he reached the country of the Zuni Indians, where the expedition gradually became dispersed. García López de Cárdenas, with 12 men, was sent up toward the Colorado River where he and his companions saw the Grand Canyon, but were unable to cross the formidable barrier. Another exploratory party under Rodrigo Maldonado was sent down to the coast at the northern end of the Gulf of California, then known as the Vermilion Sea, where ships under the command of Hernando de Alarcón were meant to keep in contact with Coronado. However, the planned meeting did not work out, although Alarcón's men learned from Indians that Coronado's men had already reached the country they called Cibola.

When Coronado and his main expeditionary force had finished their first winter in the north, a decision was taken to strike off northeastward from the main force with 30 horsemen across the great plains, where huge buffalo herds provided the Plains Indians with an unusual nomadic way of life. After sharing considerable hardships with their

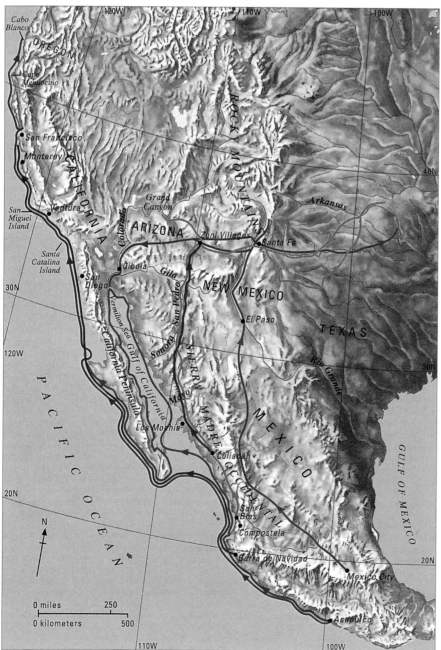

◄ **Villages** with many-storeyed houses in the country of the Zuni Indians were described by Fray Marcos on his return to Mexico. They were regarded as evidence that there were many rich kingdoms to the north, and this helped to encourage the spawning of a series of expeditions during the years 1539–43.

▶ **Among the expeditions** driven by a desire to find gold was that of Francisco Vásquez de Coronado in 1540–42. He opened up a vast expanse of the southwest, but the region was not to be colonized until the end of the century.

Indian companions, Coronado and his men reached the banks of the Arkansas River in modern Kansas, and so came within 300 miles (480 kilometers) of the present state of Arkansas where Soto's expedition from Florida passed the winter. Coronado's efforts were not considered a success when he returned to Mexico, but they resulted in a remarkable understanding of the main contours of the southern half of the continent, a result which was reflected in contemporary maps.

Coastal exploration

Between 1539 and 1543 it was established that California was a peninsula rather than an island, and familiarity with the Pacific coast of California grew apace with voyages of men such as Francisco de Ulloa and Juan Rodríguez Cabrillo. In 1539–40 Ulloa sailed north from Acapulco, followed the coast of the Gulf of California, and explored part of the Pacific coast of Lower California. Cabrillo's expedition set out from Barra de Navidad in 1542, and when his men came in contact with the native inhabitants as far north on the coast as San Diego, Santa Catalina Island, and Ventura, the Indians made it clear through sign language that they were aware that other white men were exploring the interior.

Cabrillo appears to have sailed northward parallel to the coast until his ships were blown off course somewhere near Monterey or San Franciso, and he returned to spend part of the winter at San Miguel Island where he died. After his death, at least one of his ships reached a latitude of about 42°30′, before sailing back to Barra de Navidad in the spring of 1543.

The next major exploratory expedition up the coast was under a Basque captain, Sebastián Vizcaíno, in 1602. He left Acapulco with three ships, and reached Cabo Blanco at a latitude of 43° where the crew suffered from excessive cold and scurvy. According to Fray Antonio de la Ascensión, one of the Franciscans on board, there were not more than six men well enough to sail the ship that he was on. From 1565 onward, however, under normal circumstances the crews of the Manila galleons returning from the Philippines and following the sailing directions of Fray Andres de Urdaneta (another Basque) had often sighted land at Cape Mendocino, but they had not experienced quite such appalling conditions as those suffered by Vizcaíno's crews. The problems that arose during his

expedition of 1602–3 were due to the fact that the highest latitudes were reached in the coldest months – December and January.

The first colonies

While the west coast was gradually acquiring Spanish names for capes and bays, the Indian settlements on the western slopes of the Rocky Mountains were becoming better known to potential Spanish colonists, in particular the Franciscan friars who had at heart the founding of missions to the Indians. Two residents of Mexico led the way in half-colonizing and half-exploratory projects. In 1582 Antonio de Espejo came across turquoise and silver mines in the Arizona mountains, and in 1598 Juan de Oñate led a very large colonizing party across the Rio Grande near El Paso. By 1609, a mission and a settlement had been founded at Santa Fe.

▲ **The Grand Canyon** was reached by Garcia López de Cárdenas and his men after they had left Coronado's main expedition to follow a route to the Colorado River.

Champlain and his Contemporaries

During the second half of the 16th century, after the explorations of Cartier and Soto, there were no substantial additions to the cartography of eastern North America except in Arctic waters. Some local exploration and mapping took place in the 1560s along the northeast coast of Florida near the failed colonies of René de Laudonnière and Jean Ribault, and, in the 1580s, around Sir Walter Raleigh's attempted colony in Virginia. However, it was only with the arrival of Samuel de Champlain at Tadoussac on May 24, 1603, that the mind of a talented geographer began to be focused on the intricacies of the American Indian trade routes, which were to be the basis of all future exploration in the northern half of the continent over the next two centuries.

The contribution of the American Indians

The summer months of 1603 did not allow Champlain enough time to do more than consolidate and slightly enlarge the knowledge of the area along the St Lawrence Gulf, previously explored by Cartier and a few fur traders. On his return to France, he reported that he had only been about 12 leagues (37 miles/60 kilometers) up the Saguenay, and 5 or 6 leagues down the Richelieu toward the lake that, in 1609, he would call Lake Champlain. But it is clear from his first Canadian book, *Des Sauvages, ou, Voyage de Samuel Champlain*, published in the autumn of 1603, that, although he had not yet tackled any new routes, he owed to his American Indian traveling companions an almost uncanny understanding of the various watersheds that drain regions from the sea in the north (soon to become known as Hudson's Bay) to Virginia in the south, and westward at least as far as three of the Great Lakes.

The dependence of Champlain on his Indian guides cannot be sufficiently stressed. He seems to have been quite unafraid of committing himself to long journeys with his Montagnais and Huron allies, either alone or with only one or two French companions. The fact that he was able to share their lifestyle, their food, and methods of travel was remarkable at a time when examples of trust and friendship among Europeans and the indigenous people in other parts of the continent were rare.

Cartographic achievements

Between 1604 and 1607 Champlain concentrated on the coastal areas that ran from Cape Breton Island to just south of Cape Cod. He was based during the first winter on the island of Sainte-Croix and then for two more winters at Port Royal, under the command of Pierre du Gua de Monts. His general map of the region, drawn in 1607, was well in advance of those drawn by other contemporary cartographers, although the work in 1614 of the Dutch fur trader Adriaen Block soon filled in the part of the coast from the area of Champlain's surveys southward to the area below Manhattan Island, which would become part of the colony of New Netherlands.

In 1608 Champlain, as the delegate of Gua de Monts, had laid the foundations of the new trading post at Quebec (soon to become the capital of New France), while the following year exploration which was undertaken by the English captain Henry Hudson opened the way for a new Dutch colony. In September 1609 the *Half Moon*, with a mixed Dutch and English crew, sailed up the Hudson River and anchored just below the present town of Albany. In doing so, they came close to the area explored by Champlain, for earlier that summer, not far from the headwaters of the Hudson River, Champlain and two French companions had helped his Montagnais and Huron allies to defeat a large band of Iroquois.

Exploration of inland waterways

Champlain's next important voyage was in 1613, up the Ottawa River and through adjacent lakes as far as the Ile aux Allumettes. However, this traditional Indian trade route was controlled by powerful Algonquins who did their best to discourage Champlain from continuing his journey. It was not until the spring of 1615 that he was able to make his way further upriver and across to Lake Nipissing, where he was entertained by a local chief and then taken via a small river to the shores of Lake Huron, which he called "The Fresh Water Sea." Delighted by the beauty of this eastern part of Lake Huron, the region round Georgian Bay, Champlain wandered from village to village, compiling a mass of ethnographic information.

▶ **Champlain** (above) and two French companions were able to win a battle against a large band of Iroquois, at the southern end of Lake Champlain, by killing two chiefs with an arquebus. In this engraving of the battle, the canoes in the foreground are barely more accurate than the palm trees in the background.

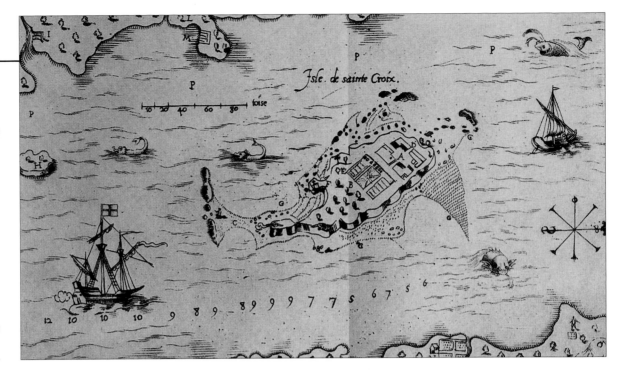

► **The island of Sainte-Croix** near the "Baye Francoise" (Bay of Fundy) was drawn by Champlain during his first winter in Canada in 1604-5. While staying on Sainte-Croix and, in the following two winters, at Port Royal, he carefully explored 375 miles (600 kilometers) of the east coast. He drew 16 detailed maps and plans of harbors along the coast, and wrote descriptions of his journeys.

▼ **Champlain's idealized drawing** of the settlement on Sainte-Croix corresponds to position A on the larger plan.

At Carhagouha that August he found Father Joseph Le Caron, a Franciscan who had started a mission to the Hurons. Later in the fall, after Champlain had been persuaded by his allies to join a war party against the Iroquois, near Lake Ontario, and had recovered from a wound inflicted during the fight, Champlain and Le Caron spent part of the winter months visiting many of the villages in the region. Both men showed impressive fortitude in spite of the cold and other hardships.

Finally, in the spring of 1616, Champlain had to retrace his route to Quebec and then to France, where the politics at Court often made his life unnecessarily difficult. The most vital period of Champlain's voyages was over, but when he returned to Quebec his work as administrator of the new colony kept him fully occupied. Apart from the period 1629–33, Champlain continued to spend most of his time in the colony and sent younger men to continue the exploration he had always encouraged.

Jean Nicollet, "coureur de bois"

Champlain had often employed young men like Etienne Brûlé, Nicolas Marsolet de Saint-Aignan, and Jean Nicollet de Belleborne as interpreters after they had spent several years living with Algonquin or Huron tribes, and these tough, capable *coureurs de bois* ("runners of the woods") helped to spread the French trading network over an

ever-growing area. In 1634 Nicollet was sent on a voyage of exploration to the region south and west of Lake Huron, far beyond Champlain's own most westward point, in order to make peace among the warring tribes on the western shores of Lake Michigan and to persuade them to be allies of New France. Passing near the future site of Fort Michilimackinac, he explored southward to the end of Green Bay and along the Fox River in the hope of finding a water route to the sea. Even though he failed to reach the Wisconsin or the Mississippi, he learned of their existence and could certainly claim to have been the first European to penetrate what is now the American Midwest.

With an imaginatively theatrical touch, Nicollet had taken on this arduous voyage a long robe made of Chinese damask, embroidered with flowers and birds. When he appeared among the Winnebagoes in this extraordinary attire, they were very alarmed. Apparently taking him for a god, they promised to hold a meeting of four or five thousand men from the surrounding tribes, a meeting which concluded in a peaceful agreement.

Champlain died on Christmas Day 1635, a few months after Nicollet's return to Quebec. The dream of finding a route to China had not been fulfilled in his lifetime, but it must have given the old explorer immense satisfaction to know that a new generation was traveling and living with the Indians as he had done.

KEY TO ROUTES

— Champlain 1604–7
— Champlain 1608–16
— Nicollet 1634–35

Charting Northern Waters

The exploration of the northeast coast of America is closely linked with the desire of the English, French, and Dutch to find a northern route to the riches of the "South Sea" and Cathay (China) at a time when the southern route was controlled by the Spanish and Portuguese. The first expedition to search for a sea passage round the top of the American continent was led by the Englishman Martin Frobisher. He set sail in 1576, and although two of his three small ships were lost, he managed to reach Baffin Island in the *Gabriel* and sailed into a bay which he believed to be the strait leading to Asia. Here the ship's company encountered hostile Inuit and some of the men were killed. One Inuit was captured, however, and Frobisher took him back to England, along with some rocks said to contain gold.

A second voyage simply involved collecting more of this ore, but on a third voyage he encountered bad weather and his ship was pushed into what was subsequently to be called Hudson Strait. Frobisher did not sail on through the Strait, however, leaving the important discovery at the end of it to the Englishman Henry Hudson.

Henry Hudson's first voyage

Hudson set sail in 1609 with orders from his employers, the Dutch East India Company, to continue the search for a northeastern route to the Indies, round the top of Europe. However, his small ship, the *Half Moon*, met with so much ice that the crew threatened to mutiny unless he changed the direction of his search. Thus with a total change of plan,

▼ *In spite of their guns, several of Frobisher's men were killed during Inuit attacks. John White apparently witnessed this incident in 1577.*

but a similar objective, Hudson sailed across the Atlantic and found himself, on September 11, 1609, alongside the island of Manhattan, which would soon become the first Dutch fur-trading post in North America, and eventually the site of New York City. He then sailed up the Hudson River far enough to realize that it was not the desired strait leading to Cathay.

The second voyage

Hudson made one more attempt (which was to prove fatal) in 1610 to look for a waterway that would lead westward from the strait that the Englishman John Davis had found in 1585. But although Hudson, in his *Discovery*, opened up – as Cartier had done – a vast interior sea which, with its tributary rivers, would take traders from Europe halfway across the continent, his lack of leadership qualities led to a tragic ending for the expedition. During the wintering in James Bay, Hudson demoted Robert Bylot who was his second-in-command and the only other man aboard apart from Hudson with the capacity to navigate the ship safely on the return journey. This ill-considered act played directly into the hands of the mutinous members of the crew. They persuaded Bylot to remain on their side when the decision was made to abandon Hudson in a small boat, with the sick and the loyal members of the ship's company.

It was Bylot who not only brought back the eight survivors but also took part in the subsequent expeditions of Sir Thomas Button (1612–13), of William Gibbons (1614), and of William Baffin (1615 and 1616). These voyages received their main financial support from the "Company of the Merchants of London, Discoverers of the North-

and lost only two men to scurvy, which had been the main cause of death among wintering parties in the northern part of America since Jacques Cartier lost 25 of his men to the illness in 1535–36. Cartier had learned from the Indians near his fort at Quebec of a miraculous cure: a drink made from the bark of an evergreen tree. James's men recovered from the privations of the winter by eating the vetches and scurvy grass that appeared with the spring.

In his account of his travels, James also expressed the opinion that even if there were a Northwest Passage, it would have to be at a latitude of at least 66°, and that as "there is much Land to the Westward … this Streight must be very long and the Weather so cold, that it will not be durable." Moreover, in August and September the wind is inclined to be contrary so progress would be slow – "neither can any great Ships, which are fit for carrying of Merchandize endure the Ice, and other Inconveniencies, without extraordinary Danger." James insisted that it would be quicker to sail 1000 leagues (about 3000 miles/ 4750 kilometers) southward and round the Cape of Good Hope than to attempt 100 leagues (about 300 miles/ 475 kilometers) in Arctic seas, and that "in Navigation, the farthest Way about" was often the safest and the best.

The negative reports of Foxe and James as to the feasibility of a Northwest Passage so discouraged the London and Bristol merchants who had backed these expeditions that no more funds were forthcoming for three decades. Then, the next series of Hudson Bay voyages had an entirely different purpose: the fur trade.

KEY TO ROUTES

— Frobisher 1576
— Frobisher 1578
— Hudson 1609
— Hudson 1610–11
— James 1631–32

◄ **Henry Hudson**, his son and a handful of loyal men were cast adrift in a small boat by a mutinous crew after they had endured a hard winter in James Bay.

▲ **Thomas James** was responsible for one of the most successful winterings in Canada before the arrival of European settlers, losing only two of his crew.

West Passage" (or North-West Company), which was given a royal charter in 1612. None of these expeditions nor those sponsored by Christian IV of Denmark, between 1605 (under the Scottish captain, John Cunningham, with two other English captains, James Hall and John Knight) and 1619–20 (when Jens Munk wintered in the estuary of the Churchill River), resulted in the discovery of any Northwest Passage either at the head of Baffin Bay or out of Hudson Bay. And yet the hope lingered on in the minds of other navigators such as Luke Foxe (1631) and Thomas James (1631–32) that somewhere a passage existed, in spite of the facetious remark that Foxe said he had made to James when they met in the southwest corner of Hudson Bay: "You are out of the way to Japon, for this is not it."

The wintering of Captain Thomas James

James and his crew were to spend an appallingly hard winter on Charlton Island, near the mouth of the Rupert River, an account of which later appeared in his published journal. They built a house in a sheltered spot, digging stakes into the earth, between which they wove boughs and over which they stretched their mainsail. They insulated the outside of the house with a 6-foot (2-meter) layer of trees and bushes. By mid-December it was almost entirely covered with snow; icicles hung on the inner walls and the beds were covered with hoar frost. The casks of vinegar, oil, and wine were all frozen solid, and the cook had an incredible problem with soaking and rinsing the salt meat. As James said of their brass cauldron: "The side which was next the fire was very warme, and the other side an inch frozen." But somehow they went out every day for food and water,

Missionaries and Traders

▲ *John White's painting of Indians fishing features a dugout canoe. It was, however, the birchbark canoe that was to become the form of transport most frequently used by explorers throughout North America. It came in all shapes and sizes, and had the great advantage that the materials for making and repairing it were available everywhere – birchbark, resin, or gum to make the seams watertight, and split roots of the spruce fir with which to "sew together" parts of the canoe.*

Among the many Frenchmen who were in close touch with the Indians and made a major contribution to the exploration of North America in the 17th century were missionaries – in particular, members of the Recollet and Jesuit orders. The work of the Recollet fathers (a branch of the Franciscan order), four of whom arrived in Canada in 1615, started with the founding of a mission to the Hurons at Carhagouha, on Georgian Bay. There the first mass in central Canada was celebrated by Father Joseph Le Caron, who, as well as exploring locally, accompanied the geographer Champlain on a visit to the Petun Indians in 1616.

It is evident that evangelization would have been unsuccessful without command of one or more Indian languages, and most of the missionaries acquired remarkable proficiency wherever they were sent. Father Le Caron, for example, compiled with Nicholas Viel a dictionary of the Huron language, while the Fathers Gabriel Sagard and Christien Le Clercq wrote a number of books in which they described the customs and behavior of the Indians. Sagard's books cover the first period of exploration and evangelization by the Recollets in central Canada, from 1615 to 1629, while Le Clerq's volumes belong to the period when the Recollets returned to Canada after 1669.

During the major part of the four decades when the Recollets were absent, it was the Jesuits who bore the brunt of the Huron reaction to both the devastation caused by epidemics and the Iroquois destruction of the Huron confederation. The Hurons blamed the epidemics on the French missions with which they had developed a close relationship, and their shamans fomented a fierce distrust of the new religion.

Groseilliers and Radisson

Evangelization, exploration, and trade all suffered from 1649, as missionaries and Hurons alike had to flee from the Iroquois massacres in Huronia, until about 1660 when the situation began to change. However, during the latter half of that decade the exploits of Médard Chouart des Groseilliers and his brother-in-law, Pierre-Esprit Radisson, opened up new trade routes out of range of Iroquois attacks. Between the fall of 1659 and the summer of 1660 these two redoubtable men explored along the southern shore of Lake Superior, spending the winter at a small lake just beyond the western extremity of Lake Superior, and then six weeks in early spring with the Sioux Indians. Radisson claimed that he had also made a rapid journey from the northern shore of Lake Superior up to James Bay, but he may have made this claim in order to persuade either James II of England or some London merchants to provide finance for a trading expedition to Hudson Bay by sea. Over the next few years, he and Groseilliers were to encourage merchants in New England and London to take part in trading ventures by sea to Hudson Bay, because they were enraged by the fact that the French Governor had embargoed their furs when they returned from their voyage of 1660–61. In 1668 the first English post was established at Fort Charles, and in May 1670 the Hudson's Bay Company received its charter.

Fathers Ménard and Allouez

When Groseilliers and Radisson arrived at Montreal in canoes laden with furs, it was obvious to local merchants that the western voyage was financially viable again, but it was the Jesuits who were perhaps most delighted with the information they received from the voyagers. That very fall, Father René Ménard joined a group of Ottawa Indians who were returning to the west with five French traders. He was the first known priest to visit the Lake Superior Indians, and he founded a mission halfway along the southern shore at a place that he called Chassahamigan (Keweenaw Bay, Michigan). Unfortunately, he was lost in the woods in August of the following year, and it was not until 1665 that Father Claude Allouez was able to continue the work that Ménard had begun.

The mission that Allouez started was even further west at Chequamegon Bay, and from there he not only established other missionary posts in the interior of what is now the state of Wisconsin, but also voyaged across Lake Superior and upriver to Lake Nipigon. During his 24 years as a missionary he is said to have covered more than 3000 miles (4750 kilometers) of the Great Lakes region and to have been in contact with 23 different Indian nations.

Father Charles Albanel

In 1671 the Jesuit Father Charles Albanel left the mission at Tadoussac and, with Montagnais guides, made his way up to Lake Mistassini, across to Nemiskaw and down the Rupert to James Bay. There he had found an English vessel and two deserted houses, but no Europeans since they were apparently all on a hunting expedition.

It had been an exhausting voyage – 800 leagues (about 2400 miles/4000 kilometers) to and from the Bay – and the worst winter, Albanel said, of the ten that he had spent in the woods with the "Savages." But no sooner had he returned to Quebec than a new voyage was planned by the Governor, Frontenac, whose report of November 13, 1673, shows the extent to which missionary zeal was made use of by the Government of New France: "I have availed myself of the zeal shown by Father Albanel, Jesuit, to set off on a mission to those quarters in order to try to deflect the

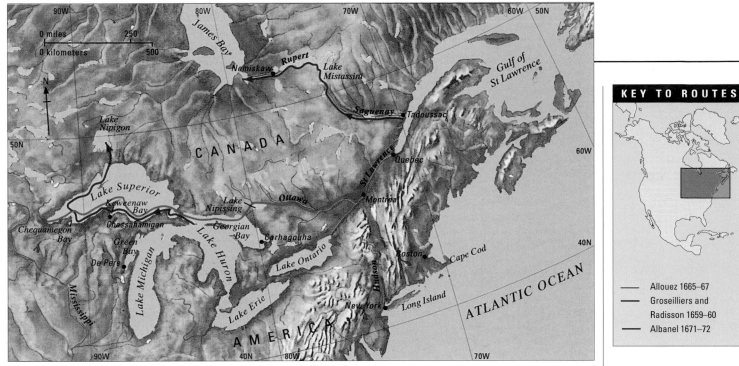

KEY TO ROUTES

——— Allouez 1665–67
——— Groseilliers and
    Radisson 1659–60
——— Albanel 1671–72

Savages … from taking this route for the English commerce. The said Father Albanel must sound out Des Groseilliers if he meets him and try to see whether he can make him take up our interests again."

Armed with a polite letter from Frontenac, Albanel made another onerous journey overland to the Rupert River, a journey with 200 portages, which for a man of over 50 proved a terrible trial. When he arrived in August 1674 at the English fort at the mouth of the Rupert, he found that he was far from welcome. Charles Bayly, the first resident Governor of the Hudson's Bay Company, suspected the motives of this French envoy. Since the con-

versions of Father Albanel, both spiritual and commercial, on his previous visit had already succeeded in deflecting some of the English trade southward, the missionary was put firmly aboard a ship to England.

The English allowed Albanel back to France after he had promised to refrain from activities hostile to the Hudson's Bay Company, and he appears to have kept his word. Although he returned to Canada in 1676, as Superior of the St Francis-Xavier mission (now De Pere, Wisconsin), he confined himself to spiritual activities. He died aged 80, remarkable for someone who when he was barely 50 had already looked worn out from voyaging.

◄ **Snowshoes** were an Indian invention which was adapted by Europeans for the winter months when the lakes and rivers were frozen over. However, traveling on them with a 90-pound (45-kilogram) pack plus a gun did not make for rapid progress.

Jolliet's Journeys

Until 1670, nearly all exploration in New France had been undertaken as private enterprise by traders or missionaries, without any official backing from the government. However, with the founding of the English Hudson's Bay Company this situation changed, and men were commissioned to lead expeditions with the promise that they would be rewarded with the post of commandant of a fort or trading establishment, or with a *seigneurie* (a feudal estate). Financial support was rarely forthcoming.

Aware that it was vital to prevent English traders from gaining control of western trade routes, the Intendant of New France, Jean Talon, with the full approval of the Governor, Frontenac, commissioned Louis Jolliet to lead an expedition southwestward from Lake Michigan. The existence of the Mississippi River had been known ever since the explorations of Jean Nicollet in 1634, but there was no knowledge of where this river discharged into the ocean. Having promised Frontenac that he would find the mouth of the "Great River," Jolliet had first to draw

up an agreement for a trading company with several Quebec merchants to defray the cost of the voyage, before setting out in the fall of 1672 for Fort Michilimackinac, where he was to pick up his remarkable traveling companion, Father Jacques Marquette.

Jolliet delivered a letter to Marquette from the superior of the Jesuits in New France ordering him to join the expedition, an order which fitted perfectly with Marquette's plans. The three powerful motivating forces that lay behind the astonishing expansion of New France were thus united in the seven men who set off in two canoes in mid-May 1673. Political, commercial, and religious motives were all represented on this journey, which was to open up as important a waterway as those found by Cartier and

▲ **Father Marquette** was determined "to seek out new nations that are unknown to us so that they shall be made to know our great God."

His ability to speak six Indian languages greatly facilitated communication with the Indians who joined Jolliet's expedition (below).

▲ **On approaching the confluence** of the Mississippi and Arkansas rivers, Jolliet and Marquette decided to turn back. Marquette was unable to communicate with Indians as far south as the Arkansas Indians. Moreover, these were people who traded with the Spaniards, into whose hands they did not wish to fall.

Hudson, and to frustrate the expansion of the English colonies westward for nearly a century.

The Mississippi

Jolliet and Marquette did not, in fact, reach the mouth of the Mississippi. After passing two important tributaries, the Missouri and the Ohio, they decided when they were close to the confluence of the Arkansas and the Mississippi that they had gone as far as it was wise. So, having discovered that the Mississippi definitely flowed into the Gulf of Mexico, the expedition turned round and paddled back against the current well over 1000 miles (1600 kilometers) upstream, returning to Lake Michigan via the Illinois River and the portage across to Chicago. Jolliet named a mountain after himself to the south of Chicago, and a large town nearby also now bears his name.

During the winter of 1673–74, Jolliet stayed at the Sault Ste Marie mission, making copies of his journal and map. Leaving these duplicates in the hands of the Jesuits, he set off for Quebec in the spring, but his canoe was overturned at Sault St Louis. He was the sole survivor of the accident, but the copies of the maps and journals that he had with him were irretrievably lost. To compound this misfortune, the copies he had left at Sault Ste Marie were destroyed in a fire.

Overland to Hudson Bay

With or without maps and journals, Jolliet had built up a sound reputation as an explorer by 1679, and in that year he was commissioned to survey or inspect "all the nations and lands in the King's Domain." This commission really meant that he was to sound out the extent to which the native population of the Hudson Bay basin had come under the influence of English traders. However, another ostensible reason for this northern voyage was to establish a mission and trading post at Nemiskaw, on the Rupert River.

The expedition in this case was not covering entirely new ground, since Father Charles Albanel had already made the journey five years previously, but it is interesting that when Jolliet and his companions arrived at the English fort, Governor Bayly received him with a civility he had not shown toward Albanel. It would seem that Bayly had heard of Jolliet's explorations down the Mississippi and was trying to persuade the Canadian to change sides. However, born in Quebec, Jolliet appears to have had the well-being of the colony more closely at heart than most of the officials sent over from France, and his loyalty never wavered.

The Labrador coast

As a merchant Jolliet had a strong interest in the fur trade, and he joined forces with a number of Quebec merchants to form a company for trading along the north coast of the St Lawrence. He was conceded a *seigneurie* that finally included the whole of the north shore of the St Lawrence up to the western end of the Strait of Belle Isle, where the Basques had formerly exploited their whaling establishments. In 1694 he set off on his travels again, this time to map and describe in detail, in a journal left for posterity, the Atlantic coast of Labrador for 106 leagues (about 320 miles/500 kilometers) north of the eastern end of the Strait of Belle Isle.

The Basques seem to have always enjoyed good relations with the Montagnais Indians along the southern Labrador coast, but trading with the "Eskimaos" (Inuit) was another matter. There was some trade, apparently in sealskins, but the exchanges were extremely cautious with little trust displayed on either side. This is why Jolliet's

journal of his exploration up the Labrador coast as far as latitude 56°1′ is of particular interest. He and his companions do not appear to have had a moment of fear during the whole month that their small ship was on the coast. They were invited into Inuit houses, and the Inuit women entertained them with singing and dancing, while the Recollet father who accompanied Jolliet repaid this kindness by intoning hymns, which apparently delighted their Inuit hosts.

Jolliet's journey up the Labrador coast, and his comfortable relationship with the Inuit, was all the more remarkable when compared with descriptions of fierce Inuit attacks on European fishermen in the Strait of Belle Isle throughout the first half of the 18th century, often brought on by the fishermen's over-reaction to Inuit pilfering. It was only in 1764–65, when the first of the Moravian missionaries – who were able to communicate with the Inuit in their own language – arrived in the area, that a peaceful atmosphere was again restored between the Inuit and Europeans.

La Salle and the Mississippi

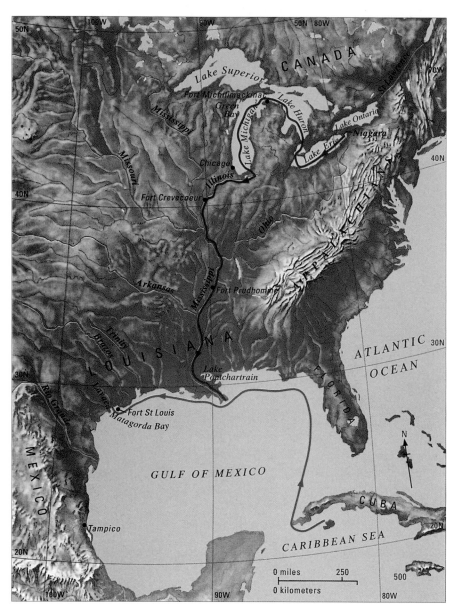

men, several of whom made notable contributions to the journey, particularly in the early stages.

The Great Lakes

The expedition began with Dominique La Motte de Lucière and Father Louis Hennepin being sent ahead to the eastern end of Lake Erie to choose a site for a fort on the Niagara River, and a suitable place above the falls for the building of a ship. The construction of *Le Griffon*, the first ship to sail the Great Lakes, was certainly La Salle's idea, but he had little to do with the execution of the project that began in midwinter and was completed in August 1679. Other business kept La Salle at Fort Frontenac until just before the launching of *Le Griffon*, a vessel of about 60 tons with seven cannons.

It soon transpired that the ship had not been built simply to carry the members of La Salle's expedition up to Fort Michilimackinac and on to Green Bay. In total contravention of the king's orders that there was to be "no commerce with the Savages called the Ottawas or others who bring their beaver and other furs to Montreal," La Salle loaded *Le Griffon* with a cargo of furs and sent it back from Lake Michigan to the fort at Niagara, but, to La Salle's despair, it never arrived.

Considering that exploratory expeditions had to be self-sustaining and received no financial support from the crown, La Salle could perhaps be forgiven for contravening orders. He was heavily in debt by 1680. Not only had he lost *Le Griffon*, but another ship bringing him 20,000 francs' worth of merchandise for trade had been lost in the St Lawrence. Other men might well have given up at this point, and further calamities were to follow. During a first attempt at descending the Illinois River at the beginning of 1680, La Salle had established a fort which he had suitably called "Crevecoeur" or Fort Heartbreak. While he was away in Montreal, trying to arrange his financial affairs, some of the men he had left at the fort mutinied and the place was destroyed.

Down the Mississippi

A final attempt was made in January 1682 to complete the Mississippi project, which was now into its fourth year. With his faithful lieutenant, Henri de Tonti, plus 23 Frenchmen and 18 American Indians, La Salle made his way from Fort Crevecoeur to the junction of the Illinois and the Mississippi. There, the melting of the ice in the middle of February allowed the expedition to use canoes for the rest of the journey, which went extraordinarily well apart from a hold-up of ten days while they searched for a missing member of their party, Pierre Prudhomme, who had gone astray while hunting. He eventually turned up, starved and exhausted, floating downriver on a piece of wood. Many leaders of expeditions would have been infuriated by the wasted time, but La Salle had employed some of his men in building another fort during the search period, and celebrated the return of the stray man by naming the establishment "Fort Prudhomme."

Relations with the Indians who lived on either side of the lower Mississippi were excellent. After a brief moment of menacing drums and war cries, the Arkansas Indians decided to smoke a pipe of peace with the newcomers, and plied them with welcome provisions. La Salle with due protocol took possession of their territory for the crown of France, and similar ceremonies took place further downriver with the Taensas and the Coroas. Tonti wrote glowingly of the impressive dignity and beauty of the Taensas, and the generosity of most of the tribes almost overwhelmed the explorers.

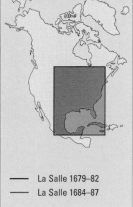

KEY TO ROUTES

— La Salle 1679–82
— La Salle 1684–87

Although most contemporaries of Jolliet and La Salle gave full honor for the discovery of the Mississippi to Jolliet, the glory of having followed the great river to its mouth, and of claiming Louisiana for the French, put La Salle's explorations into a specially dramatic category. Unfortunately, La Salle's own exaggerated sense of drama led in the long run to his downfall.

During most of his 15 years in New France, La Salle had received considerable support in his trading activities from the authoritarian Governor, Frontenac, and in 1673 he had become commandant of a fort which he renamed Frontenac. However, his passionate adherence to the Frontenac camp made him many enemies, and has resulted in some very biased versions of both his life and the value of his contribution toward the exploration of North America. It is incontestable that he built various forts at strategic places which acted as staging posts in his expedition down and up the Mississippi. However, to what extent he did or did not discover the Ohio River, for example, is a matter still under discussion by historians. That he was arrogant and self-glorifying there is no doubt. A point which distinguished La Salle from explorers such as Jolliet and Father Albanel is that instead of voyaging quietly with just two or three Indian guides and one or two other companions, his major expedition started with well over 30

The expedition's goal was attained at last when they arrived in view of the sea, but the high point of La Salle's career came three days later, on April 9, 1682, when, dressed in a scarlet coat and to the sound of solemn hymns, he took possession of Louisiana in the name of Louis XIV.

Plans for the founding of a colony

La Salle had attached to the crown, without a blow, a stretch of territory that almost doubled the size of New France. The new territory ran from the Appalachians, in the east, southwestward to the Spanish territories, and included the Mexican coast as far south as Tampico.

But Louis XIV was not at all pleased by La Salle's tremendous efforts. He seems to have feared that the frontiers of New France had become over-extended. Returning to France just before Christmas 1683, under a cloud of disapproval, La Salle immediately got in touch with men whom he hoped would support his new project for a French colony in the region of the Taensas, the Indians who had welcomed his expedition with such warmth and civility. Fortunately, an account of his expedition had already reached France and La Salle's plan was presented favorably to the king. Suddenly he was back in favor and he was put in charge of a grandiose project to which the king contributed two ships with their crews and 100 soldiers with their officers. The convoy carried over 320 people, including a few women and children.

Unfortunately, however, La Salle miscalculated the location of the Mississippi's mouth and headed westward along the northern shore of the Gulf of Mexico, relying on inadequate maps. After various misadventures, the major part of the expedition found itself in Matagorda Bay.

On the Lavaca, one of the rivers that flow into the bay, La Salle erected his last fort, and established the little colony there in May 1685. The next two years were spent in fruitless exploration: the search for the Mississippi. Finally, after several unsuccessful journeys from the base at Fort St Louis, La Salle decided in January 1687 to try to fetch help from his fort on the Illinois River. Leaving 25 men, women and children, the remnants of the colony at Fort St Louis, La Salle and 16 men started northeastward,

▲ *La Salle* proudly claimed Louisiana in the name of King Louis XIV. However, far from being flattered by this gift, the king wrote that in future such useless enterprises must be stopped.

but on March 19, near the Trinity, a river that flows south from Dallas to the Gulf, La Salle and three of his men were killed by some of the angry and disillusioned members of the expedition. It was left to Pierre Le Moyne d'Iberville to rediscover by sea the mouth of the Mississippi in 1698 and over the next few years to establish a successful colony there.

◄ *The launch* on Lake Erie of Le Griffon, *whose construction was ordered but not overseen by La Salle, was an impressive sight.*

Crossing the Appalachians

▶ **This palisaded village** was among the many scenes of Indian life in Virginia which were drawn by John White in the 16th century.

The first English colonists in North America knew little of their future home beyond its coastline. It was not a very inviting one, being mostly rocky or thickly forested, and the site which they selected for their settlement – Jamestown in Virginia – was swampy, malarial, and hard to defend. Their first concern was survival. Otherwise, to the disgust of Captain John Smith, they were chiefly interested in hunting for gold. They had undertaken to look for a passage to the "East India Sea," and before he left to pick up more colonists, Christopher Newport sailed up the James River as far as the site of Richmond and made contact with Powhatan, chief of a confederation of Indian tribes.

The tottering colony was saved by Smith, who took over as Governor in 1608 although, after an accident with his gunpowder pouch, he left for England the following year. With 14 men in an open boat, Smith had made two trips up Chesapeake Bay, encountering "grimme and stout Savages with long poles like Javelings" and sustaining a nasty wound from a stingray that he speared with his sword. He found no strait to the western ocean which was believed to lie beyond the mountains.

The Blue Ridge

By 1650 the colony of Jamestown was safe and prospering on the tobacco crop. In search of more land suitable for crops, two landowners, Edward Bland and Captain Abraham Wood, with local guides, journeyed southwest to Roanoke Rapids, opening up trade. Probably many hunters and traders were on the move westward by this time, but records are scanty. A more genuine explorer was John Lederer, a scholarly young German interested in North American culture, who made several scouting trips at the behest of the Governor in 1670. He reached the top of the Blue Ridge, the climb taking all day, and was disconcerted to see "my sight ... suddenly bounded by Mountains higher than I stood upon." Making contact with hitherto unknown peoples, including the Tuscarora, he was taken along some of the trails through the southern Appalachians and reached the Catawba River near the present Rock Hill. Contemporary maps showed a large lake in this area, and Lederer – otherwise reliable – confirmed its existence, though he did not state that he had actually seen it.

Lederer's success encouraged other expeditions, sponsored by local magnates like Captain Wood. Thomas Batts and Robert Fallam, escorted by an Appomattox chief, Perecute, crossed the Blue Ridge in 1671 and followed the westward-flowing New River, which they hoped would lead them to the "Western Sea": they claimed they had seen it in the distance. James Needham, described by

▶ **Daniel Boone** was among the many frontiersmen who in the 18th century explored the area to the west of the Appalachians. Here he is shown escorting a band of pioneers traveling west in their search for good farming land.

Wood as "this heroyick English man," led a party to near the present Asheville, but was killed by the Occaneechi. His companion, a youth named Gabriel Arthur who could not read or write, spent a year living and traveling with the Tomahitans between Florida and the Ohio.

Many others were drawn west in pursuit of furs, and the "Western Sea" soon ceased to be a realistic objective. Most expeditions faced demanding challenges, but some had the air of a jaunt. Alexander Spotswood led a party of Virginia gentlemen across the Blue Ridge to the Shenandoah, which they called the Euphrates, in 1716. They spent a lot of time firing off celebratory volleys and toasting the king. "We had several sorts of liquor, viz. Virginia red wine and white wine, Irish usquebaugh, brandy, shrub, two sorts of rum, champagne, canary, cherry, punch, water [sic], cider, etc."

Carolina

Meanwhile, colonists had settled in the Province of Carolina, between Virginia and Spanish Florida, indeed encroaching on Spanish territory. One of the first settlers, Dr Henry Woodward, was sent to Port Royal in 1664 to learn local languages. The Spaniards captured him, but he escaped during a raid by English buccaneers and, after spending some time with them, returned to Carolina in time to take part in the founding of Charles Town (Charleston). This lively and able man led several ventures west and north, discovering promising territory and, on the whole, relating amiably to local tribes. In 1685 he set up a trade center on the Chatahoochee at Coweta (Columbus), among Creek tribes. Hearing of his presence, the Spaniards sent a large expedition from St Augustine, but he got away before they arrived, leaving the message: "I am very sorry that I came with so small a following that I cannot await your arrival." Next year he was back in business.

New York

The Dutch in New Amsterdam were slow to penetrate westward largely because of their small numbers. They were at Schenectady by the 1660s, though driven out again by the French in 1690. Among the pioneer travelers in western New York was Arnout Viele, who journeyed many miles between 1682 and 1694, reaching the Wabash, but left no account of his travels. Viele also explored the area west of the Susquehanna. Many traders were already operating there in the early 18th century, the most enterprising of them being George Croghan from Philadelphia, who had a post on the Miami River before 1750. Later, after the French and Indian War, Croghan was to lead a mission to Pontiac and fall into the hands of the Illinois. He survived a blow from a tomahawk because "my Scull being pretty thick the hatchett wou'd not enter."

Traders from Albany, the chief center of the fur trade, ventured into the Great Lakes region, sometimes guided by French renegades. Joannes Rosebloom reached the Straits of Mackinac, between Lake Huron and Lake Michigan, in 1685, although when he repeated the trip the following year the French were waiting for him.

Routes west

By 1700 Englishmen from the southern colonies were infiltrating almost to the Gulf Coast, and many people had crossed the Appalachians. A Carolina trader, Thomas Welch, reached the Mississippi in 1698. John Lawson covered 600 miles (960 kilometers) of the Carolina back country in 1700–1, before being killed by the Tuscarora. The naturalist Mark Catesby ranged as far as the Savannah River, sending plants, seeds, and marvelous watercolors

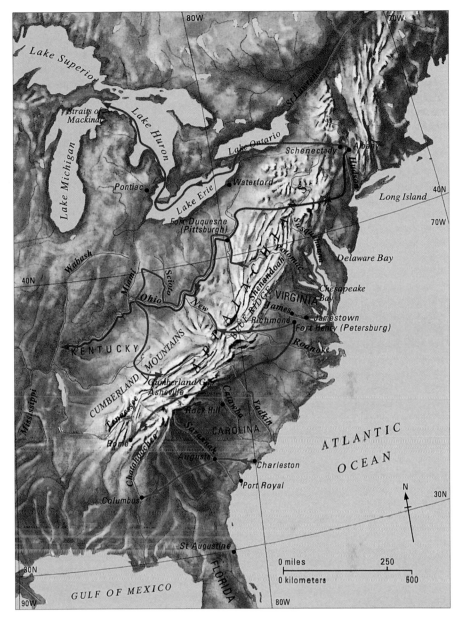

back to England. Unrecorded traders followed the streams, rivers, and narrow Indian trails through the forests.

Further discoveries were made in the 18th century by agents of commercial companies scouting the unexplored lands granted to their employers. Dr Thomas Walker, on behalf of the Loyal Land Company of London, found a useful break in the Cumberland Mountains in 1748 – the Cumberland Gap – through which the settlers of Kentucky were to pass in their thousands. Walker recorded many adventures with animals, especially hunting exploits: in just over a month he killed "13 Buffaloes, 8 Elks, 53 Bears, 20 Deer, 4 Wild Geese, about 150 Turkeys, besides small Game." Rattlesnakes did their best to redress the balance, but their only victims were horses.

Christopher Gist, a well-known frontiersman born in Maryland who had settled with his family on the Yadkin River, was hired by the Ohio Land Company to explore the Ohio River system in 1750. He met with George Croghan on the Scioto River, and together they negotiated rights for settlement on the east bank of the Ohio before Gist returned through the Kentucky Blue Grass Country. Later, Gist was employed by George Washington as a guide on his mission to Fort Le Boeuf (Waterford, Philadelphia) in 1753.

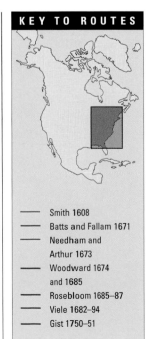

KEY TO ROUTES

— Smith 1608
— Batts and Fallam 1671
— Needham and Arthur 1673
— Woodward 1674 and 1685
— Rosebloom 1685–87
— Viele 1682–94
— Gist 1750–51

Journeys to the Northwest

There is no doubt that the original exploration of the lands to the west of Lake Superior was by French Canadian traders who were primarily driven by the necessity of finding new, unexploited areas of beaver and other fur-bearing animals. However, it was also spurred on to a marked degree by the efforts of La Vérendrye and his sons to establish a route from Lake Superior to Lake Winnipeg and then along a river which the Indians said would lead to the "Western Sea."

La Vérendrye and his sons

With the approval of the French Minister of Marine and Colonies, Comte de Maurepas, La Vérendrye first set about

establishing a chain of forts between Lake Superior and Lake Winnipeg. In his reports he and his family feature prominently, but much of the pioneering was done by the *coureurs de bois* ("runners of the woods") he employed. He did not reach Lake Winnipeg himself until 1737. Maurepas was getting impatient, suspecting, not without reason, that La Vérendrye was "less interested in the Western Sea than in a sea of beaver."

La Vérendrye took his exploratory obligations more seriously after the Massacre of the Lake of Woods, when 21 of his men, including his son Jean-Baptiste, were ambushed and killed by the Sioux (a disaster not unconnected with the fact that La Vérendrye had been arming their enemies). With a party of 50, further augmented by Assiniboine groups met *en route*, he visited the Mandan villages on the Missouri in 1738, a journey of 300 miles (500 kilometers) on foot. In 1739 his son Pierre reconnoitered north of Lake Winnipeg, investigating another big river, the Saskatchewan. Two other sons, François and Louis-Joseph, in company with the Bow Indians, covered the region between the Little Missouri and Cheyenne rivers as far south as the Black Hills in 1742.

Under increasing pressure from Maurepas, La Vérendrye lost or resigned his position as Commander of the Western Posts in 1742, complaining, probably with some justice, that he was poorer than when he had begun his exploration. When Maurepas fell from power in 1749, La Vérendrye was restored, but he died later that year.

The importance of Indian cooperation

A remarkable map of the Indian routes from Lake Superior to Lake Winnipeg, drawn by the Indian, Ochagach, for La Vérendrye in 1728, shows the extent to which Indian knowledge and cooperation was still vital for explorers, just as it had been in the days of Champlain in the 17th century. Indeed, this was still true for explorers in the early 19th century. There are, for example, two maps redrawn by Peter Fidler, a Hudson's Bay Company trader, from sketches prepared by Blackfoot Indians at Chesterfield House on the South Saskatchewan River in 1801 and 1802. They show the relationship of western rivers such as the Missouri, the Milk, and the Bow to the Rocky Mountains, and in one case the rivers flowing from the Rockies to the Pacific with the names of many of the tribes living on both sides of the mountains. In a third case Fidler redrew a map by a Chipewyan called "Cot aw ney yaz zah," which showed the canoe routes between the Churchill River and Lake Athabasca.

During this period of exploration in the northwest, the opening up of new routes was quite definitely a joint venture, with Indian experience of how to make the maximum use of favorable currents, and of where to make the best portages, clearly an essential element in the rapid expansion across the continent. Northern exploration had an efficiency and a sense of purpose that was mutually understandable to traders and Indians alike – the former needed furs, and the latter needed guns and other manufactured articles – and on the whole the only major disputes arose when one Indian nation wanted to prevent another from receiving arms and ammunition.

Samuel Hearne

By 1769 the Hudson's Bay Company had been in existence for just on a century, but it had not earned a reputation for discovery or the opening up of new territory. It had in fact been criticized for lack of initiative in this matter, and to remedy the situation it was proposed that Samuel Hearne should be sent on "an inland journey, far

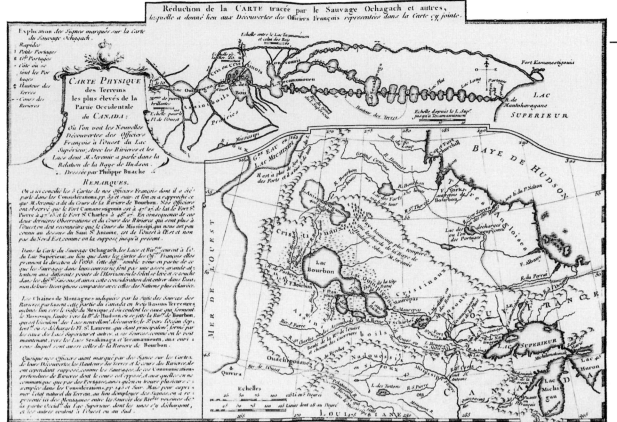

◀ **This map of Canada,** published in 1764, includes the Indian routes from Lake Superior to Lake Winnipeg which were drawn for La Vérendrye in 1728. The Western Sea is shown too close to Hudson Bay.

▼ **Samuel Hearne** journeyed through a huge expanse of unmapped territory before reaching the most northern point of North America.

to the north of Churchill to promote an extension of our trade, as well as for the discovery of a North-West passage, copper mines, etc." A few of the Company's traders had gone westward as far as the North and South Saskatchewan rivers, but no one had yet gone far northward toward the river which, according to Indian reports, led to the country of the copper mines.

Samuel Hearne had been sent out to Fort Prince of Wales, at the mouth of the Churchill River, as a young man of about 20 and was not more than 24 when he was entrusted with this important mission. He had had considerable experience trading with Inuit on the northwest coasts of Hudson Bay, and had demonstrated his ability to get on well with them. Unfortunately, during his first attempt at the journey in November and December 1769, his Indian companions deserted him "nearly 200 miles [320 kilometers] from Prince of Wales' Fort," stealing most of his supplies. With admirable tenacity of purpose, Hearne set out once more in February with a smaller and more faithful troop, and this time managed about 500 miles (800 kilometers) before an unfortunate occurrence made him retrace his steps to the Churchill again. His quadrant had been blown over and broken, and Hearne felt there was no point in continuing the journey if he was unable to continue with his mapping.

The third attempt began in December 1770, in the company of a distinguished leader of men, called Matonabee. It was a complete success in an exploratory and geographic sense. However, humanly, in Hearne's view, there were moments of appalling disaster. Not far from the Great Slave Lake, what appeared to be hundreds of Indians joined Hearne's and Matonabee's party, and it suddenly became evident that the exploratory expedition had turned into a military one, with the over-riding purpose of making surprise attacks on any unsuspecting Inuit and seizing their copper implements. Hearne thus became an unwilling witness to the slaughter of a group of Inuit men, women, and children who were fast asleep in their tents. He ends his description of the attack by saying: "My situation and the terror of my mind at beholding this butchery, cannot easily be conceived … though I summed

up all the fortitude I was master of on the occasion, it was with difficulty that I could refrain from tears."

Hearne pursued his survey to the mouth of the river, where "For the sake of form … after having had some consultation with the Indians, I erected a mark, and took possession of the coast, on behalf of the Hudson's Bay Company." Fifty years later, Sir John Franklin, accompanied by Sir John Richardson and Sir George Back, surveyed the lower part of the Coppermine River, and found, exactly as Hearne had described, the Bloody Falls where the massacre had taken place with skulls and bones "strewed about the ground near the encampment." It was at a latitude of 67°42′, and Hearne had unquestionably found the Arctic Ocean at a point just opposite the island that was later to be called Victoria Island.

▲ **Fort Prince of Wales** was one of a number of forts established by the Hudson's Bay Company in the late 17th century to serve as centers for the fur trade. Hearne was captured here in 1782 by the French explorer and soldier La Pérouse, who insisted that Hearne should publish an account of his travels.

The North Pacific Coast

▲ **George Vancouver**
spent three years carefully
surveying the northwest
coast and thus contributed
greatly to British claims
to the region.

▼ **Remarkable totems,**
such as those of the Kwakiutl
Indians on the northwest
coast, deeply impressed
European explorers.

During the 16th century the Spaniards in Mexico had made some progress in exploring the coast of California, and in 1603 Sebastián Vizcaino's expedition had entered Monterey Bay and reached as far north as Cape Blanco in southern Oregon. These maritime probes, however, had not been exploited. The Spaniards did not need new lands for settlement, and the Pacific coast seemed to offer little potential. Monterey was not settled until a Franciscan mission arrived there in 1770, when Spanish interest in the northwest coast was rekindled by fears that the territory to which they laid claim was about to fall into the hands of other Europeans.

The threat came not from the sea but overland, as two great expanding movements converged from east and west. The spread of Europeans across the North American continent had not yet reached the Pacific, although Samuel Hearne reached the Arctic Ocean in 1771. The advance from the west was more pressing. Russian trading ventures to the Aleutians had followed Bering's and Chirikov's voyages to Alaska in 1741. The first permanent settlement, on Kodiak Island, was not founded until 1784, but as the sea otters and blue foxes declined in numbers, the Russian traders ventured further east and south.

Spanish advance

Reports, perhaps exaggerated, of the profits of the Russian fur trade activated a Spanish response, launched from a new port at San Blas in Mexico. After some preliminary voyages along the Californian coast, Juan Perez was instructed to search for likely sites for settlement further north. He had a single ship, the *Santiago*, which left San Blas in January 1774. After lengthy stops at San Diego and Monterey, by mid-July she was in the vicinity of the Queen Charlotte Islands, doing noisy but friendly trade with the Haida. On the return journey, Perez probably discovered Nootka Sound in Vancouver Island, which, like Cook later, he assumed to be part of the mainland. With the crew weakened by scurvy, a perennial curse on the Spanish Pacific voyages, the *Santiago* reached Monterey in a sorry state in late August.

Perez was soon off again, this time under the command of Bruno Hezeta, with two vessels, the *Santiago* and *Sonora*, the latter commanded by Juan Francisco de la Bodega y Quadra. Bad weather and various mishaps, including a rare but bloody confrontation with indigenous people on the coast of Washington, caused delays, and the chances of reaching their objective of 65°N receded. Separated from the *Sonora* by a storm, the *Santiago* turned back to Monterey. Bodega y Quadra, more resolute, "pressed on, taking fresh trouble for granted," as he put it. He reached 58°N and proclaimed Spanish sovereignty in Salisbury Sound, before cold, storms, and scurvy forced a retreat. In 1779 he made a second voyage, with Ignacio Arteaga in overall command of a pair of new frigates, pushing as far northwest as Kayak Island, and landing at several points to establish Spanish possession.

The last voyage of Captain Cook

Bodega y Quadra's 1779 voyage almost overlapped with that of Captain Cook, who spent the summer of 1778 reconnoitering the coast for the Northwest Passage, though Hearne's journey to the Arctic Ocean had made the existence of such a strait in lower latitudes improbable. He avoided California as a Spanish preserve, but he spent a month refitting in Nootka Sound before sailing along the Aleutian chain and north through Bering Strait until he was stopped by ice at 70°44'N. Landing briefly on the Asian shore, he returned to the Aleutians and had some interesting conversations with Russian traders, in spite of the lack of a common language, before retiring to Hawaii for the winter. He intended to return the following year but was killed in Hawaii (see pages 160–61). Charles Clerke, himself a dying man, took over command of Cook's *Resolution* but made no advance on Cook's discoveries: really, there was none to be made.

In the course of his great world voyage which was to end in disaster in 1788 (see pages 160–61), the Comte de la Pérouse followed Cook's track in 1786, but in the opposite direction, sailing south along the coast. He claimed the land for France at Lituya Bay, and was surprised to find that the people he met showed evidence of earlier contact with Europeans, no doubt Russian traders. After spending some time at Monterey, he turned west across the Pacific to sell furs in Macao, returning for another sweep through the north Pacific the following year.

Nootka Sound

Cook had noted the profusion of sea otters and other fur-bearing animals around Nootka Sound and, even before publication of his report, English traders were cashing in, with the usual deleterious effects on the indigenous animals and human beings. However, it was not the fur traders but rumors of Russian expansion which provided the main motive for the voyage of Esteban Martinez in 1787. He sailed as far as Prince William Sound, and made contact

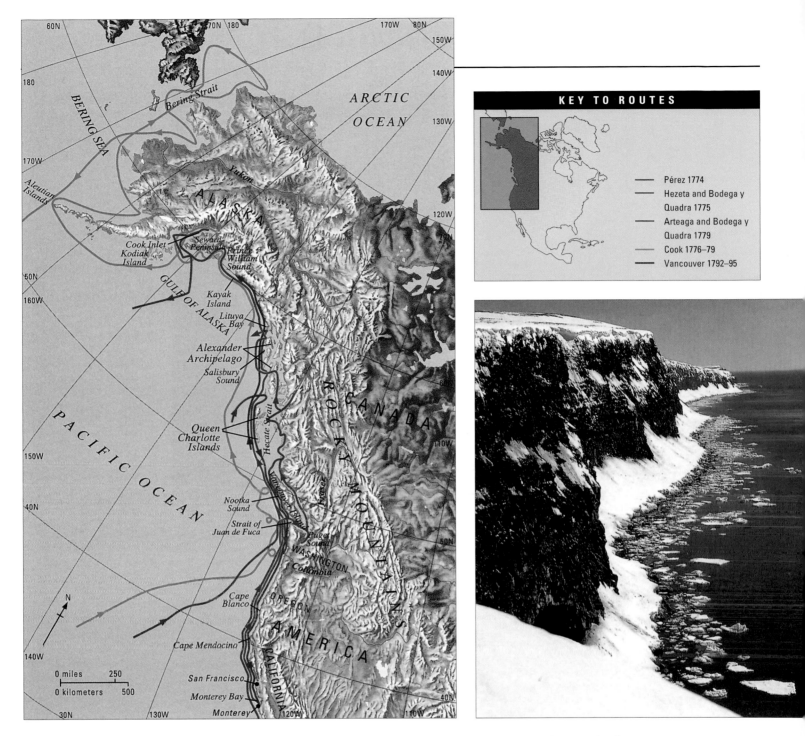

KEY TO ROUTES

———— Pérez 1774
———— Hezeta and Bodega y
        Quadra 1775
———— Arteaga and Bodega y
        Quadra 1779
———— Cook 1776–79
———— Vancouver 1792–95

with a Russian settlement where he learned that plans were already laid to take over Nootka. When he brought this news to Mexico, the Viceroy, without waiting for instructions from Madrid, ordered him promptly to Nootka to reassert Spanish control. He confiscated a couple of British ships, an act which incensed the British Government and led to demands for compensation and the abandonment of Spanish claims in the northwest. After a certain amount of saber rattling, the Nootka Convention (1790) resolved the affair more or less in Britain's favor.

George Vancouver

The diplomatic fuss prompted further exploration. In 1792 George Vancouver circumnavigated the island named after him, and in succeeding summers meticulously charted the coastline between 56°44′ and 35°N. The Spaniards were equally active. Alfrerez Manuel Quimper, in one of the British ships confiscated by Martinez, explored the Strait of Juan de Fuca in 1790, and a Spanish map of 1791 shows a large part of the east (strictly, north) coast of Vancouver Island. Jacinto Caamano's charts of the northern Queen Charlotte Islands (1792) were seen by Vancouver, who, in

the Strait of Juan de Fuca, met Dionisio Galiano in the *Sutil*, employed on the same task as himself. They exchanged charts and information, and actually operated as a team for a short time. Galiano, with Cayetano Valdes, sailed along the east coast of Vancouver Island in this same season (1792), but they emerged by a different channel and at a later date. Moreover, Vancouver's account was published first! Vancouver learned from many others, including Alessandro Malaspina, an Italian in Spanish service who set up an observatory in Nootka Sound during his world voyage of scientific research in 1792, and Bodega y Quadra, who was on his last trip north. The two men entered into a lively correspondence while in Nootka Sound. Vancouver also came into contact with Robert Gray, a US trader who is usually credited with discovering the mouth of the Columbia River. (Hezeta had seen it in 1775 but had mistaken it for the mouth of a strait.) Part of Gray's commission was to negotiate details of the Nootka Convention on the spot, and his opposite number was Bodega y Quadra. Agreement on the Convention proved difficult, but social relations were "most agreeable."

▲ *The coast of Alaska* was first explored by Alexei Chirikov and Vitus Bering, on behalf of Russia, in 1741. Reports of their journeys led to the belief that Alaska was an island, separated from the mainland by a strait which might be the entrance to the Northwest Passage – a belief that was only finally disproved in the 1790s.

Crossing the Canadian Rockies

◀ *The Canadian Rockies presented more than a physical obstacle to David Thompson in his attempts to find a route to the Pacific. He also had to contend with the opposition of the Piegan Indians, who on one occasion only decided not to attack him after he sent their chiefs large quantities of tobacco and a particularly "fine pipe." Despite such difficulties, he succeeded in surveying the entire length of the Columbia River.*

▶ *Alexander Mackenzie, on reaching the Pacific Ocean, used a mixture of vermilion and melted grease to inscribe a brief memorial to himself. No mention was made, however, of the six French Canadians, two Indians, and his second-in-command, Alexander Mackay, who had journeyed with him.*

By the late 1780s a realistic estimate of the shape and immense size of the continent of North America had been obtained, but it had not yet been crossed from coast to coast by any European, nor is it likely that any indigenous North American had journeyed from Hudson Bay or the St Lawrence over the Rocky Mountains to the Pacific. Both feats were to be achieved in the next two decades, notably by expeditions led by the Scotsman Alexander Mackenzie, the Welshman David Thompson, and the Americans Meriwether Lewis and William Clark.

The explorations of these men have been recognized because they left journals describing their expeditions, while the contributions of other equally intrepid men have often been ignored because they left no published accounts. It is clear, however, that their success depended to a large extent on the network of trading establishments that had gradually been set up by fur traders. Moreover, they also often relied on "Métis" guides, the sons or daughters of French traders, and their Indian wives.

Alexander Mackenzie

In 1789 Alexander Mackenzie, a partner in the fur-trading North West Company, set out from Fort Chipewyan on Lake Athabasca with the goal of finding a waterway route to the Pacific. He had with him four French Canadians, two of them with their Indian wives, and an Indian chief with two of his wives. For part of the journey Mackenzie was also accompanied by another French trader called Laurent Leroux, who had set up the first trading post on the Great Slave Lake. Alexander's cousin, Roderick Mackenzie, had built Fort Chipewyan in 1788. However, the first known trader in the Athabasca district was actually Peter Pond, who had been born in Connecticut but by the end of the 1770s knew more about the northwest than any of his contemporaries. He was aware, for instance, that the Peace River flowed east from the Rocky Mountains. Unfortunately, he had also come to the conclusion that the great river that flowed westward out of the Great Slave

Lake had its outlet in the Pacific Ocean, even though the Indians had correctly informed him that it flowed north.

It was Pond's information that led Mackenzie to believe that by following this great river, which was eventually to be called the Mackenzie, the expedition would emerge at a point on the west coast coinciding with the mouth of a large river that had been seen by Captain Cook. That his valiant expedition finally discovered not the "Western Ocean" but a new part of the Arctic Ocean was a matter of considerable disappointment to Mackenzie, but he remained undaunted.

The journey to the Pacific

In October 1792 Mackenzie embarked on another expedition which would attain his desired goal, via the Peace River and a section of the Fraser River to Bella Coola. He both started and ended his journey to the Pacific at much higher latitudes than any other man attempted to do during the 18th or early 19th centuries, setting out from Fort Chipewyan at a latitude of nearly 59° and finally arriving on a branch of the sea leading to Queen Charlotte Sound, at 52°20′48″, according to his own reckoning "by the natural horizon." There on a rock he inscribed, in large characters, this brief memorial: "Alexander Mackenzie, from Canada, by land, the twenty-second of July, one thousand seven hundred and ninety-three."

David Thompson

David Thompson arrived at Churchill in 1785, aged 14, and in the next 26 years gained extensive knowledge of the region between the Great Lakes and the Pacific, building on the work of Mackenzie and helped on many journeys by his Indian wife (with whom he was to have 13 children). Parts of the country he covered, such as the area north of Lake Winnipeg, were scarcely visited by other Europeans for a century or more. He took great pains as a surveyor – one of his companions remarked that he traveled more in the style of a geographer than of a fur trader – and his map

MACKENZIE

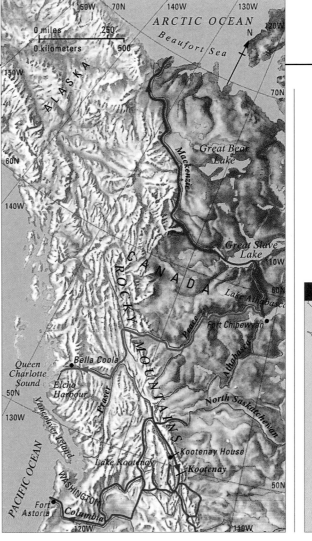

of the northwest, drawn in 1814, remained the standard authority for many years. Some of the Indians apparently called him "the Star Man" due to the incessant number of observations he took for ascertaining the latitude and longitude of points on his journeys. However, the Hudson's Bay Company failed to appreciate his worth, and in 1797 he joined the rival North West Company, for whom he undertook his most famous journeys.

From the headwaters of the Saskatchewan, he crossed the Rockies to the headwaters of the Columbia, surveying the whole river system of southern British Columbia and following the Kootenay River through Idaho to its outlet in Lake Kootenay, which he reached in 1807. Progress was delayed slightly by Thompson's careful methods and also by difficulties with the local people. The Piegan Indians, with whom Thompson had been trading for several years, became profoundly disturbed at the thought of him crossing the Rockies and guns being obtained by tribes on the western side. While Thompson and his men were building the log-hut settlement called Kootenay House, delegates from the Piegans arrived to check on his activities. Thompson showed them the strength of the stockades and bastions, and told them: "I know you are come as Spies and intend to destroy us, but many of you will die before you do so; go back to your country and tell them so." This they apparently did, and Thompson noted in his Narrative, "We remained quiet for the winter."

In the spring, however, events took a more serious turn when about 40 Piegans were sent by the tribal council to besiege the trading post. The party was held up for some time and, in order to avoid Piegan attacks on his canoes, Thompson had to change his plans and find a way to the Columbia which first involved going north. He had many more misadventures before eventually reaching the mouth of the Columbia on July 14, 1811. A few months earlier, a trading post called Fort Astoria had been built there by agents of Jacob Astor's Pacific Fur Company, who had endured a long voyage from New York and around

Cape Horn. It must have been a considerable surprise for them when Thompson and his party appeared in sprightly condition after their overland trek.

Thompson had done a brilliant job of surveying the whole length of the Columbia and its tributaries. He was to conclude with justifiable pride: "Thus I have fully completed the survey of this part of North America from sea to sea, and by almost innumerable astronomical Observations have determined the positions of the Mountains, Lakes, and Rivers, and other remarkable places of the northern part of this Continent; the Maps of all of which have been drawn, and laid down in geographical position, being now the work of twenty seven years."

▲ *Fur traders* and their Indian wives often acted as guides and provided valuable information to the explorers of the northern Rockies in the 18th and early 19th centuries.

Surveying the West

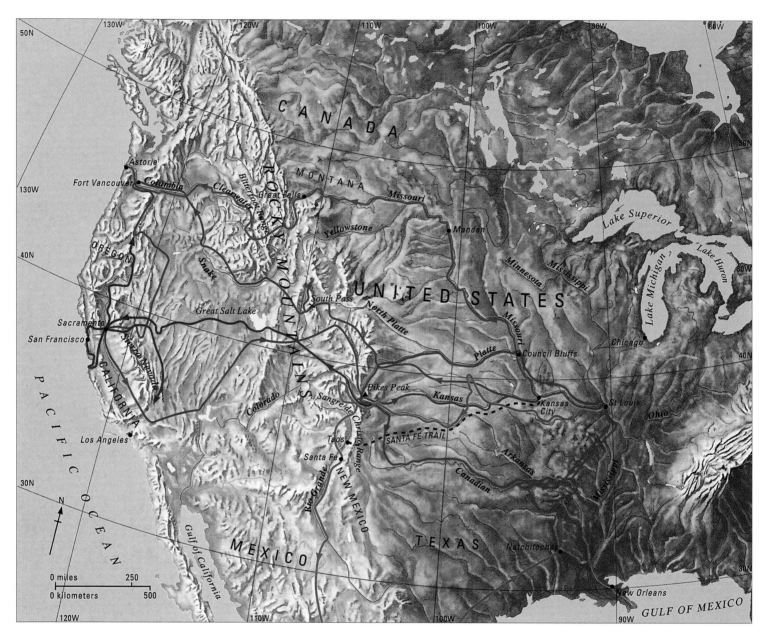

KEY TO ROUTES

—— Lewis and Clark 1804–6
—— Pike 1806–7
—— Long 1817–20
—— Frémont 1842–44
—— Frémont 1845–46

President Thomas Jefferson had contemplated the exploration of the West even before the American Government's purchase of the Louisiana Territory from France extended the size of the USA by over 800,000 square miles (2 million square kilometers). He had the men to do it – his private secretary, a young ex-army officer named Meriwether Lewis, and William Clark, a friend of Lewis from army days. The other members of what we now know as the Lewis and Clark expedition were mainly soldiers, some enlisted for the purpose and chosen from "good hunters, stout, healthy, unmarried young men, accustomed to the woods."

Up the Missouri

Explorers had been sponsored by governments before, but the Lewis and Clark expedition was the first in the New World that could be called a national enterprise. The main purpose was to find a route from the Mississippi to the Pacific, and roughly the first half of the journey – up the Missouri – was well known. The explorers knew they would ultimately encounter mountains, but hoped the Missouri might flow through them. The Rockies turned out to be a more formidable barrier than they anticipated.

In fact, the expedition was to prove that no route such as Jefferson hoped for existed, but it fulfilled other purposes, the chief one being to make contact with more than 50 native tribes and nations. Science was not ignored, and the expedition sent back numerous specimens of hitherto unclassified plants and animals. In an otherwise well-organized enterprise, it was perhaps strange to take no qualified scientists, nor a doctor, though Lewis undertook an intensive study of botany and zoology before they left, and both he and Clark coped with medical problems admirably. They could do nothing about a ruptured appendix, however, which killed Sgt Charles Floyd. He was their only casualty, although Lewis suffered a flesh wound in Montana when one of his men mistook him for an elk.

After spending the winter of 1803–4 in training at St Louis, the expedition paddled upstream to the Mandan villages, where they spent the following winter. They hired two guides from the *voyageurs* (French-Canadian hunter-traders) in the Mandan villages, one of whom was married to a 16-year-old, heavily pregnant Shoshone girl, who came along too. Her name was Sacajawea, and she was to prove the most valuable member of the entire party. She could not only communicate with many of the unknown

▼ *Trappers and hunters* led an isolated existence and many adopted Indian customs. Their travels frequently resulted in geographical discoveries.

peoples they encountered, but she also had some know-ledge of the passes through the Bitterroot Range into Shoshone country. It was with the help of her people, and others, that the "Western Expedition" eventually reached the Columbia River, via the Clearwater and the Snake. However, they had been forced to make long portages, and their canoes, made on the spot, had to negotiate some intimidating rapids.

On November 7, Clark wrote in his diary, "Great joy in the camp. We are in view of the Ocean." They arrived at the site of Astoria (founded by Jacob Astor's fur traders in 1811) a few days later. That was approximately the date anticipated, but they were forced to winter there, relying on their own resources – building a substantial log cabin (Fort Clatsop), making flour from arrowroot and candles from a stranded whale. Although it had been far from certain at the outset where they would strike the coast, it seems surprising that no supply ship was sent to keep watch.

The way back

The return journey began on March 23, 1806. After cross-ing the mountains, they separated, Clark following the Yellowstone River to the Missouri while Lewis took the shorter, more northerly route, via Great Falls and through Blackfoot country. This led to trouble, when a hunting party, camped nearby, tried to steal guns and horses during the night. In the fracas, two men were killed. Lewis and his party then rode without stopping for 62 miles (100 kilometers) to put themselves out of reach of possible pursuers. They met Clark below the mouth of the Yellowstone and reached the Mandan villages a few days later. There Sacajawea left them.

On September 23, 1806, the expedition arrived at St Louis, to "a harty welcom" (spelling was one of the few skills Clark had no talent for). They had traveled nearly 8000 miles (over 12,000 kilometers), much of it through unknown country, and revealed the river system of the northwest. They had also observed the cultural degradation of coastal peoples, after a few years of contact with Europeans, compared with the proud and vigorous communities of the mountains and the plains.

Zebulon Pike

Jefferson encouraged other military forays, notably that of Lt Zebulon Pike, another army acquaintance of Lewis, to investigate the upper Mississippi in 1805. Having accom-plished this mission successfully (though he failed to identify the great river's source), he departed again from St Louis, three months before Lewis and Clark returned, this time bound for the southwest. With a party of 20, he

followed the Arkansas River into the Rockies, discovering Pikes Peak, which he considered unclimbable, then turned south to the Sangre de Christo range and was arrested by the Spanish authorities in New Mexico in 1807. They eventually returned him to US territory, but not before he had noted the weakness of the Spanish capital, Santa Fe, and the economic opportunities in the southwest that were to attract US pioneers into Texas.

Other official, usually military, explorers of the early 19th century included Stephen Long, who surveyed the area between the Platte and Canadian rivers in 1817–20, and the controversial John C. Frémont, future presidential candidate of the Republican Party, who carried out extensive surveys in the West in the 1840s.

The mountain men

His great fame notwithstanding, Frémont discovered little if any unknown territory in the course of his extensive travels between the Mississippi and the Pacific. Apart from the native inhabitants, whose knowledge of the country was, in general, much greater and wider ranging than is often assumed, the old western trails were first followed by travelers who left few records of their movements.

The mountain men were trappers and hunters who, for one reason or another, disliked the society from which they sprang and preferred a solitary life in the wilderness. They made many incidental geographical discoveries, and some deserve to be remembered as genuine explorers. Jedediah Smith discovered the South Pass and pioneered the route to California over the Sierra Nevada; he was later killed by Comanches when leading a wagon train on the Santa Fe trail in 1831. Jim Bridger, in 1824, was the first white man to see the Great Salt Lake. Its saltiness made him think it must be an arm of the ocean. Mountain men had a reputation for spinning extremely tall stories, but Bridger complained that people called him a liar for accurately describing natural features like the geysers of Yellowstone National Park.

In the 1830s there may have been as many as 3000 mountain men roaming the West. Their numbers fell during the 1840s with the decline of the fur trade and increasing settlement.

▲ *The Oregon Trail* was one of a number of trails to the West that were opened up by explorers and traders following in the footsteps of the Indians through whose territory they traveled.

The expedition that was led in 1802–4 by Meriwether Lewis (above) and William Clark (below) was essentially of a military nature, although not the least of its achievements was to do almost no fighting.

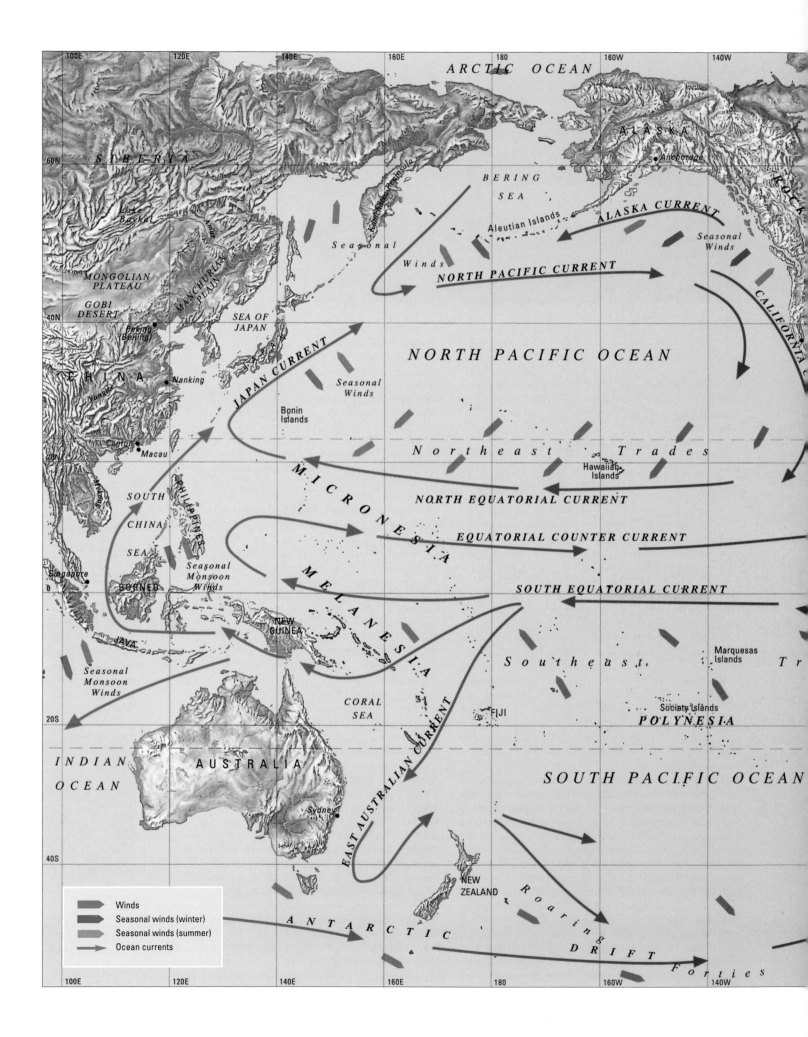

ARCTIC OCEAN

SIBERIA

Lake Baykal

MONGOLIAN PLATEAU

GOBI DESERT

Peking (Beijing)

CHINA

Nanking

MANCHURIAN PLAIN

Amur

Kamchatka Peninsula

SEA OF JAPAN

Canton
Macau

Mekong

SOUTH CHINA SEA

Singapore

PHILIPPINES

BORNEO

JAVA

Seasonal Monsoon Winds

Seasonal Monsoon Winds

BERING SEA

Aleutian Islands

Seasonal

Winds

JAPAN CURRENT

Bonin Islands

Seasonal Winds

MICRONESIA

Seasonal Monsoon Winds

MELANESIA

NEW GUINEA

CORAL SEA

ALASKA

Anchorage

ROCK

ALASKA CURRENT

Seasonal Winds

NORTH PACIFIC CURRENT

CALIFORNIA C

NORTH PACIFIC OCEAN

Northeast Trades

Hawaiian Islands

NORTH EQUATORIAL CURRENT

EQUATORIAL COUNTER CURRENT

SOUTH EQUATORIAL CURRENT

Southeast

FIJI

Marquesas Islands

Society Islands

POLYNESIA

Tr

EAST AUSTRALIAN CURRENT

INDIAN OCEAN

AUSTRALIA

Sydney

SOUTH PACIFIC OCEAN

NEW ZEALAND

Roaring

ANTARCTIC

DRIFT

Forties

	Winds
	Seasonal winds (winter)
	Seasonal winds (summer)
→	Ocean currents

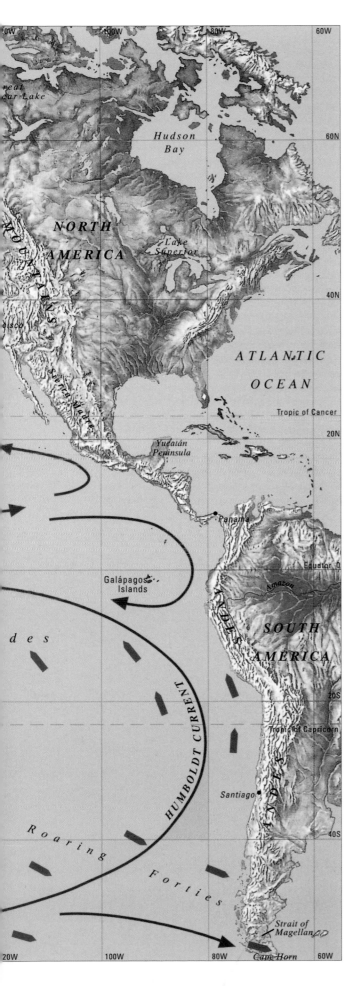

THE PACIFIC, AUSTRALIA, AND NEW ZEALAND

The Pacific Ocean occupies roughly one-third of the Earth's surface, stretching about 10,500 miles (17,000 kilometers) from east to west and slightly less from north to south. Sheer size was the greatest obstacle to those seeking to explore it. The prevailing winds were another. The predominant winds, with seasonal variations, are the Southeast and Northeast Trades in the tropics, and the Westerlies in the higher latitudes. Sailors entering the Pacific via Cape Horn or the Strait of Magellan were unable to maintain a westerly course, due to the combination of the Humboldt Current and the opposing wind. This particular difficulty helps to explain the persistent belief in an enormous, undiscovered *Terra Australis* occupying the South Pacific.

The Pacific was not to be found on European maps until the 16th century. Columbus learned of its existence in 1502–3, but the first European to set eyes on it was Vasco Núñez de Balboa, who crossed the Darién Isthmus in Central America in 1513 and called the ocean the "South Sea." Until Magellan's voyage from South America to the Philippines in 1520–21, Europeans were to believe that the Pacific was a fraction of the width of the Atlantic.

While the size of the ocean was to come as a shock to Europeans, others, living in closer proximity, were already aware of it. Chinese junks, Japanese fishing boats, Arab dhows, and Malayan proas had long cruised the western fringes. The Chinese had voyaged far from their native shores, as far afield as Africa, but there was little to tempt them, even in their most expansionist era, into the vast, empty waters to the east. Nor did the Japanese undertake serious maritime ventures: the Bonin Islands, only 500 miles (800 kilometers) away, were not permanently settled until the 19th century. Nevertheless, long ocean voyages had been made in the South Pacific many centuries before Magellan.

The Pacific contains a vast number of islands, probably more than 25,000, but except in the southwestern sector those islands are small – tiny by comparison with the vastness of the surrounding ocean – and scattered. Yet nearly all, no matter how remote, that were capable of supporting human population were inhabited when Magellan made the first recorded Pacific crossing, and had been inhabited for many centuries.

Voyages of the Polynesians

Those who first settled New Guinea and Australia did so after a short sea crossing at a time, about 50,000 years ago, when the sea level was considerably lower than it is today. The small and widely scattered islands of Polynesia, however, could only have been reached by long voyages across the ocean.

Ancestors of the Polynesians

It is now generally accepted that the ancestors of the Polynesians came from Southeast Asia and the East Indies. Voyages on balsawood rafts exploiting the South Equatorial Current from Peru, as tested by the Norwegian Thor Heyerdahl and *Kon-Tiki* in 1947, may have been possible (and it is still a mystery how the sweet potato, native to America but unknown in Asia, came to the South Pacific islands), but a vast amount of evidence (linguistic, biological, archeological) supports the hypothesis that the Polynesians originated from the East Indies.

The ancestors of the Polynesians probably came via Fiji to Samoa and Tonga about 3000 years ago. Many centuries after that, perhaps impelled by land shortage, groups of them set out on a migratory voyage to the east. There are a number of theories about the route that these oceanic explorers took. The most firmly established is that they first landed and settled in the Marquesas: a voyage of over 1875 miles (3000 kilometers), with winds and currents largely unfavorable.

This success must have given them confidence, for during the next thousand years or so the process was repeated many times: Hawaii, Tahiti, New Zealand, Easter Island – all were apparently colonized from the Marquesas.

No doubt some islands were settled by chance, as a result of boats being driven off course, but such long voyages as these – Hawaii is over 2185 miles (3500 kilometers) and

New Zealand is about 3125 miles (5000 kilometers) from the Marquesas – must have been planned. Food and water, besides livestock, seeds, even pottery (which provides the strongest evidence of their movements), had to be carried. How was this accomplished by a people whose technology belonged, in many respects, to the Stone Age?

Boat design

The basic Polynesian vessel was the dugout canoe. The ocean-going versions were double-hulled, with fiber-sewn planks to give added freeboard. The two hulls were joined by a central platform that accommodated a cabin as well as a mast (sometimes two masts) which carried a triangular sail. And they were large. One that James Cook measured in Tahiti in 1770 was 108 feet (33 meters) long, slightly longer than his own ship. With a good wind they could do about eight knots, and their paddles ensured some forward movement in conditions that rendered a European sailing ship helpless.

The capacity of Polynesian double-hulled canoes for long ocean voyages has been demonstrated by replica expeditions in the *Kon-Tiki* tradition, notably in 1976, when such a vessel, with 17 men and a cargo of plants and animals, sailed from Hawaii to Tahiti. Her captain, Mau Piailug, used traditional Polynesian navigational techniques and reached his destination unerringly.

Methods of navigation

The Polynesians had no navigational instruments as we think of them – not even a magnetic compass – but they were highly skilled navigators who possessed gifts of sea-manship (apparent to some degree also in early European navigators) and enjoyed an almost mystical communion with the sea and the cosmos. They navigated by the stars. They had names for about 200 fixed stars and knew where

KEY TO ROUTES

— Possible routes of the Polynesians

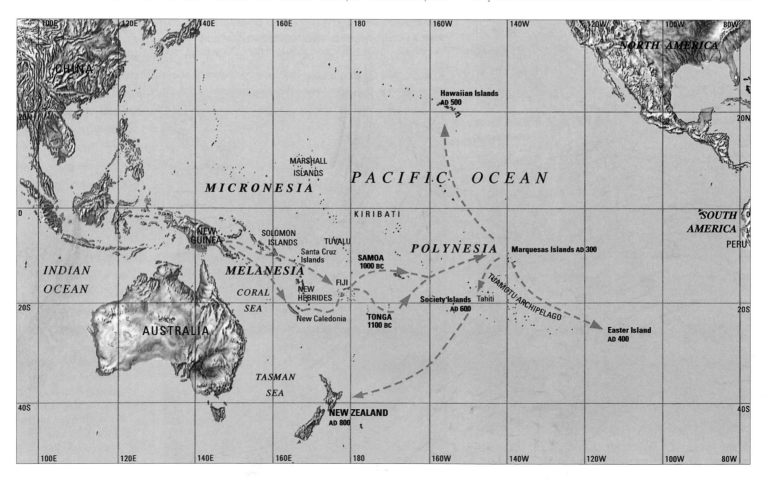

certain stars rose and set, and how this varied according to latitude. They understood equinox and solstice, and the variation in the position of the rising sun according to season – though not, of course, the reasons for these phenomena. They had no conception of longitude and latitude, but were able to calculate the latter by their system of "on-top," or zenith, stars: thus, the "on-top" (directly above) star for Tahiti was Sirius, conveniently bright, and any navigator seeing Sirius directly above him knew he was in the same latitude as Tahiti and could find it by sailing west or east, following that star. Like European navigators until the late 18th century, however, the Polynesians had no adequate system for calculating longitude.

Polynesian navigators, members of an elite group who gained their knowledge from their fathers, even had charts of a kind. These were made from palm sticks tied with coconut fiber, with shells threaded on to the sticks to indicate islands. The navigators also had a sidereal compass which enabled them to set a course by lining up a pointer with a fixed star.

Thus they were able, within limits, to navigate between fixed points, and there is evidence to show that return voyages, for purposes of commerce, culture or even war, were made between, for example, Tahiti and the Tuamotus, and between Samoa, Tonga, Tuvalu, Fiji, and other islands in western Polynesia. A return voyage between Tahiti and New Zealand may have been possible, though unlikely – certainly very risky. Hawaii to Tahiti, as Mau Piailug demonstrated, was certainly possible. A return voyage to Easter Island, from almost anywhere, is almost inconceivable due to adverse sailing conditions and the small size of the objective.

The first settlers

The question remains: how did the original settlers of these distant islands find them in the first place? It seems most unlikely that large expeditions set off from the Marquesas or elsewhere with nothing more than a hope of finding new islands. They must have had good reason to believe that they would find land, and of all the theories advanced, the most likely seems to be that they observed the flight of migrating land birds.

The migratory path of golden plovers takes in Hawaii and Tahiti; long-tailed cuckoos and several other species pass between Tahiti and New Zealand. The early Polynesians who, like the Aborigines, were attuned to nature in profound ways that are incomprehensible to post-industrial humanity, may have set a course from the observed flight of the birds. Even so, there would have been a danger of missing the land – finding Easter Island seems well-nigh miraculous – but their sympathy with the ways of the sea, awareness of subtle changes in the ocean swell caused by waves breaking on a distant shore, plus the evidence of cloud banks, bird life, and floating debris, would have pointed them toward the shores they sought.

As practical seamen and long-distance voyagers, the Polynesians were far ahead of any other people until the European Age of Discovery. Others, notably the Chinese, *could* have made such voyages. They were in many respects better equipped. But they never did.

Magellan's Voyage

▶ **Ferdinand Magellan** was the first European seaman to command a voyage across the Pacific. He thus became the first man to sail around the world, for his early career had taken him to islands in the Moluccas which were further east than the Philippines, where he was later to lose his life.

▲ **Of the five ships** that set out from Seville in 1519, the *Victoria* was the only one that returned home. It did so under the command of Juan Sebastián del Cano.

When Columbus reached the Caribbean islands, he was convinced that they were the East Indies. It soon became apparent, however, that his discoveries were part of a New World, and that it would be necessary to travel further west in order to reach the lands of the Orient, although it was not clear how far. It was widely assumed that they were quite close, and that a strait could be found through the American obstacle, giving easy access.

The first person to find such a strait was Ferdinand Magellan. He had visited the Moluccas (Spice Islands) in Portuguese service, but was convinced that according to the Treaty of Tordesillas of 1494 the islands belonged to Spain rather than Portugal. Failing to get the recognition for his services which he felt he deserved from King Manuel of Portugal, he offered to lead a Spanish expedition to the islands around South America.

He set sail in September 1519 with five ships and a somewhat motley crew. After crossing the Atlantic, he sailed down the east coast of South America, led his ships through the strait which now bears his name (see pages 94–95), and in November 1520 saw the Pacific for the first time. The immensity of the ocean – "a sea so vast that the human mind can hardly comprehend it" – was then gradually and painfully revealed. For 98 days they saw no land except for two small uninhabited islands which offered no sustenance. Antonio Pigafetta, a gentleman volunteer, graphically described the hardships: "We ate old biscuit, reduced to powder and full of grubs, and stinking from the dirt which the rats had made on it when eating the good biscuit, and we drank water that was yellow and stinking." Rats changed hands at two for a ducat. They also ate sawdust and the leather covers on the yards, soaking them in seawater for several days before roasting them on a firebox. Every man suffered from scurvy, so that they could not chew their grisly substitutes for food, and 19 men died of the illness. Pigafetta concluded that, "If Our Lord and His Mother had not aided us in giving us good weather … we should all have died of hunger in this very vast sea, and I think that never man will undertake to perform such a voyage [again]."

Finally, they reached Guam in the Marianas, which Magellan named the Ladrones ("Thieves"). In order to regain possession of a ship's boat, he burned a village and killed half a dozen people. This was but a small and insignificant episode in the long and terrible list of crimes against the local inhabitants as the Europeans strove to conquer the world. Magellan was not, by common standards, a particularly brutal man.

Death in the Philippines

After recovering from the rigors of the voyage, Magellan and his crews sailed on to the Philippines. They were kindly received on Cebu where the king, having heard something of European guns, was quick to embrace Spanish overlordship and the Christian religion. Some of his subjects, however, were not so obliging. Magellan allowed himself to become involved in local quarrels and felt bound to assist his new ally in an attack on the neighboring island of Mactan, where the opposition proved stronger than anticipated. Fighting with the fearless bravado characteristic of his time and class, Magellan staged a rearguard action against vastly superior numbers. According to Pigafetta's vivid description, he received a poisoned arrow in the thigh, two blows from spears that knocked off his helmet, a lance wound in the face and another under the right arm, but was still fighting when he was finally overwhelmed.

Magellan's death prevented him from leaving his own record of his exploits, and his voyage – perhaps the greatest in maritime history – raises some interesting questions. What, for instance, was he doing in the Philippines anyway? It was said to have been the destination recommended by the people of the Marianas, but why did Magellan set a course across the Pacific that would inevitably carry him into higher latitudes than his alleged objective, the Moluccas? One recent theory is that Magellan had learned, perhaps from Chinese in the Moluccas, of the route necessary for sailing ships to cross the Pacific from west to east – a route not discovered by the Spanish until 1565 – and that his diversion to the Philippines was planned to reconnoiter that route and establish a friendly base on the way. If true, this hypothesis would settle another question: how was Magellan planning to get home? It seems unlikely that he planned to sail on around the world, as that would take him into hostile, Portuguese waters, where he personally would have been especially at risk. But if Magellan was really planning a return voyage by sailing north to catch the Westerlies, he apparently confided in no one, as the later fate of the *Trinidad* confirms.

The homeward journey

Compelled by their depleted numbers to abandon one ship, the survivors sailed on, via Brunei, where there was more trouble with the local inhabitants, until they finally reached their destination: Tidore, an island in the Moluccas, in November 1521. After taking on a cargo of cloves and arranging trade and "protection" agreements, they set out for home. Though the Portuguese were not yet in control, a fleet was out looking for the Spaniards. The *Trinidad* was in need of a complete overhaul, and it was decided that, when repairs were completed, she should return to the east, making for Darién, which was still thought to be within easy reach. Forced back by the contrary Trade winds, the *Trinidad* fell into unsympathetic Portuguese hands.

Meanwhile, the *Victoria*, under Juan Sebastián del Cano, made her labored way around the Cape of Good Hope and back to Spain, arriving at Seville in September 1522 with just 18 men. A few from the *Trinidad* later got back too. The world had been encompassed, though at great cost and, some felt, to little purpose. Spanish attempts to repeat the voyage failed, as did attempts to make the crossing from Mexico or Peru, until the return route was discovered in 1565.

KEY TO ROUTES

— Magellan 1519–21
— Del Cano 1521–22

INDO-CHINA (VIETNAM)

SIAM (THAILAND)

PHILIPPINES

Cebu

MICRONESIA

MARIANAS

MARSHALL ISLANDS

Hawaiian Islands

PACIFIC OCEAN

BRUNEI

BORNEO

MOLUCCAS

Tidore

SUMATRA

EAST INDIES

JAVA

CELEBES

NEW GUINEA

SOLOMON ISLANDS

MELANESIA

POLYNESIA

Marquesas Islands

SOUTH AMERICA

PERU

INDIAN OCEAN

TERRA AUSTRALIS (AUSTRALIA)

TUAMOTU ARCHIPELAGO

NEW ZEALAND

CHILE

San Julián

Strait of Magellan

Tierra del Fuego

Cape Horn

Planting the Cross

▲ *The Marquesas Islands*
were first briefly visited by
Europeans in 1595. It was
to be almost 200 years
before Europeans landed
on their shores again.

▲ *Francis Drake was the*
second man to command a
voyage around the world –
more than 50 years after
Magellan's fleet set sail.

Magellan's voyage showed that it was possible to reach Asia by sailing west, but his route was too long and too dangerous. Spanish hopes of establishing an eastern trade depended on finding a route across the central Pacific, from Mexico to the Philippines. The outward voyage, exploiting the Northeast Trades, was straightforward, apart from the inescapable hazards of so long a voyage. Returning was more of a problem.

André de Urdaneta
The solution was not found until 1565, coinciding with the permanent settlement of the Spaniards in Manila. The man responsible was André de Urdaneta, a monk removed from his monastery to lead the voyage. From the Philippines he sailed north, parallel to the Japanese coast, until he found the Westerlies to carry him back across the ocean at about 37°N. He then sailed south along the Californian coast to Acapulco. This was the route followed henceforth by the Spanish galleons.

Mendaña and Sarmiento
Meanwhile, legends of lands in the Pacific rich in gold, combined with the European belief in a great southern continent – one of the most stubborn fictions in the history of exploration – provided the motive for the voyage of Alvaro de Mendaña and Pedro de Sarmiento in 1567.

They set out from Lima in two ships, carrying about 150 men, including several Franciscan friars. They were gone for almost two years, in the course of which they sailed about 7000 miles (11,500 kilometers), often with only the vaguest notion of where they were. They were

charged with "converting the heathen," but in spite of the protests of the devout and well-meaning Mendaña, the Europeans found it easier to shoot them. Conflict, as always in Pacific voyaging, was caused by the naive supposition of the Europeans that a delicately balanced island economy was capable of providing food for large numbers of hungry sailors and soldiers on demand.

The chief discovery of the voyage was the Solomon Islands, at first thought to be a spur of the "southern continent." In spite of the sufferings of the voyage, Mendaña became fired with the ambition to found a Christian colony in the lands he had discovered. This was the objective of his second great voyage, in 1595.

In the meantime, the Englishman Francis Drake had made the second circumnavigation of the globe (1577–80), having failed to find a strait in northern California which would lead him back to the Atlantic. Exploration was not the main purpose of Drake's voyage and his only discovery of real importance was that Tierra del Fuego is an island, as suspected by Magellan, though others thought it was part of the "southern continent."

Mendaña and Quirós
Mendaña, leaving Callao, the port of Lima, in April 1595, had the advantage this time of a first-rate pilot and second-in-command, the Portuguese Pedro Fernandez de Quirós. (The crowns of Spain and Portugal had been temporarily united in 1580, although this by no means ended Portuguese–Spanish competition abroad.) Nevertheless, the voyage was an almost total disaster, a grisly tale of pain and horror, as recorded by Quirós.

Mendaña was unable to find the Solomons again (nor could anyone else for nearly two centuries), and, having discovered the Marquesas, at first took them to be the Solomons, though they are half an ocean away – a good example of contemporary difficulties in measuring longitude. He was unable to establish a colony there, or in the Santa Cruz Islands, which he stumbled upon next, because of resistance from the native inhabitants. Mendaña himself died, along with many others, and Quirós managed to get what was left of the expedition to the Philippines, a considerable feat considering the state of the men and the ships, and his ignorance of the region.

Quirós's voyage

Quirós, who shared both Mendaña's religious zeal and the common belief in a "southern continent," gained support for another voyage in 1605. His three small ships carried nearly 300 men, and his first objective was the Santa Cruz Islands. The usual problems arose – incipient mutiny, storms that threw them off course, desperate shortage of water and food – and these were exacerbated by Quirós's poor health and inability to enforce discipline. Several new islands were discovered (their identity now uncertain), but Quirós became increasingly vague about their destination: "God will guide [the ships]," he said.

They discovered Espíritu Santo in the New Hebrides (Vanuatu) Islands just in time to avert a mutiny. The islands were rich, though the inevitable battle had to be fought to establish Christian ascendancy, and it may have been this which turned Quirós's mind; he began to display signs of a kind of religious megalomania. Then, one day, in the course of some local exploration, Quirós's ship was blown out of sight of land. It never reappeared in the area but eventually made the voyage back to Mexico. Some mystery surrounds this – possibly involuntary – defection.

Meanwhile, command of the expedition fell to Luis Vaez de Torres, a more resolute leader and as good a navigator. He continued, according to the orders of the Viceroy of Peru, to look for the "southern continent," in spite of vociferous resistance by one and all, who wished to make for Manila right away. Having reached 21°S without sighting the continent he sought, Torres turned north, meaning to sail along the known northern coast of New Guinea to the Philippines.

Unable to make it round the east point, he coasted westward along the south coast, thus proving that New Guinea is an island. Like a number of other momentous discoveries in the history of exploration, the existence of Torres Strait was registered – and ignored. (The Spanish, of course, kept their discoveries secret.) History, too, unfortunately must ignore Torres from the moment he finally reached port: no word of him is heard thereafter.

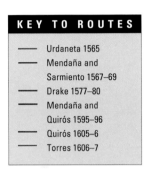

KEY TO ROUTES

— Urdaneta 1565
— Mendaña and Sarmiento 1567–69
— Drake 1577–80
— Mendaña and Quirós 1595–96
— Quirós 1605–6
— Torres 1606–7

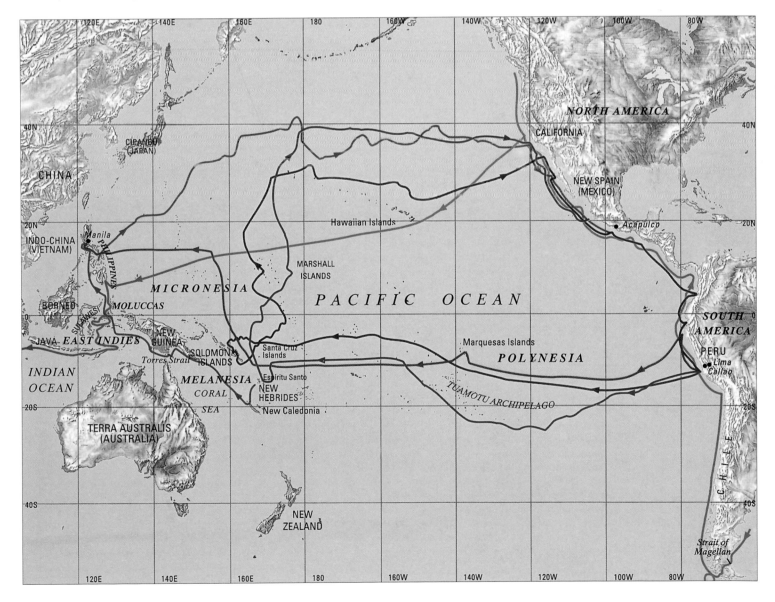

The Dutch

▲ **This sketch** of the first contact between Maoris and Europeans in 1642 appears in a copy of the journal of Abel Tasman. After initially appearing friendly, the Maoris attacked some of Tasman's men in Golden Bay on North Island, killing four of them.

By the beginning of the 17th century Spain's golden age was coming to an end. The Dutch were in the process of displacing the Portuguese in the East Indies, and their base at Batavia (Jakarta), commanding the Sunda Strait, was established in 1619. The agent of expansion was the Dutch East India Company, then a formidable organization – practically an arm of the government. The interest of the Company was in profit, not exploration, but in the circumstances discoveries were inevitable, especially as the Dutch adopted a fast, southerly route from the Cape of Good Hope. The haziness about longitude ensured that some ships would be carried on to the shores of Australia.

Due both to accident, and more deliberate probes, the Dutch soon knew the Australian coast north as far as Cape York Peninsula, west and south as far as the Great Australian Bight. They were not impressed. The inhabitants they regarded as "wild, cruel savages" (the latter actually tried to defend themselves), and the country appeared to lack valuable natural resources, even water.

Le Maire and Schouten

In 1615 Isaac Le Maire, a maverick Dutch merchant, set up a company to trade in the Far East. He aimed to circumvent the East India Company's monopoly of trade by finding an alternative passage to the Strait of Magellan and the Cape. The plan worked perfectly when the ship commanded by his son Jacob, with Willem Schouten, an experienced navigator, as second-in-command, discovered Le Maire Strait and became the first to pass Cape Horn, so named after Schouten's home town.

By April 1616 they were among the Tuamotu and Tongan islands, where the inevitable clashes with the inhabitants occurred. Soon afterward they discovered Horn Islands, between Fiji and Samoa, where the native people were friendly, though never more so than when they saw the signs of the Dutchmen's imminent departure.

Le Maire then wanted to head west in search of the Solomons and Quirós's "southern continent," but Schouten (knowing nothing of the Torres Strait and fearing embayment in New Guinea) insisted on a more northerly course. They coasted the north of New Ireland (thinking it was New Guinea) and by the end of October were at Batavia, having lost only three men on the whole, excellently conducted, voyage.

They had a poor welcome. The East India Company's Governor-General impounded ships and cargo, and sent the men home in a Company ship. Jacob Le Maire died on the voyage home, but his father, Isaac, embarked on a legal vendetta against the Company which ended in full restoration of the confiscated property, with interest.

Abel Tasman

The chief discoveries of the Dutch were due to another governor at Batavia, Anthonio van Diemen. In 1642 he despatched an expedition commanded by Abel Janszoon Tasman, an experienced skipper, piloted by Frans Jacobszoon Visscher. The plan was to search for the "Southland" by sailing east in a latitude of 52°S or 54°S (from the staging post of Mauritius). Van Diemen's instructions also contained the command that in any contact with strange people they should "be patient and long-suffering, no ways quick to fly out." For once this admonition was observed; Tasman's voyage was unusual in that more casualties through violence were suffered by the explorers than the explored.

They were unable to keep to as southerly a track as planned, and in fact sailed between 50°S and 42°S, arriving at the land named after Van Diemen by Tasman but now bearing his own name. They followed the coast until it bore away northwest (into the wind) then turned east

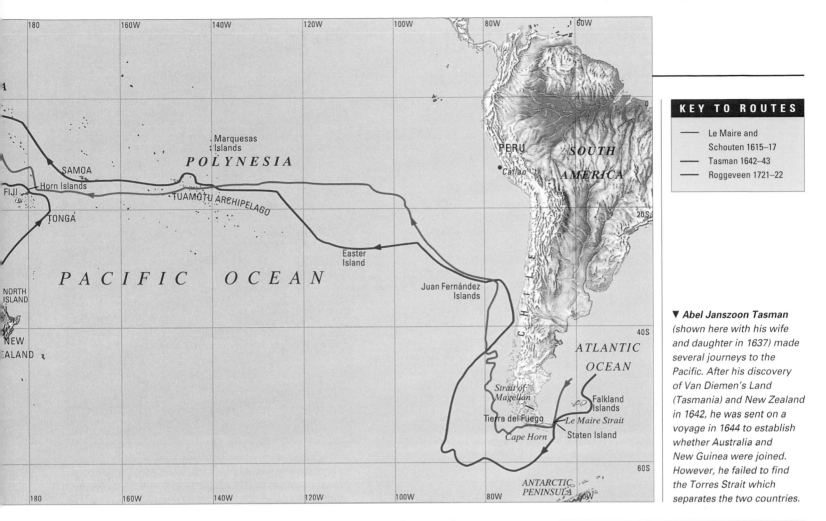

KEY TO ROUTES

— Le Maire and
    Schouten 1615–17
— Tasman 1642–43
— Roggeveen 1721–22

▼ **Abel Janszoon Tasman** (shown here with his wife and daughter in 1637) made several journeys to the Pacific. After his discovery of Van Diemen's Land (Tasmania) and New Zealand in 1642, he was sent on a voyage in 1644 to establish whether Australia and New Guinea were joined. However, he failed to find the Torres Strait which separates the two countries.

again. Within a few days they discovered more new land (New Zealand) and, anchoring in a bay, were approached by canoes. The men seemed friendly at first, but suddenly attacked a longboat, killing four Dutchmen. Tasman left "Murderers' Bay" (Golden Bay) hastily. It was a sad first contact between Europeans and Maoris.

They coasted north, wondering if this were part of Le Maire's Staten Land (the island east of the tip of South America) and looked for a strait that would provide a passage to Chile. They entered what was later to be called "Cook Strait," but did not recognize its nature. Rounding the northern tip of North Island, they were forced northeast by the wind. Following Le Maire, they found Tonga, and got into a terrible tangle amid reefs and rocks in the Fiji group. After failing to find Torres Strait, still unknown outside Spain, they coasted northern New Guinea and reached Batavia ten months after they had set out.

Celebrations were muted. Tasman was criticized for not investigating more closely the lands he had discovered, and in any case the Company already had more commercial opportunities than it could cope with, and feared that promising new discoveries would just be exploited by others, such as the English. In the words of the historian J. H. Parry, "Trade, which in the 16th century had been a prime stimulus to exploration, became its enemy in the 17th century."

It is therefore not surprising that the progress of discovery hardly advanced in the remainder of the century, nor that the only other really important Dutch voyage of exploration was carried out by a non-Company man.

Jacob Roggeveen

Jacob Roggeveen, following rather late in life (he was 62) an idea of his father's for new sources of trade in the South Sea, was backed by the West India Company (a much less grand institution than the East India Company). In pursuit of the great "Southland" he entered the Pacific in 1721 via Le Maire Strait, took a look at the Juan Fernández group of

islands, 300 miles (485 kilometers) off the coast of Chile, and searched for a coast, reported by a buccaneer, at a latitude of 27°S.

He found no continent, but did find, on Easter Day, a small island whose inhabitants are said to have believed their nearest neighbors were on the Moon. Most astonishing were the giant carved stone figures, the significance of which still puzzles experts today. After a week they sailed on, failing to find the continent but wandering for over a month among the Tuamotus. Having lost one ship and a number of men, Roggeveen decided to head for Batavia, touching on the pleasant Samoan group on the way.

The English and the French

From the end of the 17th century there was intense interest in the Pacific in England and France. William Dampier, a buccaneer and famous author of *A New Voyage Round the World* (1697), was commissioned to undertake a voyage of discovery to find the "southern continent." During his journey of 1699–1700, however, he only succeeded in discovering the Dampier Strait between the Bismark Sea and the Solomon Sea. Otherwise, interest in the area was largely confined to talk until 1763, when the Seven Years War between the two great colonial and commercial rivals came to an end. At this point it was decided to put ships and men to better use than war, and the golden age of Pacific exploration began.

John "Foul-weather Jack" Byron

In 1764 John Byron, grandfather of the poet, set sail in the *Dolphin* with orders to check the Falkland Islands as a possible base, which he did, and to sail up the west coast of North America to look for a strait from Hudson's Bay. He decided not to do this, and instead set off west to look for the "southern continent." He put in to the island of Takaroa in the Tuamotus, touched on various other small islands, including one in the Gilberts (Kiribati) that still bears his name, and rounded the Philippines to reach Batavia (Jakarta), by then a large but unhealthy city, when he sailed home via the Cape. The voyage had taken under two years – a record.

Samuel Wallis

Before the year was out the *Dolphin,* refitted, was off again, this time commanded by the rather more reliable Samuel Wallis – the true forerunner of Cook. Like Cook, he took

good care of his crew and was the first captain to keep scurvy at bay on such a voyage; ironically, as both Wallis and Cook found, the most dangerous place in terms of casualties was the "European" city of Batavia. The *Dolphin* was accompanied by the sloop *Swallow,* commanded by Captain Carteret, a veteran of Byron's voyage. Unfortunately, the *Swallow* sailed like a barrel; the ships became separated after passing the Strait of Magellan and completed the voyage independently.

Wallis followed the customary northwesterly route across the Pacific, but in the Tuamotus he was somewhat further south than most previous travelers and thus encountered Tahiti. This moment may be regarded as something of a turning point in the exploration of the Pacific by Europeans. To the sailors who landed there, Tahiti seemed a kind of paradise. But from the time Wallis's ship dropped anchor in Matavai Bay, the traditional society of Tahiti was, of course, doomed.

After staying in Tahiti for over a month, Wallis sailed west for a time, naming numerous islands after royal dukes and eminent admirals, until the poor condition of his ship and crew made him decide on a course for Batavia.

Carteret and the *Swallow*

Meanwhile, the little *Swallow,* against all odds, was making her own way around the world. Her tardy progress enforced a trans-Pacific voyage at the worst season, and, like everyone else, Carteret was compelled to sail in a more northerly latitude than he wished. He was, however, well to the south of Wallis, and discovered Pitcairn Island, soon to be made famous as a result of the mutiny on the *Bounty.* He rediscovered Quirós's Santa Cruz Islands, and sailed

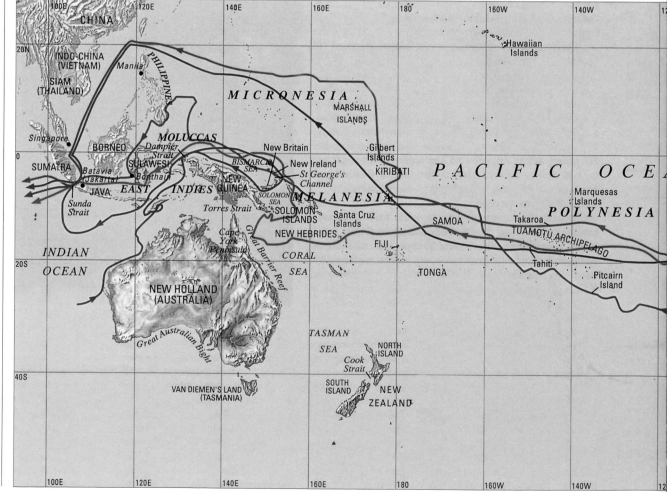

through the Solomons without recognizing them. He found St George's Channel, thus proving that New Ireland and New Britain are separate islands, but, further north, contrary currents prevented him entering Dampier Strait.

After spending five months in the small Dutch port of Bonthain in Sulawesi, he was able to sail to Batavia, where his ship, by now severely battered, was repaired. He was still forced to spend six weeks at the Cape (not entirely unwelcome) to revive his crew, before setting out on the final stage in January 1769. North of Ascension Island he was swiftly overhauled by the gallant Comte de Bougainville in the French frigate *Boudeuse*.

The Comte de Bougainville

Bougainville had also been round the world, his course in the central Pacific running close to that of Wallis. He, too, had the good luck to strike Tahiti, but he remained there for little more than a week before sailing due west again. Unlike practically every navigator in the previous century and a half, he was willing to risk embayment on a lee shore of New Guinea/Australia, but there were to be moments when he regretted his boldness. He touched the outer fringes of the Great Barrier Reef, surmised that much land, probably islands, lay beyond, and, working his way north, sighted the coast of New Guinea.

He was on the verge of rediscovering Torres Strait, but his crew was in a poor condition and he was intent on reaching a port as soon as possible. However, working his way out of the Gulf, in order to round New Guinea, was a nightmare – storms, poor visibility, shoals everywhere. He sailed through the Solomons, without realizing their identity, and eventually found a haven off New Britain,

where there was wood and water, though not much food. By an extraordinary coincidence, he discovered the remains of Carteret's camp about 5 miles (8 kilometers) away.

Unlike Carteret, Bougainville did not recognize St George's Channel as a strait (Dampier had recorded it as a bay), and therefore passed to the north of New Ireland. Within five weeks he reached a Dutch base in the Moluccas, where the men ate their first decent meal for many weeks. Batavia was reached 12 days after Carteret had left, and the *Boudeuse*, having left its storeship behind, gradually closed the gap, until the *Swallow* was sighted in the Atlantic on February 25, 1769.

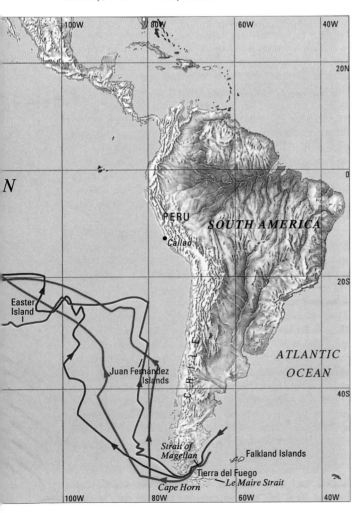

Comte de Bougainville
Despite the murder of some of their countrymen by French sailors, the Tahitians continued to offer their hospitality to Bougainville.

A thorough gentleman and son of the Enlightenment, Bougainville (1729–1811) was distinguished by personal charm as well as courage and high scientific intelligence. He had been a soldier before his voyage around the world and had established, at his own expense, a French settlement in the Falklands. After his circumnavigation, in which he lost only seven men, he was for a time a royal secretary, served in North America, but was disgraced after the French defeat at the Battle of Saints in the Caribbean (1782). He narrowly escaped the Terror and sat out the Revolution on his Normandy estates, until finding favor again under Napoleon.

James Cook

▶ *During Cook's second voyage* he crossed and recrossed the Antarctic Circle and identified many of the Polynesian islands found by earlier explorers. The Resolution *and* Adventure *are shown here anchored in Matavai Bay, Tahiti, in 1773.*

▶ *Captain James Cook was not only a fine seaman and an accomplished surveyor, but had a more enlightened attitude than many of his contemporaries toward the cultures of the people he encountered.*

In the 250 years since Magellan's voyage in 1519–22, much had been learned about the Pacific, yet much was still unknown. Exploration had been unplanned, and the secrecy maintained by the various powers about their own discoveries had led to much unnecessary repetition. Roughly half the ocean had never seen a European ship, and some questions had not been resolved. Chief of these was the matter of the "southern continent," and its relationship to Australia and New Zealand, regarded by some as a continental cape. These questions were to be conclusively answered by the Englishman James Cook (1728–79), son of a Yorkshire laborer, who joined the Royal Navy at the age of 27 after an apprenticeship in a Whitby collier.

Cook had risen fairly fast as a result of his natural abilities; he become known to the Admiralty through his meticulously accurate charts of Newfoundland waters and to the Royal Society through observations of an eclipse of the sun. He was, however, a compromise choice to command a voyage in 1768, whose immediate object was to observe the transit of Venus across the sun, from the vantage point of Tahiti. After these observations were completed, his instructions were to sail south as far as 40° to discover the supposed continent. If he found nothing, he was to sail west until he reached the eastern coast of New Zealand. Having investigated that territory, he should return home by whatever direction he thought best.

The Admiralty provided Cook with a ship called the *Endeavour*. Built as a Whitby collier, she was strong and spacious, though not swift. She carried 94 people, including a bright young botanist, Joseph Banks.

The first voyage

The *Endeavour* left Plymouth in August 1768, rounded the Horn in January, and from a record southerly latitude sailed almost directly northwest toward Tahiti – thus taking a further slice off the hypothetical continent. In Tahiti they spent three months, building an observatory and a fort, and enjoying the now expected hospitality of the people.

Banks and his fellow naturalists found much to fascinate them. Cook, who in four visits to Tahiti learned to speak the language after a fashion, was troubled by feelings of guilt. He had no doubt of the "fatal impact" of European civilization, but knew there was no going back.

When the observations were completed and several islands had been charted, the *Endeavour* sailed south, beyond 40°S, but without catching sight of the "southern

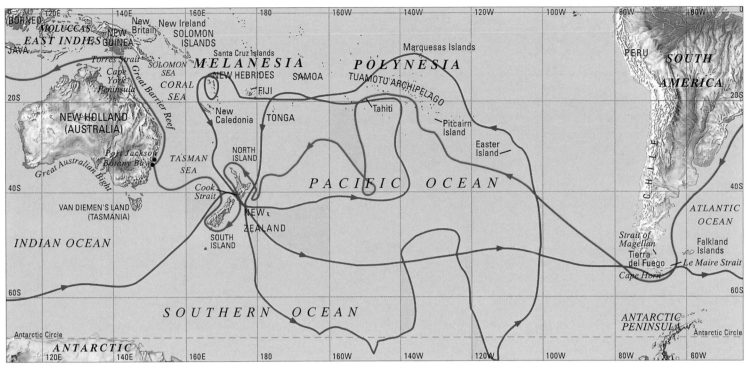

Harrison's chronometer
Until the invention of an accurate marine chronometer, an assessment of a ship's longitudinal position was very difficult, if not impossible.

Longitude is measured by working out the difference between the local time (taken from the sun) and Greenwich mean time (for example) – every hour's difference equaling 15° longitude. On his second voyage Cook carried a copy of the fourth chronometer of John Harrison, a Yorkshire carpenter who had set out to gain the prize of £20,000 offered by the Board of Longitude for an accurate marine timepiece.

KEY TO ROUTES
—— Cook 1768–71
—— Cook 1772–75

beyond the understanding of Europeans. Banks regarded them as "one degree removed from the brutes" but Cook, as usual, was more appreciative of another culture: "They may appear ... to be the most wretched people on earth but in reality they are far happier than we Europeans .... They live in a tranquillity which is not disturbed by the inequality of condition."

Sailing north again, Cook noted and named Port Jackson (Sydney), though he did not investigate the splendid natural harbor. Bougainville had approached Australia further north, and had been prevented from sighting the coast by the Great Barrier Reef. Cook, coasting up from the south, was inside the Reef, which soon began to close in on him. He was in terrible trouble, and it was a miracle that the *Endeavour* did not sink after being grounded on the coral for 24 hours; they reached the shore by using a sail as a sling to cover the hole.

Patched up, the *Endeavour* resumed her nerve-racking progress, dependent on the vagaries of the wind and currents within a labyrinth of shoals and reefs. Still, Cook was determined to find out whether or not New Holland and New Guinea were joined, and in August 1770 he became the second European captain to sail through the Torres Strait, taking a more southerly passage than Torres himself. Sadly, the worst was yet to come. Cook had not lost one man through sickness, but at Batavia the crew was decimated by fevers. Before he reached the Cape nearly 30 were dead, and scarcely a dozen were fully fit.

The second voyage
Cook had made by far the most fruitful voyage in the whole history of Pacific voyages of discovery, yet the devotees of the "southern continent" theory were not discouraged by proof that New Zealand was an island. There was still a vast expanse of the southern ocean in which the continent might be lurking. The French were also showing signs of unwelcome activity in the south Pacific.

Cook was therefore sent on a second voyage (1772–75), this time with two ships, *Resolution* and *Adventure*. On this voyage, in some ways even more remarkable than his first, Cook finally despatched the "southern continent" theory by sailing around the world in a hitherto unvisited latitude, twice crossing the Antarctic Circle, and only missing sight of Antarctica by chance. He also rediscovered the Marquesas, unvisited by Europeans since Mendaña's day, and discovered New Caledonia in the Pacific, and South Georgia and the South Sandwich Islands in the Atlantic.

continent." Cook turned to the west and in October reached the North Island of New Zealand. Early contacts with the Maoris were unhappy, though friendly relations were established later. Cook then embarked upon his masterly, six-month survey of the coasts of New Zealand.

Australia
By March 1770 Cook's main tasks had been completed. He now opted to return via the East Indies by sailing westward, to try to find the east coast of New Holland (Australia). He aimed for Tasmania, but a gale drove the ship north and landfall was made near Botany Bay, where they went ashore. The culture of the Aborigines was

The North Pacific

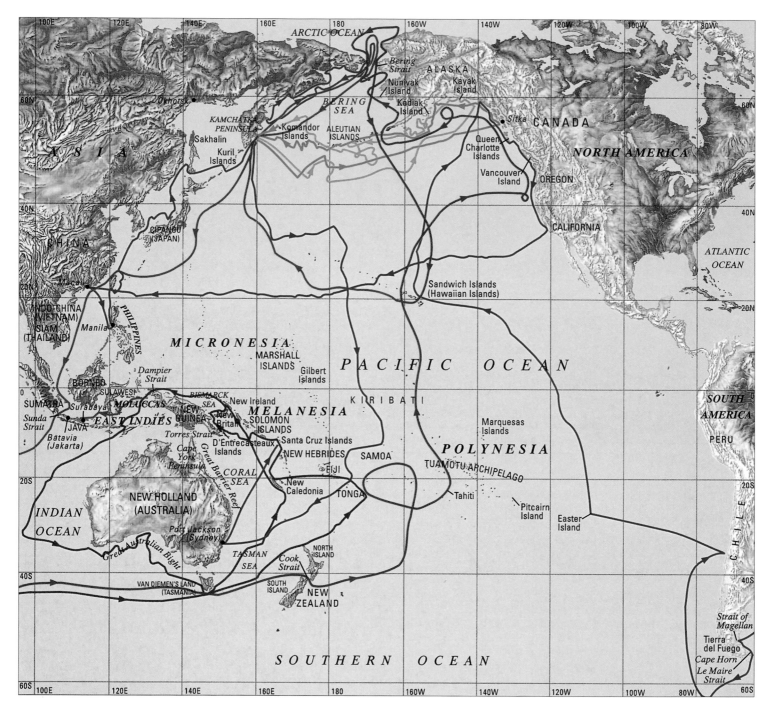

At the beginning of the 18th century there were several unresolved questions regarding the North Pacific, one of them being whether Asia and North America were joined. Peter the Great of Russia, intent on expanding Russian territory to the east, charged the Danish explorer Vitus Bering with the task of finding the answer. Bering left St Petersburg in 1725, but took almost two years to reach Okhotsk, his forward base. Embarking on his voyage in 1728, he sailed as far north as 67°, but owing to fog he missed the American coast.

The Russians were anxious lest they were forestalled commercially in the North Pacific by the French or the English, so Bering tried again. While his lieutenants made somewhat ineffectual voyages to the Kurils and Japan, Bering, with the more energetic Alexei Chirikov, at last set out for America in June 1741.

Their two ships became separated and Bering made landfall on Kayak Island, close to the coast of Alaska.

Conditions on board were deteriorating, and many were down with scurvy, so they prepared to return. In a grim state, they were forced to winter on Bering Island, heart-breakingly close to their base in Kamchatka. Bering himself was not among the survivors.

Meanwhile, Chirikov had sailed to a point beyond modern Sitka, further east than Bering had achieved, and returned safely, though in poor condition. Not much had been learned about the coast, but Alaska was, at least for the time being, Russian.

Cook's third voyage

Cook's third voyage (1776–80) aimed to solve another long-standing question: the possible existence of a Northwest Passage around or through North America. Numerous mariners had sought the passage from the Atlantic; Cook was to search from the Pacific. From his favorite base in Tahiti, Cook sailed more or less due north,

◄ **The vast area** covered by Cook and La Pérouse in their Pacific voyages is reflected in this engraving of the inhabitants of the many lands they visited.

and in January 1778 made his last great discovery – Hawaii – named by him the Sandwich Islands. Friendly relations were established, and Cook was moved to ponder, not for the first time, how a single race of people came to be scattered so widely over the Pacific.

According to his instructions, Cook turned east about 40° and headed for the North American coast. Sighting the coast of what is now Oregon, he turned north and began his search for the elusive passage. In spite of Bering's travels, the coasts of Canada and Alaska were virtually unknown; Cook was therefore charting the last major section of continental coastline on the world map, apart from those in polar regions.

He followed the line of the Aleutians, then turned north to Bering Strait, landing briefly on the Asian coast before continuing until the ice stopped him, in 70°44′N. He searched briefly for a passage, but the waning summer and a shortage of wood and water made him break off. Coasting the Asian shore, he crossed to the Aleutians, where he had an informative meeting with Russian traders.

He decided to winter in Hawaii, and found a suitable anchorage in Kealakekua Bay. Cook having been adjudged to possess divine status, relations with the Hawaiians were good, but they soon began to enquire when their guests were leaving, since supplies were growing short. Cook therefore sailed to find another anchorage, but was at once caught in a gale which sprung the foremast of the *Resolution* and the ships were forced to return.

They were not welcome, and in a fracas resulting from a stolen boat which Cook was partly responsible for provoking, he was struck down and killed.

The voyage continued, now under the command of Charles Clerke, a first-rate captain but, at 31, already suffering from a lung disease which after another summer exploring in the Arctic proved fatal. No advance was made on Cook's discoveries, and the ships returned to England in October 1780.

In the 11 years of Cook's voyages, he virtually completed the discovery of the Pacific; it held no more great secrets. Although the motives for his work were largely political and strategic, the results were mainly scientific and geographical – a striking reversal of the usual result of European exploration. His greatness was universally recognized: the French government requested its commanders and officials abroad to give Cook free passage, even in time of war.

La Pérouse and Entrecasteaux

Of Cook's French contemporaries, probably the finest maritime explorer, besides Bougainville, was La Pérouse, who sailed on a Pacific voyage, charged with establishing the position of the Solomons once and for all, in 1785. After carrying out various preliminary surveys with outstanding accuracy, La Pérouse put in at Port Jackson (Sydney) soon after the arrival of the British First Fleet. His appearance caused some consternation, quickly allayed by the great charm of the Frenchman, his obvious concern with scientific rather than political results, and not least his frank admiration for the work of Cook. He sailed for the Solomons in February 1788 and disappeared. Wreckage was found of his two frigates on a reef off the Santa Cruz Islands 30 years later.

His work was to be completed by Entrecasteaux, sent to search for La Pérouse in 1791. At last Mendaña, the subject of much complaint by navigators over the centuries, was vindicated, as Entrecasteaux fitted physical features to the Spaniard's description of the Solomons.

▼ **John Cleveley** has provided us with this depiction of Cook's death at Kealakekua Bay, Hawaii. It was based on a sketch made by Cleveley's brother, James, a carpenter on the *Resolution*.

The British in Australia

Cook's discovery in 1770 of New South Wales was timely for the British because the success of the American colonists in fighting to gain their independence in 1781 meant that convicts could no longer be sent to North America. The land described by Cook appeared to be an acceptable alternative, and in May 1787 the First Fleet, consisting of 11 ships, set sail carrying nearly 800 convicts. Also on board were the first Governor, Captain Arthur Phillip, a large number of sailors and marines (plus families, in some cases), and stores for two years. After a trouble-free journey, the fleet arrived at Botany Bay in January 1788 and then moved north to establish a settlement where there was better farming land, at Port Jackson or, as it was to be called, Sydney Harbour.

An air of fantasy hovers around this operation and the marvel is that, despite severe hardship, the settlement somehow survived and eventually prospered. The Governor and his men knew virtually nothing about the continent to which they had been summarily despatched, neither the land nor the Aborigines who had inhabited it for some 50,000 years.

In 1788, when the First Fleet arrived, the Aborigines probably numbered more than 300,000. They were divided into many different groups, speaking different languages, and occupying distinct regions marked by natural features such as rivers and mountain ranges. They lived in close affinity with nature and understood their own land in a profound, mystical way that was beyond the ken of Europeans. They also knew a great deal about its geography, for although they lived within their own clearly defined territories, there were many contacts between different groups, and long journeys were undertaken for trading or cultural purposes.

The beleaguered settlers at first made little effort at exploration. Some years passed before anyone reached the Blue Mountains, 37 miles (60 kilometers) away, many more before the interior was understood. Exploring the coasts was more urgent, as the French were showing interest in New Holland and the British wished to lay claim to the whole continent. The task was undertaken by Matthew Flinders, an explorer in the Cook tradition – intelligent, humane, and determined.

Flinders's first voyage

Flinders, a midshipman, arrived in Sydney in 1796 on the same ship as his friend George Bass. At 21, he was already an experienced sailor. With the Governor's encouragement, Flinders and Bass sailed in a sloop to discover if, as was widely suspected, Tasmania was an island. They sailed through what was subsequently named Bass Strait and circumnavigated Tasmania, exploring the valleys of the Tamar and Derwent.

Flinders's second voyage

In 1800 Flinders returned to England, where he gained the support of Sir Joseph Banks for a projected exploration of the whole coast of New Holland. At Banks's urging, the Admiralty issued the relevant order and provided Flinders with a ship, the *Investigator*. She was an ex-collier, like Cook's *Endeavour*, but proved abominably leaky despite her

▼ **The discovery,** by Matthew Flinders and George Bass, that Tasmania was an island, took a week off the voyage time from the Cape to New South Wales.

▶ **This sketch map** of Sydney Cove, Port Jackson, was made by one of the convicts deported there in 1788. The First Fleet is shown at anchor in the bay.

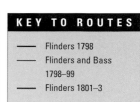

refit. Several scientists and other experts sailed with him, but the astronomer, a martyr to seasickness, left at Cape Town with the result that Flinders and his brother Samuel made all the astronomical observations. In the process, they added significantly to the science of navigation, most notably to knowledge of magnetic variation.

Along the south coast

From Cape Leeuwin, the *Investigator* made a six-month cruise along the south coast, hugging the shore, most of it virgin. Flinders sometimes walked 20 miles (30 kilometers) to a suitable hill from which to take bearings. They explored Spencer Gulf, which turned out not to be a strait, as some believed, dividing New South Wales and New Holland. Soon after, the *Investigator* encountered Nicolas Baudin in the *Géographe*, exploring the coast between Bass Strait and Encounter Bay on behalf of France. Despite language problems, they exchanged information amicably. Both missed the Murray River; in fact Flinders failed to spot the outlets of any of the great rivers, encouraging speculation that they drained into a huge inland lake.

After ten weeks' recuperation at Port Jackson, Flinders set out north along the east coast. He narrowly beat the monsoon to Torres Strait, and found a new route through that notoriously hazardous waterway. His belief that it would become a valuable short cut between the Pacific and Indian Oceans failed to take account of the fact that few captains possessed his navigational skills.

In the Gulf of Carpentaria which, like Spencer Gulf,

offered no strait, the state of the ship was found to be desperate. Nevertheless, Flinders continued up the western shore, hitting rocks now and again, and along Arnhem Land. Though he made every effort not to antagonize the Aborigines, an attack on Groote Eylandt, in which a sailor was speared, was repelled by guns and one man was killed. Off Arnhem Land, in one of those encounters that reminds us that European explorers often went where others had long been accustomed to go before, they came across a group of Malay fishermen. Flinders named an island Pabassoo, after their leader.

Flinders had come to the reluctant conclusion that to continue his survey would invite disaster, and in March 1803 he sailed from Arnhem Bay to Timor for stores, thence back to Sydney, completing his circumnavigation.

Return to England

He sailed for England, but was wrecked on the Great Barrier Reef and returned to Sydney, where he was given a 30-ton schooner, the *Cumberland*. He set out once more, via Torres Strait, which he passed through in three days. Forced into Mauritius for repairs, he was imprisoned by the French Governor. (Although the *Investigator* had a safe-conduct from the French, who were at war with the British, the Governor deemed it not to cover the *Cumberland*.) Flinders remained in captivity for over six years, not reaching England until 1810. In poor health, he managed to complete his account of *A Voyage to Terra Australis*, dying the day it was published in 1814.

Across the Blue Mountains

crossed, by Gregory Blaxland who, unlike earlier pioneers, elected to keep to the high ground instead of following the valleys. Even so, he and his companions made slow progress, sometimes covering only a mile or two all day, but after nearly three weeks they saw, from Mount York, the desirable prospect of lush green land stretching before them. The Governor sent others to follow up Blaxland; there was a road to Bathurst by 1815, and in 1818 John Oxley, having failed to get far down the Macquarie River, turned east and discovered the Liverpool Plains.

By this time, restrictions on settlement having been removed, British emigrants were flooding in, increasing pressure for more land. Hamilton Hume, a native Australian, traveled from Sydney to near modern-day Melbourne in 1824, though greatly harassed by insects and Aborigines. The botanist Allan Cunningham discovered the rich pastures of the Darling Downs in 1827 and went almost as far north as modern Brisbane, west of the Great Dividing Range.

Sturt and Macley

Just as people nowadays speculate about conditions on other planets, formerly they evolved theories about unexplored lands on Earth. The exploration of Australia's coastline had indicated a remarkable lack of outflowing rivers (partly because they were overlooked), and this gave rise to the theory that the island-continent contained a great inland sea, into which its rivers drained. The problem of the New South Wales' drainage system was largely solved by the outstanding figure among the first generation of explorers of Australia: Charles Sturt, who was a 33-year-old soldier on the Governor's staff when he was chosen for the task in 1828.

▲ **Europeans,** mounted on horseback and equipped with guns, had little difficulty in quelling any threat from the Aborigines, as shown in this painting by Thomas Baines, official artist to an expedition in northwest Australia in 1855.

The first efforts to penetrate the interior of Australia were made from Sydney and were motivated by the growing need to find more grazing land. The task was not easy, as the settlement was fenced in by mountains shrouded in a bluish haze, the effect of the oily eucalyptus trees, which to the unhappy convicts seemed to signify a paradisal land beyond (how wrong they were).

It was not until 1813 that the Blue Mountains were

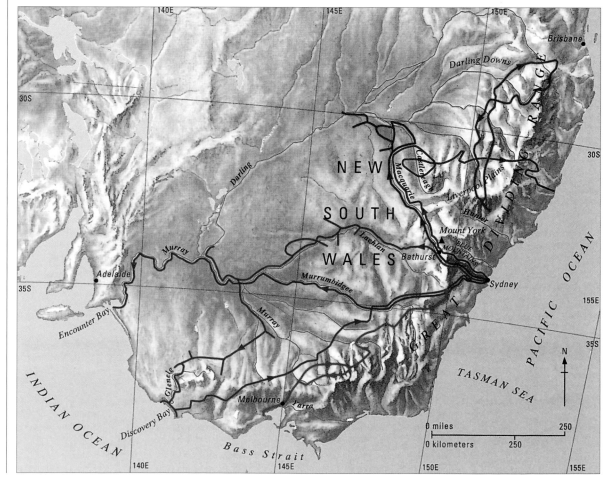

KEY TO ROUTES	
——	Blaxland 1813
——	Oxley 1818
——	Hume 1824–25
——	Cunningham 1827
——	Sturt and Hume 1828–29
——	Sturt 1829–30
——	Mitchell 1836

► *Twenty-five years elapsed* *between the first settlement in Sydney and Blaxland's successful crossing of the* *Blue Mountains. The Three Sisters rocks, shown here, give an idea of the difficulty of the terrain.*

His first journey took him, with Hume, down the Macquarie River, beyond the swamps that had defeated Oxley. His account is full of the hazards that were to become familiar to explorers of Australia: intense heat, scarcity of water, aggressive insects, and hostile Aborigines. In February 1829 he reached the Darling River, but confessed he could not hazard a guess about its course.

On his second journey, Sturt took a more southerly route, along the Murrumbidgee and then the Murray rivers. His chief companion this time was George Macley (or M'Leay), a young, red-headed naturalist who got on so well with the Aborigines that they were convinced he had once been one of their race. But as they proceeded west, the Aborigines became more hostile. In a famous incident, the explorers were confronted by some 600 armed people, clearly on the point of launching an attack. Sturt was about to shoot one of the leaders, hoping to discourage the rest, when Macley stopped him, indicating the sudden appearance of four other men from another direction. "Turning round, I observed four men at the top of their speed. The foremost of them, as soon as he got ahead of the boat, threw himself from a considerable height into the water. He struggled across ... and ... stood in front of the savage against whom my aim had been directed. Seizing him by the throat, he pushed him backwards, and forcing all who were in the water upon the bank, he trod its margin with a vehemence and agitation that were exceedingly striking." Violence having been averted by this fortuitous ally, the 600 became friendly. This was often the way: Aborigine hostility, though certainly sometimes fatal, was short-lived; they could often be distracted from imminent assault by something that amused them.

But the sensational events of this day were not over. Sturt and Macley had allowed their boat to drift on to a shoal and, having pushed her off, "our attention was withdrawn to a new and beautiful stream coming apparently from the north." They proceeded up the new river, accompanied for some way by a noisy but now amiable multitude on the bank, and Sturt concluded, correctly, that it was the Darling. He then turned back and followed the Murray for nearly 400 miles (650 kilometers) to its mouth.

South from the Murray River

Sturt had opened up plenty of well-watered land to the colonists. His discoveries were followed up by Thomas Mitchell, surveyor-general of New South Wales, who doubted Sturt's identification of the Darling. After two failures, due to attacks by Aborigines, his third expedition in 1836 proved that Sturt was right. He then struck off on his own, south from the Murray, found the Glenelg River, and sailed down to the sea at Discovery Bay.

His journey opened up another large and desirable stretch of land to European farmers, though this region was not entirely virgin territory. Whalers had established a small settlement on the coast and a few colonists from Tasmania were also in residence, without permission from the authorities in Sydney. In 1835 John Batman had noted a site at the mouth of the Yarra River as suitable for a village and had "bought" 600,000 acres of land from the local Aborigines. In 1836 Bourke, the Governor of New South Wales, vetoed Batman's purchase, named the place Melbourne and had a plan of streets drawn up, with building lots measured and offered for sale.

The overlanders

Early exploring expeditions in Australia were largely motivated by the need for grazing land, and initial discoveries were quickly followed up by men driving their "mobs" of sheep or cattle to new pastures, or to settlements where meat was scarce and prices high. The "overlanders" frequently undertook long treks through country which, if not totally unknown, was unmapped, and they played a significant part in opening up Australia to white settlement. Among the most notable feats was that of Patrick Leslie, who moved nearly 6000 sheep from a station in the Hunter Valley westward to the Darling Downs in 1840.

Into the Interior

By the end of the 1830s much of the southeast of Australia was settled. But the bulk of the continent, not only the interior, was still a mystery. Future exploration was devoted to two main objectives. In the first place, it was desirable to establish overland routes to the settlements which had arisen around the coasts as a result of coastal exploration. In the second, it was necessary to learn the nature of the interior and to find a route across the continent.

The northwest coast was explored between 1837 and 1839 by George Grey (later a notable colonial governor) partly from the sea, partly on land. However, the first substantial colony in Western Australia was established in the southwest corner of the country. Pressure began to grow to establish a land connection between the new colony and New South Wales, and in 1840 the job was offered to Edward Eyre.

Edward Eyre

Eyre had already traveled about the country, driving cattle from Sydney to remote settlements, and declared that the proposed route, along the Great Australian Bight, would be impossible for stock. Eyre undertook an expedition into the interior, instead, discovering Lake Torrens and Lake Eyre (though he thought they were one) before his horse sank up to its belly through the salt crust and he gave up.

The following year, however, not put off by his experience, he decided to attempt the journey overland around the Bight, from Adelaide to Albany, if only to prove that it was useless. All went well as far as Fowler's Bay, because a boat accompanied them that far, carrying their stores. Thereafter there were no more anchorages, and the stores had to be carried on horseback. He reduced his party to four – one European, John Baxter, and three Aborigines – and, in the height of summer, set out. Sometimes they marched through the scrub, sometimes along the cliffs, sometimes on the beach. By the time they were halfway to their destination they were discarding coats, weapons and cooking pots, and eating their horses. Baxter wanted to turn back before they had passed the point of no return; Eyre dissuaded him.

The two younger Aborigines disappeared for a couple of days but were driven back by starvation. A few days later, while Eyre was away from camp rounding up the horses, they shot Baxter – possibly by mistake or in panic at being caught stealing – and made off with his and Eyre's guns, as well as much of the food and water. Eyre and Wylie, the remaining Aborigine, continued. Fortunately, Eyre still had a rifle, without which they could scarcely have survived because they were now largely forced to live off the land. One marvelous day he managed to shoot a kangaroo. Wylie, with his remarkable digestive powers, consumed innards, hind legs, and even the hide. By the end of May the weather had changed; it became cold and wet, a welcome change. The horses recovered sufficiently to be ridden, and they began to encounter green grass.

Early in June they spotted a boat, the *Mississippi*, which they hailed, and within an hour, Eyre noted, "I had the inexpressible pleasure of being again among civilized beings, and of shaking hands with a fellow-countryman." That night he lay in a comfortable bunk but could not sleep. For nearly two weeks they lived in what seemed like utter luxury on the *Mississippi*. When they left, they carried as much food and supplies as they could possibly need, including a gift of six bottles of wine.

The weather became dreadful, wet and stormy, and they had to wade through seemingly endless swamps. Nevertheless, within three weeks they reached the little settlement of Albany on King George Sound. The expedition had discovered nothing of importance and had merely established what was known, certainly to Eyre, already: that the route was unviable as a trail for livestock. But that does not diminish Eyre's achievement. And it was, after all, the first overland link between east and west.

Ludwig Leichhardt

In 1844 Ludwig Leichhardt, a German who had arrived in Australia at the age of 30 only the year before, set out with a party of nine to establish an overland route from Brisbane to a military outpost on the Cobourg Peninsula, Arnhem Land. The party, which included two Aborigines and two youths, covered 2500 miles (4000 kilometers) in its remarkable journey, arriving in Port Essington in December 1845.

Leichhardt achieved his objective in spite of severe difficulties. However, he was a most inefficient explorer, with almost no ability to calculate his position accurately. Unlike Sturt and Eyre, he had little sympathy with the Aborigines, for whom he expressed some contempt – an extraordinary attitude when traveling in the bush. He also failed to ration his supplies, so that before long his men had

▼ *Charles Sturt* was one of the most intrepid of the Australian explorers, enduring, with his companions, the extreme heat of the Stony Desert.

J Macfarlane

F.A. Sleap sc

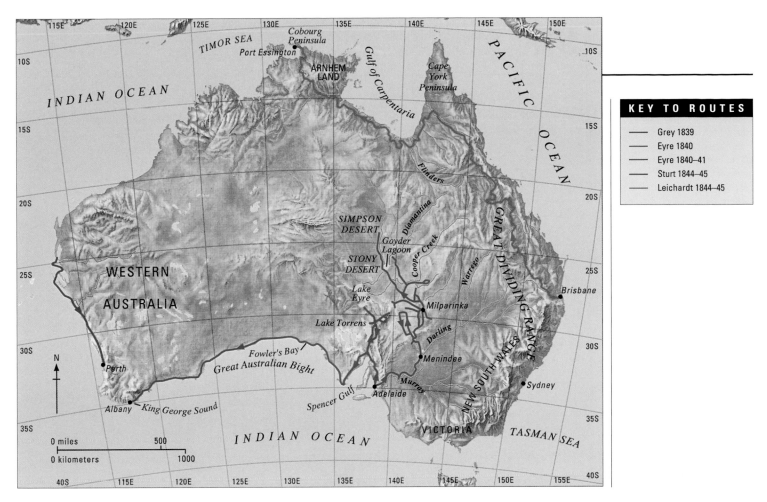

—— Grey 1839
—— Eyre 1840
—— Eyre 1840–41
—— Sturt 1844–45
—— Leichardt 1844–45

to depend largely on what wildlife they could kill. In 1848 he set out to cross the continent from east to west. He crossed the Warrego River but soon after disappeared and was never seen again.

Sturt's expedition

In 1844 Charles Sturt made an attempt to cross the continent. Hoping to avoid the problem of the salt lakes encountered by Eyre, he went up the Darling River to Menindee, then walked north to Milparinka before turning northwest. It was a particularly hot summer, all the water holes were dry, and Sturt and his companions were compelled to remain near Milparinka for six months, living part of the time in an underground chamber which they dug to escape the ferocious sun. Writing was extremely difficult because, in the intense heat, ink evaporated from the pen almost immediately.

It was July 1845 before enough rain fell to risk an advance. They covered about 400 miles (650 kilometers) when Sturt decided to turn back. He was in fact on the edge of the Simpson Desert and to have gone further would probably have been fatal. He made another attempt the following summer, taking a more easterly route. At Cooper Creek a thermometer which registered up to 127°F (53°C) was shattered.

Returning across the Stony Desert nearly killed the whole party. When Sturt eventually arrived in Adelaide he was almost blind, burnt black, sick with scurvy, and unable to walk (he was carried on a cart). Nevertheless, he lived to the age of 74, dying at Cheltenham, England, in 1869.

In the late 1840s Australia was entering a period of rapid change. The principle of self-government was conceded, the colony of Victoria was founded, and deportation to the eastern colonies was abolished. But no less important than these political advances was the discovery of gold. The population increased rapidly, as did roads and railroads. Yet still no one had succeeded in crossing the continent. After the fever of the gold rush had died down, this became an urgent ambition.

▲ **The Aborigines** received little understanding from most Europeans, explorers and settlers alike. Edward Eyre, however, deplored their persecution: "It is a most lamentable thing to think that the progress and prosperity of one race should conduce to the downfall and decay of another ... and still more so to observe the apathy and indifference with which this result is contemplated by mankind in general."

Across the Continent

▶ **The departure** of the expedition of Robert O'Hara Burke was a very public event, with crowds turning out to see them off. Such scenes of gaiety must quickly have faded from their memories, however, in the face of the appalling conditions they encountered on their trek.

▼ **Burke, Wills, and King** returned to Cooper Creek in 1868, only to find that Brahe and his companions had left earlier that day. The physical condition of the three travelers, and the state of their clothing, must actually have been somewhat poorer than depicted here by Nicholas Chevalier. Of the three, John King was the only one not to die during the expedition.

The first expedition to succeed in crossing the continent was much the most elaborate and expensive ever mounted in Australia. It is also the most famous, not so much because of its success as of its dramatic failures. It was backed by the government of Victoria and the people of Melbourne, who together contributed about £10,000. Its leader was Robert O'Hara Burke, a former soldier, prospector, and currently police superintendent at Castlemaine. He was by no means an obvious choice, being without any experience of real exploration, and

critics have accused him of recklessness. Accompanying him was William John Wills, a young English surveyor who became a close and loyal comrade.

Burke and Wills

Burke was in a hurry. He knew that another expedition was setting off with the same objective from Adelaide (this was led by John McDouall Stuart, who actually started first), and there was prize money as well as glory awaiting the first man to cross the continent. The expedition arrived at Menindee, the last outpost of European settlement, in October 1860. Summer was approaching, but Burke could not afford to wait until the fall, so he took a party of eight ahead to Cooper Creek (discovered by Charles Sturt 30 years before), leaving William Wright to bring up stores later.

He set up camp in the shade of a coolibah tree and built a stockade to keep out animals and Aborigines. Here there were reeded waterholes, wild flowers, and flocks of brilliant birds, but there were also troublesome insects and rats. The latter made it necessary to hang food on strings from the trees and they also threaded the ground with their burrows, endangering the legs of camels and horses.

When Wright did not appear, Burke decided to press on with Wills, John King (a former British soldier), and Charlie Gray, whom he had picked up on the way. They took supplies for three months, and each man had his gun and a sleeping roll. But they took little spare clothing and – a bad mistake – no tents. The small party had to cross desert, plains, woods, and rocky ridges in every kind of vicious weather from blistering heat to withering gales. In 57 days they were floundering through salt marshes near the mouth of the Flinders River. They knew by the tidal movements that the sea could only be a few miles away, but they turned back without actually seeing it.

Most of their food had gone and they had little luck as hunters, though they boiled the plant portulaca as a vegetable to keep scurvy at bay. Both the men and the animals were very tired, the result of malnutrition as much as physical effort, and the constant rain meant that they were never dry. Burke had an attack of dysentery, but recovered in time to give Gray a beating after Wills had reported him cheating on rations. A few days later Gray was found at dawn dead in his bed roll. The only horse had to be shot, leaving two tottering camels.

Return to Cooper Creek

The lure of the camp at Cooper Creek kept the three of them going, and on the last day they marched 30 miles (50 kilometers) to reach it. Unfortunately, William Brahe, left in charge, had waited four months fending off the rats but had eventually assumed that Burke and his party were dead, or had taken a ship from the Queensland coast. Just eight hours before the three exhausted travelers staggered into the camp, Brahe and his company had ridden out. They had left some food but little else, not even spare clothes.

Burke and Wills tried to follow Cooper Creek to the west, but it soon split up into small channels that disappeared among the rocks. Meanwhile, Brahe and his party, having met Wright coming up belatedly with supplies, returned to the camp but, finding no sign of Burke, they rode away again. Burke dared not attempt a 150-mile (250-kilometer) march across the desert without water. The Aborigines offered some help; they gave them fish and showed them how to make *nardoo* (pounded seeds).

When Brahe reached Melbourne, a search party was organized. It made good time to Cooper Creek where they found, among the Aborigines who greeted them, a white man, burned almost black, fleshless, and practically speechless. It was John King. Burke and Wills had been dead for two months.

John McDouall Stuart

John McDouall Stuart was six years older than Burke and less lavishly supported, but he was a more experienced traveler. He had been with Charles Sturt on his last expedition and had since made several lesser trips on his own. Setting out in March 1860, he took a route that was not only much longer but also tougher. He headed for the center, found Chambers Pillar, a natural monolith he named after one of his patrons, and crossed the Macdonnell Ranges, named after the Governor of South Australia. In April 1860, he reached the center of the continent, and with one of his three companions climbed the hill now named after him (although he originally named it after Charles Sturt), where he planted the flag.

Soon afterward the party was forced to turn back to Adelaide by Aborigines who set fire to the bush. There he heard of the departure of Burke and Wills in August, which spurred him to renewed effort. He set off again in November, this time with the official backing of the South Australian government, but when he had gone 100 miles (160 kilometers) or so beyond Attack Creek, he was once more forced to turn back. By the time he reached Adelaide, the search party for Burke and Wills had already departed from Melbourne.

Less than a year after the start of his second attempt, Stuart set off again, with nine men this time and even more determined to achieve his goal. Once they had found a way through the rough country which had daunted him the previous year, the going became comparatively easy – "extensive plains, well grassed, and of beautiful alluvial

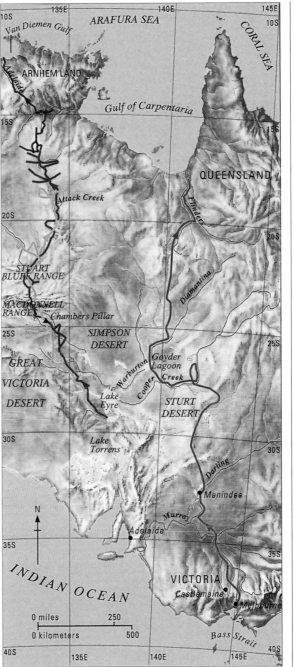

soil" – and in July they reached the sea near the mouth of the Adelaide River. "I advanced a few yards on to the beach, and was gratified and delighted to behold the water of the Indian Ocean in Van Diemen Gulf, before the party with the horses knew anything of its proximity. Thring, who rode in advance of me, called out 'The Sea!' which so took them all by surprise, and they were so astonished, that he had to repeat the call before they fully understood what was meant. Then they immediately gave three long and hearty cheers."

They then had to get back about 2000 miles (3250 kilometers) to Adelaide, and Stuart's health was so poor that he could not keep going a full day, even on horseback. His men had to make a sling between two horses in which he was carried. The expedition arrived on the same day that the bodies of Burke and Wills were being carried through the city on their way to burial in Melbourne.

Within ten years, a telegraph line was in existence between Adelaide and Darwin, following Stuart's route.

Europeans in New Zealand

European interest in New Zealand after Cook's visit of 1769 was desultory. Potential settlers were deterred by the Maoris, a more formidable population than the Australian Aborigines. However, sealers and whalers found welcome bases on New Zealand's coasts, where they could refit their vessels and replenish their stores, while pioneer traders sold goods, particularly guns, to the Maoris, and set up timber and flax production in North Island for processing in New South Wales.

Charting the coasts

The efficiency of Cook meant that New Zealand's coasts were remarkably well charted from the very beginning, although there was much detail to fill in. Rough weather had prevented Cook from surveying the east coast of South Island as thoroughly as he would have wished, and what Cook had named Banks Island, for example, turned out to be a peninsula when investigated by Captain Chase in 1809. In the same year Captain Stewart carried out a close survey of the island now named after him; Cook had not spotted the strait dividing it from the mainland, though he seems to have suspected its existence.

Early exploration of North Island

In 1814 a mission was established by Samuel Marsden at

▼ *Ekehu* was the Maori guide and companion of Heaphy and Brunner on their exploration of South Island. His skill at living off the land helped to ensure their survival in the very difficult terrain.

the Bay of Islands. From there he and other missionaries made several journeys into the interior of North Island, and within 30-odd years had penetrated to the center. The most resolute traveler was William Colenso, missionary and botanist, who, among other journeys, reached Lake Taupo from Napier in 1847.

European explorers did not, however, travel alone. As in other parts of the world they were accompanied by natives of the country concerned. Since the Maoris were, naturally, far more knowledgeable about the land of the long white cloud than were the Europeans, and a great deal more adept at living off the land, the achievements of the European explorers appear somewhat less remarkable than they would if the islands had been uninhabited.

European settlers

With the arrival of the first European settlers at Port Nicholson in 1840, the search for land began. Some of the settlers had other interests, however. Ernst Dieffenbach, a naturalist, set out to climb Mount Egmont in the summer of 1839–40 but had great difficulty in persuading Maori guides to accompany him, as the mountain was taboo; when he did get them to do so they refused to go further than the snowline. Dieffenbach reached the top with a whaler named Heberly, but the summit was enveloped in fog and the spectacular view was hidden from them.

On North Island, sheep farming expanded rapidly after 1842, when Charles Kettle and Alfred Wills crossed from Wellington, via the Manawatu Pass, to Lake Wairarapa, and discovered excellent, and apparently uninhabited, grazing lands. On South Island, the founding of Nelson on

KEY TO ROUTES

—— Heaphy, Brunner, Fox, and Ekehu 1846
—— Heaphy, Brunner, and Ekehu 1846
—— Brunner and Ekehu 1846–48
—— Colenso 1847
—— Harper 1857

Tasman Bay was soon followed by the discovery of the Wairau Valley, beyond the Richmond Range. The land was already occupied and European settlement there provoked the first serious clash with the Maoris over land.

Heaphy, Brunner, and Ekehu

The rigors of travel in the first half of the 19th century, especially on the larger, more rugged South Island, were considerable. Scarcity of water, the bane of Australian explorers, was seldom a problem; the rivers being numerous and often exceedingly fast, death by drowning was a notoriously common end for travelers in New Zealand.

The most demanding journeys in the early years were those of Charles Heaphy and Thomas Brunner (surveyors employed by the New Zealand Company), and their Maori guide Ekehu. In 1846 the three of them, in search of uncontested land, traveled south from Nelson to a point beyond Lake Rotoroa, and later that year they ventured down the coast, through very rough country, as far as the Arahura River. It was winter, and there rains and snow forced them to turn back, but in December Brunner set out on his most famous journey, accompanied by Ekehu and another Maori, and their wives.

Brunner's objective was the great tableland in the south which the Maoris spoke of, and the plan was to descend the Buller River and thence go south more or less parallel with the coast. Neither topography nor vegetation aided rapid progress, and in spite of Ekehu's hunting skills food soon became scarce. It took them about eight months to reach the mouth of the Grey River, where they overwintered. On reaching Tititira Head in November, Brunner was knocked over by a wave and damaged his right leg, which dissuaded him from continuing south.

In January 1848 they started on their return journey, but Brunner's condition began to deteriorate rapidly. As the southern winter approached, he became partly paralysed and his vision was badly affected. They found a cave, where they sheltered until Brunner's condition improved and he was fit to travel again. They made good progress and, 18 months after they had begun, reached Nelson in June 1848.

Across the mountains

Attempts to cross the mountainous spine of South Island were first made as early as 1850, and in 1852 an enterprising sheep farmer drove his flock from the vicinity of Nelson to Hanmer Plain on the east coast. The Harper Pass is named after Leonard Harper, who crossed from east to

▲ *The missionary* and explorer Samuel Marsden conducted his first service at his mission at the Bay of Islands, North Island, on Christmas Day, 1814.

▼ *Mount Cook,* known to the Maoris as Aorangi, is the highest peak on South Island, and towers above Lake Pukaki. It was first climbed in 1894.

west by that route in 1857, descending the Taramakau River to the coast below Greymouth.

In the far south, the Southern Alps presented an insuperable obstacle. In 1863 a group of gold miners, led by A. J. Barrington, attempted to find an east–west route. In the high mountains, one man was lost and another slid two miles down a glacier on his back without serious injury. Food was practically non-existent at this altitude, and a rat was consumed with relish, yet, perhaps surprisingly, they eventually survived to recount their exploits. They had proved, beyond much doubt, that no real pass existed.

In the years that followed, individual bushmen contributed odd bits of topographical information, though often without official recognition. One famous character in the 1880s and 1890s was Charles "Mr Explorer" Douglas, who spent much of his adult life traveling through some of the toughest country in Westland Province, mapping hundreds of unknown valleys, sometimes employed by the government, sometimes following his own inclination.

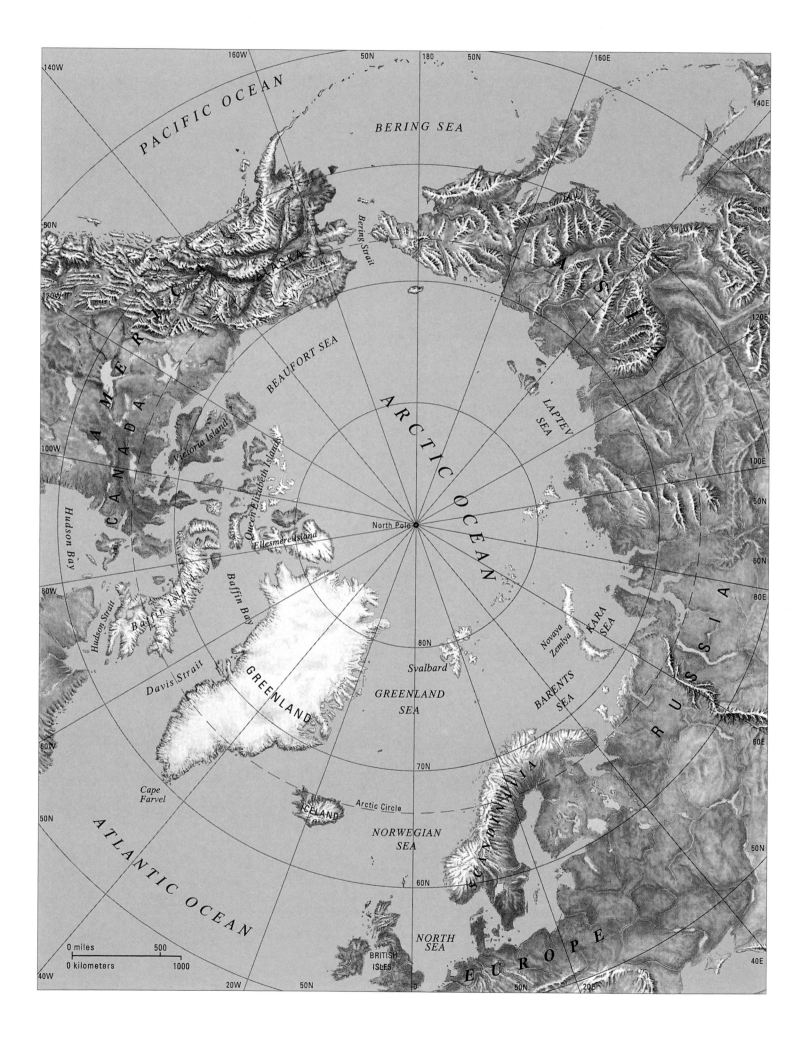

THE ARCTIC

Pytheas, a Greek trader from Marseilles, journeyed to Britain around 320 BC seeking tin ore. Hearing about a northern land, he sailed toward the Arctic Circle and reported "a land where the sun shines at midnight and the seas around it are curdled in winter." Unfortunately, when he returned home nobody believed such unlikely traveler's tales.

Centuries later, around AD 870, Othere, a nobleman living in the northwest of Norway, became curious about the extent of the empty land beyond his home. He took a ship east along the coast and then south into the White Sea, where he found so many walrus that his party killed 60 in three days, providing a cargo of fine ivory tusks.

By the end of the 10th century, Vikings had settled in Greenland's fertile southwestern valleys, supported by annual trading ships from Norway. These colonies died out in the 15th century, unable to survive the worsening climate, the loss of contact with Norway, and the hostility of the Inuit people.

In the following centuries European voyagers described the Arctic's spectacular landscapes and awe-inspiring grandeur, the clash and rumble of the ever-moving ice, and the mighty whales. However, they only found it possible to visit the region in the summer. Navigation by sun and stars was difficult in these high latitudes, where fog often obscured the sky and refraction created disturbing optical effects. The magnetic compass in its primitive form was unreliable so far north and was in any case disturbed by the iron stoves, harpoons, stanchions, and other gear in whaling vessels. And while the indigenous people did not want for food, fuel, and shelter, Europeans were slow to adopt the diet and skin garments of the Inuit. Any ship caught by the onset of winter risked being crushed by the ice, and would certainly run short of food.

Search for a Northern Seaway

Britain and Holland, both active maritime trading nations during the 16th and 17th centuries, found the southern seaways to the Far East barred by the power and might of Spain and Portugal. Trading companies were obliged to seek another route into the Pacific Ocean – one which passed north of Russia or America, or even directly over the Pole – if they were to have safe access to the ports of China and Southeast Asia.

Search for the Northeast Passage

In 1553 three English ships, commanded by Sir Hugh Willoughby, sailed on behalf of the Muscovy Company in search of a Northeast Passage to the Pacific. The vessels became separated and Willoughby was "frozen unto death" off Lappland, but Richard Chancellor reached the White Sea and traveled overland to Moscow, where he established trade relations with Russia before returning to England in 1554. Chancellor went to Russia again in the following year, but on the way home he and most of his crew were lost when his ship was wrecked off Scotland. In 1556 Stephen Borough, a veteran of Chancellor's first voyage, took his small ship as far as the Kara Sea before ice and bad weather forced him to turn back and winter on the Russian coast.

By this time trade with Moscow was prospering and the Muscovy Company lost interest in a route to the Orient, leaving the Dutch to take up the quest for a Northeast Passage. The most successful of the Dutch explorers was Willem Barents. Already an experienced Arctic pilot, he sailed, in 1596, via Bear Island (Bjornoya) to Spitsbergen (Svalbard), and from there went on to Novaya Zemlya. He and his men pressed on for some weeks, round the northern tip of the island, seeking a way to the Kara Sea, before their ship was finally broken up by ice. They then had no alternative but to camp on Novaya Zemlya, where they became the first Europeans to survive an Arctic winter. They returned in two open boats in June 1597, but Barents died before they were rescued.

Search for the Northwest Passage

Attempts to find the Northwest Passage began when, in 1576, Martin Frobisher sailed from England for the Labrador region. Two of his three small ships were lost, but he took the *Gabriel* across to Baffin Island and into a bay which he believed to be the strait leading to Asia. Here some of his crew were killed in an encounter with hostile Inuit and Frobisher returned to England, taking with him one Inuit captive and some rocks said to contain gold. The prospect of wealth encouraged his backers to send him back twice for more ore, but this was later proved to be worthless.

New patrons were found to support John Davis, who directed his search for the passage from a more northerly latitude. In 1585 he sailed up the west coast of Greenland, crossed over the strait named after him to Baffin Island, and discovered Cumberland Sound before bad weather forced his return. His second voyage followed much the same route, but his third, in 1587, took him as far as 72°N before confronting the ice barrier.

Davis had established a record for northerly travel, but Henry Hudson penetrated further west than his predecessors when he sailed *Discovery* into what is now Hudson Bay in 1610. He followed the coast south to James Bay, where his ship was beset by ice. After enduring a hard winter, his crew mutinied. Hudson and his son were set adrift in a small boat and the crew sailed back to England. Several voyages were made to follow up these various early discoveries, the most rewarding being that of 1616, when Hudson's old ship *Discovery* sailed, with William Baffin as pilot, to explore the northern portion of Davis Strait. They were able to reach 78°N and to coast the islands north of Baffin Island. These early voyages put Davis Strait and Baffin Bay on to the chart, together with the three great seaways of the Canadian Arctic: Smith Sound, Lancaster Sound, and Jones Sound.

By the mid-17th century it was clear that while neither the Gulf of St Lawrence nor Hudson Bay opened into the

▶ **Willem Barents** and his men survived an Arctic winter by building a large wooden hut, 30 feet by 20 feet (10 meters by 6 meters), from the trunks of trees that had been washed up on the shore. Even though they had a fire burning in the middle of the hut, the men's clothes would become white with frost as they slept. Despite the intense cold, each man bathed weekly in a Turkish bath made of wine barrels.

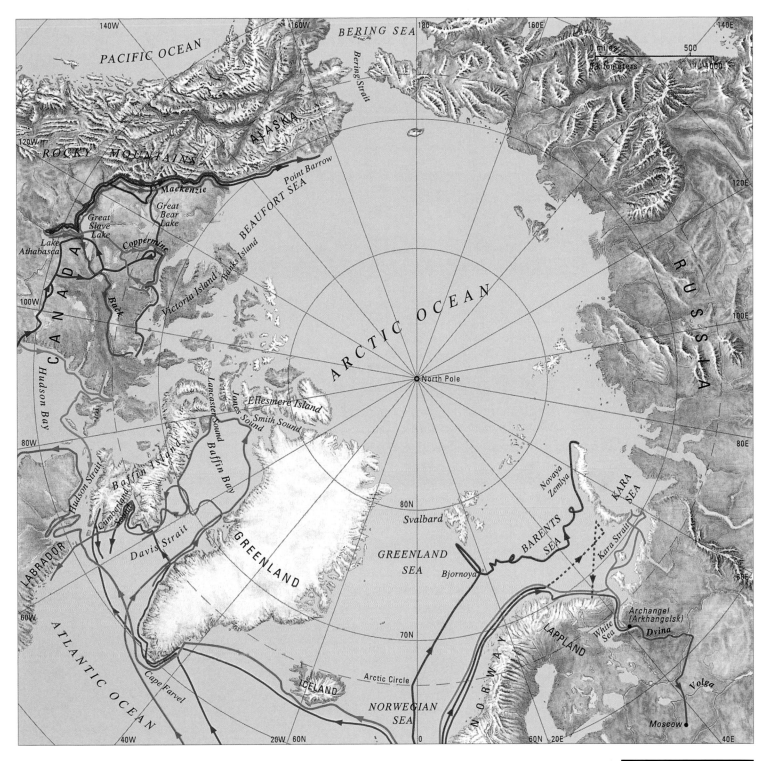

desired northern seaway, both were gateways to the vast forests of northern America. Denied the riches of the Orient, the traders bartered just as profitably with native trappers for furs, copper, and other local products. Several companies were formed to handle this trade, the most successful being the Hudson's Bay Company.

The Company did not announce its discoveries lest other shipowners should be attracted into the region. In 1741 the British Admiralty, uncertain how far this exploration had progressed, sent Christopher Middleton, a former Company servant, into Hudson Bay, with HMS *Furnace* and HMS *Discovery*, where he searched unsuccessfully for a northwestern exit to the Bay.

No further attempts on the passage from the east were to be made until the next century. Attention was focused instead on the western end of the passage, explored briefly by Vitus Bering in 1741, and by James Cook in 1778 (see pages 160–1). Expeditions to the north coast of America by river were to provide further information, which would prove so useful in subsequent attempts at the passage.

Expeditions on land

Hudson's Bay Company posts were being established further north and west although not, as yet, in the high latitudes which the ships had reached. In 1771–72 Samuel Hearne traveled to the Coppermine River and the Arctic Ocean, and in 1789 Alexander Mackenzie of the North West Company took the more westerly route down the Mackenzie River to the same ocean. The Royal Navy was represented by John Franklin's expeditions of 1819–22 and 1825–27 (which charted large sections of the coastline), and by George Back, who explored the Great Fish River (now the Back River) in 1833–34.

In 1837–39 Peter Warren Dease and Thomas Simpson, both Hudson's Bay Company servants, made extensive discoveries in the interior and on the coast between the Mackenzie and Great Fish rivers. They also discovered what they called Victoria Land, now known to be a great island. By the mid-19th century the Arctic coast of mainland North America and parts of its adjacent islands were therefore fairly well explored.

British Admiralty Expeditions

The shortest route from Europe to the Pacific, as the crow flies, passes over the North Pole. In the 18th century there were a number of enthusiastic supporters of the theory that the Pole lay in an open temperate sea, and in Britain the Royal Society proposed to the Lords of the Admiralty the investigation of this "interesting point in geography."

A route to the Pole

Two sturdy bomb vessels, HMS *Racehorse* and HMS *Carcass*, were further strengthened to protect them in the ice. Commanded by Constantine Phipps, the expedition left for the North in June 1773, with orders not to proceed beyond the Pole. In fact the ships got no further than 80°48'N when the onset of bad weather forced them to turn for home. On calm days during the passage, however, Phipps was able to investigate the depth of the sea. He also attempted to measure its temperature, for which task he had been issued with a rather primitive thermometer in a water bottle – a device that failed to work. (Phipps tried wrapping a wine bottle in a cloth so that he could bring up the seawater with its temperature unchanged and take a reading on deck.)

His natural history observations, including those on the polar bear, were considered of great value by zoologists, and his narrative of his voyage was also of considerable scientific interest; it was widely read and influenced many who followed him into these northern waters.

The continuing search for the Northwest Passage

The 19th century was the great age of British naval expeditions. England had triumphed in the Napoleonic wars and when it was reported in 1817, by William Scoresby Jnr, that the Arctic Ocean was less ice-bound than in former years, the Admiralty decided to back further searches for the Northwest Passage. The first expeditions were purely exploratory, but gradually their scope widened to include new types of scientific observation. In its turn this requirement stimulated the invention and improved construction of scientific instruments and apparatus.

In the spring of 1818 the Admiralty despatched four ships in an attempt to reach the Pacific. HMS *Dorothea* and HMS *Trent* under the command of David Buchan and John Franklin were to keep a northerly course through the Greenland Sea in the hope of breaking through into the supposedly ice-free polar region. HMS *Isabella* and HMS *Alexander*, commanded by John Ross and W. Edward Parry respectively, were to turn into the Davis Strait and to seek a route north of the American continent.

On entering Lancaster Sound Ross saw what appeared to him to be a range of mountains closing its far end. Some of his officers wondered if this were but one more example of the mirages frequently encountered in the region, but Ross would not be contradicted nor investigate further. He dubbed the range the "Croker Mountains" in honor of the First Secretary of the Admiralty and resolutely set sail for home. Buchan and Franklin found no open polar sea, of course. Their ships were battered by gales and continually beset by pack-ice. They did little scientific work and finally they too returned to England.

John Ross's report could only be checked by sending another expedition. Official incentives were offered to crews willing to endure the harsh conditions and isolation of the high Arctic. An Act of Parliament of 1744 had offered £20,000 for the discovery of a Northwest Passage; that of 1776 had offered £5000 for reaching 89°N by sea. An Act of 1818 confirmed these figures and authorized smaller rewards for partial successes.

Edward Parry

Edward Parry, who was one of those to challenge Ross's vision of the "Croker Mountains," led the expedition of 1819 in HMS *Hecla* and HMS *Griper*. He sailed into Lancaster Sound, over the supposed position of the "Croker Mountains" and on into Viscount Melville Sound. Crossing 110°W, the ships' companies became eligible for the Parliamentary reward of £5000.

Shortly after that it became clear that the expedition needed to find a safe anchorage for the ships. Channels were cut in the ice and the ships were towed into a safe haven. Parry and his men then settled down to winter in their ships – a time that must have tested the qualities of officers and men to the full. In fine weather the men exercised on the floe, went off on hunting trips or cut ice for drinking water, while the officers made scientific observations. Afterward there were talks and writing lessons for the men, and lectures for the officers. A ships' newspaper was produced, and all hands joined in the theatricals which were the winter highlight.

The ships broke free of the ice on August 1, 1820, but, having made little progress in finding the Northwest Passage, Parry returned home. However, in 1821 he set sail again. He began a survey working northward from Hudson Bay, but he was unable to break through and connect the two regions then charted.

After Ross's expedition, the whalermen who had previously stayed in Davis Strait followed his track and found excellent fishing north of Melville Bay. Parry's third voyage led them into the equally lucrative Prince Regent Inlet.

Magnetic North

While Parry's reputation grew, the career prospects of John Ross had been dashed by the episode of the "Croker Mountains." Hoping to regain favor, he persuaded a wealthy distiller, Felix Booth, to support an expedition. In 1829 he took ship in *Victory*, an erratic paddle-steamer whose machinery gave endless problems before she froze immovably into the ice at Felix Harbor.

In 1831 John Ross and his nephew James Clark Ross were on the Boothia Peninsula when they realized that the Magnetic North Pole – then some 1250 miles (2000 kilometers) from the geographical North Pole – was close at hand. James Ross set out with a sledge party of Inuit to identify the very spot, which he reached on June 1, 1831.

By 1832 food was running short so the Rosses trekked north to find the stores that Parry had left after the wreck of his ship *Fury* in 1825. These provisions lasted through the winter; in 1833 they left Fury Bay in small boats and were fortunate enough to be picked up by a whaler.

▲ *Ross and Parry* met a group of Inuit, with whom they tried to communicate.

The scene was painted by John Sacheuse, an Inuit who accompanied the expedition.

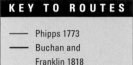

KEY TO ROUTES

— Phipps 1773
— Buchan and Franklin 1818
— Ross and Parry 1818
— Parry 1819–20
— Parry 1821–23
— Ross 1829–33

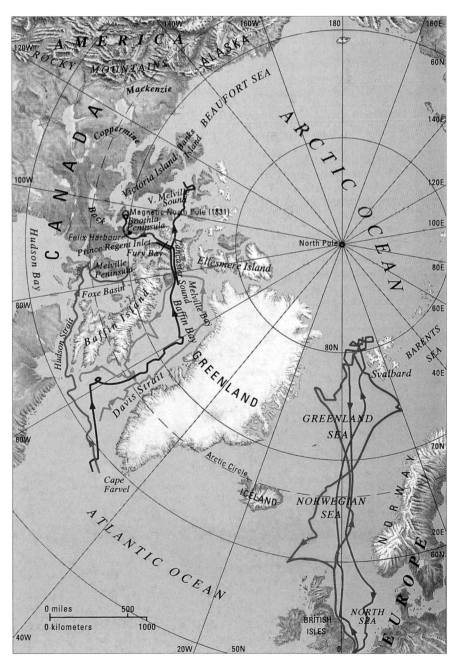

Charting the Northwest

Following the success of the Antarctic Expedition of 1839–43 (see page 189), the British Admiralty decided to send another expedition to resolve the question of the Northwest Passage. In 1845 John Franklin, then aged 59, sailed with the HMS *Erebus* and HMS *Terror*, newly equipped with steam engines and screw propellers. His ships were last seen by a whaler in Baffin Bay in July of that year. In 1848, when no more news had reached England, official anxiety and public concern mounted. The first of a series of relief expeditions was despatched, but no one even knew which route Franklin had followed, or where to begin to look for him.

After the disappearance of John Franklin (above), his wife Jane (below) gained the respect of the British public with her continuing efforts on his behalf.

The search for Franklin

The search parties were organized by both the British Government and private individuals, including Franklin's wife. Six parties traveled overland and 34 expeditions used ships and sledges. They searched from the Bering Strait and from the eastern Arctic. Sledging techniques were developed and some thousands of miles of coastline were seen and mapped for the first time. Robert McClure was only prevented from navigating the Northwest Passage in HMS *Investigator* by a narrow sector of obstructing ice, and his crew eventually received a £10,000 award for their achievement.

In 1850 graves of the first three men to die were found, pointing to where Franklin had spent his first winter. In 1854 Dr John Rae of the Hudson's Bay Company arrived home with personal belongings from the expedition. He had obtained these from some Boothia Inuit, who told him

Keeping healthy in the Arctic

Adequate nutrition was essential for survival in the Arctic. Extreme cold and the tremendous exertions of sledging journeys demanded a high-calorie diet, while the balance of that diet, especially its fat and vitamin content, had a direct effect on the men's health, strength, and ultimately their sanity.

Franklin's Canadian guides introduced him to pemmican, a mixture of dried pounded meat and melted fat – the ideal food for such journeys. Canned meat, soup, and vegetables were also available from the early 19th century, and were welcome additions to salted and dried provisions.

Fortunate crews might hunt large or small game, fish, and marine mammals. On the margins of the high Arctic, where the snow melts in summer, wild rice, scurvy grass, and other edible plants grow. It is also possible to make "spruce beer" from a species of juniper tree, as an alternative to lemon juice for the prevention of scurvy. But the large numbers of men needed to sail ships through the Arctic seaways could not find all the fresh food that they needed and suffered accordingly from their restricted diet.

how some years previously they had passed a party of 40 starving white men dragging a sledge.

With this information, Lady Franklin sponsored the expedition of 1857–59, under Leopold McClintock, which found, in a cairn on King William Island, messages telling of Franklin's death on June 11, 1847, and of his companions' intention to march south. A sad trail of skeletons and relics along their route showed that the last man had perished by the mouth of the Back River.

Through the Northwest Passage

In the opinion of Dr John Rae, expeditions as large as Franklin's were handicapped by the number of people involved, and by the correspondingly large amount of provisions that had to be carried. Consequently, many of the expeditions that followed involved a far smaller number of people, who found ways of living off the land. One such expedition was led by Roald Amundsen. After studying medicine in his native Norway, he bought *Gjøa*, a small motorized sailing ship, and in 1903 set sail with six companions and six dogs, determined to take her through the Northwest Passage. They passed serenely through Lancaster Sound, but then in the James Ross Strait a storm drove *Gjøa* aground at high tide. After several nerve-wracking days, jettisoning some of their precious stores to lighten ship, another high tide lifted her from the rocks.

Winter found them close to the Magnetic North Pole, in their snug base in Gjøa Haven, where they built huts for themselves and the recording instruments, mapped the surrounding area, took game for the pot, and enjoyed the company of Inuit. The summer of 1904 proved too cold to melt the ice, but in August 1905 *Gjøa* was once more under way, heading westward. It was not until August 1906, however, after yet another winter spent in the ice during which Amundsen trekked overland to send news of his feat, that the *Gjøa* finally made it into the Pacific.

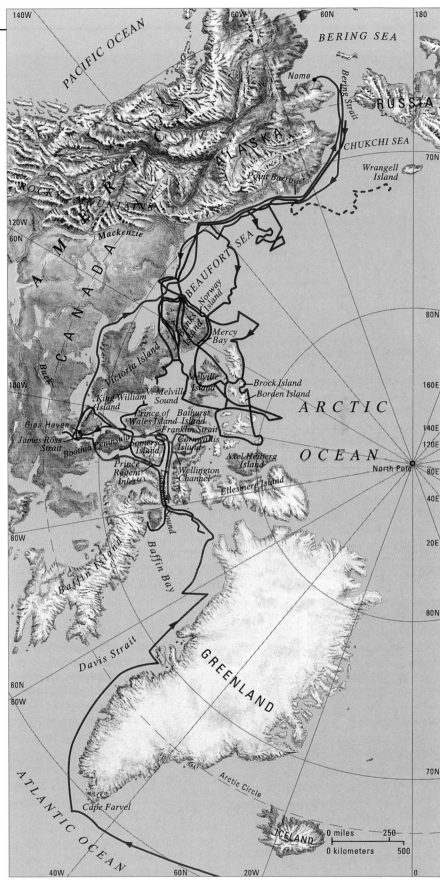

▲ Robert McClure *and the crew of the* Investigator *made their ship fast to an iceberg in Mercy Bay, Banks Island, in the fall of 1851. They had eventually to* abandon ship in the spring of 1853, but were rescued and returned to England – the first men to complete the Northwest Passage, albeit in more than one ship.

Living off the land

Another explorer who demonstrated how it was possible to "live off the land" was Vilhjalmur Stefansson. He was an anthropologist who lived for many years among the Inuit, and was one of Canada's most remarkable explorers. Stefansson commanded the ill-starred Canadian Arctic Expedition of 1913–18, whose main objective was to explore the Beaufort Sea, the last blank space on the map. Misfortune struck, however, after the expedition's principal ship, the *Karluk*, disembarked one party at Point Barrow, and Stefansson and a few men went off to hunt. The ship became hemmed in by ice, and when a storm blew up the *Karluk*, locked in the floes which grew daily thicker and more dangerous, began to drift along the coast of Alaska and then toward Wrangell Island.

The dogs lived on the ice alongside, leaving 20 Europeans and a small number of Inuit on board. It was only a matter of time before the *Karluk* would be fatally crushed; supplies were got ready and when the inevitable happened, men, women, and children set out in the dark and bitterly cold winter night across treacherous, shifting, and incredibly rough pack-ice. Only nine survived the 60-mile (100-kilometer) trek to Wrangell Island.

Stefansson, meanwhile, unaware of the fate of the *Karluk*, spent the summer on Norway Island, hunting caribou and preparing meat and skins. When the *Karluk* failed to arrive, Stefansson took his men south, finding the crew of one of his support ships, which had also been damaged.

Over the succeeding years, this party of 17 men traveled thousands of miles surveying and mapping the territory, including the previously unknown Borden and Brock Islands. They also found many cairns and stores left by previous explorers, and sometimes grim testimony of their fates. The land and sea provided their food, clothing, fuel, and shelter. On the final leg of their journey, they hitched a 400-mile (650-kilometer) lift by camping on a drifting floe, and came at last over the pack-ice to reach solid ground in Alaska.

KEY TO ROUTES

— Franklin 1845–47
— McClure 1850–54
— McClintock 1857–59
— Amundsen 1903–6
— Stefansson 1913–18

Reaching for the Pole

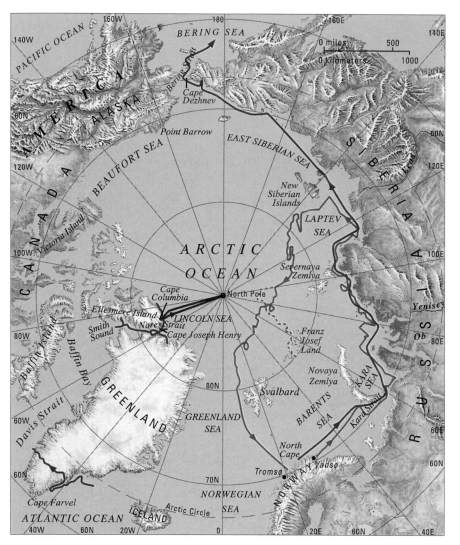

KEY TO ROUTES

— Nares 1875–76
— Nordenskjöld 1878–79
— Nansen 1888
— Nansen 1893–96
— Peary 1909

As it became clear that the Arctic ice did not hide an open sea, attempts to reach the Pole were made on foot. In 1827 Edward Parry sailed to Svalbard and headed north with two small boats which could be set on runners and towed as sledges. The ice surface was rougher than expected, however, and to make matters worse, the ice was drifting south nearly as fast as the men progressed northward. After struggling for 680 miles (1100 kilometers), they had reached only 82°45′N. By July 22, the Pole was still 500 miles (800 kilometers) distant, and Parry had to admit defeat.

The next serious attempt on the Pole was made by the British Arctic Expedition of 1875–76, commanded by George Nares, who took the steam sloop *Alert* and the steam whaler *Discovery* to what is now known as Nares Strait, between Greenland and Ellesmere Island.

Nares sent out sledging parties to explore and survey the northern coast, and one of his teams, led by A. H. Markham, crossed rough hummocky ice and deep powdery snow to reach a new furthest north of 83°20′N off Cape Joseph Henry. At the end of the first year a serious outbreak of scurvy forced Nares to return. The expedition had failed in its declared aim, but it had succeeded in gathering valuable geological and natural history collections

Nordenskjöld and the Northeast Passage

Another man to make an attempt on the Pole was Nils Nordenskjöld, a Swedish-trained chemist and geologist, and the first great scientist-explorer of the Arctic. The

attempt, however, was unsuccessful, and Nordenskjöld is best remembered today as the man who succeeded in taking a ship the full extent of the Northeast Passage, following a coastline that had been charted by the Great Northern Expedition of 1733–42 (see pages 48–49).

He and a multinational team of scientists set off on their voyage in the 300-ton steam-sailing ship *Vega* in July 1878, carrying supplies for two years. They reached the mouth of the Lena River by late August without encountering any problems. During September, however, navigation became increasingly difficult due to fog and snow, and just before Cape Dezhnev they ran into heavy ice. Tantalizingly close to the end of their journey, the ship's company had to resign themselves to spending a winter in Siberia. It was not until July 1879 that they broke through the ice and, within two days, had passed Cape Dezhnev and fulfilled their task.

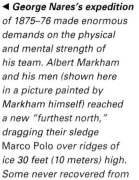

◄ *George Nares's expedition* of 1875–76 made enormous demands on the physical and mental strength of his team. Albert Markham and his men (shown here in a picture painted by Markham himself) reached a new "furthest north," dragging their sledge Marco Polo over ridges of ice 30 feet (10 meters) high. Some never recovered from the experience.

Nansen and the *Fram*

Further explorations of the Arctic region were made by the Norwegian Fridtjof Nansen. A zoologist by training, he combined a scientific mind with physical strength and practical skills which stood him in good stead in his expeditions into the frozen Arctic. He also received the encouragement of the veteran Nordenskjöld.

Following a crossing of Greenland on foot in 1888, Nansen embarked on his North Polar Expedition of 1893–96. This was a bold attempt to demonstrate that a transpolar current moved across the Arctic from Siberia to the Norwegian Sea. The *Fram* was built to resist ice-pressure and Nansen sailed her round the coast of Siberia before putting her into the ice in September 1893, just north of the New Siberian Islands. She proceeded to drift in a generally westerly direction, while the men on board monitored ice and weather conditions, and measured, with painstaking accuracy, the depth, temperature, and salinity of the water through holes in the ice. Nansen found the Arctic Basin far deeper than he had anticipated. The scientific reports from this expedition, which filled six large volumes, gave the first picture of circulation in a frozen ocean.

Nansen's bid for the Pole

Nansen himself, accompanied by Hjalmar Johansen, left the *Fram* early in 1895 in an attempt to walk to the North Pole. They took three sledges, pulled by dogs, adopting the tactic of killing off the weakest dog every few days to feed to the rest. By mid-April, however, they were forced to abandon their attempt and turn south again, reaching Franz Josef Land in July. Here they spent the winter, building a stone hut and laying in supplies of meat. When the spring came they started to travel southward, in kayaks, along the coast, intending to head across the sea to Spitsbergen (Svalbard). Fortunately, they met the Englishman Frederick Jackson on April 13, 1896 (the very day that the *Fram* was breaking free from the ice north of Spitsbergen), and were given a welcome lift to Tromsø, where they were reunited with the rest of their party.

Robert Peary

Robert Peary trained with the US Coast and Geodetic Survey before joining the Civil Engineering Corps of the US Navy. He organized and led six Arctic expeditions between 1891 and 1909, each time pushing further north, via Smith Sound and Nares Strait. His explorations settled the question of Greenland's northern limits, showing it to be an island.

Peary was driven by the desire to be the first man at the Pole, an ambition which he apparently achieved at his third attempt, on April 6, 1909. Earlier in 1909 relaying support parties of 24 men, 19 sledges, and 133 dogs advanced from a land base at Cape Columbia to clear a trail, erect camps, and lay stores. This enabled Peary and his Inuit companions to have an easy march up to the forward point, saving their energies and supplies for the final dash for the Pole. Following the departure of the final support party, Peary sped over the 150 miles (250 kilometers) to the Pole, and the 485 miles (780 kilometers) back to base, allegedly covering the whole distance in 16 days.

Unfortunately, Peary was not universally believed. Some doubted that he could have traveled so fast; others considered that his navigation had not allowed for ice-drift, while Frederick Cook claimed to have reached the Pole in 1908. Recent re-examination of the evidence, however, appears to support Peary's claim to have been at the Pole on the date shown in his log.

▼ *Peary and Cook* fought a long and hard war of words for the honor of being first to the Pole. Initially, Cook won the media battle, with his gallant message of congratulation to Peary, to which Peary responded by calling him a liar; the public disliked Peary's arrogance and were sceptical of his claims. Scientific opinion, however, subsequently came down on the side of Peary.

Expeditions in the 20th Century

▶ **Wally Herbert,** leader of the British Trans-Arctic Expedition of 1968–69 described the terrain they traveled over as "an area with a fantastic amount of pressure-ice movement – a lead would open up and come together again to form a pressure-ridge; then the floe would split in opposite directions and build another pressure-ridge at right-angles to it. By the time this had been going on all winter there would be an absolute chaos of ice."

In the 20th century attempts to reach the Pole were made not only on foot but also in the air. In 1897 the Swedish aeronaut Salomon Andrée had set out from Svalbard in a drift balloon. He was never to be seen again, but his remains, and those of his companions, were discovered in 1930 on White Island, only a short distance from their departure point. According to their diary, the balloon had landed further to the northwest and the men had sledged to the island, where they later died.

An American journalist, Walter Wellman, made the first dirigible balloon flights in 1906, but he never got far from his Svalbard base. In 1925 Roald Amundsen and Lincoln Ellsworth attempted to reach the Pole in two seaplanes. They flew for eight hours, by which time half their fuel had been consumed, and got within 100 miles (160 kilometers) of the Pole, before landing. They then abandoned one plane and transferred the remaining fuel to the other, which carried both crews back to base.

Although flight in the Arctic region obviously had its problems, it was an effective way of making large, sweeping surveys of the area. On the outward leg of their journey Amundsen and Ellsworth had flown over 38,600 square miles (100,000 square kilometers), and could confirm that there was no previously undiscovered land there.

In 1925 Richard Evelyn Byrd made a number of flights over Ellesmere Island and the Greenland ice cap. The following year he and Floyd Bennett flew the 850 miles (1375 kilometers) from Svalbard to the Pole in about eight hours. Such was the accuracy of their navigation that the plane returned exactly to its point of departure.

Umberto Nobile

In the same year Umberto Nobile, an Italian engineer and aeronaut, flew in his dirigible balloon *Norge* from Svalbard to Alaska with Amundsen, Ellsworth, and others. Nobile was well provided with instruments to make gravity, magnetic, and weather observations. His route crossed unfamiliar regions and where the sky was clear of fog, he was able to take photographs.

In 1928 Nobile went back to the Arctic with the balloon *Italia*. A few days after a flight toward the Siberian coast, he took off again and flew over the North Pole. Then disaster struck and the balloon crashed on the ice floe. Six of the crew were killed, but Nobile and the rest survived, along with clothes, food, radio, and even a tent. They radioed for help, but their message went unnoticed for several days. When they were at last heard, an extensive international rescue operation was launched, and eventually (almost a month after the crash) a Swedish pilot managed to land on the ice and airlift Nobile to safety. Unfortunately, his plane was damaged on the return journey, so another month went by before Nobile's crew were

rescued by the Russian ice-breaker *Krassin*. Nobile subsequently returned to Italy in disgrace, an embarrassment to Mussolini's regime.

The disaster was compounded by the tragic disappearance of Amundsen, who left Tromsø in a seaplane to go to Nobile's rescue and was never seen again.

Land expeditions

Subsequent journeys to the Pole have been many and varied. The largest and most enterprising was the well-supported British Trans-Arctic Expedition, under the command of Wally Herbert, that crossed the Arctic from Alaska to Svalbard in 1968–69. They left Point Barrow in February 1968 and crossed 80 miles (130 kilometers) of mush ice to the polar pack, where they encamped for the summer, taking meteorological, geophysical, and marine observations as their floe drifted north. When the sea froze once more, the men sledged toward the Pole each day until the onset of darkness, when they received a scheduled air-drop of food, fuel, and supplies, including a prefabricated hut. Throughout the winter more scientific work, including accurate stellar position fixes to show their line of drift, kept them fully occupied. Their intention was to reach Svalbard by May 1969, but the threat of melting ice led to their being rescued by helicopter a few miles short of their destination.

By way of contrast were Naomi Uemara's solo journey to the Pole in 1978 and Will Steger's 1986 expedition, which was the first unsupported party to reach the Pole since Peary. Ranulph Fiennes's Transglobe expedition, in 1981–82, circumnavigated the world via both Poles.

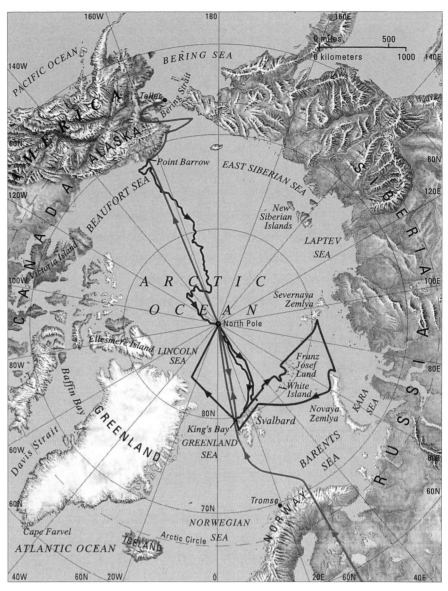

◀ **The remains of Andrée's** attempt on the Pole in 1897 were found 30 years later. They included his diary in which he had written: "Shall we be thought mad or will our example be followed?"

▼ **The Italia *left King's Bay*** on May 15, 1928, but crashed after flying over the North Pole. Ten men were flung clear, but six were blown away with the wreckage and were never seen again.

KEY TO ROUTES

——— Nobile 1926
——— Byrd 1926
═══ Nobile 1928
—— Herbert 1968–69

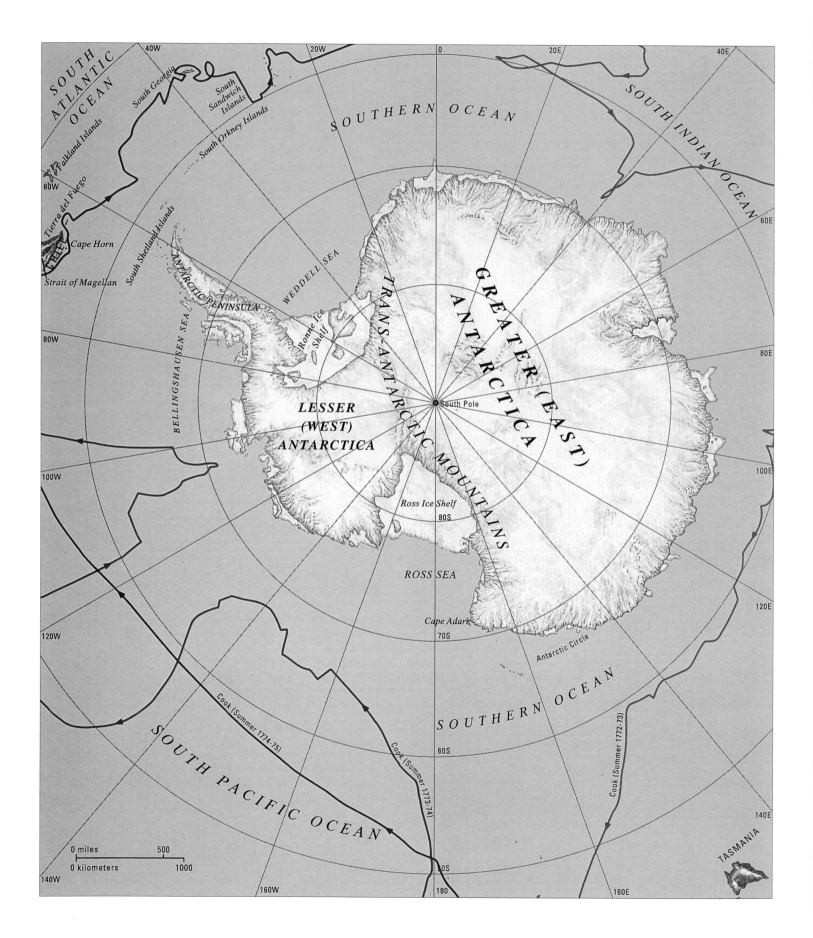

SOUTH
ATLANTIC
OCEAN

40W

South Georgia

20W

South
Sandwich
Islands

0

20E

SOUTHERN OCEAN

40E

SOUTH INDIAN OCEAN

Falkland Islands

South Orkney Islands

60W

Tierra del Fuego

Cape Horn

CHILE

Strait of Magellan

South Shetland Islands

ANTARCTIC PENINSULA

WEDDELL SEA

Ronne Ice
Shelf

GREATER (EAST)
ANTARCTICA

60E

BELLINGSHAUSEN SEA

80W

TRANS-ANTARCTIC MOUNTAINS

80E

LESSER
(WEST)
ANTARCTICA

South Pole

100W

Ross Ice Shelf

80S

100E

120W

ROSS SEA

Cape Adare

70S

Antarctic Circle

120E

Cook (Summer 1774-75)

Cook (Summer 1773-74)

SOUTHERN OCEAN

Cook (Summer 1772-73)

SOUTH PACIFIC OCEAN

60S

140E

0 miles   500
0 kilometers   1000

140W

160W

50S

180

160E

TASMANIA

THE ANTARCTIC

At the bottom of the globe lies a frozen continent, separated from the rest of the world by the stormy Southern Ocean. It is encircled by pack-ice and huge tabular icebergs, and covered by an ice sheet, several miles deep in places. Not surprisingly this so-called "Seventh Continent" was the last to be explored. Even at the beginning of the 20th century there was discussion as to whether the Antarctic really was a continent or only a great mass of ice resting on islands.

The sea defenses of Antarctica were first penetrated by wooden sailing ships, and then by specially strengthened vessels and powerful ice-breakers. In the early years of the 20th century – the "heroic age" of Antarctic exploration – the first sledging journeys were made by men, dogs, and ponies into the great frozen interior of this land. Then followed tracked vehicles and also the airplane, from which not only the surface of the continent has been mapped, but also its shape under the ice. Most recently, satellite imagery has provided further refinement to the maps.

The charts and globes of geographers in the 18th century and earlier had often outlined a vast southern continent extending to quite temperate latitudes, where there is now known to be nothing but sea. Successive forays further and further south by a number of mariners, over several centuries, however, had failed to discover the land mass they were seeking. The great English navigator James Cook sailed round the world in high southern latitudes, in the *Resolution* and the *Adventure*, through icy and tempestuous seas. He encircled, but did not sight, the true Antarctic continent and disproved altogether the existence of a temperate land mass. His journal entry of February 21, 1775, has become famous in the history of polar exploration: "I had now made the circuit of the Southern Ocean in a high Latitude and traversed it in such a manner as to leave not the least room for the Possibility of there being a continent, unless near the Pole and out of the reach of Navigation …. That there may be a Continent or large tract of land near the Pole, I will not deny, on the contrary I am of opinion there is, and it is probable that we have seen a part of it…."

First Sightings of the Continent

▲ *In 1822 James Weddell, a British sealer who had been Master in the Royal Navy during the Napoleonic Wars, sailed to the Antarctic as captain of the 160-ton brig* Jane, *accompanied by the 65-ton cutter* Beaufoy *(right).*

KEY TO ROUTES

—— Bransfield 1819–20
—— Bellingshausen 1819–21
—— Weddell 1822–24

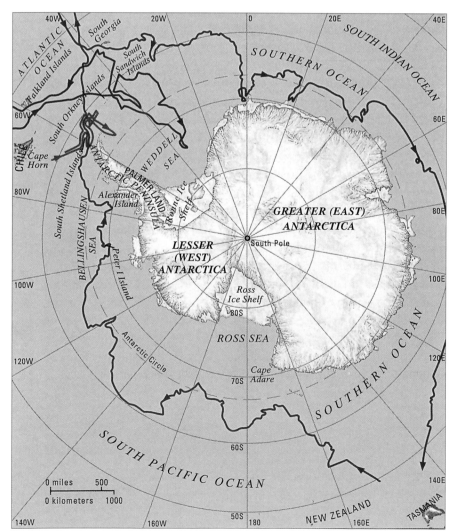

James Cook discovered South Georgia in 1775, following which first British, and then American, sealers began the slaughter of thousands of fur seals (for their pelts) and of sea elephants (for their oil) on the island and elsewhere in the Southern Ocean. By the early 1820s the fur seals were almost extinct. The sealers were, of course, rivals and tended to keep their discoveries secret, but the number of vessels engaged in the work makes it certain that various islands and much of the northwestern part of the Antarctic Peninsula became known to them.

Historians and geographers have argued about who first discovered the Antarctic Peninsula, the long "tail" of Antarctica, which stretches north toward the tip of South America. It is quite certain, however, that Edward Bransfield, in the trading brig *Williams*, discovered part of the northwestern coast of the peninsula, which he named "Trinity Land" on January 30, 1820. The first chart of this area of the coast of Antarctica was a result of his survey. In November of the same year, the American sealer Nathaniel Brown Palmer, in the shallop *Hero*, reported land, which was later called "Palmer Land," a name now transferred to the southern Antarctic Peninsula.

James Weddell

Leaving the port of Leith in Scotland in 1822, a British sealer, James Weddell, in the brig *Jane*, with the cutter *Beaufoy* in company, penetrated the sea which now bears his name, as far as 74°15′S, the furthest south yet attained. On a previous voyage, Weddell had visited the South Shetlands (northwest of the Antarctic Peninsula). His chart of those islands, of the South Orkneys (also off the Antarctic Peninsula) and, in particular, of his voyage in what became known as the Weddell Sea, can be found in his book, which went into two editions, and was entitled *A Voyage towards the South Pole, performed in the years 1822–24, containing an Examination of the Antarctic Sea, to the seventy fourth degree of latitude....*

Of a scientific and enquiring mind, Weddell made many interesting observations. Few navigators have found the Weddell Sea so relatively free from ice and it is to his great credit that he made the most of his opportunity. Another British sealer, George Powell, also published a chart of the South Shetlands. He and the American sealer Nathaniel Palmer first discovered and charted the South Orkneys during their joint voyages of 1821–22.

Thaddeus Bellingshausen

A worthy successor to James Cook was the Russian naval officer Thaddeus Bellingshausen, who circumnavigated the Antarctic continent in a high southern latitude in 1819–21. The tracks of his ships, *Vostok* and *Mirnyy*, complemented those of Cook 50 years before, and he discovered the three northern islands of the South Sandwich Islands that had escaped Cook. Bellingshausen took care to navigate in seas not sailed by Cook and in fact traveled much further than him within the Antarctic Circle.

An English translation of the narrative of the expedition was not published until 1945, so that for many years its achievements were little known in the English-speaking world. In the introduction to this book, *The Voyages of Captain Bellingshausen to the Antarctic Seas*, the editor, Frank Debenham, wrote of Cook and Bellingshausen: "Between them the two great navigators therefore covered about 60° of longitude within the Circle, one sixth of its circumference, yet were unlucky enough to miss the mainland entirely."

Debenham explains one of the reasons for their failure to get close enough to identify Antarctica as solid land as a combination of the effect of the wind and weather on the sailing ship: "When the wind comes from the north in those latitudes, while helping the ship to sail south it invariably brings thick and snowy weather, so that land cannot be seen. When, on the other hand, the south and east winds bring clear weather, they hinder the sailing ship

The "crow's nest"

The "crow's nest" was a special feature of polar ships. Believed to have been invented some 200 years ago by Captain William Scoresby Snr, for use when whaling in the Arctic, it was a canvas or wooden structure, sometimes a large barrel, which was lashed to the fore or mainmast. Entry to the crow's nest was through a trap door in the bottom.

Protected overhead by a canvas awning and relatively well sheltered by the barrel's sides, the mariner could survey the surrounding sea-ice with his telescope.

in getting south, and bring out the loose ice from the coast, fending the ships off from a close approach."

It must be said, however, that the Russians did in fact sight the ice edge of Greater (East) Antarctica in January and February 1820. Opinion differs as to whether this constitutes the discovery of the continent or not. Like Cook, Bellingshausen discovered and surveyed a number of islands in the Southern Ocean, in particular Peter I Island, the first land seen within the Antarctic Circle, and Alexander I Land (Alexander Island). Both are west of the Antarctic Peninsula on the margins of what is now called the Bellingshausen Sea.

Charting the Coastline

▲ **Members of Dumont d'Urville's party** planted the French flag on a rock just off the coast of Terre Adélie on January 21, 1840.

▶ **Jules Dumont d'Urville** named Terre Adélie after his wife "to perpetuate the memory of my profound regard for the devoted companion who has three times consented to a long and painful separation in order to allow me to accomplish my plans for distant explorations."

The first indisputable sighting of land in Greater (East) Antarctica was by the Briton John Biscoe, in the brig *Tula* on February 28, 1831. In his journal he described his discovery of Enderby Land (named after the well-known London sealing and whaling firm which financed the voyage) as follows: "4 p.m. saw several hummocks to the southward, which much resembled tops of mountains, and at 6 p.m. clearly distinguished it to be land, and to considerable extent; to my great satisfaction what we had seen first being the black tops of mountains showing themselves through the snow on the lower land."

The mountains were what are now called "nunataks" – peaks which stick up through land-ice. Biscoe circumnavigated the Antarctic, accompanied by the cutter *Lively*, commanded by George Avery, and a year later discovered Graham Land (part of the Antarctic Peninsula), Adelaide Island, and the Biscoe Islands. Biscoe was "firmly of the opinion" that he had found "a large continent," off which he had coasted for 300 miles (485 kilometers).

Another British sealer, Peter Kemp, in *Magnet* may have discovered icy and desolate Heard Island (53°S 73°20′E), as well as Kemp Land, in Greater Antarctica, in November and December 1833. A few years later, in February 1839, another Enderby sealing venture discovered the Balleny Islands, which guard the entrance to the Ross Sea. The expedition's captains, John Balleny in the *Eliza Scott* and Thomas Freeman in the *Sabrina*, also reported an "appearance of land" near what was later called Sabrina Coast, Greater Antarctica. (The Enderby Company actively encouraged its captains to explore the Antarctic region and published their findings.)

National expeditions

Three national expeditions, French, American and British, between 1837 and 1843 took an important step forward in charting the Antarctic coastline. Both the French and the American expeditions did the greater part of their work in the warm waters of the Pacific. J.-S.-C. Dumont d'Urville, commanding the *Astrolabe* with the *Zélée* (under C.-H. Jacquinot) in company, discovered and named Terre Adélie after his wife. The little Adélie penguins are reminders of her too. At least one egg of an Emperor penguin was collected by the French expedition and brought back home. A splendid atlas and other volumes were later published in Paris, in the pages of which can be seen pictures of the French sailors and their officers on the rocky coast in January 1840. The French ships also visited and surveyed part of the Antarctic Peninsula and adjoining islands, notably Trinity Peninsula and the South Orkney Islands.

The United States Exploring Expedition of 1838–42 consisted of a squadron of five ships. They too returned with a harvest of charts and collections, one of the indirect results of which was the founding of the great Smithsonian Institution in Washington, DC. However, there was much controversy both about its leader, Charles Wilkes, who was court-martialed on his return (although cleared of any serious charge), and about its charts, on which some land was shown in positions that were later sailed over by other explorers. Wilkes's poorly equipped ships sailed westward along the coast, discovering and charting what was later called Wilkes Land between 160°E and 98°E – a great arc of the Antarctic Circle.

James Clark Ross

Neither Dumont d'Urville nor Wilkes had earlier navigated in icy seas. The third and greatest of the three national expeditions of 1837–43 was commanded by a man who had served a long Arctic apprenticeship as a midshipman and a lieutenant in the Royal Navy, James Clark Ross. His ships, HMS *Erebus* and HMS *Terror*, were "bomb vessels," stoutly built to withstand the recoil of heavy mortars on deck and additionally strengthened for work in sea-ice.

At the instigation of the British Association and the Royal Society, the Admiralty despatched Ross (who had already reached the Magnetic North Pole in the Arctic) to find the Magnetic South Pole, the location of these points being of great importance to science and navigation.

A magnetic observatory named Rossbank was set up in Tasmania, where the British colony's Governor was John Franklin, the man who five years later would himself command HMS *Erebus* in an unsuccessful attempt to find the Northwest Passage (see page 178).

Ross was told of the expeditions of Dumont d'Urville and Wilkes, and, determined not to follow in their footsteps but to seek new waters to chart, he took a more easterly direction than originally planned. On January 5, 1841, his two ships were the first to pass boldly through a belt of pack-ice into what was to be called the Ross Sea. To Ross's disappointment, land barred the way to the Magnetic South Pole, so he was unable to proceed with his original mission. He did, however, make some remarkable discoveries – notably Victoria Land, Mount Terror and Mount Erebus (an active volcano amid the ice and snow), and the cliffs of the extraordinary "Great Icy Barrier," now known as the Ross Ice Shelf.

Ross made two further southern sweeps, but he did not make any discoveries as dramatic as those in his first season of Antarctic exploration. The survival of his vessels in such inhospitable conditions is, however, evidence of the skill of the shipwrights who built them, and of the captains and crew.

Ross's second-in-command was F. R. M. Crozier, who was to perish in the Arctic with the Franklin expedition. The assistant surgeon of HMS *Erebus* later became an eminent botanist and traveler, Sir Joseph Dalton Hooker.

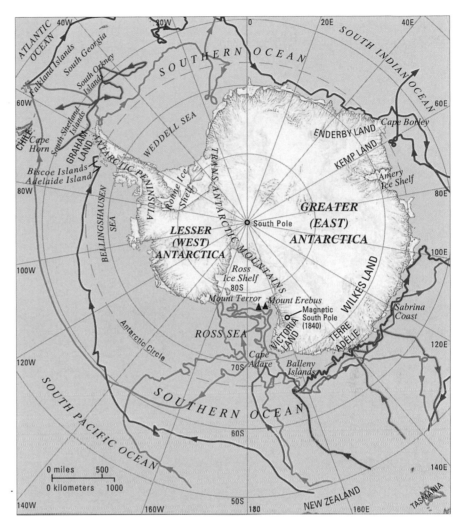

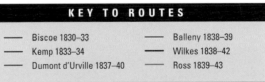

KEY TO ROUTES

- Biscoe 1830–33
- Kemp 1833–34
- Dumont d'Urville 1837–40
- Balleny 1838–39
- Wilkes 1838–42
- Ross 1839–43

▶ *The narrow escape* of HMS Erebus and HMS Terror, in March 1842, was sketched by J. E. Davis, cartographer on the Terror. The Erebus, turning suddenly to avoid hitting an iceberg, crossed the bows of the Terror and a collision was unavoidable. The two ships, their rigging entangled, were dashed against each other. Ross described how the Terror "rose high above us, almost exposing her keel to view, and again descended as we in our turn rose to the top of the wave, threatening to bury her beneath us." Eventually the ships parted and, through a mixture of skill and luck, narrowly missed the iceberg and made for open sea.

Scientific Voyages

The expedition led by the Briton James Clark Ross in 1839–43 to find the Magnetic South Pole was followed by two notable scientific voyages. The first was led by T. E. L. Moore who, in the *Pagoda*, made important magnetic observations, complementing those of Ross, in the South Atlantic and southern Indian oceans in 1844–45; the second was that of HMS *Challenger* which, during her great oceanographic circumnavigation of the world in 1872–76, became the first steam vessel to cross the Antarctic Circle. This voyage of the *Challenger* aroused the interest of scientists and geographers in the Antarctic regions, and resulted in the revival of exploration there at the beginning of the 20th century.

Searching for whales

At the very end of the 19th century, four Scottish vessels from the Dundee whaling fleet and the *Jason*, commanded by C. A. Larsen, from the Norwegian port of Sandefjord, made unsuccessful whaling reconnaissances in the Antarctic Peninsula area, based on Ross's reports of whales observed years before. Some scientific and survey work was undertaken, and Larsen collected fossils on Seymour Island, proving that the Antarctic climate had not always been frigid. He returned the following season (1893–94) and managed to sail the *Jason* down the Weddell Sea coast of the Antarctic Peninsula to 68°10′S, a latitude which remains the most southerly penetration by ship along that coast. This voyage was important geographically: when linked with Biscoe's in the west, it showed the narrowness of the land until well south of the Antarctic Circle.

At the opposite side of the continent, the first landing on Victoria Land was made in January 1895, at Cape Adare, by other Norwegians engaged on a whaling recon-

▼ *James Clark Ross* was the nephew of John Ross. He had served on expeditions led by his uncle and W. Edward Parry in the Arctic before being appointed to lead the British Antarctic expedition of 1839–43.

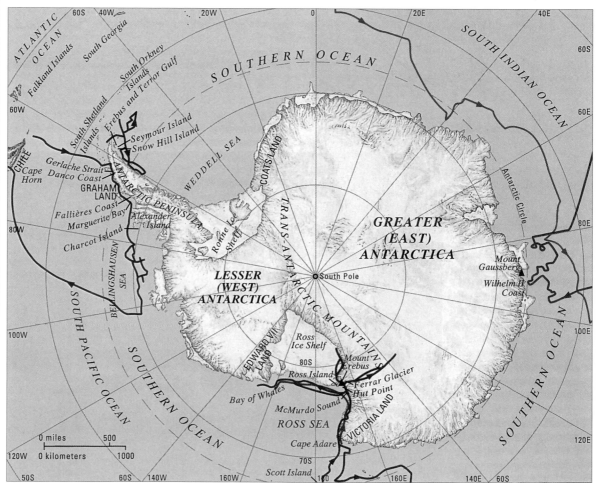

◄ **Adrien de Gerlache** and the crew of the Belgica spent a year beset by ice in the Bellingshausen Sea. They were ill-prepared, both mentally and physically, for the Antarctic winter, and appear to have been troubled by the perpetual night. One of the crew later described the experience as "hellish."

naissance, this time in the Ross Sea area. Three years later a British party, financed by George Newnes, wintered at this spot under the leadership of C. E. Borchgrevink. They were the first scientists to do so intentionally. Their ship, the *Southern Cross*, sailed along the Ross Ice Front, which was found to have receded since Ross's day. A small group landed to reach a new high latitude, using dog teams in Antarctica for the first time.

Another privately financed expedition, a Belgian one, organized and led by Adrien de Gerlache de Goméry in 1897–99, explored the waters to the west of the Antarctic Peninsula, discovering Gerlache Strait and the Danco Coast. Their ship, the *Belgica*, was beset by ice and drifted for a year in the Bellingshausen Sea, involuntarily becoming the first expeditionary vessel to winter in the Antarctic. (The mate was Roald Amundsen, later to win fame as the first navigator of the Northwest Passage and the first man to reach the South Pole.)

German and British expeditions

The turn of the century saw a clutch of exploratory and scientific expeditions sent to the Antarctic. A German and a British expedition went south in a spirit of scientific cooperation. Led by Professor Erich von Drygalski in the *Gauss* (the second vessel to winter in the Antarctic pack-ice), the Germans carried out much scientific work and discovered an extinct volcano, the Gaussberg, on what they called Kaiser Wilhelm II Land (Wilhelm II Coast).

The British expedition was sponsored partly by the Royal Society and the Royal Geographical Society, and partly by the British Government. Its ship, the *Discovery*, wintered for two seasons in a sheltered bay near what was named Hut Point, McMurdo Sound, at the head of the

Ross Sea, under the shadow and smoke plume of Mount Erebus. The expedition had earlier discovered King Edward VII Land at the far end of the Ross Ice Shelf.

It did much scientific work, making the first discovery of a rookery of Emperor penguins and collecting the first fossils found at high southern latitudes, and is notable for accomplishing the first extensive land journeys in Antarctica. Its leader was Robert Scott, whose sledge party reached beyond 82°S, tracing a range of great mountains beside the Ross Ice Shelf. The following season, Scott and two companions sledged up the Ferrar Glacier through these mountains, on to the plateau of the immense ice sheet over which they trudged for some distance.

The expedition's relief ship, the little *Morning*, made two voyages to the Antarctic, under William Colbeck, remarkable in their own right. On the first (1902–3), Scott Island was discovered near the entrance to the Ross Sea.

Other national expeditions

A Swedish, a Scottish, and two French expeditions were also in the area at the beginning of the 20th century. All carried out comprehensive scientific programs, and made geographical discoveries in their field of operation.

The Swedish Antarctic Expedition of 1901–4, led by Otto Nordenskjöld, made a major contribution to our knowledge of Graham Land. Their ship, the *Antarctic*, was beset and sank in the pack-ice of Erebus and Terror Gulf. The three parties into which the expedition separated eventually met at Snow Hill Island and were rescued by the Argentinian *Uruguay*.

The Scottish National Antarctic Expedition of 1902–4, in SY *Scotia*, was led by W. S. Bruce. It made the first systematic oceanographical exploration of the Weddell Sea, discovering Coats Land. The team wintered in the South Orkneys and there set up the first permanent station in the Antarctic, which has been maintained since 1904 by the Argentine weather service.

The French expeditions were both led and commanded by J.-B. Charcot in the *Français* (1903–5) and the *Pourquoi-Pas?* (1908–10), each a specially built three-masted wooden sailing vessel. Both ships made considerable contributions to the exploration of Graham Land and adjoining islands. Charcot in the *Pourquoi-Pas?* discovered Marguerite Bay, the Fallières Coast, and Charcot Island (to the west of Alexander Island).

▲ **The Discovery** (shown here wintering in McMurdo Sound) was built in 1900. Her hull structure was described by Scott as follows: "The frames, which were placed very close together, were eleven inches [28 centimeters] thick and of solid English oak; inside the frames came the inner lining, a solid planking four inches [10 centimeters] thick; whilst the outside was covered with two layers of planking, respectively six and five inches [15 centimeters and 12.5 centimeters] thick, so that, in most places to bore a hole in the side one would have had to get through twenty-six inches [65 centimeters] of solid wood."

The Heroic Age

▲ *Scott (on the right) is shown here with Evans, Bowers, and Wilson, relishing a hot meal inside their tent during their journey to the Pole. Bowers and Wilson are wearing their sledge-hauling harnesses.*

▼ *The food Scott took* on his expeditions was chosen for the ease with which it could be transported, rehydrated, and eaten. It was heated on a fuel-efficient stove designed by Fridtjof Nansen. It did not, however, provide the explorers with either variety or the necessary vitamins.

Exploration of the interior of the continent made great progress just before the First World War, during what has been called the "heroic age" (1900–16) of Antarctic exploration. On the first extensive journeys into the interior made by the British National Antarctic Expedition of 1901–4, under the leadership of Robert Scott (see page 191), dogs and men were both used in teams to pull the sledges, which were lightweight and flexible, made to the design of the Norwegian Arctic explorer and scientist Fridtjof Nansen. The selection of clothing and equipment for this and subsequent expeditions was largely based on Nansen's experience and advice, which in its turn derived to an extent from the native people of the Arctic.

One member of the party was Ernest Shackleton, who in 1907–9 led a sledge party from Ross Island to within 100 miles (160 kilometers) of the Pole. The Trans-Antarctic Mountains were seen to continue alongside the Ross Ice Shelf, and a route to the polar plateau was found up the Beardmore Glacier. A scientific party sledged to the Magnetic South Pole, in Victoria Land; the crater of Mount Erebus, an active volcano, was also reached.

The race to the Pole

Spurred on by Shackleton's near-success at reaching the Pole, Scott's ship, the *Terra Nova*, left Wales for the Antarctic in 1910 and, after battling through terrible storms and unusually heavy pack-ice, reached McMurdo Sound at the beginning of 1911. The men immediately embarked on the business of laying depots for the attempt on the Pole.

The Norwegian Roald Amundsen, meanwhile, made for the Bay of Whales and also laid down depots, reaching some 200 miles (320 kilometers) further from his base than Scott, on what was an unknown but shorter route. Amundsen launched his attempt on the Pole on October 9, 1911 – a party consisting of five men, with four sledges and 52 dogs. His journey was fairly straightforward and he reached the South Pole on December 14, 1911.

Scott's party, on the other hand, had not left until November 1, and were encountering difficult conditions. As planned, the expedition was reduced in size as it advanced, with "support parties" being sent back to base,

▲ *The efficiency and speed of Amundsen's expedition owed much to his experience in the Arctic. He had actually been heading there in 1910 when news of Peary's success in reaching the North Pole (see page 181) caused him to turn his attentions to the South Pole. He was practised in the handling of dog sledges – and in the use of dogs as food – and this is generally considered to have been his major advantage over Scott.*

and ponies shot and eaten when there was no more fodder for them. Eventually, five men – Scott, "Bill" Wilson, "Titus" Oates, Edgar Evans, and "Birdie" Bowers – continued southward for the final assault, dragging their sledge.

They arrived at the South Pole on January 17, 1912, to find Amundsen's black flag and tent erected there. Having failed in their attempt to be first to the Pole, they were now faced with the 800-mile (1280-kilometer) return journey. The extent to which the depressed mood of the men affected their physical resilience will never be known, but they became increasingly unable to cope with the terrible conditions. Frostbite and snow blindness caused great discomfort, and shortage of food left them weak.

Evans was the first to die – on February 17. By mid-March, "Titus" Oates had also reached such a state that he could no longer continue. Knowing that Scott and Wilson would not leave him, he walked out into a blizzard, uttering the immortal words: "I am just going outside and may be some time."

By March 21, the remaining three men were confined to their tent by a blizzard, unable to walk the final 11 miles (18 kilometers) to their supply depot. Realizing that they were not going to survive, Scott wrote farewell letters and a Message to the Public in those last few days, huddled in his tent. These, together with his diary, provide a moving account of the expedition which was to capture the public's imagination in a way that Amundsen's never did.

The bodies of Scott and his two companions were found the following November and were buried beneath a cairn where they lay. News of their deaths did not reach the outside world until early in 1913.

German and Japanese expeditions

Contemporary with Scott and Amundsen was the German South Polar Expedition of 1911–12 in the *Deutschland*, led by Wilhelm Filchner. The *Deutschland* was beset in the Weddell Sea for nine months. The German expedition's principal discoveries were the Filchner Ice Shelf at the head of the Weddell Sea and the Luitpold Coast.

A Japanese expedition in the *Kainan-Maru*, 1910–12, sledged some distance over the Ross Ice Shelf from the Bay of Whales, and also landed on King Edward VII Land.

Means of transport

Different methods of transportation were used on these expeditions. Shackleton took ponies on his expedition of

1907–9, and although they proved problematic, Scott did likewise in 1910. Mules used in the Himalayan snows by the Indian Army were imported for the summer of 1912–13, in the belief that they were likely to be better beasts of burden than the ponies, but neither was terribly successful. Scott's decision not to use dogs to haul his sledges has often been given as the reason for his failure and Amundsen's success. Scott and his men hauled their own sledges, once they had been forced to kill and eat their ponies, using up enormous amounts of precious energy, each sledge weighing nearly half a ton.

Scott pioneered the use of tracked vehicles, while Shackleton tried an air-cooled Arrol-Johnston car as early as 1908. Neither of these forms of mechanical transport was successful, but did portend what was to come.

Supplies of food

The men of the "heroic age" were largely unaware of the need for vitamins, so that scurvy became a scourge on long journeys, where no fresh food was available. Vitamin pills later overcame this terrible affliction. Pemmican (pounded dried meat) long remained a staple of the polar diet on lengthy sledge journeys. On the expeditions of 1901–4, the daily allowance per man was about 30 ounces (850 grams) water-free weight (that is, in concentrated form). The food also included biscuit, oatmeal, pea flour, cheese, chocolate, cocoa, sugar, tea, onion powder, pepper, and salt.

Weight was a great consideration, and even though the daily ration was cut to a minimum, food took up three-quarters of the payload on a sledge. Seals and penguins could often provide food on coastal journeys, but inland there were no sources of nourishment. For this reason, a system of depot-laying was developed. Food and fuel were left in these depots, which were usually laid in the fall before the main sledging season. It was, of course, vitally important to be able to locate them on the return journey. Scott's party died during a prolonged blizzard from scurvy and starvation, within a few miles of a depot that had been laid further to the north than was originally intended.

◄ *An ice-cave* formed in an iceberg was one of the many natural wonders that Herbert G. Ponting photographed during Scott's expedition of 1910–13. The Terra Nova *can be seen in the background.*

KEY TO ROUTES	
——	Shackleton 1907–9
——	Amundsen 1910–12
——	Scott 1910–13
——	Filchner 1911–12

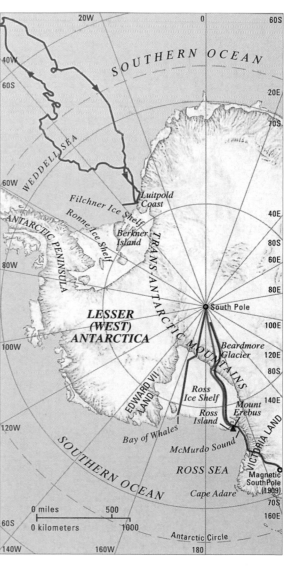

Mawson and Shackleton

▲ *Shackleton and his men dragged their whaleboat up the beach before setting off to cross the mountains of South Georgia, described by James Cook as a land "doomed to everlasting frigidness."*

▲ *Mawson's resilience and resourcefulness were demonstrated on his extraordinary journey of 1911–12, during which he suffered – and survived – terrible privations.*

Douglas Mawson, the Australian explorer of the "heroic age" (1900–16), combined the ability to organize and explore with the discipline of scientific work. Born in Yorkshire in 1882, he emigrated to Australia with his parents two years later. After graduating from Sydney University, he was appointed lecturer in mineralogy and petrology by the University of Adelaide in 1905, and remained on its staff for the rest of his working life, becoming Professor of Geology and Mineralogy in 1921.

Mawson's first experience of polar exploration was in 1907–9, when he took part in Shackleton's *Nimrod* expedition. On his return, he initiated, organized, and then led the Australasian Antarctic Expedition of 1911–14. This accomplished much in the way of geographical exploration and scientific work in the area of the Antarctic to the south of Australia (later claimed as Australian Antarctic Territory), including the discovery of a second rookery of Emperor penguins. (The first had been found by the British Expedition of 1901–4.)

The main base was set up at Commonwealth Bay (where the hut still stands), and others were established on the Shackleton Ice Shelf and on Macquarie Island, halfway between Australia and the Antarctic. George V Land and Queen Mary Land were discovered and explored, while a party sledged to the Magnetic South Pole.

Mawson set out on a sledge journey beyond the Mertz and Ninnis glaciers, named after his two companions. Ninnis was lost in a crevasse – the snow giving way after Mawson and Mertz had unwittingly walked across it – along with a dog sledge carrying most of the food and the tent. Mawson and Mertz were left 300 miles (480 kilometers) from base with scant supplies. They set off on the return journey, but after eating the dogs they were still over 100 miles (160 kilometers) from base. Mertz weakened and then died, and Mawson, after cutting his sledge in half to lighten the load, struggled back alone to Cape Denison. He arrived to see the expedition's ship, the

Men wanted for polar expeditions
Well aware of the dangers posed by exploration in Antarctica, Shackleton is said to have drawn up the following advertisement for the *Endurance* expedition:

"Men wanted for Hazardous Journey. Small wages, bitter cold, long months of complete darkness, constant danger, safe return doubtful. Honour and recognition in case of success."

Above, Shackleton is pictured with Francis Hurley, camping out on the ice after they had been forced to abandon the *Endurance*.

Aurora, which had waited as long as she was able, vanishing into the distance. Five men had volunteered to wait for him and the six of them wintered there, until they were eventually picked up and returned to Australia in 1914.

Ernest Shackleton

The *Aurora* was later purchased for the Imperial Trans-Antarctic Expedition which left Britain just a few days after the outbreak of the First World War in August 1914. The aim was to cross the continent from Vahsel Bay in the Weddell Sea to the Ross Sea. A party was sent to the Ross Sea in the *Aurora* to lay stores for the latter stages of the transcontinental journey. Unfortunately, it was a particularly bad winter for ice in the Weddell Sea and the expedition's other ship, the *Endurance*, became caught up in it. The ship drifted further south and then northward, and was eventually crushed, forcing everybody to camp out on the ice until they were able to launch their boats. They eventually reached Elephant Island in April 1916. Shackleton and five companions then sailed in an open boat, the *James Caird*, to seek help for the rest.

They covered 800 miles (1280 kilometers), finally arriving on the coast of South Georgia. They then had to cross the island on foot before reaching the whaling community. Here, Shackleton "borrowed" a whaling ship and attempted to return to Elephant Island but was prevented by ice. He made for the Falkland Islands, where he took charge of a Uruguayan trawler, and managed to get within sight of Elephant Island, but no further. He then traveled to the Strait of Magellan, where he chartered a schooner, but to no avail. Finally, the Chilean Government lent him a tug and he succeeded in getting through.

Shackleton, however, had still not finished his rescue operation. The expedition to lay supplies for him from the Ross Sea had run into difficulties in May 1914, when the *Aurora* had been torn from her moorings, leaving ten men stranded at Cape Evans on Ross Island. She eventually reached New Zealand in December 1916, where she was extensively refitted before being used by Shackleton to rescue the stranded men.

Neither Shackleton's Weddell Sea party in the *Endurance*, which discovered the southern part of the Caird Coast, first seen by the Scottish National Antarctic Expedition of 1902–4, nor the Ross Sea depot-laying party in the *Aurora*, contributed much to the exploration of Antarctica. The example of the "Boss," as Shackleton was known, in extricating his men against all odds has, however, never been forgotten. Raymond Priestley's aphorism regarding the three principal figures in Antarctic exploration has often been quoted: "For swift and efficient travel, give me Amundsen; for scientific investigation, give me Scott; but when you are at your wits' end and all else fails, go down on your knees and pray for Shackleton." It omits Sir Douglas Mawson, whom some would claim, as explorer, leader and scientist, to be the greatest of them all.

▼ **The end of the Endurance** was described by Shackleton as follows: "The ship was bending like a bow .... The floes, with the force of millions of tons of moving ice beneath them, were simply annihilating [her]."

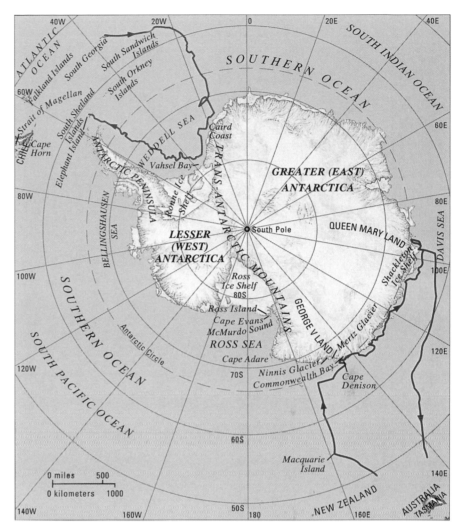

KEY TO ROUTES
— Mawson 1911–14
— Shackleton 1914–16

Expeditions Since 1918

▲ *Richard Evelyn Byrd was one of the most experienced of the polar explorers of the period before and immediately after the Second World War.*

The 1920s and 1930s saw a number of expeditions using aircraft to explore the continent. One of the first was that of the Norwegian Riiser-Larsen, who in 1929–30 sailed from South Georgia to Queen Maud Land, and then discovered and charted from the air Kronprins Olav Kyst and Kronprinsesse Martha Kyst.

In 1929–31 Mawson's British Australian and New Zealand Antarctic Research Expedition (BANZARE) combined traditional transport in the form of Scott's old ship, the *Discovery*, with the new, a Gypsy Moth float plane. The latter would take off from pools in the pack-ice, thus extending the range of the expedition, and as the "eyes" of the ship discovered the Banzare Coast, Mac.Robertson Land, and Princess Elizabeth Land. A similar combination was used by the British Graham Land expedition of 1934–37, led by the Australian John Rymill, which in addition made some fine dog sledge journeys along and across the Antarctic Peninsula.

Richard Byrd

The same period also saw a revival of American interest in the Antarctic in the person of Richard Evelyn Byrd. Byrd established his base camps near the Bay of Whales, Ross Ice Shelf. They were called "Little America I" (1928–30) and "Little America II" (1933–35). The area to the east of Edward VII Land was explored by sledge and plane, and called Marie Byrd Land.

Byrd also established an "Advance Base" from which to take meteorological observations, and decided to winter there alone during 1934. Unfortunately, the chimney of

his hut became blocked with ice, and fumes from his generator and stove gradually began to poison him. His men, in Little America, eventually realized that something was amiss from Byrd's peculiar radio messages, and traveled 120 miles (200 kilometers) through the Antarctic winter to rescue him. Byrd was too ill to make the return journey for two months.

A first flight by Byrd over the South Pole was made on November 29, 1929, piloted by Bernt Balchen. Pioneering flights were also carried out at this time by the Australian Hubert Wilkins, piloted by A. H. Cheesman, and the American Lincoln Ellsworth, piloted by C. B. Eielson and H. Hollick-Kenyon.

Scientific and national expeditions

Meanwhile, in 1925–27, the *Discovery* and her successor *Discovery II* made a series of major oceanographic voyages (Discovery Investigations), with the aim of establishing a scientific basis for the protection of the whale, which was being hunted in thousands by both Norwegian and British whaling companies. Besides exploring the life of the Southern Ocean, Discovery Investigations charted large areas of unknown waters.

The year 1939 witnessed the outbreak of the Second World War, but from 1939 to 1941, the United States Antarctic Service Expedition, led by Byrd, operated from "Little America III" on the Ross Ice Shelf and from Marguerite Bay, on the west of the Antarctic Peninsula. Flights and sledge journeys extended Byrd's previous work and that of the British Graham Land Expedition.

In 1943–44 permanent British weather stations were established by the Royal Navy at Port Lockroy and Deception Island under the wartime code name "Operation Tabarin" in Lesser (West) Antarctica. From this, after the War, the Falkland Islands Dependencies Survey (later the British Antarctic Survey) developed.

The immediate post-war years saw the arrival of the massive United States naval "Operation Highjump" in the southern summer of 1946–47. Byrd was in overall command. Thirteen vessels (including a submarine) took part, divided into three groups from which numerous flights were made, including Byrd's second to the South Pole on February 15, 1947. "Little America IV" was established near the Bay of Whales, from which overland journeys were made to the Rockefeller Mountains.

Many other, mainly national, expeditions were sent out to establish permanent stations on the continent and its surrounding islands after the Second World War. Particularly notable are the Australian National Antarctic Research Expeditions (from 1947 onward), which have accomplished much exploratory and scientific work in the huge expanse of Australian Antarctic Territory. The French have done likewise in Terre Adélie, although, sadly, the construction of a runway for aircraft between the little islands off the coast has disrupted the breeding grounds of eight species of penguins and other birds studied assiduously over many years by French biologists.

International Geophysical Year

The Norwegian–British–Swedish Antarctic Expedition of 1949–52, led by the Norwegian John Giaever, was the first international expedition to Antarctica. "Maudheim" base was established on the ice shelf of Queen Maud Land (the "Norwegian sector"). Field parties operated from there and from an advance base situated to the south.

It could be said that this successful scientific and survey expedition was a forerunner of the International Geophysical Year of 1957–58, organized and coordinated by

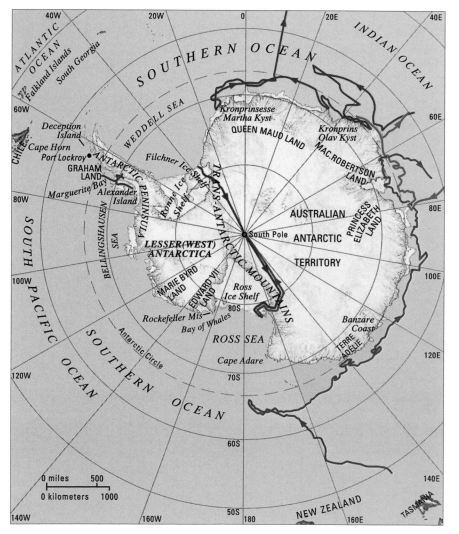

▲ **Vivian Fuchs's team** had to cope with frequent blizzards on their leg of the Trans-Antarctic Expedition of 1957–58.

▶ **The "sno-cat"** tracked vehicles used by Fuchs's team had to be able to cope with the numerous crevasses encountered on the crossing.

▼ **Hjalmar Riiser-Larsen,** the Norwegian aviator, was one of the first to use the float-plane as an aid to surveying in the Antarctic.

the International Council of Scientific Unions. (The IGY, as it came to be known, was itself the successor to the International Polar Years of 1882–83 and 1932–33.) All the IGY nations (Argentina, Australia, Belgium, Chile, France, Japan, New Zealand, Norway, South Africa, the United Kingdom, the United States, and the USSR) carried out meteorological and other scientific work during this specially designated period – and many continued for years, indeed even decades, after it.

This spirit of peaceful cooperation was to form the basis of the Antarctic Treaty, which came into force in June 1961, having been signed by all 12 nations in December 1959.

Trans-Antarctic Expedition

The first overland crossing of the continent was made by the British Commonwealth Trans-Antarctic Expedition of 1955–58, under the leadership of Vivian Fuchs. The crossing party started from the head of the Weddell Sea (Filchner Ice Shelf) on November 24, 1957, and arrived at the Amundsen–Scott station at the South Pole within a few hours of their projected arrival time. They were joined there on January 5, 1958, by a support party led by the New Zealander Edmund Hillary, who had driven from the Ross Sea to the South Pole in tractors. The combined expeditions arrived at New Zealand's "Scott Base" on the Ross Sea on March 2, 1958, to a tremendous welcome and much public attention. Fuchs's party had traveled 2150 miles (3475 kilometers) and had realized Shackleton's dream of 40 years earlier when he had led the Imperial Trans-Antarctic Expedition of 1914–16.

The Fuchs expedition used light aircraft for recon-naissance and supply, but made the actual crossing by large yellow tracked vehicles called "sno-cats," plus one dog sledge team. Seismic and other observations were carried out *en route*. A single-engined Otter aircraft, piloted by J. H. Lewis of the RAF, flew across the continent from Weddell Sea to Ross Sea on January 6, 1958.

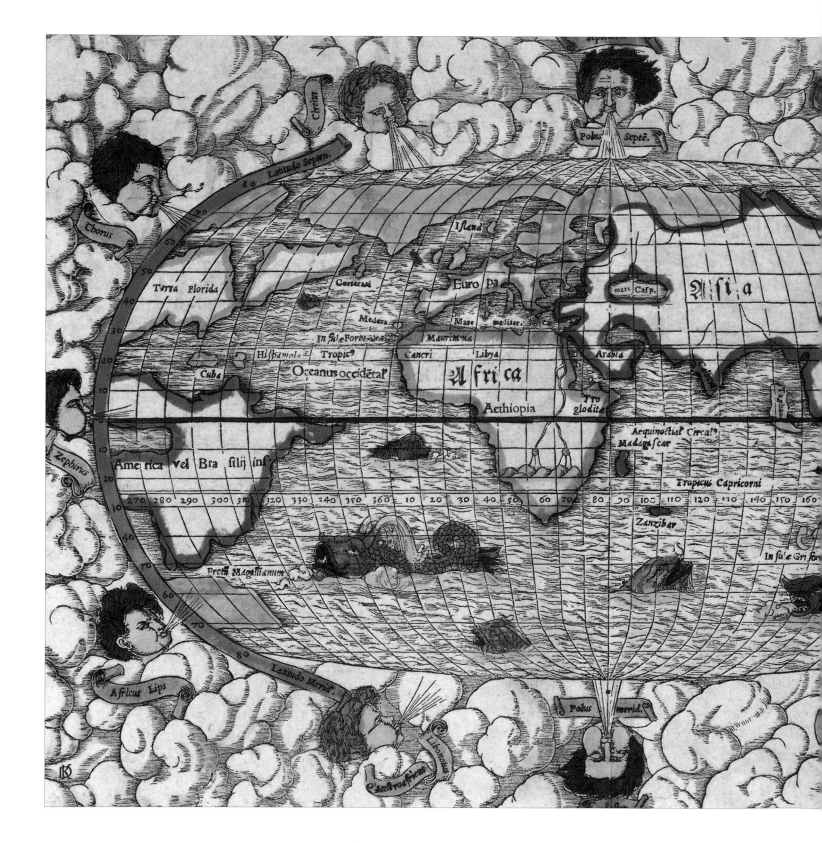

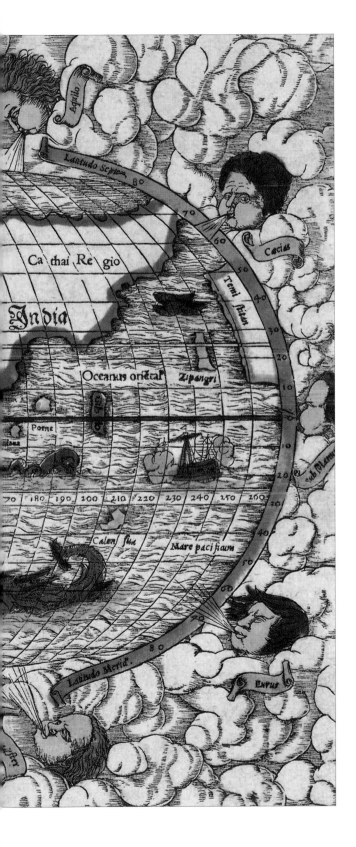

OCEANOGRAPHY

The oceans cover 72 percent of the Earth's surface. They have been described as the dynamo of climate and carry 50 percent of the sun's heat between the tropics and the poles, yet they are the least-known environment on this planet.

The ocean deeps never attracted explorers in the way that far-off lands did. These inaccessible regions held no wondrous kingdoms, no fabled mines of gold or gems. Neither warring tribes nor pagans ripe for conversion to the true faith inhabited their depths. Yet the oceans certainly had a place in most early mythologies.

Plato spoke of the city of Atlantis, submerged 9000 years previously for having made war against Athens. It was also thought that the ocean depths were home to a strange and wonderful range of monsters, which, being generally considered hostile to mankind, were best left undisturbed. These monsters were used to decorate the empty spaces on early maps, where they served to lead the eye toward the distant coastline.

In medieval and Renaissance times concepts of the oceans were shaped by two lines of philosophical thought. One drew largely on Old Testament writing, where a flat Earth, its continents separated by the Red Sea, the Persian Gulf and the Mediterranean, was bounded by the ever-flowing world ocean. The other, based on rational argument, favored a spherical Earth with water filling the hollows – an idea held by many of the classical Greek philosophers and never entirely lost during the Dark Ages.

When, at the end of the 15th century, Portuguese navigators ventured along the African coast, past the Equator and into the southern hemisphere, the flat Earth theory passed into oblivion. Yet centuries more would pass before cartographers could be confident that they knew exactly how large the Earth was and what proportion of its surface was covered by water. The map opposite, dating from 1550, is illustrative of the misconceptions that persisted.

First Observations

▲ **Corals** *were wrongly believed by Marsigli to be plants rather than animals after he put a branch of coral into a bucket of water and saw its '"flowers" emerge.*

Rational thinkers from Classical Greece onward believed that nature obeyed certain laws. Wise people might therefore hope to discover how the oceans were formed, what shape their basins were, why the water was salty, and what caused the waves and tides and the currents that were seen to flow through the Bosphorus and the Strait of Gibraltar.

Many early ideas were subsequently attributed to Aristotle, whose works, together with those of Pliny, were required reading for scholars throughout the Middle Ages. Neither man had been outside the Mediterranean, and they relied on hearsay or imagination in their depiction of what lay beyond its shores. Aristotle knew that oceans occupied depressions on the globe but found it hard to account for their saltiness. He examined the marine creatures brought ashore by Greek fishermen and was the first to classify them into those with blood and those without.

From speculation to observation

In the 17th century new attitudes toward the natural world led to the formation of the Royal Society in London and similar academies in other European cities. Experiment and observation replaced speculation.

When preparing his *Tracts* about the globe, published in 1671, Robert Boyle tried to establish whether, being so far from the sun's rays, the sea was frozen at the bottom, or whether, being so close to the subterranean fires that erupted through volcanoes, it was actually hot. He wondered whether the sea became deeper the further one went out from the shore. If so, how could he account for midocean islands? Boyle questioned men who dived on wrecks, but they knew nothing of the deep sea. This would have to be explored by means of apparatus, sent down on the seaman's hemp line. Indeed, for almost three centuries underwater exploration was carried out at the end of a very long line, the results dependent on what technical progress had been made. The scientists were often in doubt about the records brought back by their instruments and apparatus because they simply did not know what to expect.

Seamen regularly sounded to a depth of 50 fathoms (300 feet/90 meters) with the ship under way, and greater depths were possible when the ship was stationary. The sounding was confirmed if sediments came up on the dab of tallow put on the base of the lead. The line was hauled in with great effort against the friction of the water, and if it broke, both lead and line were lost.

When the Royal Society turned its attention to the exploration of the sea, it had first to provide suitable apparatus. The task of designing various instruments fell to its Curator of Experiments, Robert Hooke, who tested his inventions in the Thames estuary.

In its *Directions for Seamen bound for Voyages*, published in 1662, the Royal Society subsequently recommended the use of the instruments developed by Hooke and his colleagues. Ships' captains were requested to investigate the deep sea and report their findings to the Society. But 17th-century technology was not equal to the demands of underwater work, and such random methods with unsuitable wooden apparatus were unproductive.

The discoveries of Marsigli

The first planned underwater exploration was carried out along the Mediterranean coast of France by Count Louis-Ferdinand Marsigli in 1706–8. Marsigli was an Italian nobleman who had been a military surveyor for Emperor Leopold of Austria, fighting the Turks in eastern Europe. Between campaigns he wrote a history and geography of the Danube region. He came to believe in the essential unity of geological structure, and went to Montpellier in 1706 in order to confirm his ideas by looking at the geology of coasts and the adjacent seabed.

As Marsigli examined the offshore sediments, he discovered curious growths, now known to be invertebrates: sponges, corals, and bryozoa. For centuries sponges and coral had been gathered and sold dry, but Marsigli had never seen them in their natural habitat. At first he thought they were minerals that grew like the stalactites he had found in caverns.

Members of Montpellier's Académie des Sciences were also curious about the nature of coral, which was a valuable harvest for fishermen off the rocky Provençal coast, but they disputed Marsigli's views. To resolve the matter, Marsigli undertook a comprehensive survey of the coast. As he did not have his own ship, he went out with the local coral fishermen who manoeuvred their traditional

▶ **During his study** of the Mediterranean coast, Marsigli drew the coral structure (below), mapped the seabed where it grew, and sketched the nets used to bring it to the surface. He wrote up his findings in his Histoire Physique de la Mer, which was the first book devoted entirely to the sea. In it Marsigli described the structure and sediments of the sea's basin, the nature of the water, the waves, tides and currents, and the "marine plants." The manuscript languished for many years, until Marsigli went to Amsterdam where he arranged for its publication in 1725.

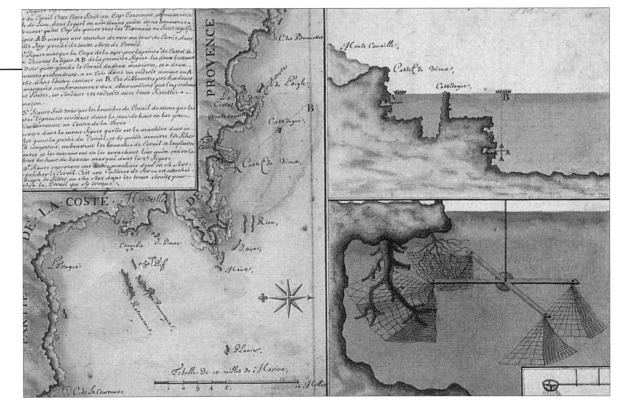

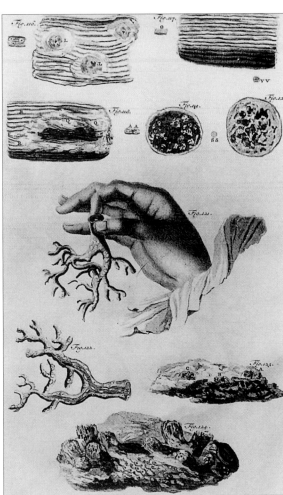

scoops and nets into the underwater caverns and rocky ledges where the coral was believed to grow upside down. He collected whatever came up in the nets, taking home specimens to examine under his microscope and to analyse by the primitive methods then available. However, his examination of the corals led him to think that they were marine plants, a view discarded later in the 18th century when the "flowers" of coral were identified as colonial animals living in a stony growth of their own making.

Hooke's sounder and Six's deep-sea thermometer

Robert Hooke invented his sounder in 1667. It consisted of a wooden ball coupled by a wire spring to a stone or iron sinker, and when dropped overboard it sank to the bottom where the spring opened, the sinker fell off, and the ball returned to the surface. Hooke tested his sounder in water of known depth to find its rate of travel, and he believed that this rate would hold for deeper soundings. In later years he proposed adding a pressure-measuring device, or a geared mechanism to register the distance traveled.

The Englishman James Six spent several years perfecting a self-registering thermometer for weather observations before modifying one for use under water in about 1780. He wrote about the air thermometer in 1782 and described the marine thermometer in his book published posthumously in 1794. Such a thermometer would have been of great value to Marsigli who, in an attempt to discover whether the deep water in the Mediterranean warmed in summer, had occasionally lowered his thermometer into the depths. When his thermometer had been broken he had been forced to abandon the project, for in the early 18th century no two thermometers were the same.

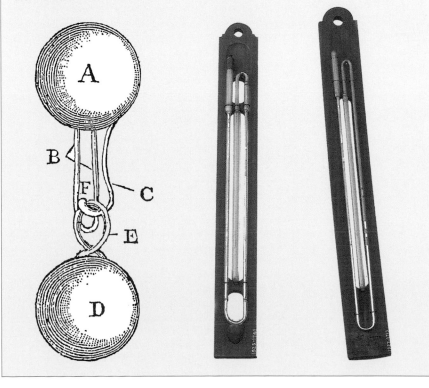

Charting the Ocean Depths

▶ **The first map** of an ocean basin was compiled by Matthew Fontaine Maury and appeared in his book The Physical Geography of the Sea, *published in 1855. Based on soundings made with Brooke's detaching-weight sounder, it contains a number of errors but is less misleading than reports of previous soundings.*

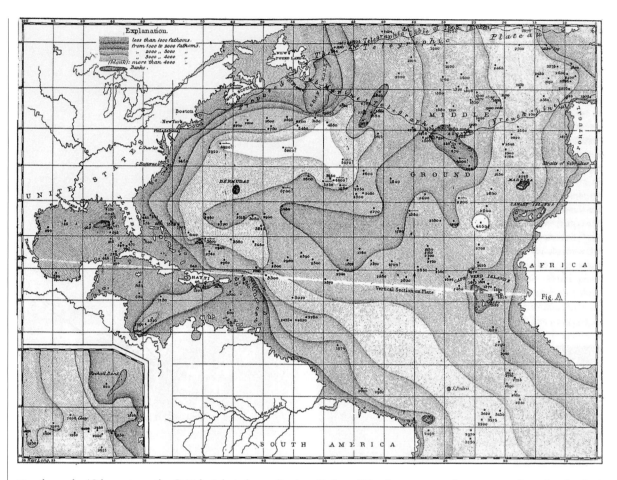

In the early 19th century, the British Admiralty realized that marine science might benefit Arctic exploration. John Ross, sailing into Davis Strait in 1818 on his search for the Northwest Passage, hoped to distinguish between rivers and seaways by measuring the temperature and salinity of the water beneath the surface-ice meltwater. Estuarine deep water would be cold but fresh, that of marine channels would be slightly warmer and saline. Such measurements could be important aids to exploration in areas where ice and snow masked the landscape, where visibility was hampered by fogs, and the magnetic compass erratic. The Admiralty was optimistic of success, for the ships had been issued with Six's marine thermometer (see page 201) and Massey's sounder, both invented some years previously. Massey's sounder consisted of a series of counting-wheels that were turned by vanes as they sank through the water. The mechanism was slipped out of gear by the action of hauling it up, leaving the pointer to show what Massey claimed was a true vertical depth.

Global charting

Beyond home waters, ships' captains relied on their charts to indicate the way into unfamiliar harbors, to warn of dangerous submerged rocks and sandbanks, and to identify good "holding ground" for safe anchorage. Soundings were noted on charts from the 16th century onward, and this was eventually to lead to government-sponsored continuous hydrographic global charting, an activity that has continued right up to the present day.

The best hydrographic charts offered a great deal of information about the ocean over the continental shelves. Near-shore underwater features were located by triangulation, and lines of closely spaced soundings gave a good picture of the nature of bottom sediments. Further out to sea, charting was far more arduous. The British Captain

Robert Wauchope reported on a sounding that he had made in 1816 when he attached a water-sampler to 1435 fathoms (8610 feet/2624 meters) of rope, weighted by seven cannon-shot spaced down the line and with a 72-lb (33-kg) sinker. The rope itself was 2.5 inches (6.3 centimeters) thick, increasing to 3.5 inches (8.9 centimeters) near the surface. It took 22 minutes to veer this cumbersome assembly overboard and then the efforts of 100 men working the capstan for 1 hour 20 minutes to haul it in, due to the great friction between rope and water. Consequently, such soundings were seldom made and the few that were made were judged worthy of report.

Soundings were made far apart, and their location relied on the navigator's accurate observation of his position at the time. Charts also recorded isolated rocks and reefs that had been reported by ships' captains on earlier voyages but whose existence was doubtful. These "vigias," as they were called, might be only icebergs or clumps of weed, glimpsed through fog or driving rain, but they remained on the charts, as a precaution, until modern sounding techniques proved or disproved their existence.

French and Russian expeditions

During the 19th century French and Russian expeditions were also active in charting the oceans. When the Russian ships *Rurick* (1815–18) and *Predpriatie* (1823–26) sailed round the world from their Baltic home port to Russia's Pacific settlements, their captains sounded the deep water along their routes. French ships visited the Pacific and nosed down toward the Antarctic continent. Jules Dumont d'Urville explored and collected botanical specimens on his two expeditions in *Astrolabe* (1826–29 and 1837–42) but did not neglect the water beneath his keel.

Abel Dupetit-Thouars was despatched in *Vénus* (1836–39) on a political mission to help and protect French

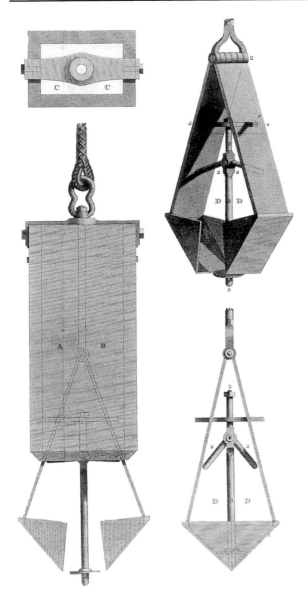

The American Civil War (1861–65) delayed progress in deep-sea exploration, but US surveyors soon caught up and by the third quarter of the 19th century they had taken a leading position.

Some ancient concepts of the sea died hard. Professor Charles Wyville Thomson, later to become one of the world's most famous marine biologists, recounted, "There was a curious popular notion ... that, in going down, the seawater became gradually under the pressure heavier and heavier, and that all the loose things in the sea floated at different levels, according to their specific weight: skeletons of men, anchors and shot and cannon, and last of all broad gold pieces wrecked in the loss of many a galleon on the Spanish Main ... beneath which there lay all the depth of clear still water, which was heavier than molten gold."

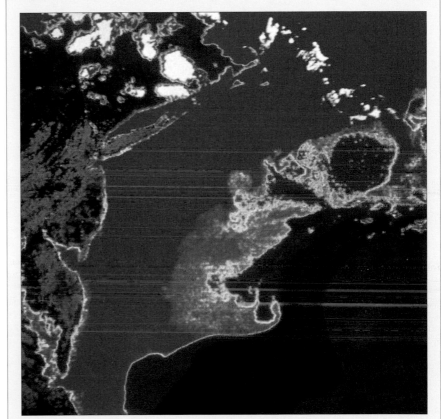

▲ *John Ross* had this "clamm," or grab, made on board his ship during his search in 1818 for a *Northwest Passage. It was intended to help him determine when he was in a seaway rather than a river.*

The Gulf Stream

Captains of sailing ships had known for some time about the existence of a great current that flows from the Gulf of Florida to Europe when, in 1765, it was first marked on a chart by William Gerard de Brahm. Ten years later, Benjamin Franklin noted the marked change in water color and weed content when his ship entered the warm current, and he persuaded his seafaring cousin Timothy Folger to mark the course, dimensions, and velocity of the Gulf Stream on a chart.

Survey ships were borne along by the very current whose depth they sought to measure until 1876, when the American lieutenant John Pillsbury devised a method of anchoring in deep water; he then lowered a heavy current meter into each level of the Stream far below his keel. Modern survey ships drop neutrally buoyant floats, with transmitters attached, into each level of the Gulf Stream. These floats rise and fall with changing temperature and salinity, and travel with the current, transmitting their position.

Heat-sensing radiometers on satellites create images of the warm water of the Gulf Stream as it flows north (as in the picture above). Along its western flank the stream flows at 60 miles (100 kilometers) or more per day. Meanders develop on the ocean side, breaking off in eddies that spin out into the open water. They create boundaries between water masses of differing qualities, which are similar to the atmospheric fronts of our daily weather systems.

whalers in the Pacific but, as his route led through regions seldom visited by naval ships, he was also ordered to spend some time on hydrographic work.

American endeavors

Lt Matthew Fontaine Maury, head of the US Depot of Charts and Instruments (later the US Naval Observatory) from 1842 to 1861, enlisted the help of his ships' captains to compile his charts of surface currents and winds, and asked them to make deep soundings. Maury was suspicious of many of the great depths reported and hoped that the detaching-weight sounder invented by his assistant, John Brooke, would give more reliable results. However, his claim that there was "between Cape Race in Newfoundland and Cape Clear in Ireland, a remarkable steppe which is already known as the telegraphic plateau" was to be proved wrong. Some of his soundings were simply erroneous, none had registered the deeper basins, and others had landed on the rocky midocean ridge. Maury's *Physical Geography* was influential, but some of his statements owed more to his religious beliefs than to reality.

Exploration for Commercial Needs

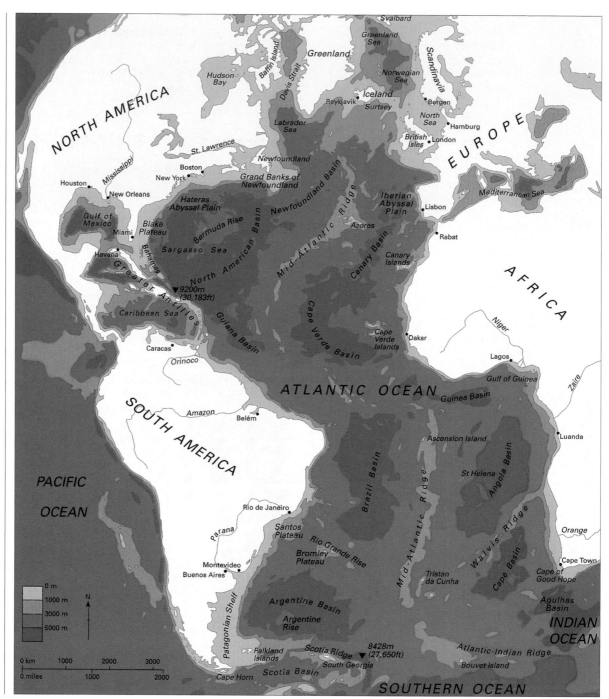

▶ **Ridges, gullies, and basins** are all features of the ocean floor which began to be charted in the second half of the 19th century in response to the requirements of telegraph companies. In the satellite image (below) of the floor of the South Atlantic Ocean, the red, yellow, and green areas are higher than the mean sea height, while the blue and magenta are lower. The black areas on the left are the tip of South America (top) and the Antarctic Peninsula (bottom). The southern end of the Mid-Atlantic Ridge can be seen in the upper right-hand corner.

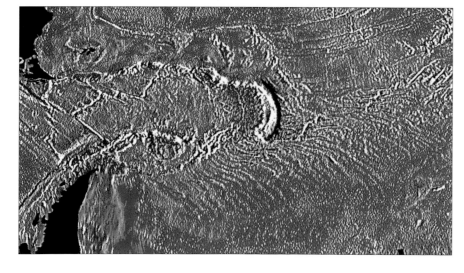

A true three-dimensional underwater landscape took shape during the second half of the 19th century, following the invention of telegraphy. From modest beginnings in the 1840s, cable networks were extended until the American and European cable companies were talking about a transatlantic link. The advent of the steam engine made this a feasible project. Steamships could hold to a predetermined course against wind and weather while their donkey-engines drove the heavy cable-handling gear. But the initial step was to obtain an accurate profile of the sea floor, so that sufficient cable could be manufactured. This could then be paid out from the ship at a rate that allowed it to sink through several miles of water and come to rest evenly on the bottom.

Sounding surveys

The first sounding survey was made by Lt Berryman in USS *Arctic* in the summer of 1856, with the new Brooke sounders. Berryman worked across the Atlantic and back but produced two very different profiles. The following year Lt Dayman repeated the exercise in HMS *Cyclops*. Since the laying ships would have to follow his track, Dayman took more care than Berryman over his own position fixes at the time of each sounding. He also used a variety of sounders, hoping in this way to reduce errors caused by defective apparatus. After several false starts, the transatlantic cable was laid and functioning.

Meanwhile, the British Admiralty was sounding other cable routes through the Mediterranean Sea and along the Red Sea to India. Cables linked Britain to its offshore islands and to Europe and Scandinavia; they crossed the Mediterranean from France to North Africa.

Invention of the wire sounding machine

Time was money; fast yet reliable surveys were essential, and new apparatus was therefore urgently needed. Sir William Thomson, better known as Lord Kelvin, Professor of Natural Philosophy at Glasgow University, telegraph engineer and consultant, answered this need by inventing the wire sounding machine (among many other devices) in 1872. Previous attempts to sound with wire had failed because it had been impossible to manufacture long runs of strong wire. Thomson succeeded because recent progress in wire-drawing technology had given him the quality of wire that was needed.

Cable engineers devised a range of sampling tubes for their own or Kelvin's sounding machines. They could now complete each operation in minutes rather than hours, the ship being able to steam to the next position while the wire was reeled in, since the friction between wire and water was negligible. If a cable broke or became faulty, ships searched for it by steaming back and forth over its position until they hooked it. As these "grappling runs" were charted, wide areas of seabed topography were delineated, and the same process took place when cables were duplicated.

The cables running along tropical coasts were laid beyond the continental shelf in cold water, where they were undisturbed by fishermen or ships' anchors. Thus the continental slopes, and the canyons that scored through their flanks opposite the major river mouths, were added to the list of submarine topographical features.

Mapping the underwater landscape

The cable engineers sounded the approaches to volcanic islands carefully, seeking the safest place to bring the cables ashore. This work revealed, for the first time, the true structure of these rocky midocean peaks. The cable ships also explored the deep-water shoals. Some of these had been known since the 18th century, by the sudden chill in the surface water caused by deep cold water rising up their flanks. They could then be mapped, one more element in an underwater landscape that was proving to be as diverse as any on dry land.

The abyss was not a smooth basin carpeted with mud but contained mountains and valleys, scarps and plains, volcanoes and freshwater springs, still water and swift-flowing currents, each unit with its distinctive ground cover of bare rock, gravel, shells, or clay.

Before long it was apparent that the seabed was far more dynamic than had been supposed: cables were frayed by strong currents moving gravel across them or broken by landslips on the continental rises. A great debate ensued as to whether the currents were driven by differences in the density of water masses, by surface winds, or some other force. Much more information had to be gathered before a density-driven ocean circulation system was accepted. On

the global scale, dense cold polar water sinks and drifts slowly toward the Equator, where it rises, warms, and returns toward the Pole. Regional circulation systems form where global currents are deflected, for example by a rise in the seabed. The resulting pattern is complex and is still being studied.

Introduction of echo-sounders

Prior to the First World War there was on average only one sounding per 5400 square miles (14,000 square kilometers) in the Atlantic and one per 10,000 square miles (26,000 square kilometers) in the Pacific and Indian oceans. Even along cable routes, depth measurements obtained by lead and line were so far apart that they gave a misleading impression of a smooth basin occasionally interrupted by peaks or trenches.

More detailed information was provided by echo-sounders which were developed during the war and fitted to survey ships in the 1920s. Early models generated sound pulses as hammer-blows on the ship's hull; these pulses traveled down to the seabed and the return echo was detected by a microphone on the ship. The speed of sound through water being known, the time taken for each pulse to make its double journey was an indication of the depth of water under the keel. In later models, silent ultrasound pulses replaced the hammer-blows, and by 1958 side-scan techniques were being used. Side-scan sonar transmits pulses sideways from a ship, or from a towed "fish." In the latter case, returning echoes are converted to electrical signals and sent up a cable to the usual inboard recorder, where the trace builds up line by line into an image resembling a photograph. At short range the system picks up small ripples in sand or the texture of bare rock. Long-range systems can image objects 15 miles (24 kilometers) distant and are used for rapid general surveys.

One of the most notable expeditions made by a ship fitted with an echo-sounder was that of the *Mahabiss* in 1933-34. The echo-sounder was of the primitive audible type, and her crew had to endure 25 soundings per minute over most of her 22,000-mile (35,400-kilometer) voyage to the Red Sea and Indian Ocean. They were rewarded by traces showing systems of parallel ridges and gullies, and an extension to the Carlsberg Ridge – discoveries of major importance scarcely appreciated at the time.

What *Mahabiss* had recorded was later seen to be a vital piece in the jigsaw of the Earth's crustal plates, whose boundaries are the great ocean ridges and deep trenches. Acoustic sounding eventually revealed the global extent of these, Earth's mightiest physical features.

▲ *The transatlantic cable was laid in 1857–58 after the topography of the ocean floor between the British Isles and Newfoundland had been charted by Lt Dayman in* Cyclops. *His instructions had been to sound closely in water less than 100 fathoms (60 feet/180 meters), every 10 miles (16 kilometers) until deep water was reached, then every 40 or 50 miles (68 or 80 kilometers) until he approached the Newfoundland shore. The subsequent profile was more accurate than any produced in previous years.*

Life in the Depths

◄ **A team of scientists** traveled for three and a half years on board HMS Challenger, shown here in a watercolor painting taken from a personal diary. The ship contained a small laboratory in which dredge samples were examined, drawn, and preserved.

▼ **This delicate sponge,** Rossella velata, *was dredged by HMS* Porcupine *in the Strait of Gibraltar in August 1870. Until the middle of the 19th century most scientists had believed that life could not survive below around 400 fathoms (2300 feet/ 700 meters), but during her North Atlantic voyage HMS* Porcupine *brought up objects from as great a depth as 2500 fathoms (15,000 feet/4600 meters).*

The oceans contain the largest ecological regime on the planet. Marine life ranges in size from microscopic bacteria to the giant whales and squid. Some plants and animals are closely related to those living on dry land; there are also free-floating plants and whole classes of animals that spend their life anchored to the seabed. The majority of fish, reptiles, and mammals that inhabit the sea live close to the surface, sustained by a food chain that begins with green plants (phytoplankton) growing in the sunlit area. Until recently, naturalists knew nothing of those species which spend their lives in the utter blackness of the abyss.

Marine plants and animals are collected as food, as objects of biological study, and for the sake of their rarity and value – pearls, red coral, and murex shells have been prized since prehistoric times. For many years naturalists puzzled over the identity of corals, these curious stony growths which had no parallel ashore. In the early 18th century, the Italian naturalist Marsigli believed that they were plants; later in the century two French naturalists, Jean-André Peyssonnel and Bernard de Jussieu, correctly transferred coral to the animal kingdom.

Investigating the deep sea

Dredging the open sea was no weekend pastime for the amateur naturalist. A powerful ship was needed to tow a heavy dredge over the seabed and then haul it up. The few experiments made in the early 19th century were tantalizingly inconclusive – the creatures might have been captured anywhere between the surface and the seabed.

Edward Forbes joined HMS *Beacon*, in 1841–42, in the Aegean, where he found that the number of species and their populations decreased between the surface and 300 fathoms (1800 feet/550 meters), below which he supposed that life was absent. By this time many starfish and other bottom-dwelling creatures had been brought up clasped to the sounding line, but naturalists were reluctant to admit the evidence.

In 1860 some 40 miles (65 kilometers) of a telegraph cable, laid across the Mediterranean three years previously, was pulled up for repair. Parts of this cable had lain in the

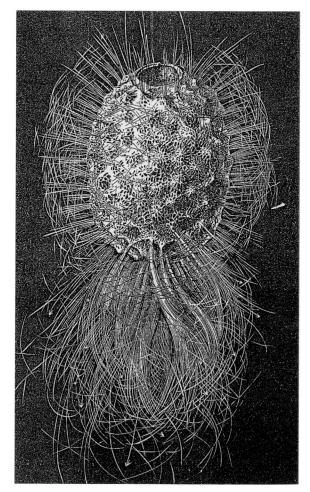

blackness of water up to 1200 fathoms (7200 feet/2200 meters) deep, yet this had not prevented shells, corals, and other organisms from growing to maturity on it.

Between 1868 and 1870, HMS *Lightning* and HMS *Porcupine* were sent to dredge in the North Atlantic. Varied and abundant life was found throughout the expedition,

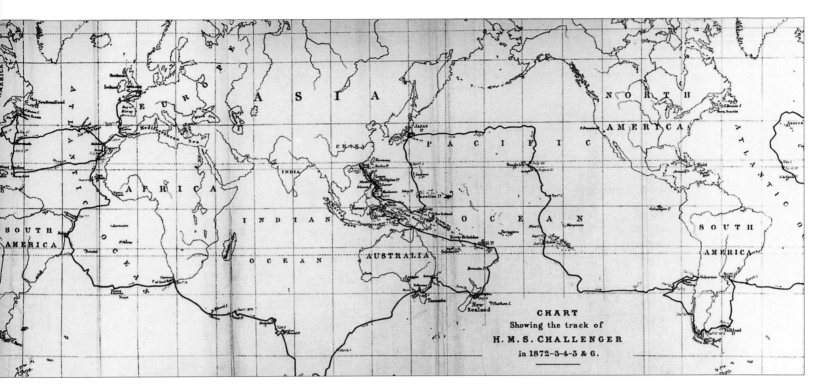

CHART
Showing the track of
H. M. S. CHALLENGER
in 1872-3-4-5 & 6.

and it emerged that the deep-water temperature was not uniform. The scientists found distinct bodies of water in slow movement, each contributing to a grand oceanic circulation, and each with a characteristic fauna.

HMS *Challenger*

The success of the HMS *Lightning* and HMS *Porcupine* cruises encouraged British scientists to press for a comprehensive survey of the major oceans. The Admiralty agreed to refit HMS *Challenger*, and she sailed in December 1872, with Captain G. S. Nares in command and five scientific staff under Professor Charles Wyville Thomson.

In all, HMS *Challenger* sailed 68,890 miles (110,870 kilometers), obtained 492 soundings, and made 133 dredgings and 151 trawls. Not all the equipment on board gave good results, but the new reversing thermometer that was invented in 1874 heralded a new era in underwater temperature measurement.

The scientists on board found the remains of living organisms and volcanic fragments in sediments brought up from the abyssal depths. In the Pacific, strange manganese nodules came up from the deep ocean floor south of Japan, and in the Atlantic it was established that a central range of mountains divided the ocean into an eastern and a western province, each with distinct water masses and fauna.

The *Challenger* returned to England in May 1876, having passed through all except the Arctic regions and skirted the permanent ice of Antarctica. Her collections were sent to specialists at home and abroad, and their reports came out in a series of 50 volumes published between 1880 and 1895. Marine biologists still consult these reports for their detailed information and beautiful illustrations.

The oceanographer prince

A growing interest in the oceans as a dynamic system, like the atmosphere, created the need to study its changes with time. Prince Albert I of Monaco led the way, returning to survey particular areas every year. He acquired his schooner *Hirondelle* in 1873, and by 1875 had decided to devote his life to marine science. For the next 40 years his summer cruises took him through the Mediterranean or out into the North Atlantic, even into the Arctic.

He faced many adventures: once a storm washed the bottled specimens from the day's catch round the ship's deck; on another occasion he ran on to a rock off the desolate coast of Svalbard, to be saved in the nick of time by a high tide. The *Hirondelle* was replaced by the steam

yacht *Princesse Alice*, fitted with laboratories and deep dredging and sounding gear. She helped to bring up from the record depth of 19,800 feet (6035 meters) a new species of fish, to be named in honor of the Prince's family, *Grimaldichthys profundissimus*.

Prince Albert developed new apparatus, including closing nets for capturing fish in midwater and photometers that measured the penetration of light within the sea. The results of his work were reported in a series of lavishly illustrated volumes. Albert also responded to the call for a world chart of ocean depths and supervised its production. The first edition of his *General Bathymetric Chart of the Oceans* was published in 1903. In 24 sheets, at a scale of 1:10 million, it was based on 18,400 soundings. A second edition followed in 1912.

The chain of life in the oceans

In the late 19th century a network of shore biological stations backed by survey ships was established in Germany; Swedish biologists made long-term observations of the Baltic; and the famous Naples Zoological Station was founded and offered its facilities to visiting scientists of all nationalities.

Zoologists began to investigate the whole chain of life in the sea, beginning with the complex inorganic molecules that, with sunlight, sustained microscopic plant life – the "grass of the sea" – on which minute herbivores grazed before they were in turn eaten. This stratum of floating marine life had no identity until 1887, when Victor Hensen coined the term "plankton" to describe it.

Fish depend ultimately on plankton, a fact of interest to the governments of Scandinavia, Germany, and Britain which were becoming worried about the declining catches of fish. The Plankton Expedition of 1889, organized by the great German zoologist Ernst Haeckel, crisscrossed the Atlantic, sampling and comparing plankton from tropical and temperate waters.

The migration of plankton and fish across national boundaries meant that international cooperation was essential if stocks were to be managed and breeding grounds protected. Consequently, in 1902 the maritime nations of northern Europe set up the International Commission for the Exploration of the Sea (ICES). Each participating nation sent fisheries research vessels to its designated areas four times a year. They employed standard apparatus, designed in the ICES laboratory, and their results were published rapidly and to an agreed format.

▲ *HMS* **Challenger** *sailed 68,890 miles (110,870 kilometers) in 1872–76, in a voyage that laid the foundations of the modern science of oceanography.*

Seeing for Ourselves

The human body is not adapted to life in the sea. We are clumsy swimmers, and our bodies cannot withstand the sudden changes in pressure or the numbing cold. Over the centuries, therefore, numerous diving machines have been invented to enable us to repair underwater structures or to salvage material from wrecks. These were the forerunners of today's free-ranging apparatus which now permit divers to venture into the remotest regions of the underwater world.

The development of diving apparatus

The first practical diving apparatus consisted of a surface air-pump supplying an open helmet or full suit known as a Siebe suit. Such tethered suits were issued in the 1830s to divers working on HMS *Royal George*, wrecked in 1782. An obvious disadvantage was that the divers, drawing their air from the surface, could not walk far. In 1825 the first self-contained compressed-air diving apparatus was invented by the Englishman William James. The diver wore a full suit and helmet, but carried his air supply in a metal container strapped to his body. There is, however, no record of the apparatus ever being used.

In 1865 Benoît Rouquayrol and Auguste Denayrouze devised a pressure-regulating valve which delivered air at a balanced pressure and only when the wearer inhaled. Within two years a diving suit equipped with this apparatus was in commercial production. This was the outfit that Jules Verne gave his characters in his book *20,000 Leagues under the Sea*, published in 1870. Verne's underwater explorers traveled at will, but most diving is limited to around 100 feet (30 meters) where sunlight penetrates and the water is not too cold.

In 1943 Jacques-Yves Cousteau and Emile Gagnan fitted the Rouquayrol–Denayrouze demand-valve to high-pressure liquid-air cylinders, and this is the Self-Contained Underwater Breathing Apparatus (scuba) used today. In exchange for their freedom, scuba divers can wear a helmet, telephone, TV camera and lights, supplied by cable from a support ship.

Deep-sea craft

In 1930 the American naturalist William Beebe climbed into a pressurized steel "bathysphere" and was lowered 3000 feet (900 meters) into the depths, the first man to look upon the living creatures of this dark and alien world. Just 30 years later USS *Trieste*, a free but non-powered craft, carried Jacques Piccard and Lt Don Walsh down through the icy water into the very bottom of the Mariana Trench. The two men sat in a tiny capsule beneath a huge buoyancy tank. Cast off at 08.15 hours, they sank down, anxiously waiting for their echo-sounder to warn them as they neared bottom, which they reached at 13.06 hours.

Switching on their floodlight, Piccard was amazed to find a flat fish watching him – proof that life could exist in the greatest depths of the ocean. Twenty minutes later, their ballast released, *Trieste* began her slow ascent, breaking the surface at 16.56 hours. Their descent of 14 miles (22 kilometers) had taken eight-and-a-half hours.

▼ **The invention** of the aqualung by Jacques-Yves Cousteau and Emile Gagnan in 1943 gave divers the ability to move freely underwater. It is still used today, along with a neoprene wet suit which preserves body warmth.

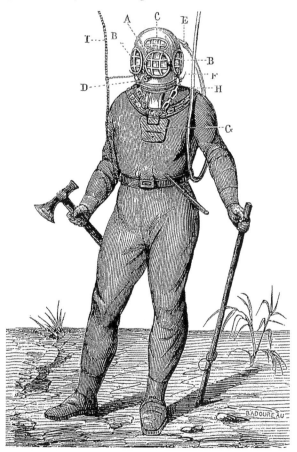

▲ **The Cabirol suit** was used in the 1850s in the eastern Mediterranean and elsewhere by divers searching for new sponge-fishing banks. Like the Siebe suit, it was not self-contained and required divers to be tethered to the surface by an air pipe and a control rope, thus limiting their freedom to explore.

During the 1930s a US submarine named *Nautilus* failed in an attempt to penetrate below the floating Arctic ice. The first successful crossing was made in 1958 by a nuclear-powered submarine also called *Nautilus*. In the same year, USS *Skate* went under the ice and surfaced near the Pole where an American drift-station had been set up. Submarines from various navies now patrol regularly through the Arctic Ocean, using their sonar to map the basin floor and the undersurface of the ice. These surveys have shown the ocean bed to consist of a series of deep basins divided by ridges. Changes in the thickness of the floating ice cap are seen to reflect past climatic change, and to influence the weather of the northern hemisphere.

Reaching for the ocean floor

Divers working to 165 feet (50 meters) can breathe air; for deep dives, oxygen is supplied with other gases. Under increasing pressure, nitrogen dissolves in the divers' blood. The longer and deeper their dive, the more decompression stops they must make during their ascent to allow this gas to leave their bodies; otherwise they will suffer a painful or possibly fatal attack of "the bends." Subject to such precautions, divers at ambient pressure can now work at 1000 feet (300 meters) and will soon be able to go much deeper. One-atmosphere armored suits and submersibles are able to operate at 2100 feet (650 meters); cable-controlled manned vehicles reach deeper zones.

In 1972–75, Project FAMOUS (French–American Mid-Ocean Undersea Study) sent manned submersibles to examine the formation of the ocean crust on the Mid-Atlantic Ridge, where the American and African plates are separating at a rate of 2–3 inches (5–7.5 centimeters) each year. A bathymetric map constructed from echo-soundings and underwater photographs disclosed promising dive sites, and the French craft *Archimède* and *Cyane* and the USS *Alvin* made 30 dives. FAMOUS demonstrated that submersibles could undertake detailed geological mapping of rough deep-sea terrain, for the survey revealed the structure of the ridge, with its 1.6-mile (2-kilometer) deep central rift valley, lava flows, and the transform faults that displaced the rift as the continental plates continued to move apart.

Submersibles diving on the Galápagos rift in 1977 discovered warm mineralized springs surrounded by colonies of bacteria. In 1978–79, near the Gulf of California, hot vents were found emitting dark plumes of sulfide-rich

water at 662°F (350°C) through chimneys built up of silica and metal sulfides. Biologists were amazed to find these vents colonized by tube-worms, clams, and other creatures, a veritable oasis of life which flourished despite the total absence of oxygen or sunlight.

Exploration from space

Today the ocean is explored from space, with satellites sending back information on surface temperature, movements of icebergs, and the presence of fish and plankton. Long-running multinational projects continue to investigate the global ocean–atmosphere coupling that controls our climate, the effects of increasing pollution, and changes to the ecological systems which include fisheries. Basic surveys continue; the ocean floor is still less well known than the face of the Moon.

▲ *In 1960* the bathyscaphe Trieste *was used by Jacques Piccard and Don Walsh to go to a record depth of 35,800 feet (10,900 meters) in the Mariana Trench in the southwestern Pacific.*

EXPLORATION TODAY

Today a third of the world's surface area is still considered to be wilderness – land primarily shaped by the forces of nature. However, exploration as Livingstone, Columbus or Cook would have defined it is now mainly confined to the deep oceans, underground caves and, of course, space. Today's explorers are facing a challenge of a different nature. It is no longer a matter of just filling in the blanks on the map, but of discovering how the Earth functions and how better to manage the world's diminishing natural resources. Consequently, today's explorers are not loners pitting their skills against the elements. Rather, they are multidisciplinary teams of scientists who, with a wide range of new technologies available to them, seek to extend the boundaries of our knowledge and understanding.

We are now discovering more about our world than ever before, particularly the processes that regulate the planet and its four main component parts – the atmosphere, geosphere, biosphere, and hydrosphere. The more we explore these processes, the more we learn about the way in which each is really one part of a complex whole. The emphasis on studies of the Earth as an integrated system – global environmental research – is taking us into a new age of discovery, in which the collection of data is a priority. There is an "environmental Everest" to climb, and yet, in comparative terms, we have only just achieved the "hobnailed boots and tweed jacket" stage reached by those trying to conquer the mountains in the 1920s.

As the world's population grows, the scale of environmental degradation caused by human activities is immense. In March 2005 the *Millennium Ecosystem Assessment*, a global inventory of the state of the world's ecosystems, was published. Containing the findings of some 1400 experts from 95 countries about the effect of human activities on the planet, the inventory makes frightening reading. It appears that 60 percent of the world's natural ecosystems on which people depend for their health and well-being are damaged. Already 40 percent of rivers have had their flow interrupted by water extraction or dams, 20 percent of coral reefs have been lost, and our climate has been disrupted. There has never been a more urgent need to discover better ways of managing the world's natural resources.

Tropical Forests

▼ *Scarlet and red-and-green macaws (Ara macao and Ara chloroptera) are among the vast number of animal species to be found in the rain forests. The biodiversity of these forests is such that while they cover only 6 percent of the Earth's surface, they contain, for example, between 70 and 90 percent of its insect species.*

Naturalists have played a major part in the history of exploration since the mid-19th century, collecting plants and animals from every corner of the globe. But despite the efforts of taxonomists, only 1.75 million species of plants and animals have been named to date. No one actually knows how many species live on the planet, but recent studies suggest the figure may be as high as 14 million, leaving some 87 percent of the world's flora and fauna to be described and named.

Of the different habitats, tropical forests are among the most biologically rich, and yet studies using satellite imagery show that they are being cut down at an alarming rate. Fortunately, the importance of the Earth's natural resources has been recognized; the 1992 Convention on Biological Diversity was initially signed by 150 countries.

The first step toward the sustainable use of these resources is to establish what is actually there, and the coming years will see a flurry of activity to record and monitor biodiversity. Field scientists and taxonomists have never been busier.

Conservation International, which specializes in carrying out rapid assessment surveys in biologically rich but little-known regions, sent out a team in December 2005 to the Foya Mountains of Irian Jaya (western New Guinea). In just a few weeks the biologists found dozens of previously unknown species, including frogs, butterflies, plants, and what is thought to be the first new bird from New Guinea in more than 60 years, as well as a golden-mantled tree kangaroo, not previously found in Indonesia.

Investigating the forest canopy

Until the 20th century, exploration of forests was limited to the understorey, but reaching and working in the forest canopy is the ultimate frontier. Attempts to reach the canopy were pioneered by the British Oxford University expedition of 1929 to British Guiana (now Guyana). Using rocket-firers and line-throwers, the team tried to get a rope-and-pulley system erected in the branches of trees 100 feet (30 meters) high, but found the assistance of local climbers with spikes tied to their feet to be more effective. Little else was tried until the 1960s, when Dutchman Adrian Kortlandt, with the help of Zairois pygmies, constructed a platform from which to observe chimpanzees. After that a few scaffolding towers, tree ladders, and short walkways were built. Balloons and dirigibles were also tried, but with limited success.

In 1989 the Smithsonian Tropical Research Institute erected a huge tower crane which raised and lowered a module on a 260-foot (80-meter) arm, enabling scientists at their research site in the Panamanian forest to work in the canopy for an area of 12 acres (5 hectares). In 2006 there were ten such cranes at sites around the world, and a further ten were being planned by the network of scientists who make up the Global Canopy Program. These scientists

▶ *The tropical forests of Borneo were cut down at a rate of 10.5 million hectares (roughly the size of England) during the 1980s and 1990s. Among the inhabitants of the forest whose traditional way of life is consequently under threat are the Penan – nomadic hunter-gatherers.*

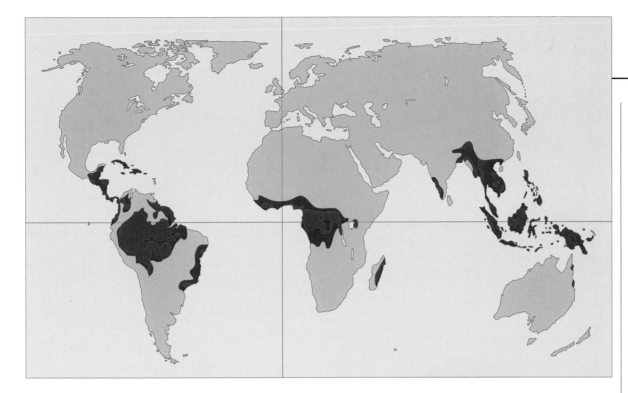

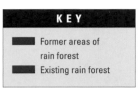

KEY

■ Former areas of rain forest

■ Existing rain forest

are confident the cranes will at last enable them to access tropical ecology's last frontier – the tree canopy where most of the photosynthesis and pollination takes place.

A wide range of research projects

Tropical forest expeditions are being organized by a large number of private and public institutes. Their scale and operations vary enormously, from small teams of taxonomists visiting an area for one season, to long-term international taxonomic research schemes. Begun in the early 1990s, the Flora Mesoamericana Project, coordinated by the Missouri Botanic Garden, Britain's Natural History Museum and the University of Mexico, is attempting to document the 20,000 native and cultivated vascular plants of Mexico and Central America. About 10 percent of these were previously unknown. The results of this work are being published in Spanish and on the Internet to help local scientists better manage and conserve the area's biodiversity.

The complexities of the forest and the number of specialists needed to understand them have encouraged a proliferation of field study centers where scientists can base themselves for a period of time. These are often financed and administered by major international institutes. As well as the long-running Smithsonian Tropical Research Institute project in Panama, there is the Organization for Tropical Studies, which operates three field centers in Costa Rica and, over the last 40 years, has trained several thousand North American and Latin American scientists and students. In Africa, the Worldwide Fund for Nature proposed a $10 million plan to found the Korup National Park in Cameroon. Opened in 1990, this comprises 493 square miles (1265 square kilometers) of one of the most biologically diverse areas of lowland forest in Africa.

A number of countries with significant forest resources are now able to fund their own centers. In Brazil, the National Institute for Research in the Amazon (INPA) employs over 1000 people, while in Brunei, in the Batu Apoi forest reserve of Temburong, the Kuala Belalong Field Studies Center functions as a "university in the rain forest." Built for the Brunei Rain Forest Project of 1991–92, a joint initiative between the University Brunei Darussalam and the Royal Geographical Society, it has a continuing program of school visits, undergraduate training, and research. These centers attract scientists of international standing and enable longer-term monitoring of the processes occurring within the forest itself rather than just the component parts.

◀ **As part of the Global Canopy Program**, a crane carries scientists in a gondola over the Wind River in Oregon in the United States. Erecting cranes has made it possible to explore and study the ecosystems at the top of some of the world's tallest trees.

Exploration for conservation

It is not only large international organizations that can make a difference. In September 1999 Michael Fay, an American biologist, set off with a group of Bambendjellé Pygmies on a 1250-mile (2000-kilometer) trek on foot through the forests of Equatorial Africa. The stunning photographs and data collected during the 465-day trek helped persuade the government of Gabon to create 13 new national parks. Many of the new parks will be developed for ecotourism as an economic alternative to exploiting the country's forests for timber.

Hot Deserts

▲ **Plants and animals** are being surveyed in the drought-stricken central area of Australia, partly to find out why some 17 mammal species have become extinct since Europeans first arrived in the country.

Many discoveries continue to be made today in the world's desert regions. Teams looking for minerals and oil are joined by those searching for clues to help predict the changing shape of the world's arid regions. Well-equipped expeditions and scientists working at permanent research centers all contribute to the understanding of desert processes, for which there is an urgent need. One-third of the Earth's land surface is arid or semiarid and is home to more than 2 billion people. Desertification has become one of the most pressing environmental issues. Most at risk are sub-Saharan Africa (Sahel, Horn of Africa, and southeast Africa) and Central Asia. In China it is estimated that some 27 percent of the country's land mass is degraded, with an average of 950 square miles (2460 square kilometers) of land being lost to advancing deserts each year.

Modern technology to aid exploration

Great exploratory desert expeditions are now rare. Those that do take place are mainly conducted by university-

based teams undertaking earth- and life-science studies. Expedition teams with efficient four-wheel drive vehicles, satellite navigation, and good radios can drive to almost any corner of the great deserts.

New techniques continue to be pioneered, and hot-air balloons, microlights, and motorbikes have all been used to facilitate access to difficult locations in the Arabian, Australian, and Saharan deserts. Reliable vehicles with special sand tires, balloon jacks, sand ladders, and accurate satellite navigation now make it relatively easy to traverse the most difficult of desert terrains. Small, lightweight all-terrain vehicles (ATVs), with three or four balloon tyres at very low pressure, made the first crossing of the Grand Erg Occidental in Algeria in the early 1980s.

The dustiest place on Earth

In 2005, seven researchers set off on an expedition to the Bodélé Depression in Chad after the Total Ozone Monitoring Satellite (TOMS) had identified it as the dustiest place on Earth. Their aim was to study what happened when the Harmattan wind lifts dust from a dry lake bed of some 9650 to 13,510 square miles (25,000 to 35,000 square kilometers) and blows it across the Atlantic Ocean. The samples they collected will be used to understand the role that dust plays in cloud formation, and in controlling the temperature of the planet.

Dust also plays an important role in soil formation and the supply of nutrients such as iron, potassium, phosphorus, and calcium to the oceans. Dust from the Bodélé is thought to be the main source of nutrients in Sahelian farming systems and Ghanaian forests, and an important source of nutrients as far away as the Amazon in Brazil.

Centers of desert research

Growing scientific interest in deserts has led to the establishment of several centers of desert research, many of which welcome international scientists. These include the University of Arizona, the Hebrew University of Jerusalem, the Negev Institute of Desert Research in Israel, several universities in the Arabian Gulf, such as the Sultan Qaboos University, Oman, and the Jordan Badia Research

KEY

- Existing deserts
- Areas with a high risk of desertification
- Areas with a moderate risk of desertification

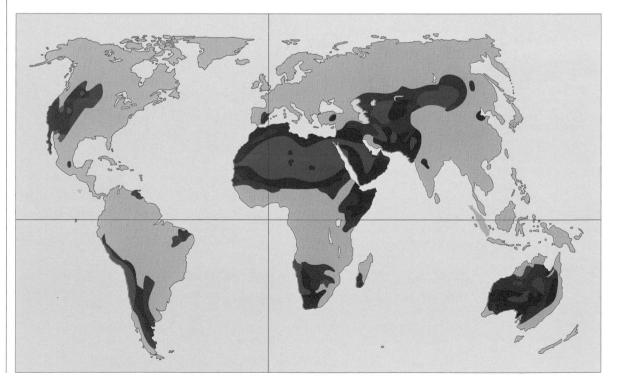

and Development Center, the Universidad del Norte in Chile, the Turkmenistan Academy of Sciences, the Desert Department of Academia Sinica in China, and the Central Arid Zone Research Institute in Jodhpur, India.

The issue of desertification was given proper recognition – along with the other key environmental challenges of climate change and loss of biodiversity – when the United Nations Convention to Combat Desertification (UNCCD) was adopted in 1994. This calls for urgent international action to assess the expansion of deserts, a matter of considerable concern since the tragic drought in the Sahel in the 1960s and the droughts that followed it in the Horn of Africa. Looking at specific scientific problems, such as erosion and overgrazing, or studying the potential resources of an area, is now high on the agenda of international desert research. Despite thorough investigations at a regional level, desertification is still little understood globally, and effective long-term solutions remain elusive.

The Oman Wahiba Sands Project

One example of a desert research project was that undertaken in the Wahiba Sands, a sand sea in the eastern region of the Sultanate of Oman, in 1985–86. Organized by the Oman Government and the Royal Geographical Society, the project's aim was to study the Sands as a stand-alone ecosystem by examining the relationships between the people, the biological resources, and the sands themselves. A multidisciplinary team of some 50 local and visiting scientists was appointed to achieve this is in just four months.

Navigation was assisted by satellite receivers in the Land Rovers. Considerable aerial and ground logistic support was provided by the Omani armed forces. A computing officer designed and coordinated a field-computing system, incorporating word processing, database, and Geographic Information System (GIS) facilities.

A six-strong survey team mapped the routes and specific areas for the geomorphologists (who were studying sand movement) and for the botanists (who were preparing a vegetation survey). The eight members of the biological resources team were experts in the areas of botany, plant physiology, entomology, herpetology, ornithology, and mammalogy (large and small). A land-use map and a vegetation map were drawn up. A broad-based earth-science team, also comprising eight people, looked at the original source and early development of the Sands, the hydrology and current geomorphology. Four expedition members prepared educational material for Omani schools, including teaching aids on sand deserts and desertification, and how animals and plants survive in this environment.

The different expedition teams met regularly to discuss the progress of the project and to coordinate their findings. Two weeks after completing the field work they presented

▲ **Jordan's Badia region** was the subject of an RGS joint UK–Jordan research program in 1992–96. This gathered the information needed for the sustainable management of the region.

▼ **Knowledge** of desert processes was developed through research in 1985–86 into the origins of Oman's Wahiba Sands.

▲ **The expansion of desert areas** means that there is a desperate need for further research into how plants and animals survive in such an environment.

a 600-page "rapid assessment document" to the Government of Oman, and a year later a full international conference to discuss the project's finding was held at the Sultan Qaboos University. The recommendations arising from this conference were subsequently incorporated into a general management plan for the area, with the purpose of helping to ensure its sustainable development.

The Polar Regions

Since the 1950s there has been growing recognition of the political, economic, strategic, and scientific importance of the polar regions, and it is now understood that these regions have a major influence on the life-support systems of our planet. The International Geophysical Year of 1957–58 was the first major post-war international program on a worldwide scale, and stimulated research programs in both the Arctic and Antarctic. The researchers were the first to monitor stratospheric ozone and atmospheric carbon dioxide levels, and to establish the thickness of the Antarctic ice sheet. Fifty years on, the International Polar Year of 2007–8 involved hundreds of research projects highlighting the importance of the polar regions. These were particularly concerned with the effects of climate change, which are likely to be greatest in the high latitudes of the polar regions.

Cooperation in the Arctic

The "Arctic-rim" nations, including the United States, Canada, and Russia, as well as a number of non-Arctic countries, have significantly increased their scientific efforts in the Arctic, and there is a marked trend toward cooperative projects which enable nations with smaller budgets to participate. In 1996 the Arctic Council was formed. Including organizations that represent the indigenous peoples – such as the Saami Council, Inuit Circumpolar Conference, and Russian Association of Peoples of the North – it compiled the Arctic Climate Impact Assessment

▶ *In Antarctica* one of the effects of the recent rise in temperature has been the disintegration of some of the ice shelves and the creation of an increasing number of icebergs.

Scientists from around 29 countries are active in Antarctic research. Below, a biologist marks the egg of an Adélie penguin;

opposite, a geologist examines rock samples as part of the research being conducted into the evolution of the continent.

in cooperation with the International Arctic Sciences Committee (IASC). Published in 2004, the Assessment shows that the Arctic is experiencing some of the most rapid and severe climate changes on Earth, changes that will affect the rest of the world through increased global warming and rising sea levels.

In September 2005 researchers from the National Snow and Ice Data Center in the United States recorded the smallest extent of Arctic winter sea ice for more than a century. This, together with reports from submarines on the depth of the ice, confirms fears that the Arctic sea ice could be shrinking by as much as 8 percent per decade. Speculation has begun that should the legendary Northwest Passage, and its Russian counterpart the Northeast Passage, become ice-free, both could open to commercial shipping for the first time. The continental shelf would also become accessible for oil and gas extraction.

The last great wilderness

The Antarctic is the highest, coldest, windiest, most remote place on Earth. Scientists working here use helicopters, fixed-wing ski-equipped aircraft, snow scooters, and ice-strengthened research vessels to aid their work, as and when the weather allows. Around 29 countries are active in Antarctic research, running programs which operate from field camps and a network of about 35 permanent research bases all over the continent. These are staffed by scientists who stay mainly for a short summer season and by a smaller number, about 800, who undertake work for a year or longer.

Ice is, of course, a major feature of the region. Some 99 percent of the continent is buried by permanent ice up to 3 miles (4.5 kilometers) thick. This flows outward from a central dome and, where it reaches the sea, may form large floating ice shelves, from which massive tabular icebergs break off and float out into the Southern Ocean. Beyond lies the pack-ice zone, which may in winter cover some 7 million square miles (20 million square kilometers).

Antarctic ice yields an archive of environmental information that goes back many hundreds of thousands of years. An analysis of core samples has highlighted issues associated with present changes in the world's climate. At the Soviet Vostok Station, in 1986, French and Soviet scientists recovered a 6500-foot (2000-meter) thick core, which provided a record extending back into the last Ice Age but one – 160,000 years ago. The results suggest a clear correlation between temperature rise and atmospheric pollution from industrial countries, which are mainly in the Northern Hemisphere. Such pollution has led to the thinning of, or "hole" in, the ozone layer which was first discovered by the British Antarctic Survey in 1980. More than any other discovery during the latter part of the 20th century, this drew attention to the urgency with which atmospheric pollution needs to be tackled.

Concerns over "global warming" are leading scientists to examine the possible effects on the stability of the Antarctic ice sheet and its role in world sea-level changes. Temperatures on the Antarctic Peninsula (as measured at the Faraday Station) have risen by 4.5°F (2.5°C) over the past 50 years, and satellite imagery has provided evidence of the disintegration of some of the ice shelves in the area. In just 50 days in 1995, 500 square miles (1300 square kilometers) of the Larsen Ice Shelf broke off, sending huge icebergs into the Weddell Sea. It is now thought that over 5000 square miles (13,000 square kilometers) of sea ice have been lost from the Antarctic Peninsula over the last 50 years. Studies such as those into the role of sea ice in climate change are initiated by the Scientific Committee

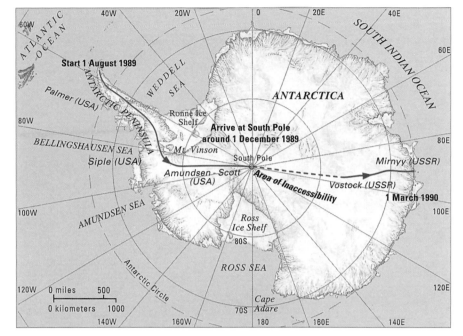

International Trans-Antarctica Expedition

On March 1, 1990, an international team completed the first unmechanized crossing of Antarctica by dog sled from west to east. Co-led by the American Will Steger and the Frenchman Dr Jean-Louis Etienne, the six-man team included representatives from six countries (the United Kingdom, France, Japan, China, the then Soviet Union, and the USA), chosen to reflect peaceful cooperation in Antarctica. Despite the arduous nature of their journey, a wide range of scientific investigations was conducted throughout the 4000-mile (6400-kilometer) overland journey, including the first measurement of ground-level ozone across the continent and of pollutants, such as aerosol deposits and DDT concentrations, in mosses and lichens.

on Antarctic Research, which provides advice on environmental protection in Antarctica.

The Southern Ocean, despite its extreme cold, is rich in nutrients and serves as a unique laboratory to help understand the biological productivity of the seas. The land, only 1 percent of which is not permanently covered by ice, supports a unique flora and fauna. Now tourists as well as scientists are being attracted to the frozen continent, and there is pressure to establish better controls to preserve the Antarctic environment.

The Marine Environment

▶ *The titanium-hulled Alvin, operated by the Woods Hole Oceanographic Institution, is the best-known manned submersible. Capable of taking two scientists and a pilot up to 14,760 feet (4500 meters) deep, it has been used to explore the wreck of the Titanic as well as many natural features on the ocean floor.*

▼ *Volcanoes such as this, with a crater 1.25 miles (2 kilometers) wide, have been revealed by unmanned towed vehicles and submersibles. Other ocean-floor features that have been explored include the hypo-thermal vents, or geysers, known as "Black Smokers."*

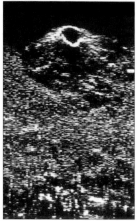

Sophisticated equipment and a great deal of money are required to explore the deep oceans. However, with increased international interest in underwater oil and mineral prospecting, waste disposal, fisheries and climate modeling, there is now considerable investment in the exploration of the seas. The military requirements of submarine and anti-submarine warfare have also been a guiding factor in underwater research, especially those aspects concerned with acoustics and the nature of sediments. This means that modern-day ocean exploration and research are largely within the domain of national institutions, the universities, and naval research establishments.

Satellites and survey ships

Instruments mounted on satellites are capable of monitoring many aspects of the ocean. Radar, photographic, and coastal zone color scanners are all used. Radar altimetry and scatterometry and associated systems can measure wind speed and direction at the sea surface, wave height, mean sea level, sea temperature, and tides and currents.

Today, much exploration of the sea is carried out from satellites, with multinational projects investigating the global ocean–atmosphere interaction that controls our climate. Yet research vessels using increasingly sophisticated unstaffed towed vehicles still have an important role to play in providing detailed information about the oceans. In the 1960s, the US Naval Oceanographic Office developed a multibeam or swath echo sounder which vastly increased the area that could be covered in a single pass (in the region of half a mile or one kilometer). Also developed – by the British Institute of Oceanographic Sciences – was GLORIA, a long-range side-scan sonar imaging system. In certain conditions this could cover up to 35 miles (60 kilometers) at one sweep and produce unique "pictures" of the seabed, including images of tectonic plates.

This technology was made available to researchers in the 1970s and, coupled with improvements in positioning systems and increased computing power, it has transformed our ability to view the ocean floor. Despite this, only 15 percent of the ocean bed has been mapped to date.

Shoals of Capricorn Program

In 1999 the governments of Seychelles and Mauritius signed an agreement with the Royal Geographical Society and the Royal Society to establish a research, education, and training program that would contribute to our knowledge and understanding of the Indian Ocean. The Shoals of Capricorn Program was the first multidisciplinary research project to focus solely on the Mascarene region in the southwest Indian Ocean. The region consists of the Mascarene Basin – more than 2.5 miles (4 kilometers) deep – to the west, the granitic islands and low-lying coral islands of the Seychelles, the extensive banks and shoals of the Mascarene Plateau (or Ridge), and the volcanic islands of Mauritius, Réunion, and Rodrigues. With much of its landmass 26–65 feet (8–20 meters) below the surface, the Mascarene Plateau is a rare example of an extensive shallow-shelf sea completely detached from land.

Over three years, the program hosted over 200 international scientists from 21 countries, at three field bases. It also provided comprehensive training in scientific, practical and marine safety skills to over 300 local people, and ran an education program to help establish marine education in the national curricula of the Seychelles, Mauritius, and Rodrigues. It is hoped that this will encourage marine research to flourish in the region in the future.

Using underwater vehicles

Priority has long been given to the development of auto-subs, robotic vehicles that are capable of exploring and sampling the deep oceans. These include remotely operated vehicles (ROVs) that remain tethered to a ship, and autonomous underwater vehicles (AUVs) that operate independently using satellites both for navigation and for relaying routine data back to base. In the mid-1990s the Woods Hole Oceanographic Institution developed the Autonomous Benthic Explorer (ABE). A true robot, this 6-foot (2-meter) long craft can monitor large areas of the deep ocean over many months, and it does so at a fraction of the cost of using manned submersibles and repeat visits by research vessels.

◄ *The first shipwrecks* to be explored were those of classical antiquity, lying in the clear waters of the Mediterranean. However, techniques have now advanced to the point where wrecks can be excavated in the dark and turbid waters around northern shores.

Developments in diving

The oil and gas industries worldwide have made advances, both in civil engineering and in saturation diving techniques, that have enabled professional divers to spend prolonged periods at high pressure without having to decompress. However, dives under these circumstances at depths greater than 1640–1970 feet (500–600 meters) are still extremely rare and very carefully supervised. From the 1970s the American aquanaut Sylvia Earle carried out research using the Atmospheric Diving Suit (ADS) systems known as JIM, WASP, and MANTIS. Other pioneering divers include the Canadian Joe MacInnes, who developed a portable diving station made of clear plastic, which enabled divers to rest and conserve air during their time underwater in the Arctic. In 1974 MacInnes became the first scientist to dive beneath the ice at the North Pole.

As leading cave divers, America's William Stone and Britain's Rob Palmer were among those responsible for extending the limits of diving technologies. While exploring the Blue Holes of the Bahamas, they experimented with new mixtures of gases and rebreathers in order to extend the period in which they could stay underwater.

Exploring ancient worlds

Shipwrecks have always fascinated divers, although it has only been possible to locate and investigate many of them with underwater vehicles. Great publicity was given to the discovery of SS *Titanic*, which sank in 1912 after her hull was ripped open by an iceberg on her maiden voyage. The ship was found in 12,500 feet (3810 meters) of water in the Atlantic in 1985 by a Franco-American expedition, under the direction of Jean-Louis Michel and Robert Ballard. The sonar of US submersible *Argos* first located the wreckage, which one year later, in July 1986, was inspected by the crew of USS *Alvin*. Thousands of photographs were taken of the great ship lying on the ocean floor.

Earth's last great unknown

In the past the study of the biology of the deep oceans focused on the phytoplankton, but it now appears that the

◄ *Caves* are among the underwater environments whose exploration has been greatly aided by advances in mixed-gas diving techniques.

oceans support a much greater biomass than had previously been understood, with bacteria and fungi living in a massive chemical-bacterial soup. As a result, attention is being focused on the organo-chemical properties and the circulation of the amino acids of the sea, along with the monitoring of contaminants and radioactivity. This and other work on, for example, plate tectonics and ocean circulation systems is adding greatly to the knowledge of that last great unknown on Earth – the oceans.

The Challenge of the Mountains

Before the First World War, mountaineering and exploration were often synonymous, since those wishing to reach high places in distant lands frequently moved through unknown country, charting new peaks, passes, and glaciers. In the mountains of Central Asia the surveyors of the "Great Trigonometrical Survey," begun in 1802 (see page 58), needed to climb to gain vantage points from which to take their measurements.

Many people considered the great mountains of the Himalayas, and especially Mount Everest, to be the last remaining challenge the Earth held for explorers. But before this challenge could be met, mountaineers had to familiarize themselves with the exact geographical features of these mountains and develop new techniques to cope with the specific problems they posed. In the interwar years several attempts were made to reach the summit of Everest, and in 1937 Eric Shipton and Frank Smythe were only 1000 feet (300 meters) away when bad weather forced them back. Success, however, remained elusive until 1953, when a well-prepared British expedition, using oxygen equipment to offset the effect of altitude, made an assault which resulted in New Zealander Edmund Hillary and Sherpa Tenzing Norgay standing on top of the world's highest mountain. Soon mountaineers of all nationalities were scrambling to make the first ascents of the 14 peaks over 26,000 feet (8000 meters). Of these the highest – Everest, K2 (in the Karakorams), and Kanchenjunga (in the Himalayas) – had all been climbed without oxygen by 1983, a feat that was unbelievable even in the early 1960s.

▼ *Brad and Barbara Washburn, shown here on the summit of Mount Bertha in the Alaska Coastal Range in 1940, have spent more than 50 years climbing and mapping mountains. Brad used aerial photography to map Mount McKinley in Alaska and then the heart of the Grand Canyon.*

The achievements of climbers

Today, mountaineering is a major international sport in its own right, with the emphasis more on the climb itself than on exploring the surrounding area. The ultimate challenge is to climb solo. In 1980 Austrian Reinhold Messner made the first solo ascent of Everest, and subsequently climbed all 14 peaks over 26,000 feet (8000 meters).

Eric Shipton and Bill Tilman are often cited as the archetypal explorer-mountaineers, and their maps and climbs in many parts of the world have acquired legendary fame. This British pair met in East Africa, where they climbed both Mount Kenya and Mount Kilimanjaro, and in the 1930s traveled extensively in the Himalayas and the Karakorams. They made the first ascent of Nanda Devi, and took part in a number of Everest reconnaissance expeditions.

Perhaps less well known, but equally remarkable, is the partnership of the Americans Brad and Barbara Washburn, which spanned more than 50 years. Brad Washburn's combined skills as a mountaineer, photographer, and cartographer resulted in some outstanding mapping, using aerial photography. His career culminated in the production of a detailed map of the Mount Everest area at a scale of 1:50 000, accurate to 33 feet (10 meters). Further maps at a scale of 1:10 000 have aided major geological and glaciological surveys of the region.

The mountain landscape

Mountain building is a very active process, and the great mountain ranges cause major disturbances through landslides, earthquakes, and even glacier surges. However, the geological and geophysical origins of mountains remained relatively unknown until the early 1960s, when the theory of plate tectonics evolved, not as a result of work in the mountain regions but on the basis of evidence taken from the floors of the oceans. The "crashing of continents" that form the great mountain ranges has also produced some of the world's most devastating natural disasters, such as the Sumatra-Andaman earthquake and tsunami in 2004, which

▼ *Wearing oxygen masks,* *Edmund Hillary and Sherpa* *Tenzing Norgay succeeded* *in reaching the top of* *Everest on May 29, 1953.*

▲ *The summit of Everest,* *viewed here from the North* *Col of Kanchenjunga, rises* *above Mount Makalu and* *Mount Lhotse on the left.*

▲ *Measurements of rainfall* *were taken by scientists* *as part of the Middle Hills* *Project in Nepal. Conducted* *in the 1990s, this long-term* *monitoring program* *provided evidence of how* *farming in the region can* *continue to be sustainable.*

depending on local agriculture and livestock to feed themselves. From the Alps to the Andes, the pressures of population growth (and in some areas tourism) are having their effect. For more than 20 years the International Center for Integrated Mountain Development (ICIMOD), based in Kathmandu, has been working to improve the livelihoods of mountain people in a region where the problems of soil erosion and deforestation are severe.

Research into mountain environments

Between 1991 and 1998, a joint British–Nepalese research project, organized under the auspices of the Royal Geographical Society and the UK's Institute of Hydrology, ran a monitoring program in Nepal's Middle Hills region. Its aim was to look at the sustainable use of land, water, and soil resources essential to the future development of managed agricultural land. Concerns that the region was in a downward spiral of degradation, caused by rapid deforestation and resulting high levels of soil erosion, were discovered to be unfounded. Overall, the communities living there have adopted sound land management practices and have stabilized the environment after a great period of change in the 1950s. There is growing evidence that while agricultural productivity is still a significant issue, low-cost alternative technologies and other appropriate development strategies make sustainable farming practices possible in these fragile mountain environments.

What is now causing the greatest concern is the effects of climate change on mountain glaciers, "the water towers of the world." Recent research indicates that China's highland glaciers are shrinking each year by an amount equivalent to all the water in the Huang He, the country's second longest river. The Chinese Academy of Science estimates that 7 percent of the country's glaciers are vanishing annually, and that as many as 64 percent will have disappeared by 2050. Approximately 300 million Chinese live in the country's arid west and depend on water from glaciers for their survival.

resulted in the death of over 280,000 people. Researchers studying seismic events, such as earthquakes, volcanic eruptions, and movements at tectonic plate boundaries, use sophisticated survey instruments to better predict where they are likely to take place. The instruments range from Global Positioning Satellites (GPS) to Electronic Distance Measurers (EDM) and tiltmeters.

Mountains cover about a quarter of the Earth's land surface, and about 12 percent of the world's population live in mountainous regions. A further 50 percent rely on mountain resources. Of these, the main one is water but they also include timber, agricultural products, and minerals. Some 90 million mountain people – almost all those living above 8200 feet (2500 meters) – live in poverty,

The Global View

▶ **The hole in the ozone layer** over Antarctica is shown in this series of satellite maps. First observed in 1980, the hole varies in size from day to day and season to season. More than any other scientific discovery, it has drawn attention to the urgent need to tackle the problem that is believed to have caused the hole: atmospheric pollution.

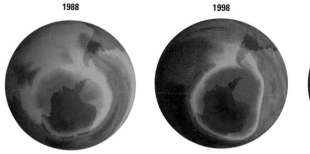
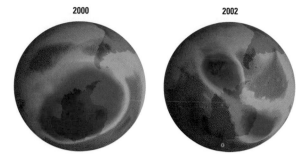

1988   1998   2000   2002

Concern for the global environment has grown at a great rate since the 1980s. Responding to the work of various pressure groups, governments have recognized the importance of the sustainable use of resources. In the scientific arena, numerous agencies are now striving, both individually and within regional, national, and global networks, to measure and predict major changes in the Earth's environment. Technological advances, especially in the use of satellites, have enabled massive amounts of data to be collected. Progress in computer technology allows this data to be analysed, to identify trends and develop models that predict future trends. Population growth, pressure on the world's natural resources, and climate change have placed explorers among those working for conservation and sustainable development.

Environmental research programs

Global environmental research falls broadly into two categories. First, there are those projects that focus on regional phenomena that are repeated worldwide, such as deforestation, desertification, acid rain, soil erosion, and changing land use; the second category is concerned with processes that are global in scale, such as the water, energy, and biogeochemical cycles. There is now an emphasis on studies of the Earth as an integrated system, in which the focus is on changes in the natural system induced by human intervention. Climate change research is a priority.

Since the 1950s the International Council of Scientific Unions (ICSU) has led the way by coordinating and supporting the efforts of scientists to carry out international environmental research programs, often working in association with UNESCO and the United Nations Environment Program (UNEP). Such programs have led to important initiatives such as the Intergovernmental Panel on Climate Change and the *Millennium Ecosystem Assessment*, which use research results to inform the policymaking process.

One of the most significant programs in terms of global processes is the World Climate Research Program (WCRP), established in 1980 by the World Meteorological Organization. Its projects have included the World Ocean Circulation Experiment (WOCE) of 1990–2002. In the field phase, which lasted until 1998, scientists from over 30 countries gathered data with the aid of satellites, ships, and thousands of moored and drifting instruments. The data was then used to analyse the role of the oceans as the dynamo of the Earth's climate. This included analysing the exchange of heat and water between the oceans and the atmosphere, and the ocean's ability to store carbon dioxide gas and drive the planet's winds.

▶ **Environmental research** draws together scientists from all over the world. Here a team takes samples from blocks of ice in the Arctic.

The oceans, through their constant motion and their capacity to store heat, are the dynamo of the Earth's climate. Their precise role in determining regional variations in temperature and rainfall is the subject of the World Climate Research Program (WCRP).

The challenge for the new millennium

It is becoming clear that targeted investment in the environment and in the restoration of damaged and degraded ecosystems has enormous long- and short-term benefits for human wellbeing. As a result, measurement of the ecosystems and their benefits is being incorporated into many organizations' research. In the words of the then UN Secretary General, Kofi Annan, on launching the *Millennium Ecosystem Assessment* in March 2005: "Only by understanding the environment and how it works, can we make the necessary decisions to protect it. Only by valuing all our precious natural and human resources can we hope to build a sustainable future."

In 2000 the United Nations Millennium Summit set out the Millennium Development Goals, which around 190 countries have since agreed to help achieve. The eight goals range from halving global poverty and hunger, to ensuring environmental sustainability. Alongside the goals, a series of 18 targets was drawn up to give the international community a number of tangible improvements to aim for by 2015. Among them are the integration of the principles of sustainable development into national policies, and reversing the loss of environmental resources.

Research for a sustainable future

The 1992 Convention on Biological Diversity set all nations the goal of reducing habitat loss by 2010. By 2006 a total of 188 had responded with "biodiversity action plans." To achieve the goals set out in these plans, many individuals and organizations – at both local and national levels – are collecting information on biodiversity in the terrestrial and marine environments. They are assessing the impact of the loss of habitats and making recommendations for improving habitat protection and land-use management. There also continues to be a challenge to

find and name the animals and plants of the world, the great majority of which have yet to be found, let alone be given a name.

A sustainable future depends on a better understanding of the processes that interlink the impact of changing land use, the availability of natural resources, and any variations in habitat cover and biodiversity. Field scientists are working hard to understand how the world's habitats are responding to global warming and changes in the natural world, and how this will ultimately affect the resources needed for our growing population. This in turn is linked to our understanding of the ability of natural systems and human communities to adapt to a changing climate. Only by having a holistic view of the interaction between climate, the land and oceans will scientists be able to predict with any accuracy the future status of the planet.

A purpose for explorers

This is the age of global thinking, and a new agenda has been drawn up. All agree that the windows through which we have traditionally viewed the world and monitored its changes are far too small. It is no wonder that scientists balk at having to provide predictions and solutions quickly and with authority. The holistic view of Earth and its biosphere has identified huge gaps in our knowledge. This gives explorers a purpose. There was never any great need to reach the Poles, climb the mountains or penetrate to the depths of the oceans except to satisfy individual curiosity. But today there is a real urgency: we need to be committed to acquiring knowledge about our planet's environments, people, and places – and to sharing this knowledge as extensively as possible – so that we can adapt, plan, and make hard decisions for tomorrow's world. Without this commitment, the wellbeing of the world's inhabitants will remain in jeopardy.

Going to the Moon

▲ *Yuri Gagarin* of the Soviet Union was the first man in space. His spacecraft, Vostok 1, completed a full orbit of Earth on April 12, 1961, in 1 hour 48 minutes.

▼ *Mercury 6,* launched on February 20, 1962, carried the first American to orbit Earth, John Glenn, into space. His flight, in the tiny capsule Friendship 7, lasted for over 4 hours 55 minutes.

Throughout human history, the Moon has been a constant companion in the sky, while the planets Mercury, Venus, Mars, Jupiter, and Saturn have been visible at various times. The more distant planets were discovered by astronomers using telescopes: Uranus in 1781, Neptune in 1846, and Pluto in 1930. Hands-on exploration of the Moon, and of space in general, only became possible with the development of rocket technology. On October 4, 1957, the Soviet Union took the lead by launching an intercontinental ballistic missile (ICBM) that carried the first artificial Earth satellite, Sputnik I. Coming at a time when the Cold War between the Communist bloc and the West was growing in intensity, this caused great consternation in the United States. The result was a space race between the United States and Soviet Union, which quickly developed into a race for the Moon.

Beginning of the Moon Race

The first attempts to reach the Moon in 1958 and early 1959 failed. However, on September 13, 1959, the Soviet Union's Luna 2 hit the Moon close to the crater Autolychus. The following month the remarkable spacecraft Luna 3 went into a deep orbit of Earth. It took images, developed and scanned them, and then transmitted them to Earth, revealing 70 percent of the far side of the Moon for the first time.

In 1961 the Soviet Union achieved another first by launching a man, Yuri Gagarin, into space. In response to

this and earlier triumphs, the newly-elected US President John F. Kennedy committed his country "before this decade is out, to landing a man on the Moon and returning him safely to Earth." This was to be Project Apollo.

While the Apollo hardware was being developed, there were several unmanned missions to the Moon to locate possible landing sites. Among them was Ranger 7, which restored US pride by taking 4316 images as it plummeted into the Sea of Clouds on July 31, 1964. It was followed by two other Rangers, which showed the Sea of Tranquillity and the crater Alphonsus in close up, and then, in 1966, the first Surveyor and Lunar Orbiter. Just ahead of these last two were the Soviet Union's Luna 9 and Luna 10. On February 3, 1966, Luna 9 landed a small capsule, which returned the first images from the surface, while Luna 10 became the first lunar orbiter. The US Surveyors and Lunar Orbiters were, however, more sophisticated machines and provided massive amounts of data about the Moon from various surface sites and orbits between 1966 and 1968.

First manned orbit of the Moon

As these missions proceeded, both the United States and Soviet Union launched manned spacecraft into Earth orbit to test systems and manoeuvers needed for Moon landings. The Soviet Union, however, began to fall behind in its plans to land men on the Moon and so devised a show-stopper. Having already demonstrated a Moon flyby and return to Earth with a Zond spacecraft, it now planned to fly two cosmonauts around the Moon and back in another Zond spacecraft. The US space agency, NASA, knew it had to respond. Consequently, after a manned Earth orbital test flight by Apollo 7 in September 1968, it was decided to send Apollo 8 to orbit the Moon.

Apollo 8 was launched on December 21, 1968, taking astronauts Frank Borman, James Lovell, and William Anders into lunar orbit over Christmas. The televised reading of the first words from the Bible's Book of Genesis by the crew, and the photos of Earthrise over the Moon, were to become two of the most memorable moments of the Space Age. Apollo 8 made ten lunar orbits before heading back to Earth and then landing in the Pacific Ocean after a flight of 6 days and 3 hours. It had been proved that humans could travel to and from the Moon. After two more test flights, Apollo 11 – with an added lunar module – was ready to try landing on the Moon in July 1969. The Soviet Union, however, was far from ready, for its giant N1 booster, developed for its manned lunar landing program, had failed in test flights.

First landing on the Moon

The Apollo 11 mission became one of the most famous events of the 20th century. This was particularly because the development of communications satellites meant that the world could share in the event, seeing live TV coverage of the famous step on to the Sea of Tranquillity by civilian test pilot astronaut Neil Armstrong. The lunar module, *Eagle*, landed on July 20, 1969. As Armstrong stepped off *Eagle*'s footpad, he uttered the memorable words: "That's one small step for man, one giant leap for mankind" (forgetting the intended "a" before "man").

Eagle's pilot, "Buzz" Aldrin, then joined Armstrong to become the second man on the Moon. In five subsequent missions a further ten US astronauts set foot on the Moon. The last was Apollo 17 in December 1972, after which the political will to continue declined and three missions were canceled. The irony is that the one mission that failed – Apollo 13 in April 1970 – was to become the most famous. An oxygen-tank explosion aborted the landing on the

◄ *One small step for a man* was taken by Neil Armstrong in July 1969 when, on leaving Apollo 11's lunar module Eagle, he became the first man to set foot on the Moon.

▼ *The Lunar Roving Vehicle (LRV)*, which was first taken to the Moon in 1971 on Apollo 15, enabled the astronauts to explore far greater areas than before. The electrically powered vehicle could travel up to a total distance of 40 miles (65 kilometers), but it never went more than 6 miles (9.5 kilometers) from the lunar module because of limitations in the astronauts' portable life-support system. Here the Apennines peak in the background is further away than it appears; distances on the Moon are very difficult to estimate.

Moon and the three astronauts managed to get home alive in a drama that captured the attention of the world.

Each Apollo landing mission deployed an array of scientific instruments on sites in many parts of the Moon to study geology, radiation, heat flow, and seismology. A total of 850 lb (385 kg) of samples was returned from sites in the Sea of Tranquillity and Ocean of Storms, both of which are large basaltic plains. A Lunar Roving Vehicle (LRV) extended exploration from feet to miles and was used on Apollos 15 to 17 in 1971–72.

The Moon had been explored in the course of 14 moonwalks, for 80 days and 12 minutes, when Eugene Cernan left the final footprints in December 1972 – and no one has been to the Moon since. Instead there have been more unmanned flights, with the Soviet Union bringing back samples of soil on return missions in 1970–76, and deploying unmanned rovers, Lunokhods.

Exploring from space stations

The end of manned flights to the Moon did not mean the end of manned missions into space. A series of space stations was sent into orbit, the first of which, the US Skylab, was manned by three successive crews in 1973–74. It was followed by the Soviet Union's Mir, which was visited by astronauts from many nations between 1986 and 2000, and the International Space Station, which began to gather huge amounts of data in November 2000.

Meanwhile, in 1998 the United States launched Lunar Prospector to conduct an orbital chemical survey of the Moon, while the European Space Agency (ESA) sent Smart 1 into orbit in 2004. There are NASA plans for a return to the Moon with astronauts by 2020, but this will depend on budgets and political will. The irony of Moon exploration is that it has given us a view of our fragile planet in space, helping to engender a greater awareness of the impact of humans on Earth's environment.

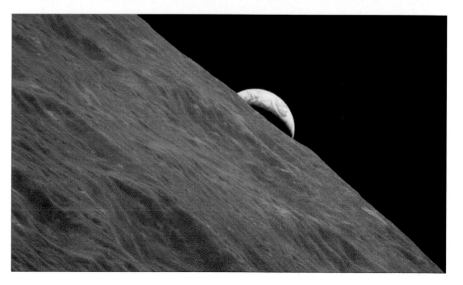

► *This picture of Earthrise over the Moon was taken* during the flight made by Apollo 17 in 1972.

Exploring the Inner Planets

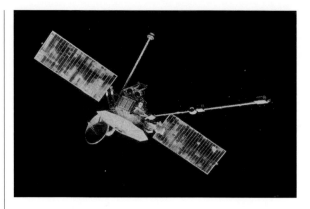

▶ *Mariner 10* flew past Mercury three times in 1974–75, when it became the first spacecraft to collect information on the planet. It was also the first to use the gravity-assist technique. It provided the only good maps we have of Mercury's surface. However, even these show less than half of the surface and so give an incomplete picture of the planet's topography.

▼ *The Pathfinder probe* was launched toward Mars in December 1996. On touching down seven months later, its "petals" opened and a small "rover," Sojourner, crawled down its ramp on to the surface of Mars. The petals and rover can be seen in this panoramic view obtained by the Mars Pathfinder Imager. The Sojourner rover is using its Alpha Proton X-Ray Spectrometer (APXS) to analyse a large rock.

Earth's neighboring planets are far enough away to ensure that exploring them presents far more problems than exploring the Moon. What is more, the positions of Mercury, Venus, and Mars in relation to Earth during their orbits around the Sun have always restricted possible explorations to specific launch windows. It is not just a question of flying across space toward a planet, but of flying off in a solar orbit that at one point will coincide with the orbit of the targeted planet.

First steps to the inner planets

The first planet to be explored was Venus, 67 million miles (108 million kilometers) from the Sun, to which it is the second closest planet after Mercury. Its diameter is 7520 miles (12,100 kilometers) – just 410 miles (656 kilometers) smaller than that of Earth. An enveloping layer of cloud makes Venus highly reflective and so, at times, the brightest object in the sky apart from the Sun and Moon. The cloud inspired thoughts of a lush jungle paradise until, on December 14, 1962, the US spacecraft Mariner 2 passed to within 21,630 miles (34,825 kilometers) of the planet. It was then discovered that Venus was a hell-hole with temperatures of 797°F (425°C) under a thick mantle of carbon dioxide. The atmospheric pressure was so great that later Soviet spacecraft were crushed before landing. However, on December 15, 1970, the strengthened Soviet Venera 7 capsule finally reached the surface, returning data that confirmed the earlier findings on temperature and establishing that Venus has an atmospheric pressure that is over 90 times that of Earth.

Veneras 9 and 10 took the first pictures of Venus's surface on October 22 and 25, 1975. They showed a rocky surface under cloud that gave lighting conditions akin to a cloudy winter's day on Earth. The two Venera mother-ships also became the first to orbit Venus. Four Pioneer Venus atmospheric probes followed on December 9, and they discovered that the atmosphere consists almost entirely of sulfuric acid. Further missions made by the radar-imaging Pioneer Venus Orbiter in December 1978, the Magellan mapping orbiter in 1989, and similar Soviet Venera craft, revealed numerous features under the thick atmosphere. They included two large continents the size of Africa and Australia, a volcano, Maxwell Montes, 6.7 miles (10.7 kilometers) high, and a tortured surface of lava flows, domes, and fractures.

After 1989 there was no mission specifically to Venus until the European Space Agency (ESA) launched Venus Express in November 2005. Five months later it went into orbit around the planet on a 500-day investigative mission. With conditions that are the equivalent of the greenhouse effect gone mad, Venus promises to offer a wealth of data on the possible effects of climate change on Earth.

Expeditions to Mercury

Mercury, the innermost planet, is 36 million miles (57.9 million kilometers) from the Sun. It was not explored until 1974, well after many of the other planets. The US Mariner 10 revealed that the planet, with a diameter of 3030 miles (4879 kilometers), is a Moon-like, cratered world with a huge metallic core. It also confirmed that Mercury has an almost non-existent atmosphere.

The spacecraft was launched on November 3, 1973, and made a flyby of Venus *en route* to a triple flyby of Mercury, so making the first "multiple" planetary flyby. On March 29, 1974, it passed to within 3582 miles (5768 kilometers) of the surface. Further flybys were made on September 21 and March 16, 1975, when the craft came to within 203 miles (327 kilometers) of the surface. A new US spacecraft, Messenger, was launched in 2004 to orbit Mercury, while Europe is planning to send an explorer to the planet in 2011–12.

Searching for life on Mars

Of all the planets, it is Mars that has most captured people's imagination, mainly as a result of a false observation by an

◄ *This photomosaic of Mercury* was created by combining 18 images taken by Mariner 10 in March 1975, when the spacecraft came closest to the planet's surface. As on the Moon, small craters generally break into larger ones. However, there are no broad plains like those on the Moon.

► *The Magellan* probe reached Venus on August 10, 1990, after a 15-month flight. The radar mapping program that began soon afterward was to cover 98 percent of the planet's surface and reveal many details, such as multiple lava flows and various other features of volcanic origin.

astronomer that on the surface there appeared to be canals. This developed into a belief that the canals represented a planet-wide irrigation system, and so were evidence of life.

The planet, which with a diameter of 4220 miles (6790 kilometers) is considerably smaller than Earth, had a lot of expectations to live up to. The first surprise came on July 15, 1965, when Mariner 4 flew past at a distance of 5962 miles (9600 kilometers) to discover that Mars had a cratered surface and that there were no signs of canals – or life. Mariner 9, which became the first Martian orbiter in November 1971, then revealed in a photographic survey that not only were the Martian moons, Phobos and Deimos, irregularly shaped bodies, but also that the Martian surface was extremely diverse. It featured volcanoes, including Olympus Mons, 16 miles (25 kilometers) high, what looked like dry riverbeds, and huge valleys – among them Valles Marineris, which dwarfs Earth's Grand Canyon.

First landings on Mars

This information just whetted the appetites of scientists. In 1976, the US Vikings 1 and 2 were launched to make the first Mars landings on July 20 and September 3 respectively. Equipped with a robot arm, the Vikings collected soil and deposited it into a chemical laboratory on the craft, which then analysed it. No indications of life were found, while the surface pictures revealed a desolate reddish-brown, rocky desert beneath a pink sky. The surface temperature was −27°F (−33°C) and the thin atmosphere consisted almost totally of carbon dioxide. Meanwhile, the two Viking orbiter motherships provided a spectacular imaging survey of the planet and its two moons.

More recently, the US Mars Pathfinder and its little microwave-oven-sized rover, called *Sojourner*, captured the imagination of the world when they landed on the Martian surface on July 4, 1997. The Pathfinder images were posted live on the Internet so that millions of people might share in the mission. Mars Pathfinder had landed as planned in what appeared to be the remains of an outwash plain of a once wet planet, near Chrys Planitia in the Ares Vallis region of Mars. While it collected data on the surface, the orbiter Mars Global Surveyor operated on a mission which began

in September 1997, returning thousands of images of almost every part of the "Red Planet." It continued to monitor the changing conditions on the surface, particularly the carbon-dioxide-ice polar caps and dust storms, until 2006.

After the success of the Pathfinder mission, the United States suffered the twin failures of a Mars Climate Orbiter and Mars Polar Lander in 1999. Tighter budgets and more realistic assessments of technical capabilities then delayed plans for an eventual Mars sample return mission.

In 2002 a new orbiter, Mars Odyssey, began a survey of the chemistry of the planet, including any evidence of water on the surface. Europe's Mars Express orbiter followed in 2003; however, its lander, the British Beagle 2, was lost on its descent. In January 2004 NASA landed two Mars Exploration Explorer rovers, called *Spirit* and *Opportunity*, which became the most successful Martian explorers in history and were still operating in early 2008. The Phoenix Mars Mission, launched in 2007 and scheduled to land in May 2008, is the first of NASA's Scout program. The possibility of life on Mars has not been ruled out, but evidence of this remains elusive.

▲ *The northern hemisphere of Venus* is shown in this false-color projection. It was created using a combination of data gathered by Magellan in 1990–93 and by the Pioneer Venus Orbiter in 1978. The general color hue comes from images provided by the Soviet Venera lander in 1972.

◄ *Mars Odyssey* was launched on April 7, 2001, from Cape Canaveral, Florida. The orbiter began a survey of Mars's chemistry the following year.

Journeys to the Giants

▲ **Pioneer 10**, top, was the first spacecraft to Jupiter. Launched on March 2, 1972, it passed the planet 21 months later. Voyager 2, above, began its journey to Jupiter on August 20, 1977. After flying by the planet, it traveled on to Saturn, Uranus, and Neptune.

In a remarkable coincidence, the era of the Space Age coincided with the very convenient relative positioning of the giant gaseous planets: Jupiter, Saturn, Uranus, and Neptune. This made it possible to use the gravitational influence of each planet to create a "catapult" manoeuver that changed the trajectories and increased the speed of spacecraft, enabling them to reach other planets much faster.

The result was that over a period of just 16 years, the four Solar System giants were explored by US spacecraft, leaving just Pluto (now classified as a "dwarf planet") to be explored in the future. This seems particularly incredible when compared with the period of 149 years – from 1781 to 1930 – that it took for astronomers to discover the existence of Uranus, Neptune, and Pluto.

First journeys to Jupiter

With a diameter of 89,350 miles (142,980 kilometers), Jupiter is the largest planet in the Solar System. The first spacecraft to be sent there was the US Pioneer 10. Launched in March 1972, it finally reached Jupiter on December 5, 1973, passing as close as 82,500 miles (132,000 kilometers) to the planet. In common with the other spacecraft to travel to Jupiter and beyond, Pioneer did not have solar panels to generate electrical power, as these would have been ineffective in the low sunlight. Instead, it was equipped with radioisotope thermoelectric generators, powered by the decay of radioactive plutonium 238.

Pioneer 10's equipment was almost crippled by the unexpectedly high level of radiation around the planet – about 10,000 times greater than that of Earth. However, the spacecraft returned over 300 images, which revealed the 24,850-mile (40,000-kilometer) wide Great Red Spot. This turned out to be a large group of thunderstorms rising several hundred miles above the highest clouds. The planet seemed to be almost entirely fluid with a small core.

Another smaller red spot was also discovered, but this had dispersed by the time the next spacecraft, Pioneer 11,

reached Jupiter almost exactly a year later, on December 3, 1974, after a launch in April 1973. The spacecraft collected data that indicated that Jupiter was made primarily of liquid hydrogen, with a core about six times the size of Earth. It was then diverted, using the "catapult" Jupiter gravity-assist manoeuver, toward a rendezvous with Saturn.

Voyager and Galileo expeditions

The twin spacecraft Voyagers 1 and 2 followed: Voyager 2 was launched first in August 1977, while the speedier Voyager 1 was launched a month later and eventually overtook its twin. Voyager 1 passed to within 220,000 miles (350,000 kilometers) of Jupiter on March 5, 1979, and Voyager 2 passed to within 400,000 miles (650,000 kilometers) on July 9, 1979.

Both Voyagers returned spectacular high-resolution images, particularly of Io, Europa, Ganymede, and Callisto, the four large moons which were seen first by Galileo in 1609. They also discovered a 14th moon of Jupiter, plus a fine ring of material encircling the planet. Reaching up to 31,000 miles (50,000 kilometers) above the clouds, it is a far less substantial feature than Saturn's rings. The shape of the Great Red Spot had changed since the Pioneer flybys. Indeed, it changed between the visits made by Voyagers 1 and 2, showing what a turbulent place Jupiter is.

Like Pioneer 11, the Voyagers were given gravity-assist diversions toward Saturn. They were followed to Jupiter by a spacecraft named after Galileo, which went into orbit around the planet on December 8, 1995, the first to do so. During its journey it had also become the first spacecraft to fly past two asteroids.

Galileo had been launched from the Space Shuttle in Earth orbit in October 1989. As it approached Jupiter, it divided into two parts: an orbiter and a probe. The latter, on its descent toward the planet's surface, confirmed the existence of an intense radiation belt at a height of 30,800 miles (49,600 kilometers). Deploying a parachute, it then

◄ **Io, Jupiter's volcanic moon**, is seen here moving across Jupiter. Another moon, Europa, is to the right. The image is one of the many superb pictures of the planet taken by the Voyager spacecraft.

▲ **This high-resolution** image of Io was taken from Galileo in September 1996. The black and bright red materials are the most recent volcanic deposits.

◀ A total of 126 images
of Saturn were obtained
by Cassini over two hours
in October 2004 to create
this mosaic. The smallest
features visible are only 24
miles (38 kilometers) across.

▲ Prometheus, one of
Saturn's moons, plus the
planet's faint and complex
F ring, appear in this image
taken on August 25, 1981.

▼ Titan's surface was
revealed as being unique
by data that the Huygens
probe collected over 72
minutes in January 2005.

plunged into the swirling clouds and experienced winds of 2000 feet (610 meters) per second. These, surprisingly, did not slacken as the probe penetrated the clouds to a depth of 100 miles (160 kilometers). The probe also detected traces of organic compounds. It sent data for about 15 minutes before presumably being destroyed by intense pressures.

Galileo continued to operate around Jupiter well into 2002, manoeuvering to make close flybys of the Galilean moons and returning stunning high-resolution images of these very different bodies. It seemed that Io is a world of active sulfur volcanoes, while Europa has the appearance of a cracked eggshell that may actually be a sheet of ice. Callisto is heavily cratered, resembling the skin of an avocado pear, while Ganymede has a smoother, dark but icy surface scarred by many features and cracks.

The United States is currently planning to send another spacecraft to Jupiter in 2010–11. Known as the Jupiter Polar Orbiter (Juno), it will investigate whether the planet has an ice-rock core and collect further data on its atmosphere, such as the amount of water and ammonia it contains.

Journeys to Saturn

Pioneer 11 made the first flyby of the beautiful ringed planet Saturn, whose diameter measures 74,900 miles (120,540 kilometers), on September 1, 1979. At a distance of 12,980 miles (20,900 kilometers), Pioneer discovered an additional ring in the famed ring system, and small moons in the rings. It was followed in November 1980 and August 1981 by Voyagers 1 and 2 respectively. These changed the image of Saturn, revealing that the rings comprised thousands of individual rings made up of ice and rock particles up to 3 feet (1 meter) in diameter, held together by the gravity of the planet. The small moons within the orbital rings appeared to act as "shepherds," keeping the particles from straying.

The Voyagers also took high-resolution images of the major Saturn moons, including Titan, which was discovered to have an atmosphere of its own. This comprised mainly nitrogen, which alone was enough information to tantalize planetary biologists.

Another spacecraft, Cassini, was launched in October 1997. It arrived in late 2004 and became the first to orbit the planet. Cassini deployed the European Huygens probe, which landed on Titan. Huygens was a spectacular success, landing against very low odds and taking images from the slushy surface of mainly methane ice.

Reaching Uranus and Neptune

The trajectory of Voyager 2's flyby of Saturn was arranged so that it was diverted by the planet's gravitational force toward a rendezvous with the next planet, Uranus, 31,760 miles (51,120 kilometers) in diameter. Voyager reached the Solar System's seventh planet on January 24, 1986, passing at a distance of 44,100 miles (71,000 kilometers). The greeny-blue, hydrogen-helium-methane Uranus did not prove to be as exciting as Saturn or, indeed, one of its moons, Miranda. This chaotic spherical body looked as though it consisted of pieces of a moon that had broken apart and somehow fused together like a misfitting jigsaw puzzle.

Having been kicked on to a new course, the remarkable Voyager 2 sped onward into the depths of the Solar System, toward a rendezvous with Neptune, which it reached on August 24, 1989, coming as close as 3115 miles (5016 kilometers). The intensely blue gaseous planet, with a diameter of 30,780 miles (49,530 kilometers), had "Scooter" clouds that raced around at 1240 miles (2000 kilometers) per hour – faster that the rotation of the planet. Voyager 2 also found that the Neptunian moon Triton consists largely of frozen and liquid nitrogen gas and has a surface temperature of –391°F (–235°C), making it the coldest body in the Solar System.

Mission to Pluto and beyond

After their missions, the venerable Pioneers 10 and 11 and Voyagers 1 and 2 continued to send data as they flew on toward the fringes of the Solar System, on course for the stars. On January 19, 2006, the United States launched the first Pluto explorer, New Horizons. It will also explore Pluto's moon Charon, before flying on into the Kuiper Belt objects at the edge of the Solar System.

▲ Uranus was photographed in January 1986
by the narrow-angle camera of Voyager 2
from a distance of 5.7 million miles (9.1
million kilometers). The blue-green color is
caused by absorption of red light by methane
gas in Uranus's extremely clear atmosphere.

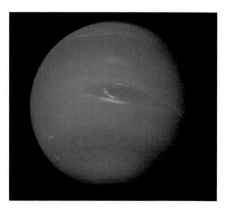

▲ Neptune was photographed in August 1989
through green and orange filters on Voyager
2's camera, from a distance of 4.4 million
miles (7.1 million kilometers). The Great Dark
Spot, its companion bright smudge, and the
Scooter clouds are among the visible features.

Asteroids, Comets, and Beyond

▲ **Mathilde**, *a main-belt asteroid, was imaged by the spacecraft NEAR in 1997. There are holes in the image because the asteroid has very little reflecting power.*

Between the orbits of Mars and Jupiter are thousands of rocky bodies – none no larger than 560 miles (900 kilometers) in diameter – called the main-belt asteroids. There are also "near-Earth" asteroids that have hybrid elliptical orbits, some occasionally passing close to Earth.

The first spacecraft to explore an asteroid was the US Galileo, launched in 1989 toward Jupiter on a route that took in ingenious gravity-assist flybys of Earth and Venus. These not only shortened the time of the flight to the ultimate target, but also made asteroid flybys possible. On October 29, 1991, Galileo passed close by the main-belt asteroid Gaspra. Images showed a rather elongated, irregularly shaped body about 12 miles (20 kilometers) long and with a smooth rounded surface, somewhat resembling a shark's head. Data indicated that Gaspra had a thick dust layer but also some craters, the largest of which was about 1.25 miles (2 kilometers) in diameter. A strong magnetic field indicated that Gaspra was made of iron or nickel.

Galileo reached another asteroid, the 32-mile (52-kilometer) long Ida, on August 28, 1993. Although similar in shape to Gaspra, Ida's surface was apparently more ancient, peppered as it was with hundreds of craters. The major surprise was the discovery that Ida had a moon, later called Dactyl, that measured about 1 mile (1.5 kilometers) in all three dimensions. Data indicated that it was not a piece of Ida that had broken away, but instead had been captured by the gravity of Ida.

First orbit of an asteroid

The US Near Earth Asteroid Rendezvous mission craft, called NEAR, was launched in February 1996 on a journey that was intended to end with it orbiting the asteroid Eros. *En route* the spacecraft was renamed NEAR Shoemaker, after the late and legendary astrobiologist Gene Shoemaker. On June 27, 1997, it passed the rather more rounded asteroid Mathilde – 38 miles (62 kilometers) in diameter – and on December 23, 1998, it came to within 2390 miles (3850 kilometers) of Eros. However, due to malfunctions the mission was waived off after 222

images had been taken. Eros turned out to be more elongated and irregular in shape than the previous asteroids. Around 20 miles (33 kilometers) long and 8 miles (13 kilometers) wide, it was covered with craters and featured deep grooves and valleys.

NEAR Shoemaker returned to Eros and on February 14, 2000, became the first asteroid orbiter. This remarkable spacecraft flew in a series of different orbits which finally took it to 1.6 miles (2.7 kilometers) above the surface. It was then decided, in February 2001, that instead of leaving NEAR in orbit at the planned end of the mission, an unprecedented attempt would be made to soft-land it on the surface. NEAR returned images until it reached an altitude of 250 feet (76 meters), at which point transmissions ceased.

Rendezvous with a comet

Comets have captured our imagination for thousands of years. Insignificant balls of dust and ice in the Solar System, some are transformed by the light and radiation of the Sun as their orbits take them close to our nearest star. Halley's Comet, which is probably the most famous, was the first to be explored by spacecraft. In 1984–85 the Soviet Union, Japan, and Europe launched spacecraft to rendezvous with Halley in March 1986 as it made its latest appearance in the skies during its 76-year journey around the Sun.

On March 14, Europe's British-built Giotto flew toward the head of the comet at a speed of 42 miles (68 kilometers) per second, coming to within 378 miles (605 kilometers) of the nucleus. It was peppered with over 12,000 particles and returned over 2000 images. The close-ups of the nucleus showed it to be a lumpy, irregularly shaped object about 9.5 miles (15 kilometers) long and up to 6 miles (10 kilometers) wide. The comet had two large jets of gas erupting from what were apparently cracks in an undulating surface that contained valleys and hills. Its main constituents were water ice and dust.

Further comet missions are presently under way, with many more planned. On July 4, 2005, the United States'

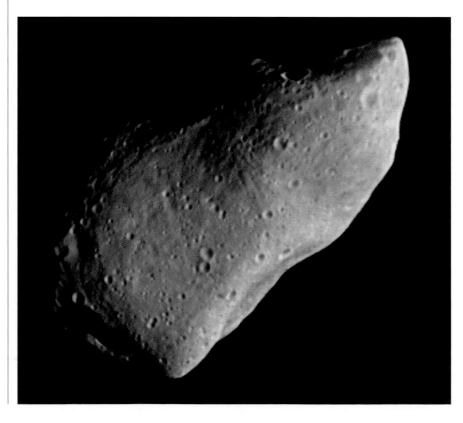

◄ **Gaspra** *was the first main-belt asteroid to be photographed at close range. This picture was obtained by the Galileo probe on November 13, 1991, from a distance of 10,000 miles (16,000 kilometers). Gaspra is irregular in shape, has a darkish, crater-scarred surface, and is about 12 miles (20 kilometers) long. It is not one of the larger asteroids. There are, however, no more than 20 main-belt asteroids – out of a total of over 40,000 whose paths have been discovered – that measure over 150 miles (250 kilometers) across. The largest, Ceres (now classified as a "dwarf planet"), has a diameter of 560 miles (900 kilometers). The irregular shape of many – but not all – of them is due to relatively frequent collisions.*

Deep Impact spacecraft sent a projectile into the comet Tempel 1, at a distance of 83 million miles (133 million kilometers) from Earth. The purpose of this was to create an explosion and so generate evidence on the composition of comets. It now appears that on Tempel 1's surface there are three small areas of water ice, while the comet's interior contains a considerable amount of organic matter.

Meanwhile, Europe's Rosetta is *en route* for a rendezvous with the comet Churyumov Gerasimenko in 2011. The United States' Genesis spacecraft came home with comet dust in 2004 and crashed, but some samples were recovered. Its Stardust spacecraft returned the following year with samples of solar wind and star dust.

Exploration beyond the Solar System

The Sun's influence extends millions of miles further into space than the far distant Pluto. Data about this area, the heliosphere, has been provided by Pioneers 10 and 11. More will be provided by Voyagers 1 and 2 as they move into the heliosheath environment, and then through the heliopause – the extent of the Sun's magnetic field and solar wind – before beginning an interstellar mission.

Both Pioneers and Voyagers will travel onward and outward, heading in different directions out of the Solar System. At the end of 2007, Voyager 1 was approximately 10 billion miles (16 billion kilometers) from Earth, with Voyager 2 about 8 billion miles (13 billion kilometers) away. Pioneer 10 is heading in the direction of the constellation of Taurus, and in 33,000 years will pass within 3.3 light years of the star Ross 248. Pioneer 11 is heading for the center of our Galaxy, in toward the constellation of

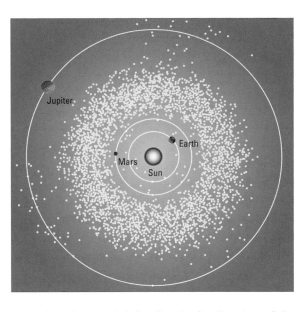

Sagittarius. Voyager 1 is heading in the direction of the constellations Ophiuchus and Hercules, and will pass a dwarf star in the constellation Camelopardus in 40,000 years' time. Voyager 2 will pass to within 0.8 light years of the star Sirius – the brightest in Earth's night sky – in 358,000 years. The Pioneers are equipped with plaques that indicate the origin of the spacecraft in the Solar System, together with a drawing of a man and a woman, while the Voyagers carry a record of the sounds of Earth – just in case.

◄ *The positions of known asteroids in 1990 are shown in this diagram, as are the orbits of Earth, Mars, and Jupiter. Most of the asteroids lie in the main belt, between the orbits of Mars and Jupiter. Among the others are some that occasionally pass close to Earth.*

◄ *Comet Hale–Bopp was discovered in 1995, beyond the orbit of Jupiter. It became brilliant in March 1997, when this photograph was taken by Akira Fujii. Clearly shown are the long blue ion tail and dust tail.*

▲ *Comet Wild 2 was photographed from the US spacecraft Stardust on January 2, 2004, at a distance of 147 miles (236 kilometers). Among the features on the comet's surface are craters and pinnacles.*

Biographical Details

This section of the atlas provides biographical details of many of the explorers, geographers, and cartographers whose achievements are described in the main text. The number(s) at the end of each entry refer to the page(s) on which further information can be found.

Alarcón, Hernando de (b. 1500)
Spanish *conquistador* and navigator whose exploration proved that Lower California was a peninsula, not an island. Despite his detailed map, his discovery was forgotten for 160 years. **124**

Albanel, Charles (1616–96)
French Jesuit missionary and explorer in Canada, who established fur trading routes after exploring the Saguenay River and Hudson Bay in 1671. His activities were a threat to the Hudson's Bay Company so the English sent him back to Europe in 1674. He returned to Canada in 1676 and spent his remaining years as Superior of the St Francis-Xavier mission. **130–31**

Albert I of Monaco, Prince (1848–1922)
Keen amateur oceanographer and patron of the sciences who made important contributions to the development of oceanography. After serving in the Spanish Navy, Albert conducted oceanographic surveys, for which he developed sophisticated equipment. He continued with this work throughout his life. **207**

Albuquerque, Afonso d' (1453–1515)
Portuguese military commander who completed the Portuguese conquests in the East. After serving as a soldier in North Africa, he was sent to India where, in 1509, he became Governor-General of the Portuguese settlement, and set out to establish control over the spice trade by taking Goa (1510), Malacca (1511), Calicut (1512), and the Malabar Coast. **39**

Aldrin, "Buzz" Edwin (b. 1930)
US astronaut. In 1966, as a member of Gemini 12's crew, he walked in space for over five hours. In 1969 he piloted the lunar module for the first Moon landing and became the second man on the Moon. **224**

Alexander "the Great", Alexander III of Macedonia (356–323 BC)
King and empire-builder. The son of Philip II of Macedonia, and tutored by Aristotle, he became king at the age of 20. After consolidating his power in Greece, he devoted 11 years to frenetic military campaigning. In 334 BC he began the Persian expedition, conquering western Asia Minor (now Turkey) and storming the island of Tyre in 332 BC. He subdued Egypt and occupied Babylon, marching north in 330 BC to present-day northern Iran and then conquering central Asia in 328 BC. In 327 BC he invaded what is now Pakistan and set about consolidating his empire. He died from a fever at the age of 33. **14–15**

Allouez, Father Claude (1622–89)
French Jesuit missionary who traveled extensively in the North American Great Lakes region. Allouez was ordained in 1655 and sailed to New France in 1658. After a period spent working in the St Lawrence River area, he was appointed Vicar-General for the Northwest and set out to establish missions in what is now Wisconsin. Toward the end of his life he lived among the Miami Indians in Michigan. **130, 131**

Almeida, Francisco de (1450–1510)
Portuguese soldier and colonial official who became first Governor-General of Portuguese India (1505–9). He set up a number of fortified trading posts and his son established a settlement in Ceylon (Sri Lanka). He was killed on his way back to Portugal. **39**

Amundsen, Roald (1872–1928)
Norwegian explorer and leader of the first expedition to reach the South Pole. In 1903–6 he sailed in the *Gjøa* through the Northwest Passage and located the exact position of the Magnetic North Pole at that time. His next expedition took him to the Antarctic, and in December 1911 he reached the South Pole. In 1925–26 he explored the Arctic region by air. He died in a plane crash while searching for the missing airman Umberto Nobile and his crew. **178, 182, 183, 191, 192–93**

Andrée, Salomon August (1854–97)
Swedish aeronautical engineer and Arctic explorer. He was killed in an attempt to fly from Spitsbergen (Svalbard) to the North Pole in a balloon. His body was found 33 years later on White Island. **182, 183**

Anson, Baron George (1697–1762)
British admiral who sailed around the world in 1740–44. He first sailed to South America with orders to stir up resistance to Spanish rule in Chile and Peru. From there he took his fleet of seven ships across the Pacific, but only one ship completed the voyage. Despite his losses he managed to seize the contents of a Spanish treasure galleon. **108, 109**

Armstrong, Neil Alden (b. 1930)
US astronaut. He was the command pilot for the Gemini 8 orbital flight in 1966, and on July 20, 1969, he became the first man to walk on the Moon. After retiring as an astronaut in 1971, he remained an influential figure in the world of aeronautics. **224, 225**

Baffin, William (1584–1622)
English navigator and explorer. In 1612–16 he led several expeditions in search of the Northwest Passage, one of which resulted in the discovery of the bay between Greenland and Canada (since named after him). He was the first person to determine longitude at sea by observing the moon. **128, 174, 175**

Baikie, William Balfour (1825–64)
British explorer and colonial administrator. He led two important explorations of the Niger River in 1854 and 1859. On the second, he set up a trading community at Lokoja, where he studied African languages. **71**

Baines, Thomas (1822–75)
English artist and traveler. In 1847–51 he was artist to the British army in the Cape and in 1855 joined an expedition to Northwest Australia. In 1858 he accompanied Livingstone on his Zambezi Expedition, and also recorded and explored the area around Victoria Falls in 1861. He returned to the Cape in 1868 and continued his work there until his death. **77, 87, 164**

Baker, Sir Samuel White (1821–93)
British explorer. He made discoveries in Ethiopia about the sources of the River Nile (1861–62) and discovered and named Lake Albert (1864). Later, as a colonial administrator, he opposed the slave trade, and led an expedition up the River Nile. His wife, Florence, traveled with him, doing much to maintain friendly relations with the people they encountered. **74–75**

Balboa, Vasco Núñez de (c. 1475–1519)
Spanish *conquistador* and the first European to see the Pacific Ocean from the Americas. He went to Hispaniola in 1500 and to Darién (Panama) ten years later, where the colonists ousted the Governor and he took control. He crossed the Isthmus and reached the Pacific in September 1513. On returning home, he was unjustly executed for treason. **98, 100**

Banks, Sir Joseph (1743–1820)
British naturalist and explorer. After graduating from Oxford University and inheriting a fortune from his father, Banks traveled extensively collecting natural history specimens. In 1766 he visited Newfoundland and Labrador. In 1768–71 he accompanied Captain Cook's expedition to the Pacific. On his third expedition, in 1772, he went to Iceland. In 1778 he became President of the Royal Society and remained in this position until his death. **68, 69, 158, 159, 162**

Barents, Willem (d. 1597)
Dutch navigator. He made three expeditions in search of the Northeast Passage (1594–97). On his third voyage he discovered Spitsbergen (Svalbard), off Norway, but after rounding Novaya Zemlya was trapped by ice for the winter. The members of his expedition thus became the first Europeans to winter in the Arctic. Barents died on the return journey. **174, 175**

Barth, Heinrich (1821–65)
German explorer and geographer. After studying Arabic he embarked, in 1845, on a two-year expedition through northern Africa, Palestine, Asia Minor, and Greece. In 1851–56 he accompanied a British-sponsored expedition through central Africa. Despite the death of his two companions, James Richardson and Adolf Overweg, Barth pressed on, studying the local topography, history, and culture. His *Travels and Discoveries in North and Central Africa (1857–58)* is considered an authoritative text. **70, 71, 84**

Bass, George (c. 1771–c. 1803)
British explorer who, with Matthew Flinders, explored parts of the coast near Sydney, Australia, that were as yet unmapped. In 1798 they circumnavigated Tasmania. The dividing strait they found is now named Bass Strait. In 1803 Bass disappeared while on a voyage to South America. **162, 163**

Bates, Henry Walter (1825–92)
British naturalist whose work on natural selection lent support to Darwin's theory of evolution. He collected 14,712 unknown species of insects on a trip to the Amazon (1848–59) and recounted his experiences in *The Naturalist on the River Amazon* (1863). **108–9**

Bellingshausen, Thaddeus (1778–1852)
Russian naval officer and explorer of the seas surrounding Antarctica. He discovered Peter I and Alexander I islands in 1821 while circumnavigating Antarctica (1820–21). At his death he was Governor of Kronshtadt. **186, 187**

Benalcázar, Sebastián de (c. 1494–1551)
Spanish *conquistador* who was with Francisco Pizarro during the conquest of Peru (1532). He founded settlements in Colombia while searching for the legendary El Dorado, and in 1541 became Governor of Popayán province. After taking part in the Peruvian civil wars he was arrested for disloyalty and sent back to Spain in 1550, where he died soon afterward. **100**

Bering, Vitus Jonassen (1680–1741)

Danish navigator and the first European to reach Alaska. Following a voyage to the East Indies in 1703 he entered the Russian navy. In 1724 Peter the Great appointed him to command an expedition to northeast Siberia to discover whether Asia and America were divided. Bering left St Petersburg in 1725, traveled overland to Kamchatka, built ships, and eventually sailed in the summer of 1728. But although he sailed north, between Asia and America, through what is now called the Bering Strait, he failed to sight land and, on returning to St Petersburg in 1730, was unable to state categorically whether there was a strait or not. He was despatched on a second expedition, and in 1741 he again sailed from Kamchatka toward North America, eventually sighting Alaska. Bering landed briefly, but he died on the return voyage, stranded by the ice on what is now Bering Island. **48–49, 140, 141, 160**

Binger, Louis-Gustave (1856–1936)

French soldier and explorer in West Africa. In 1887–89 he traveled between the Ivory Coast and the Niger, the first European to visit the city of Kong. He made further explorations in 1892, drawing up the boundaries between British Gold Coast and French Ivory Coast, becoming Governor of the latter in 1893. Bingerville, the colonial capital from 1900 to 1934, was named after him. **85**

Bingham, Hiram (1875–1956)

US archeologist whose discovery in 1912 of the Inca city of Machu Picchu in the Peruvian Andes helped historians to unravel the story of Peru before the Spanish conquest. He led many expeditions to South America and wrote *Inca Land* (1922), *Machu Picchu* (1930), and *Lost City of the Incas* (1948). **112–13**

Blaxland, Gregory (1778–1853)

British landowner who emigrated to Australia in 1805, and whose search for grazing land led him to seek a route from Sydney into the interior. He was successful in crossing the Blue Mountains in 1813. Blaxland was a keen businessman and disliked the restrictions laid down by the Colonial Office, with which he frequently came into conflict. He had some success in his farming ventures but committed suicide in 1853. **164, 165**

Borough, Stephen (1525–84)

English navigator. He took part in the expedition in 1553 under Hugh Willoughby to find the Northeast Passage. After his ship became separated from Willoughby's, he sailed into the White Sea and, with Richard Chancellor, discovered the northern route to Moscow. In 1556 he discovered the strait between the most southerly island of Novaya Zemlya and Vaygach in northern Russia and the Kara Sea beyond. He traveled again to Russia in 1560. **174, 175**

Bougainville, Louis Antoine, Comte de (1729–1811)

French navigator. An army veteran of the French and Indian wars in Canada, in 1763 he joined the navy and commanded the first French naval force to circumnavigate the globe (1766–69), making botanical and astronomical studies. He published an account of the journey in 1771–72, which was widely read. He went on to serve with the American army in the War of Independence, but was subsequently disgraced after a French defeat in the Caribbean in 1782. He sat out the Revolution on his Normandy estates, until finding favor again under Napoleon. **156, 157, 159**

Bransfield, Edward (c. 1795–1851)

English naval officer who charted the South Shetland Islands and claimed them as British. Sailing further south, he sighted the Antarctic Peninsula in 1820. **186**

Bruce, James (1730–94)

Scottish explorer. He was appointed British Consul at Algiers in 1762–65, and then embarked on an exploration of Roman ruins on the north coast of Africa, and the Mediterranean. From Alexandria he set off, in 1768, on a search for the source of the Nile. In 1770 he reached the source of the Blue Nile, and he subsequently described the Portuguese Jesuits who had reached it before him as "liars." His verbal descriptions of his travels were not well received by London society, but in 1790 he published a written account in five volumes: *Travels to Discover the Source of the Nile in the Years 1768–73*. **66–67**

Brûlé, Etienne (c. 1592–1633)

French explorer who traveled to Quebec from France with Samuel de Champlain in 1608. In the next 20 years he explored the Great Lakes and Georgian Bay, guiding French expeditions and befriending the Huron Indians, who eventually killed him. **127**

Brunner, Thomas (1822–74)

Surveyor and explorer of New Zealand who, with Charles Heaphy, undertook a number of arduous expeditions in search of uncontested land. Brunner's most famous journey (1846–48) took him and his Maori guides into the Southern Alps in search of the legendary tableland. Brunner's account of this journey was published in 1848. **170, 171**

Burchell, William John (c. 1782–1863)

English explorer and naturalist. He worked, in 1805–10, as "schoolmaster and acting botanist" on the island of St Helena, before traveling to the Cape. Here he learned the Colonial-Dutch patois before embarking, in 1811, on his travels in southern Africa, collecting specimens and making scientific observations. He traveled for four years, and on his return to England published an account of the first year's journey, as well as scientific papers. In 1825–29 he traveled widely in South America, collecting specimens. **86**

Burckhardt, Johann Ludwig (1784–1817)

Swiss explorer and scholar of Arabic language and customs, who became the first European in modern times to visit Petra in Jordan and the Egyptian temple at Abu Simbel. After studying in London and Cambridge, Burckhardt went to Syria to learn Arabic. From there he traveled to Cairo, up the Nile and through Arabia to Mecca, often in Muslim dress and under a Muslim name. He died of dysentery on his return to Cairo, while planning a journey into the desert. His records of his experiences during five years of travel were subsequently published in five volumes between 1819 and 1830. **51, 68**

Burke, Robert O'Hara (1820/21–61)

Irish explorer who led the first successful, although personally disastrous, expedition across Australia from south to north in 1860. Starting in Melbourne, he left most of his party at the Barcoo River and continued toward the north coast with a party of three. They almost reached the mouth of the Flinders River, but turned back without seeing the sea. On the return trip, Burke and two of his companions died. The fourth man, King, was eventually rescued. **168–69**

Burton, Sir Richard Francis (1821–90)

English explorer, writer, linguist, and diplomat. His extensive knowledge of the customs and languages of the Far East was obtained while serving in the army in India in 1842–49. It was put to use when, in 1853, he traveled in disguise to Medina and Mecca, becoming one of the few Europeans at that time to have visited these cities. On a trip to East Africa, with John Speke in 1857, he discovered Lake Tanganyika. He subsequently explored briefly in West Africa. In 1861 he entered the service of the Foreign Office, serving in South America, Damascus, and Trieste. The author of many books, he was best known for his 16-volume translation of *The Thousand Nights and a Night* (1885–88). **51, 72, 73, 75**

Byrd, Richard Evelyn (1888–1957)

American naval officer and aeronautic explorer. He traveled round the world (unaccompanied) at the age of 12. After naval service he went on an expedition to Greenland in 1925, gaining experience for his subsequent polar flights. In 1926 he and his co-pilot Floyd Bennett were the first to fly over the North Pole. In 1927 Byrd flew with four passengers from New York to France, but was forced to land on the sea because of poor visibility. An account of his experiences in aviation is given in *Skyward* (1928). In 1929, from a base on the Ross Ice Shelf in Antarctica, he flew over the South Pole. In 1933–34 he explored, by sledge and plane, what is now called Byrd Land. In 1939–41 he further explored the Antarctic interior and in 1955–56 he led his fifth expedition to the continent. **182, 196**

Cabot, John (c. 1450–c. 1499)

Genoese-born navigator who made the first recorded European journey to the coast of North America since the journeys of the Norse. After a period trading in the Mediterranean, he persuaded Henry VII of England to support an expedition across the Atlantic in 1497. On reaching America, he followed the coast from northern Newfoundland to Cape Breton Island, and returned to England convinced that he had found the land of the Great Khan (China). He was rewarded by the king and a second expedition was launched in 1498. Cabot did not return, but his discoveries served as the basis for English claims in North America, which led to increased trade between England and Russia. **120–21**

Cabot, Sebastian (1474–1557)

Venetian-born navigator, explorer, and cartographer, the son of John Cabot, who grew up in Bristol. He sailed across the Atlantic in search of a northern passage to China in 1508, possibly reaching Hudson Bay, and sailed down the coast of North America. He joined the Spanish navy in 1512, and in 1526 led an expedition to find a route to the Pacific from the Atlantic. In 1547 he returned to England, where he helped to found the Company of Merchant Adventurers for the Discovery of Cathay. As Governor of the Company he organized a series of expeditions in 1553–56 in search of a Northeast Passage to China. **99, 121**

Cabral, Pedro Álvares (c. 1467–c. 1520)

Portuguese navigator who was the first European to discover Brazil. In 1500 King Manuel I of Portugal sent him with a fleet of ships to the East Indies. To avoid the Gulf of Guinea, Cabral sailed westward and reached Brazil, which he claimed for Portugal. On his return to Portugal in 1501 he planned a further expedition, but was removed from this after a disagreement with the king, and replaced by Vasco da Gama. **38, 94**

Cabrillo, Juan Rodríguez (d. 1543)

Portuguese explorer of the Californian coast in the service of Spain. After taking part in the conquest of the Aztec Empire, he went to Guatemala and in 1492 sailed from northwest Mexico to explore the Californian coast. He reached San Francisco Bay but later died on San Miguel Island. **124, 125**

Caillié, René Auguste (1799–1838)

French explorer of northwest Africa, who was determined, from an early age, to visit Timbuktu. He learned Arabic and was educated in Islam before, in 1827, joining a caravan from the coast of Guinea to Timbuktu, which he reached in April 1828. Two weeks later he set off northward, across the Sahara to Fez. He was the first European to reach Timbuktu and return to tell the tale. **84, 85**

Cameron, Verney Lovett (1844–94)

British naval officer and explorer in central Africa. He spent some time as part of a naval patrol trying to suppress the East African slave trade. In 1873 he was sent by the Royal Geographical Society to give aid to Livingstone. Although he was met by news of Livingstone's death, he continued his exploration of Lake Tanganyika. He found his way to the Lualaba River, but was unable to obtain canoes from Arab slave traders to travel down to the Congo (Zaire) River, because of his refusal to countenance slavery. He therefore traveled overland to the Angolan coast, and became the first European to make the east–west crossing of Africa. He subsequently visited the Euphrates valley (1878–79) and accompanied Richard Burton to West Africa in 1882. **79, 82**

Cano, Juan Sebastian del (c. 1476–1526)

Spanish navigator who was first to circumnavigate the globe in one voyage. He commanded one of the five vessels in Ferdinand Magellan's voyage of discovery and assumed control in 1521 after Magellan's death, returning to Spain in 1522. **150, 151**

Cão, Diogo (active 1480–86)

Portuguese explorer of West Africa. He was the first European to travel up the Congo (Zaire) River and to explore the coast below the Equator, reaching Cape Santa Maria, in 1482–84. **34, 65**

Carpini, Giovanni da Pian del (c. 1180–1252)

Italian traveler and churchman. He was sent by Pope Innocent IV to the Mongol court in 1245, and on his return to Italy wrote *History of the Mongols*, in which he discredited many of the contemporary rumors concerning Mongol atrocities. **28**

Carteret, Philip (d. 1796)

British naval officer who commanded a ship on an expedition to the Pacific led by Wallis in 1766. He became separated from Wallis on entering the Pacific and took a more southerly route, encountering, and naming, many islands as yet unknown to Europeans. He returned to England after two and a half years at sea, much weakened, and after one further voyage he retired from the active list. **156–57**

Cartier, Jacques (1491–1557)

French navigator and explorer who discovered the St Lawrence River. Cartier studied navigation at Dieppe, and in 1534 was sent by King Francis I to North America, in search of gold. During this voyage he discovered the Magdalen Islands and Prince Edward Island, and explored the Gulf of St Lawrence, before returning to France. In 1535–36 he sailed up the St Lawrence River to the site of Montreal, but was forced to turn back by the rapids. The Iroquois had told him of riches to be found further west, so Cartier returned to North America a third time in 1541, as part of an expedition to secure French claims to the area. This did not prove successful, and France did not renew its claims for a further 50 years. However, Cartier's explorations formed the chief basis for later French claims on Canada. **122–23**

Champlain, Samuel de (1567–1635)

French explorer of North America and founder of New France (Canada). After a long expedition to the West Indies, Champlain went to the Gulf of St Lawrence in 1603, where he explored the St Lawrence River. He returned in 1604, bringing settlers and establishing a colony at Port Royal (now Annapolis Royal, Nova Scotia). He explored the Atlantic coast from Cape Breton to Cape Cod, making detailed maps of the area, and in 1608 he founded Quebec. He continued to explore the region for the next six years, discovering Lake Champlain in 1609 and traveling up the Ottawa River to Lake Huron in 1615. The last 20 years of his life were spent as a colonial administrator and patron of further exploration by younger men. **126–27**

Chancellor, Richard (d. 1556)

English navigator who, in 1553, commanded a ship on an expedition to find a Northeast Passage to Asia, and reached Moscow. Through his negotiations with Tsar Ivan the Terrible he laid the foundations for English trade with Russia. **42, 174, 175**

Charcot, Jean-Baptiste Etienne (d. 1936)

French explorer and physician who led two Antarctic expeditions. During the first (1903–5), he found that the Bismarck Strait connected with the sea east of the Graham coast; he also mapped the west coast of Palmer Peninsula. During the second (1908–10), he charted the Antarctic Peninsula and conducted scientific studies. In later years he carried out scientific research in Arctic waters, but in 1936 he and his crew were drowned off Iceland. **191**

Clapperton, Hugh (1788–1827)

Scottish explorer of Africa. After a career in the navy he was sent in 1822 on a government expedition south from Tripoli to explore Lake Chad and the Niger region. This was followed by a second expedition in 1825, north from the Bight of Benin, on which he died. His travels opened up new commercial possibilities in what is now Nigeria. **70, 71**

Clark, William (1770–1838)

US explorer who, with Meriwether Lewis, led a government-sponsored expedition to investigate a land route to the Pacific coast in 1803–6. In 1806 he was made Indian Agent for Louisiana Territory. He went on to become Governor of Missouri, and later Superintendent of Indian Affairs for Missouri and Upper Mississippi. **144–45**

Columbus, Christopher (1451–1506)

Genoese-born explorer often, although erroneously, credited with the discovery of America. A weaver's son with little education, the young Columbus went to sea and traveled the trade routes of the Mediterranean and the Atlantic, adopting Portugal as his home. In 1484 he went to Spain where he found support from the crown for a voyage in search of a western route to China. In October 1492 he landed in the Bahamas and called the people he found there "Indians." He founded a colony on Hispaniola (Haiti) and returned to Spain in 1493. He made three further Atlantic crossings and, in 1496, made his first recorded landing on the South American mainland, in what is now Venezuela. His final voyage, in search of a western route to the Indian Ocean, began in 1502 and took him to Panama. Here his attempts to set up a colony were thwarted by hostile Indians, and he returned to Spain, to die in poverty and disgrace. **92–93**

Cook, James (1728–79)

British naval officer and explorer who exhibited great intellectual powers (as a scientific observer and cartographer) and a humane attitude both to his crew and the native peoples encountered on his voyages. After joining the navy in 1755 he conducted surveying work on the Canadian coast. In 1768 he was appointed to lead a scientific expedition to Tahiti to observe the transit of Venus. This accomplished, he made a careful survey of the coasts of New Zealand and eastern Australia. On a second expedition to the South Pacific (1772–75), Cook reached a "furthest south," crossing the Antarctic Circle. He also established accurately the positions of many of the Pacific islands. The purpose of his last voyage (1776–79) was to discover a western entrance to a possible Northwest Passage. Passing northward through the Pacific, he discovered the Sandwich (Hawaiian) Islands. He then surveyed the Bering Strait before returning to the Hawaiian group where, in a scuffle with the native inhabitants, he was killed. **108, 109, 140, 141, 158–59, 160–61, 170, 185**

Coronado, Francisco Vásquez de (b. 1510)

Spanish explorer of North America. He went to Mexico in 1535, and in 1540 he headed an expedition to locate the seven cities of Cibola, reported to be the repositories of untold wealth. He explored the western coast of Mexico, followed the route of the Rio Grande eastward, and then headed north through the Texas Panhandle, Oklahoma, and eastern Kansas. His discoveries were impressive, but he found no gold. **124–25**

Corte-Real, Gaspar (c. 1450–1501) and Miguel (d. 1502)

Portuguese brothers who explored the northwest coast of North America. Sent by King Manuel I in 1500, Gaspar sailed to Greenland and on to Labrador and down the coast of Canada. In 1501 he made a second expedition, but failed to return. His brother, Miguel, set out the following year in search of Gaspar, but he also failed to return. The lands they had discovered, however, were recognized as belonging to Portugal, and some still bear their name. **120, 121**

Cortés, Hernán (1485–1547)

Central figure in the Spanish conquest and colonization of Mexico. After studying law at Salamanca University, Cortés set out for the New World to seek his fortune. He became secretary to Diego de Velásquez, Governor of Cuba, who sent him on an expedition to Mexico in 1518. Cortés sailed for central America with 550 men and, once landed, declared himself independent of Velásquez, giving himself the official standing and legal authority to colonize, and marched inland toward the Aztec capital. Converting many of the local American Indians into allies of his cause, Cortés was able to capture Tenochtitlán (now Mexico City) in 1521. During the following five years, Cortés brought the

Aztec lands, Honduras, and much of El Salvador and Guatemala under Spanish control. However, his personal power, symbolized by his titles and estates, was gradually eroded by the crown, and he died in Spain, a private citizen. **96–97**

Cousteau, Jacques Yves (1910–97)
French oceanographer. Best known as the co-inventor (with Emile Gagnan) of the aqualung, an independent diving unit permitting divers underwater mobility. He also invented a process of underwater television and conducted a series of undersea living experiments in 1962–65. Many of the expeditions made by his research ship, *Calypso*, were filmed by him for television and cinema. **208**

Cunningham, Allan (1791–1839)
British botanist and explorer who discovered Pandora's Pass, the Darling Downs, and Cunningham's Gap in New South Wales, Australia. Appointed as a botanical collector for Kew Gardens, Cunningham was sent to Brazil and then to New South Wales in 1816. He made many journeys by land and sea until 1830, when he returned to Britain. In 1837 he took up the post of colonial botanist in New South Wales. **164**

Dampier, William (1651–1715)
English navigator and buccaneer. An adventurous early career included a buccaneering expedition against Spanish America in 1679 and a journey across the Pacific Ocean in 1688. In 1697 he published an account of his adventures and this led to his appointment as leader of a government expedition in 1699 to the South Seas. On this journey he explored the coasts of Australia, New Guinea, and New Britain, and gave his name to Dampier Archipelago and Dampier Strait. He made two further expeditions to the Pacific, including one in 1708 when he rescued Alexander Selkirk, on whom Defoe based Robinson Crusoe, from the island of Juan Fernández. Dampier died in poverty, bitter at the way in which his achievements had been overtaken by others. **156, 157**

Darwin, Charles Robert (1809–82)
British naturalist, who originated the theory of evolution by natural selection. In 1831 he joined an expedition in HMS *Beagle*, which explored the South American coast. The observations made of the flora and fauna there, and in particular on the Galápagos Islands, formed the basis of his future work on the evolution of new species. The development of a theory similar to Darwin's own by A. R. Wallace led Darwin to present his ideas to a meeting of the Linnean Society in 1858, and he published *On the Origin of Species by Means of Natural Selection*, a detailed exposition of evolution, in 1859. His ideas reached a wider public with the publication of *The Descent of Man* (1871) and other works. **110–11**

Davis, John (c. 1550–1605)
English explorer and navigator. He made three voyages to Canada in search of a Northwest Passage (1585–87), exploring the Davis Strait, Cumberland Gulf, and Baffin Bay. In 1588 he fought against the Spanish Armada and in 1591 embarked on a further voyage of discovery, during which he reached the Falkland Islands. He published two valuable treatises on navigation, in 1594 and 1595, and the back-staff and double quadrant he designed were widely used. He subsequently undertook several expeditions to the East Indies, where he was killed by pirates. **174, 175**

Desideri, Ippolito (1684–1733)
Italian Jesuit missionary who is widely regarded as the first great explorer of Tibet. Desideri visited Lhasa in 1715 and stayed in Tibet until 1721, studying Tibetan language and culture. **45**

Dezhnev, Simon (c. 1605–73)
Russian government agent and explorer who almost certainly sailed through the Bering Strait in 1648, nearly a century before Vitus Bering reached it. The significance of his journey was not realized until the 19th century, by which time the discovery of the separation of Asia and North America had been attributed to Bering, and the Strait named after him. **47**

Dias, Bartholomew (c. 1450–1500)
Portuguese navigator. Under the commission of John II of Portugal, he led an expedition of three ships around the southern tip of Africa, thereby taking a vital step toward the establishment of the European sea route to India. He was part of the expedition in 1500 of Pedro Alvares Cabral that "discovered" Brazil by chance, but was subsequently drowned off the Cape of Good Hope. **35**

Doughty, Charles Montagu (1843–1926)
British explorer, travel writer, and poet. He traveled from Damascus to Mecca (1876–78), an account of which appears in his acclaimed *Travels in Arabia Deserta* (2 vols, 1888). His poetry includes *The Dawn in Britain* (1906) and *The Clouds* (1912). **52, 53**

Drake, Sir Francis (c. 1540–96)
English navigator and privateer. He achieved fame raiding Spanish shipping and colonies in the Caribbean (1570–72), and in 1577–80 became the first Englishman to sail around the world. He was knighted by Elizabeth I and made Mayor of Plymouth in 1581. He made further raids against Spain and contributed greatly to the defeat of the Spanish Armada in 1588. His death at sea followed a disastrous expedition to raid Spanish Caribbean settlements. **152, 153**

Drygalski, Erich Dagobert von (1865–1949)
German geophysicist. In 1892 he led a voyage to Greenland and in 1901–3 headed the German Antarctic Expedition, reaching the area that he named Kaiser Wilhelm II Land. **190, 191**

Dumont D'Urville, Jules Sébastien (1790–1842)
French navigator who made two major voyages. In the first (1826–29) he surveyed the coast of Australia and New Zealand, and visited several groups of Pacific islands. In the second (1837–40) he sailed to Antarctica, where he discovered Joinville Island and Adélie Land. He described his voyages and supplied maps in a 49-volume work which added to knowledge in a number of areas, including geology, botany, linguistics, and oceanography. He was killed in a train crash outside Paris. **188, 189, 202**

Eirik Thorvaldsson, "the Red" (c. 950–1010)
Norse explorer of Greenland. Exiled from Norway and Iceland for manslaughter, he fled in AD 982 to Greenland, which had been discovered at the beginning of the century by another Norseman, Gunnbjörn. Three years later, he brought colonists from Iceland to establish permanent settlements. Returning to Norway, he was converted to Christianity, which he attempted to introduce to the settlers in Greenland. **23, 118**

Elias, Ney (1844–97)
British civil servant and explorer who traveled extensively in central Asia. After working in an office in China, Elias set off in 1872 to return overland to Europe, accompanied by a Chinese servant. This journey was undertaken in the depths of winter and involved crossing the hostile Gobi Desert by a route never before explored. Elias was thereafter employed by the Government of India on a number of difficult journeys and delicate political missions all over central Asia. Although he was one of the greatest Asian explorers, he shunned publicity and is therefore less well known than he deserves to be. **55**

Ellsworth, Lincoln (1880–1951)
American polar explorer. He financed the Norwegian explorer Roald Amundsen, who in 1911 became the first person to reach the South Pole, and made a successful airship flight with Amundsen from Spitsbergen (Svalbard) over the North Pole to Alaska in 1926. In 1931 he explored vast regions of the Arctic Ocean and in 1935 flew over Antarctica. **182, 196**

Entrecasteaux, Joseph-Antoine Bruni d' (1739–93)
French naval officer, who commanded the French fleet in the East Indies in 1785–87, during which time he made a voyage to China. In 1787 he was made Governor of Mauritius and the Isle of Bourbon, and in 1791 was put in charge of an expedition to find La Pérouse, who had been lost since early 1788. He charted parts of Tasmania and the east coast of New Caledonia, as well as investigating the southern coast of Australia. He failed, however, to find La Pérouse, and died of scurvy off the coast of Java. **160, 161**

Eratosthenes (c. 276–c. 194 BC)
Greek geographer who was the first to calculate the Earth's circumference by geometry, arriving at an astoundingly accurate result. He administered the library of Alexandria from 234 to 192 BC, and was renowned for his work in mathematics, geography, philosophy, and literature. **18**

Eyre, Edward John (1815–1901)
British explorer of Australia and colonial administrator. He migrated to New South Wales in 1833 where he farmed before exploring, in 1839–40, the area north of Adelaide up to Lake Eyre and around the Eyre Peninsula. In an attempt to link the colonies in southwest and western Australia, he led a small party from Adelaide to King George Sound in 1841. Later, positions in the governments of New Zealand and some lesser islands led to the governorship of Jamaica in 1864. His allegedly brutal suppression of a black uprising in 1865 caused his dismissal. **166, 167**

Fawcett, Percy Harrison (1867–c. 1925)
British explorer of the Mato Grosso region of Brazil who disappeared while searching for the ruined city of El Dorado in the Amazon jungle. After surveying the frontier between Brazil and Bolivia in 1906–8, and serving in the British army in the First World War, Fawcett returned to South America to continue his explorations. In 1925 he set out with his son and a friend into the jungle. They were never heard of again, despite a rescue operation mounted in 1928. **114**

Federmann, Nikolaus (c. 1501–42)
German explorer and *conquistador* who explored the Venezuelan interior and went on to lead an expedition

into the Andes in 1537. He reached Bogotá in 1539, where he met up with Quesada and Benalcázar. He was called to Spain to answer charges against the crown, and died in prison there. **100, 101**

Filchner, Wilhelm (1877–1957)
German army officer and explorer. He traveled in the Pamir region in 1900, led the German China-Tibet expedition of 1903 and the German Antarctic Expedition of 1911–12. During the 1920s and 1930s, he made three cartographic expeditions to Tibet. His *Route-Mapping and Position-Locating in Unexplored Regions* (1957) made a major contribution to cartographic techniques. **192, 193**

Fitch, Ralph (d. 1611)
English explorer who traveled overland to India in 1583, and traded with the Mughal emperor Akbar. Three years later he became the first European to visit Burma and Siam (Thailand). **42**

Fitzroy, Robert (1805–65)
British naval commander, explorer, and meteorologist who captained HMS *Beagle* in 1828–36 on expeditions to South America. He recruited Charles Darwin as naturalist to the 1831–36 expedition. He later served as Governor-General of New Zealand. **108, 110–11**

Flinders, Matthew (1774–1814)
British navigator. He entered the navy in 1789 and in 1795 was sent on a voyage of exploration along the Australian coast. In 1798 he circumnavigated Tasmania with George Bass. In 1801 he was sent on a second voyage, during which he circumnavigated Australia counterclockwise. On his return journey to England, he survived a shipwreck off the Australian coast. Stopping off in Mauritius at the end of 1803, he was detained by the French, with whom England was now at war, and languished in prison until 1810. His account of his voyage, *Voyage to Terra Australis*, was published on the day of his death in 1814, and contains many observations regarding magnetism, meteorology, hydrography, and navigation. **162–63**

Forbes, Edward (1815–54)
Scottish naturalist, who carried out research into the relationship between geological change and the flora and fauna of the British Isles. Forbes also made an extensive study of mollusks and starfishes, taking part in several dredging expeditions to aid his research. **206**

Franklin, Sir John (1786–1847)
Naval officer and Arctic explorer. He fought at the Battle of Copenhagen (1801) and the Battle of Trafalgar (1805), but in between took part in the exploratory voyage of his cousin, Matthew Flinders, to the Australian coast (1801–3). In 1818 he was part of an ill-judged expedition to sail to the North Pole, and subsequently commanded two overland explorations of the North American coast (1819–22 and 1825–27), during which he and his team endured terrible hardship and starvation. In 1836–43 he was Governor of Van Diemen's Land (Tasmania). On his return to England he took command in 1845 of an expedition in search of a Northwest Passage. The expedition failed to return and all 129 men died. **175–79, 189**

Frémont, John Charles (1813–90)
American military explorer who was involved in the US conquest and development of California. After traveling and studying map-making with Jean-Nicolas

Nicollet, Frémont spent the early 1840s mapping the territory between the Mississippi Valley and the Pacific Ocean, and surveying much of the Northwest. His famous winter crossing of the Sierra Nevada Mountains was followed by another expedition to California, which resulted in the annexation of that state in 1846. Frémont resigned from the army and went on to make a fortune in the 1848 goldrush. He was elected one of California's first two senators in 1850. The remainder of his life was spent alternately in public office and in railroad projects. **145**

Fritz, Samuel (1653–1723)
Bohemian Jesuit missionary who worked among the Omagua and Yurimagua Indians along the Amazon River, establishing some 50 Christian settlements and charting the course of the river. He defended the Indians against slave raiders, organizing a mass exodus to the Andean watershed. **102–3**

Frobisher, Sir Martin (c. 1535–94)
English navigator and mariner. On an expedition in 1576, in search of the Northwest Passage, two of his three ships were lost but he discovered what was to be named Frobisher Bay in Canada. He returned twice (1577–78), primarily in a fruitless search for gold. He subsequently took part in the defeat of the Spanish Armada in 1588. **128, 129, 174, 175**

Fuchs, Sir Vivian Ernest (1908–99)
British geologist and explorer. He led the Falkland Island Dependencies Survey in the Antarctic (1947–50), and in 1955–58 headed the British section of the Commonwealth Trans-Antarctic Expedition, which made the hazardous 2158-mile (3473-kilometer) journey across the Antarctic. **197**

Gagarin, Yuri Alekseyevich (1934–68)
Russian cosmonaut who, in 1961, became the first man to orbit the Earth. His space flight brought him immediate worldwide fame but he never went into space again. He died in an aircrash during a routine test flight. **224**

Gama, Vasco da (c. 1460–1524)
Portuguese nobleman and diplomat who, in 1497–98, led the expedition that established the first European maritime route to India. He reached South Africa, sailed around the Cape of Good Hope and across the Indian Ocean to Calicut, but returned without having established trade links. His second voyage to India, in 1502, was more successful in this respect; following a naval battle off the Malabar coast, he forced the Indians to trade with him. On his return to Portugal, he retired from the navy, but returned to India in 1524 as Viceroy, dying there shortly afterward. **38, 39**

Garnier, Marie-Joseph François (1839–73)
French naval officer and explorer in Cambodia and Vietnam. After becoming Inspector of Native Affairs in Saigon in 1863, he played a major part in the Mekong River Expedition of 1866–68. In 1870 he served in the defense of Paris, and then entered politics and journalism. As a correspondent in China, he became caught up in the first French attempt to conquer northern Vietnam, and was killed. **62–63**

Gerlache de Gomery, Adrien Victor Joseph, Comte de (1866–1934)
Belgian naval officer who, in 1897–99, led the first expedition to winter in the Antarctic. Following this expedition (which was primarily scientific) he

collected specimens in the Persian Gulf. He made oceanographic studies of the east coast of Greenland (1905) and of the Barents and Kara seas (1909). He also crossed Greenland in 1909. **190, 191**

Gist, Christopher (c. 1705–59)
American frontiersman, soldier, and explorer. Born in Maryland, the son of a surveyor, Gist explored and surveyed the Ohio River Valley (1750–51) for the Ohio Company. He served with George Washington on the expedition to order the French out of the Ohio Valley (1753–54) and was a guide on General Braddock's ill-fated march on Fort Dusquesne (1755). **137**

Glenn, John Herschel, Jr (b. 1921)
US astronaut who, in 1962, became the first American to orbit the Earth. He subsequently became a Democratic senator and in 1998 flew his second space mission on the space shuttle *Discovery*, thus becoming the oldest person ever to travel in space. **224**

Grey, Sir George (1812–98)
British army officer who explored the northwest coast of Australia in 1837–39. Grey was an intrepid but inexperienced explorer, and his expeditions were perilous and badly planned. He made the most of his opportunities, however. He became Governor of South Australia in 1840, and subsequently secured governorships of New Zealand and the Cape Colony. **166, 167**

Heaphy, Charles (c. 1821–81)
Colonial official who explored parts of New Zealand on behalf of the New Zealand Company. Heaphy began his colonial career as a draughtsman involved in a number of surveys and road-making projects in New Zealand, and went on to become Chief Surveyor for the province of Auckland in 1864. For three years he sat as an elected member of the New Zealand House of Representatives (1867–70), and he continued as a government official until his death. **170, 171**

Hearne, Samuel (1745–92)
British fur trader and explorer of Canada. Hearne left England to navigate for the Hudson's Bay Company in 1766. Three years later, he led the first of his expeditions north from Churchill with the aim of opening up new territory for the Company. After two unsuccessful attempts Hearne set out again in 1770, making the first overland trek to the Arctic Ocean. In 1774 he helped to further the interests of the Hudson's Bay Company by establishing Cumberland House, an inland trading post. **138–39**

Hedin, Sven Anders (1865–1952)
Swedish explorer of central Asia. After serving as a diplomat in Persia, Hedin made several long and arduous journeys through central Asia. He crossed the Takla Makan Desert and discovered the remains of ancient settlements there, and in 1906–8 he traveled extensively in Tibet. He published numerous accounts of his travels, but his reputation was tarnished later by his apparent Nazi sympathies. **60, 61**

Hennepin, Louis (1640–c. 1701)
Belgian explorer and Franciscan missionary who sailed to Canada in 1675. After doing missionary work among the Indians, Hennepin was directed to explore the upper Mississippi with the French explorer La Salle. In an account of his travels, he claimed to have explored the river to its mouth, but this false claim discredited him. **134**

Herodotus (c. 485–425 BC)

Greek historian and geographer. He made lengthy journeys through the ancient world and helped to colonize Thurii in southern Italy. He is best known for his vivid history of the Persian Wars. His work, which is considered to be the beginning of Western history writing, contains an enormous amount of information. **12–13**

Heyerdahl, Thor (1914–2002)

Norwegian ethnologist who, with five companions, drifted on the balsa raft *Kon Tiki* approximately 5000 miles (8000 kilometers) across the Pacific Ocean from Peru to Polynesia (1947), in an attempt to prove that the Polynesians came from South America and not from Southeast Asia. Pursuing his theory, Heyerdahl led archeological expeditions to the Galápagos Islands (1953) and to Bolivia, Peru, and Colombia (1954). In 1970 he sailed from Africa to the West Indies in a papyrus boat. **148**

Hillary, Sir Edmund Percival (1919–2008)

New Zealand explorer and mountaineer. He participated in the New Zealand and British expeditions to the Himalayas in 1951 and 1953. In 1953 he and his Sherpa guide, Norgay Tenzing, were the first to reach the summit of Mount Everest. In 1955–58 he led the New Zealand section of the British Commonwealth Trans-Antarctic Expedition. He subsequently spent much time in Nepal, undertaking projects for the benefit of the Sherpas and becoming New Zealand's Commissioner there. **197, 220**

Hsüan-Tsang (c. 605–664)

Chinese traveler and scholar who was one of the few Chinese of his time to travel beyond the borders of China. On his 15-year-long overland journey he reached as far west as the Oxus River, and then turned south down the Kabul River and on to the Ganges. He returned via the Pamir Mountains and back across the Takla Makan Desert. During his travels he collected manuscripts and other precious objects and afterward wrote an account of his travels. **17**

Hudson, Henry (d. 1611)

English navigator and explorer. During his last four years he led several expeditions in search of the Northwest Passage to China. On his first attempt he reached Spitsbergen (Svalbard), where he discovered rich fishing grounds. On the third voyage (1609), he reached the American coast, and sailed up what was to be called the Hudson River. On his last expedition he passed through the strait that now bears his name and entered Hudson Bay. Following a winter spent icebound, he was set adrift in 1611 by his mutinous crew and never heard of again. **128–29, 174, 175**

Humboldt, Baron Alexander von (1769–1859)

German scientist, explorer, and philosopher who is particularly remembered for his expedition to South America (1799–1804). After studying at the University of Göttingen, he became a mining engineer. In 1799 he traveled to South America, where he spent five years observing, recording, and mapping various geographical features. He also formed opinions on the social, economic, and political problems of the region, objecting strongly to slavery. He and his companion, Aimée Bonpland, collected a tremendous amount of scientific data, which Humboldt spent the next 20 years collating, studying, and publishing. In 1829 he returned to his

profession and inspected mines in the Ural Mountains, before exploring central Asia. He spent the last part of his life writing *Kosmos*, a comprehensive description of the physical universe. **60, 106–7**

Ibn Battutah, Muhammad Ibn Abdullah (1304–78)

Muslim traveler and travel writer. He left his birthplace of Tangier in 1325 and traveled along the north coast of Africa to Alexandria, Palestine, and Damascus. After a pilgrimage to Mecca and Medina, he undertook several journeys in different directions: east, across the Zagros Mountains to Esfahan; south through the Strait of Hormuz; north to eastern Turkey, and then east, along the Silk Road, to Delhi. From here he traveled to Sumatra and China. He returned to Tangier in 1354, and journeyed to the Niger before spending the rest of his life dictating an account of his travels. **26, 27**

Idrisi, Abu Abdullah ash Shari al- (c. 1099–c. 1165)

Arabian geographer. Born in Spain, he studied at Cordoba and during his lifetime traveled on the Iberian peninsula, North Africa, and Asia Minor. Sometime after 1148 he was invited to the court of Roger of Sicily. From here, he and the king sent out emissaries to survey the known world, and Idrisi recorded their findings in what was to become the *The Book of Roger*, finished in 1154. He also drew a vast map in which the world was divided into seven climatic zones, each subdivided into ten parts. **25**

James, Thomas (c. 1593–1635)

English navigator. In 1631 he sailed in search of a Northwest Passage to the Indies and explored James Bay, the southern part of Hudson Bay. He wrote an account of his exploration, *Strange and Dangerous Voyage* (1633). **129**

Jenkinson, Anthony (d. 1611)

English merchant who traveled to Turkestan and Persia across the Caspian Sea. He wrote detailed descriptions of the people and places he visited, including the first account of the Tatars in the English language. **42**

Jolliet, Louis (1645–1700)

French-Canadian explorer who in 1673 became, with Jacques Marquette, the first European to travel down the Mississippi River, reaching to within 400 miles (640 kilometers) of where it flows into the Gulf of Mexico. He was handsomely rewarded for his efforts, being given an island in the Gulf of St Lawrence. **132–33**

Kingsley, Mary Henrietta (1862–1900)

British traveler, ethnologist, and writer. In 1893 she traveled to West Africa to study the religion and law of the indigenous people. She subsequently ascended the Ogowé River in the then French Congo, and ascended the Great Cameroon Mountain in Cameroon. She recorded her experiences in *Travels in West Africa* (1897) and *West African Studies* (1899), advocating the establishment of a more humane colonial government. She died of fever in South Africa while nursing prisoners during the Boer War. **89**

Krapf, Johann Ludwig (1810–82)

German missionary in East Africa from 1843. He compiled a dictionary of the Swahili language and, with Johannes Rebmann, added to knowledge of the interior of the region, including the locations of Mount Kenya and Lake Tanganyika. **72**

La Pérouse, Jean Francois de Galaup, Comte de (1741–c. 1788)

French navigator. He distinguished himself against the British (1778–83) and in 1785 led a French exploration of the Pacific Ocean, partly in search of a Northwest Passage. The expedition took him to many parts of the South Pacific as well as to the coasts of North America and Asia. He is believed to have died in a shipwreck off the Santa Cruz Islands. **140, 160, 161**

La Salle, René-Robert Cavelier, Sieur de (1643–87)

French explorer and fur trader in North America. In 1666 he sailed for Canada to make his fortune. He explored the Great Lakes area and was commander of Fort Frontenac on Lake Ontario (1675). His greatest achievement was exploring the Mississippi River to its mouth (1682) and claiming it for the King of France. He named the adjacent lands Louisiana after Louis XIV, and returned to France to gain permission to colonize the region. The king supported the project and a convoy set off in 1684, but La Salle miscalculated the position of the Mississippi's mouth, and landed in Matagorda Bay. A colony was established at Lavaca in 1685, and La Salle spent two more years trying to find the Mississippi. He was killed by some of his own men on one such expedition. **134–35**

La Vérendrye, Pierre Gaultier de Varennes, Sieur de (1685–1749)

French-Canadian soldier, fur trader, and explorer whose search for the "western sea" led him deep into the Canadian West. After joining the army at the age of 12, he fought in North America and Europe before becoming a fur trader at Lake Nipigon in 1726. With his sons he established a string of trading posts between Lake Superior and Lake Winnipeg. He bought information from the Indians about routes to the "western sea," which he and his sons attempted, and failed, to find. His achievements were not valued by the French authorities during his lifetime, but he later came to be recognized as an important explorer of the Canadian West. **138, 139**

Laing, Alexander Gordon (1793–1826)

Army officer and Scottish explorer of West Africa, he served in the Royal Africa Corps. In 1822 he traveled in Sierra Leone on a mission to try and abolish the slave trade, and later discovered the source of the Rokel River. Although he did not reach the source of the Niger, he established its location. In 1825 he was despatched to travel from Tripoli to Timbuktu, and then on to the Niger basin. He reached Timbuktu but was murdered shortly afterward. **84, 85**

Lander, Richard (1804–1834)

English explorer of West Africa. He first traveled in the region with Hugh Clapperton in 1825. On Clapperton's death in 1827 he continued his explorations, returning to England with Clapperton's journal. In 1830 he and his brother John (1807–39) established the course of the the the Niger River from Bussa to the sea. **71–72**

Le Maire, Jacob (c. 1567–1616)

Dutch maritime explorer and son of Isaac le Maire of the South Sea Company of Amsterdam. Le Maire's expedition in search of a route to the Pacific other than through the Strait of Magellan (1615–16) led to the discovery of Le Maire's Strait and Cape Horn. Le Maire himself died on the return journey. **154**

Leichhardt, Friedrich Wilhelm Ludwig (1813–*c.* 1848)

German explorer who crossed Australia from Moreton Bay (Queensland) to Port Essington (Northern Territory) in 1844–45. This exploit made him an immediate hero in Australia and donations were made in abundance for a further expedition to cross the continent from east to west. Leichhardt, however, was wholly unqualified for the task, and he and his entire team disappeared without trace. **166–67**

Lewis, Meriwether (1774–1809)

US explorer who was one of the leaders of the Lewis and Clark expedition of 1803–6. An army captain, he was selected by President Thomas Jefferson to investigate a land route to the Pacific coast and explore the land acquired by the USA in the Louisiana Purchase of 1803. He prepared for the expedition for three years, acquiring skills as a naturalist among other things. His documentation and observations of the journey paved the way for westward expansion, and in 1808 he was rewarded with the governorship of the Louisiana Territory. **144–45**

Livingstone, David (1813–73)

British missionary and explorer. Coming from a poor background, he first worked in a cotton mill near Glasgow but saved enough to take a medical degree at the age of 27. Sent to Bechuanaland (now Botswana) in 1841 by the London Missionary Society, he made strenuous efforts to combat disease and slavery. Motivated by a combination of missionary zeal and scientific curiosity, he spent the rest of his life on a series of expeditions into the African interior. In 1849–51 he explored the region round Lake Ngami, and from 1858 to 1864 he explored the eastern Zambezi River. He then set off to find the source of the Nile in 1866 and was cut off from all contact with Europe until 1871, when he was found by Henry Stanley near Lake Tanganyika. Admired by all the peoples with whom he came into contact and a fierce opponent of slavery, Livingstone died at Ilala, in modern Zambia. **76–79**

Magellan, Ferdinand (*c.* 1480–1521)

Portuguese explorer who commanded the first expedition to circumnavigate the globe; the expedition was completed after his death. From a noble family, Magellan was educated at court, and went into the service of the crown in East Africa and the East Indies. He participated in the taking of Malacca, which made possible the exploitation of the vast trade potential in the Spice Islands (Moluccas). He fell from the favor of the King of Portugal and moved to Spain, where he organized an expedition to go to the Spice Islands by sailing west. Leaving with five ships in 1519, he reached Brazil and sailed south. In November 1520 he sailed through the strait which today bears his name and reached the Philippines in March 1521, where he was killed in a local war. Just one of his ships returned to Spain in 1522, thus establishing a new route between Europe and Asia. **94-95, 150–51**

Malaspina, Alessandro (1754–1809)

Sicilian nobleman who commanded a scientific expedition to South America and the Pacific on behalf of the Spanish in 1789–94. He reached as far north as 60°N, collected a wealth of natural history specimens, and returned with some useful political intelligence. He was, however, imprisoned by the Spanish authorities in 1796 because his liberal political views were considered too radical. He was released in 1803 at the request of

Napoleon and, after refusing to serve Napoleon in northern Italy, spent the rest of his life in poverty in Sicily. **108, 109, 141**

Marchand, Jean-Baptiste (1863–1934)

French soldier and an explorer in Africa. Heading an expedition in 1898 to lay claim to a part of Sudan, he was confronted by the British in what is known as the Fashoda incident. He fought against the Chinese Boxer Rebellion (1900) and in World War I. **88**

Marquette, Father Jacques (1637–75)

French Jesuit missionary who traveled with Louis Jolliet down the Mississippi River in 1673. After studying Indian languages in Quebec (1666–68), Marquette helped to establish two Jesuit missions, at Sault Ste Marie (1668) and St Ignace (1671). In May 1673 he joined Jolliet on his expedition to follow the Mississippi River to its mouth, and came to within 640 miles (640 kilometers) of reaching it. In 1674 he set out to establish a mission among the Illinois Indians, but, after camping for the winter, illness forced him to return to St Ignace. He died on the journey at the mouth of the river now called Père Marquette. **132–33**

Marsden, Samuel (1764–1838)

British clergyman, a leading colonist in Australia and New Zealand, and chaplain of a convict colony. In 1794 he emigrated to New South Wales, where he was influential in developing agriculture and improving education. In New Zealand he established the first European settlement and mission in 1814. **170, 171**

Marsigli, Count Louis-Ferdinand (1658–1730)

Italian soldier, naturalist, and oceanographer. After long service in the Austrian army, during which he was captured, he was demoted in 1704. Thereafter, he engaged in scientific study, including, off the Mediterranean coast of Provence, the first planned underwater exploration in 1706–8. He was the founder of the Accademia delle Scienze in Bologna (1712) and became a member of the Royal Society (1722), to which he was introduced by Sir Isaac Newton. **200–1**

Masson, Francis (1745–1805)

Scottish gardener and botanist, who traveled widely, collecting plants and bulbs on behalf of Kew Gardens, London. From Cape Town he made three journeys into the African interior (1772–74) and a fourth in 1786. He also went, in 1786, to the Canaries, Azores, Madeira and St Christopher, West Indies. Many houseplants common today in Europe were brought back from his travels. **86**

Mawson, Sir Douglas (1882–1958)

Australian geologist and Antarctic explorer. He accompanied Ernest Shackleton's expedition to the Antarctic in 1907–9 and was one of the party that reached the Magnetic South Pole. In 1911–14 he led the Australasian Antarctic Expedition, returning against all odds from a journey in which two companions died. He was appointed Professor of Geology and Mineralogy at the University of Adelaide in 1921, and in 1929–31 he led a joint British, Australian, and New Zealand Antarctic expedition. **194, 195**

McClintock, Sir Francis (1819–1907)

British naval Arctic explorer. He was a member of the search parties for Franklin sent out in 1848, 1850, and 1852. In 1857 he commanded the *Fox* and succeeded

in finding Franklin's remains. Later in his career he conducted soundings of the North Atlantic for the laying of electric cable, and in his eighties he advised Scott on preparations for his first expedition to the Antarctic in the *Discovery* (1901–4). **178**

McClure, Sir Robert John le Mesurier (1807–73)

British Arctic explorer. He served in George Back's expedition of 1836–37 and then in James Clark Ross's expedition in search of Franklin in 1848–49. In 1850, in command of his own ship, he sailed round to the west coast of America, east through the Bering Strait, and discovered two possible routes to the Atlantic. He and his crew were subsequently rescued from their ice-bound ship and returned to England, thus becoming the first to pass through the Northwest Passage, although not in only one ship. **179**

Mee, Margaret (1909–1988)

British botanical artist who made 15 arduous journeys by canoe in the Amazon forests to record the extraordinary plants she found there. She explored remote tributaries of the Amazon River, and produced paintings and drawings of remarkable quality, many of which are kept at Kew Gardens, London. **114**

Mendaña, de Neira, Alvaro de (1541–1614)

Spanish explorer who discovered the Solomon Islands in 1568 while searching for a great southern continent in the Pacific. A second expedition in 1595 aimed to establish a colony there, but failed dismally, with Mendaña dying in the Santa Cruz Islands, having failed to find the Solomons again. **152–53**

Moorcroft, William (1765–1825)

British vet who worked in India for the East India Company, and who pioneered much hitherto unknown country in the Himalayas. His travels took him to Tibet, Kashmir and later to Bukhara, where he almost certainly died. **54**

Nachtigal, Gustav (1834–85)

German explorer in Central Africa. He was sent on a mission to Borno in 1869, and visited the previously unknown regions of Tibesti and Borkou. From Borno he turned eastward and traveled by way of Chad and the Sudan and then back down the Nile to Khartoum in 1874. His journey was graphically described in his three-volume book, *Sahara und Sudan*. He was Consul General for the German Empire at Tunis until 1884, when he was sent to annex territory in West Africa, as a result of which Togo and Cameroon came under the German flag. He died on his return voyage. **84, 85**

Nansen, Fridtjof (1861–1930)

Norwegian explorer, scientist, and statesman. He crossed the Greenland icecap on foot in 1888, before turning his attentions to the frozen Arctic Ocean. He designed a ship that could withstand the Arctic ice and in which he could establish the course of the Arctic drift. The *Fram* entered the Arctic ice in September 1893, and emerged in June 1896, during which time detailed scientific experiments on the Arctic Ocean had been conducted. (Nansen himself had left the ship in March 1893 in an unsuccessful bid for the North Pole.) From then until 1914 Nansen mainly continued with his oceanographic studies, but in 1918 he became a Commissioner of the League of Nations. In the early 1920s he assisted in the organization of relief to the famine-stricken Russian people, for which work he was awarded the Nobel Peace Prize in 1923. He continued to work for the League of Nations until his death. **180, 181, 192, 193**

Nares, Sir George Strong (1831–1915)
British naval explorer. He served on the *Resolute* in its search for John Franklin (1850–54). After serving in the Crimea, he was employed in surveying work. He commanded the *Challenger* (1872–74) in its deep-sea exploration. In 1875–76 he commanded an expedition to the Arctic in an attempt to reach the North Pole. He later surveyed the Strait of Magellan. **180, 181, 207**

Narváez, Pánfilo de (c. 1480–1528)
Spanish *conquistador*. He was chief lieutenant to Diego de Velázquez in the conquest of Cuba in 1514. In 1520 Velázquez sent him to Mexico to arrest Hernán Cortés, but instead he was detained by Cortés until 1522. He returned to Spain and was commissioned to conquer Florida in 1526. Leaving Spain in 1527, Narváez reached Florida after a disastrous ten-month journey, but shipwreck and starvation brought an end to the expedition, and Narváez was among those who died as a result. **97, 122, 123**

Nicollet, Jean (1598–1642)
French explorer of North America who was the first European to reach Lake Michigan and what is now the American Midwest. Nicollet left France at the age of 20 and went to New France (Canada) to work for Samuel de Champlain. After living among the Algonquin Indians on the Ottawa River, learning their language and culture, he was sent to live among the Nipissing Indians in 1620. In 1624 he became their interpreter, and remained with them for nine years. On returning to Three Rivers Settlement, Nicollet was made official interpreter to the colony. In 1634 he joined an expedition into Huron territory, and traveled by canoe through the Straits of Mackinac into Lake Michigan and on to Green Bay. There he concluded a friendship treaty with the Winnebagoes and explored the area now known as Wisconsin. He returned to Quebec in 1634 and resumed his work as colonial interpreter. Nicollet drowned in 1642 when his boat capsized on the St Lawrence River. **127**

Niebuhr, Carsten (1733–1815)
German surveyor who joined a scientific expedition to Arabia, sponsored by the King of Denmark in 1761. Niebuhr was the sole survivor of the group of six, so the task of compiling the results of the expedition fell to him on his return to Denmark. His accounts of the expedition were published in 1772 and 1774. **50–51**

Niza, Marcos de (c. 1495–1558)
Spanish Franciscan missionary and explorer of the Americas who led an expedition into New Mexico in 1539. His belief that the Zuni civilization contained the fabulous wealth of the Seven Golden Cities of Cibola led to Coronado's expedition in 1540, on which Niza served as a guide. **124–25**

Nobile, Umberto (1885–1980)
Italian aviator and army officer who commanded the dirigible balloon *Norge* in its flight over the North Pole with Amundsen and 14 companions in 1926. A second expedition to the North Pole, in the airship *Italia*, ended in a crash. Seven of Nobile's crew lost their lives and he was subsequently held responsible by an Italian Commission of Enquiry. **182–83**

Nordenskjöld, Baron Nils (1832–1901)
Swedish explorer and scientist. A geologist, mineralogist, and mapmaker, he made several scientific expeditions to Spitsbergen (Svalbard), before, in 1870, leading an exploration of Greenland's inland ice-cap. In 1878–79 he and the crew of the *Vega* successfully sailed through the Northeast Passage. In his later years he gave support and encouragement to the young Fridtjof Nansen. **180, 181**

Nordenskjöld, Otto (1869–1928)
Swedish explorer (nephew of Nils Nordenskjöld). He studied geology at university and traveled in Tierra del Fuego and Alaska. In 1901 he led an expedition to the Antarctic. He explored the Peruvian and Chilean Andes in 1920–21. **191**

Orellana, Francisco de (c. 1490–c. 1546)
Spanish soldier who undertook the first exploration of the Amazon River. Orellana was appointed lieutenant to Gonzalo Pizarro on his expedition to explore the area east of Quito (1540), but he left the main party after being sent ahead with 50 soldiers and a brigantine to find provisions. Convinced of the impossibility of returning to Pizarro, Orellana drifted with the current until he reached the mouth of the river which he subsequently named the Amazon. He returned to Spain, where he sought rights over the lands he had discovered, but was drowned near the mouth of the Amazon on his return journey. **98, 99**

Oñate, Juan de (c. 1550–after 1625)
Spanish *conquistador* and leading figure in the conquest of New Mexico. In 1598 he crossed the Rio Grande with a large colonizing party and proceeded to establish settlements north of the river. He led further expeditions westward, and reached the mouth of the Colorado River in 1605. He was appointed Governor of New Mexico, but resigned in 1608. **124, 125**

Oxley, John Joseph William Molesworth (c. 1785–1828)
Explorer and surveyor in Australia. Born in England, Oxley joined the navy in 1799 and spent 12 years sailing between Britain and Australia. In 1812 he was appointed Surveyor-General of New South Wales, and led two expeditions into the interior with the aim of tracing the Macquarie and Lachlan Rivers. Although he failed to achieve his objective, he found the rich Liverpool Plains and several hitherto unknown rivers. In 1819 he turned to carrying out coastal surveys, and explored about 700 miles (1127 kilometers) of the east coast between 1823 and 1824. **164, 165**

Paez, Pedro (1564–1622)
Spanish Jesuit missionary, sent to Abyssinia (Ethiopia) in 1603. Paez converted the negus to Roman Catholicism, which caused conflict with the native priests. In 1613 he visited the source of the Blue Nile at Gojam. **66**

Palgrave, William (1826–88)
British Jesuit priest, explorer, scholar, and spy for Napoleon III of France. Palgrave was the first European to cross Arabia from west to east. **52, 53**

Palmer, Nathaniel Brown (1799–1877)
US sea captain. In 1820, while on a sealing voyage, he became the first to sight the Antarctic mainland, which he believed to be only an island. He also discovered the South Orkney Islands. **186, 187**

Park, Mungo (1771–1806)
Scottish explorer of West Africa. After working as a medical officer on a ship engaged in the East India trade, he was asked by the African Association to explore the course of the Niger River. He explored 280 miles (450 kilometers) of the upper Niger and wrote an account of his exploration, *Travels in the Interior of Africa* (1799). Returning to Britain, he practised as a doctor until being asked by the government to undertake a further expedition to discover the course of the Niger downstream from Ségou. The expedition in 1805–6 was a disaster, with Park losing his life in the Bussa Rapids, either by drowning or in a fight with local tribesmen. **69, 70**

Parry, Sir William Edward (1790–1855)
British explorer and navigator. In 1810 he was sent by the Royal Navy to the Arctic to protect the whale population, and later published a book on the astronomical observations he made while there. He led four expeditions to the Arctic between 1818 and 1827, on the first of which he navigated more than half the length of the Northwest Passage. On his final expedition, in 1827, he attempted unsuccessfully to reach the North Pole by sledge from Spitsbergen (Svalbard). **176, 177**

Peary, Robert Edwin (1856–1920)
US Arctic explorer. He made the first of several explorations of Greenland in 1886, and between 1891 and 1902 undertook much valuable work, along with his wife, mapping the north coast. In 1902 he reached a then furthest north, which he was to extend in 1906. In 1908 he embarked on an expedition to the North Pole, which he reached on April 6, 1909. A dispute then raged as to whether he or Frederick Cook had reached the Pole first, but Peary has subsequently been awarded that accolade. **180, 181**

Philby, "Harry" St John (1885–1960)
British explorer and Arabist who crossed the Rub 'al Khali, or "Empty Quarter," of Arabia two years after the first crossing by a European was made by Bertram Thomas. Philby is remembered for his contributions to the fields of cartography, archeology, and linguistics, and as the father of Kim Philby, the double agent. He joined the Indian Civil Service in 1907 and went on to work on diplomatic missions in the Middle East before becoming an independent businessman in Arabia. In 1930 he converted to Islam and he remained in Arabia until 1939, when he returned to England to enter politics. However, he was imprisoned in 1940 for his opposition to the war and returned to Arabia in 1945, from where he was banished in 1955 for criticizing the Saudi regime. **53**

Pike, Zebulon Montgomery (1779–1813)
US soldier and explorer. Born in New Jersey, he joined the army at 15 and served at a number of frontier posts before leading, in 1805–6, an expedition in search of the source of the Mississippi River. He mapped the area with some accuracy for the first time, but failed to locate the river's source. His next expedition, in 1806–7, took him up the Arkansas River to the Colorado mountains, where he discovered Pikes Peak. The journey ended in New Mexico when he and his party were captured by the Spanish. On his return he wrote his *Account of the Expeditions to the Sources of the Mississippi and Through the Western Parts of Louisiana* (1810), which earned him some fame. He was promoted to Brigadier-General but was killed in battle during an attack on Toronto in 1813. **145**

Pinzón, Vicente Yánez (*c.* 1460–*c.* 1519)

Spanish explorer and navigator who commanded the *Niña* during Columbus's first voyage to America (1492). In 1499 he led an expedition which reached the coast of Brazil, of which he was made Governor. He was the first to report the mouth of the Amazon, and he led several futher expeditions to explore the coasts of South and Central America. **92, 93**

Pizarro, Francisco (*c.* 1476–1541)

Spanish *conquistador* who led the conquest of Peru. The illegitimate son of a soldier, he served in the Spanish army in Italy (1498–1501) and emigrated to Hispaniola in 1502. For the next 20 years he participated in various expeditions in the Caribbean, and in 1524, together with Diego de Almagro, he began to plan the conquest of Peru. After many setbacks they sailed from Panama in 1531, marching inland and taking Peru from the Incas by force. In 1535 Pizarro founded the city of Lima, but in 1538 he fell out with Almagro and open hostilities developed. Pizarro was killed by followers of Almagro in Lima. **98–99**

Pizarro, Gonzalo (*c.* 1512–48)

Spanish *conquistador*, the youngest brother of Francisco. After taking part in the Peruvian conquest in the 1530s, Gonzalo led an expedition across the Andes to the Napo River. In 1544, in defiance of Spain, he set himself up as Governor and Captain-General of Peru. He was beheaded for treason in 1548 after his defeat at the battle of Jaquijaguana. **98, 99**

Polo, Marco (1254–1324)

Italian merchant, traveler, and travel writer, whose claims to have reached China are disputed by some scholars. According to his own account, as a boy he went with his father, Nicolò, and uncle, Maffeo, on a trading mission (1275) that took them to the court of Kublai Khan, the Mongol ruler of China. While there he appears to have traveled widely, returning to Venice by ship in 1295. In 1298 he became involved in a war with Genoa and was taken prisoner, during which time he compiled an account of his travels which remained an important Western source of information on Asia for nearly 600 years. He was soon released and returned to Venice, where he spent the remainder of his life. **30–31**

Ponce de León, Juan (*c.* 1460–1521)

Spanish *conquistador* who discovered the Florida peninsula in 1513 while searching for the legendary fountain of youth. On the same expedition he discovered the Gulf Stream, which was to be of great benefit to transatlantic shipping. After a period in Spain, he returned to Florida in 1521 with a colonizing expedition and was fatally wounded when local Indians attacked his men. **120, 121**

Przhevalsky, Nikolai (1839–88)

Russian soldier and explorer whose travels in Central and Eastern Asia helped to develop European knowledge of the area. Przhevalsky was a keen naturalist and collected many botanical and zoological specimens on his expeditions. He is particularly remembered for discovering the wild camel and the wild horse, which came to be named after him. **60–61**

Ptolemy, or Claudius Ptolemaeus (*c.* 85–*c.* 150)

Egyptian-born Greek astronomer and geographer. He charted many new stars and his remarkable *Almagest*

(*c.* 1150) influenced astronomy for the next 1400 years. His *Guide to Geography*, which included Africa and Asia, also had great influence. He devised new mathematical theorems and proofs, and wrote *Optica*, a treatise on optics. **9, 19**

Pytheas of Massalia (4th century BC)

Greek navigator and geographer whose travels are reported by Strabo (Pytheas's own treatises having been lost). He appears to have sailed around the coast of Great Britain, visited a land six days north of the mainland, and to have visited the coast of northern Europe. His observations on the agricultural customs of the people in these northerly lands ties in with subsequent archeological findings. He also observed the connection between the tides and the moon, and was one of the first to fix latitudes. **12, 13**

Quiros, Pedro Fernández de (*c.* 1560–1614)

Portuguese navigator and explorer of the Pacific. After serving aboard Spanish trading ships in the Pacific, Quiros accompanied Mendaña on his voyage in search of the Solomon Islands in 1595. After Mendaña's death, Quiros led the remains of the expedition to the Philippines. In 1605 he led an expedition apparently in search of the legendary *Terra Australis Incognita*, but found instead the islands of Espíritu Santo (New Hebrides). **152–53**

Radisson, Pierre Esprit (*c.* 1630–1710)

French-born Canadian fur trader and explorer. After having a quantity of furs confiscated by the French authorities, Radisson and his brother-in-law, Groseilliers (*c.* 1632–1710) offered their services to the British. After a trip to England to gain financial support for further fur-trading ventures, Radisson returned to Hudson Bay in 1670 and established Fort Nelson. He was instrumental in convincing George III to charter the Hudson's Bay Company in 1670, but soon fell out with its administrators and led a French expedition against the English forts on Hudson Bay. Rejoining the Company in 1684, he became a British subject in 1688. **130, 131**

Rae, John (1813–93)

Scottish Arctic surveyor and qualified doctor. He worked for the Hudson's Bay Company at Moose Factory before sailing to Repulse Bay in 1846 and surveying over 700 miles (1100 kilometers) of coastline. He joined Richardson's search for Franklin in 1848, and explored and mapped a further 700 miles of coastline on the south side of Victoria Island, returning in 1851. In 1853 he commanded another expedition which proved King William's Land to be an island. He later traveled across Iceland, and in Greenland and Canada, surveying routes for telegraph lines. **178**

Raleigh, Sir Walter (*c.* 1552–1618)

English soldier, explorer, courtier, and man of letters. A favorite of Elizabeth I, he organized expeditions to North America and is credited with introducing the potato plant and tobacco to England. After the accession of James I in 1603, he was found guilty of conspiring against the king and imprisoned in the Tower of London, where he wrote his *History of the World* (1614). In 1616 he persuaded the authorities to allow him to undertake an expedition to the Orinoco River, in search of gold. When this proved both unsuccessful and politically embarrassing, he was arrested and brought back to England to be executed under the terms of his original sentence. **100, 101, 126**

Ricci, Matteo (1552–1610)

Italian Jesuit missionary and cartographer who settled in China in 1583. He spent the rest of his life there teaching science, translating many Western works on science into Chinese and writing several of his own, including a Mandarin–Portuguese dictionary. His missionary work was based on a search for common ground between Christianity and the Confucian tradition, which scandalized other missionaries. It earned him great respect among the Chinese, however, and in 1610 he received an imperial summons to Peking, becoming the first Jesuit to enter that city. **40–41**

Roggeveen, Jacob (1659–1729)

Dutch explorer of the Pacific who was the first European to visit Samoa, Easter Island, and the Society Islands. After studying theology and law in Holland, he worked in the Dutch East Indies for the Department of Justice. His expedition to the Pacific in search of the great southern continent (1721–22) took him around Cape Horn and further south than anyone before him. He saw enormous icebergs which he took to be *Terra Australis Incognita*. **155**

Rohlfs, Gerhard (1831–96)

German explorer who traveled widely in North Africa. He was the first European to traverse northwest Africa, from Tripoli to Lagos (1865–67). In 1873–74 and 1878–79 he traveled in the Libyan Desert, reaching the oases of Kufra in 1879. **84, 85**

Ross, Sir James Clark (1800–62)

British naval officer and explorer. He took part in six Arctic expeditions in search of a Northwest Passage, (under the command of his uncle, John Ross, and Edward Parry), and in 1831 was the first to identify the position of the Magnetic North Pole. In 1839 he turned his attentions to the Antarctic, discovering what was to become the Ross Sea in 1841. **177, 189, 190**

Ross, Sir John (1777–1856)

British naval Arctic explorer. His first expedition in 1818 was to explore Baffin Bay and search for a Northwest Passage. His second, in 1829, produced valuable geographic and oceanographic data. In 1850 he led an unsuccessful search for John Franklin. **176, 177, 202, 203**

Schouten, Willem Cornelis (*c.* 1580–1625)

Dutch navigator who accompanied Jacob Le Maire on a voyage to find a new trade route to the East in 1616. They became the first to sail round Cape Horn, named after Schouten's birthplace, Hoorn. **154, 155**

Schweinfurth, Georg August (1836–1925)

German explorer and ethnologist in East and Central Africa. In 1863–66 he traveled to the area between the Red Sea and the Nile, and in 1868 he explored the White Nile and the watery wastes of the Bahr el Ghazal region. He traveled overland, discovering the Uele River (1870) and encountering the pygmy Akka people. Subsequent journeys took him to the Libyan Desert (1873–74), the Arabian Desert (1876–88), and Eritrea (1891, 1892, and 1894). His studies of African history, art, and artifacts contributed greatly to European knowledge of the continent. **78, 84**

Scoresby, William Jnr (1789–1857)

British scientist and Arctic explorer. He made several voyages to Greenland between 1799 and 1822, initially as a young boy accompanying his whaler father. During these voyages he made scientific observations and collected information about the little-known coast of Greenland. His decision in 1823 to enter the Church put paid to further Arctic voyages, but he continued as an active member of the British Association for the Advancement of Science. **176**

Scott, Robert Falcon (1868–1912)
British Antarctic explorer and naval captain. His first expedition was in 1901–4, in the *Discovery*, during which he led an unsuccessful expedition to the South Pole. In 1910 he embarked on a second attempt, leaving his base at Ross Island on November 1, 1911. He reached the Pole on January 17, 1912, only to find that Roald Amundsen had got there first. Beset by blizzards, Scott and his party perished during their return journey. His diaries were published as *Scott's Last Expedition* (1913). **191, 192–93**

Scylax of Caryanda (late 6th century BC)
Greek historian and explorer, who traveled, on behalf of Darius I of Persia, down the Indus to the Indian Ocean, west along the coast of Baluchistan and Arabia, and back up the Red Sea. Scylax's account of his journey is referred to by Aristotle. **12, 13**

Shackleton, Sir Ernest Henry (1874–1922)
British Antarctic explorer. He was a member of Scott's *Discovery* expedition (1901–4). In 1907–9 he led his own expedition, getting within 97 miles (155 kilometers) of the South Pole. In 1914 he led another expedition, with the intention of crossing the Antarctic Peninsula, but his ship was crushed in ice in the Ross Sea. The expedition members reached Elephant Island, from where Shackleton and five companions sailed to South Georgia Island. Following many difficulties, he rescued the rest of his team. He died while embarking on his third Antarctic expedition. **192, 193, 194–95**

Smith, John (c. 1580–1631)
English soldier, explorer, and colonist who played a leading part in establishing Jamestown settlement in Virginia. He was instrumental in obtaining maize from the local Indians, thus saving the colony from starvation during the early years of hardship. He first traveled to Virginia in 1605, and undertook a number of river surveys, hoping to find a river route to the Pacific. In 1608 he was elected leader of the Virginia colony. **136, 137**

Soto, Hernando de (c. 1496–1542)
Spanish *conquistador* who fought in Peru with Francisco Pizarro and went on to lead an expedition into the North American interior. Leaving Spain in 1538, he landed in Florida in 1539 and traveled through present-day Georgia, North and South Carolina, Tennessee, Alabama, Mississippi, Arkansas, and Louisiana. In 1541 he became the first European to reach the Mississippi River. **122, 123**

Speke, John Hanning (1827–64)
British soldier and explorer of Africa. After service in India, during which time he explored the Himalayas and crossed into Tibet, he led expeditions in Africa with Richard Burton. During the second of these he discovered Lake Victoria (1858) and asserted it (correctly) to be a source of the Nile. This claim was disputed by Burton and was not resolved during Speke's life, which ended with an accident in which he shot himself on the day before he was due to take part in a public debate with Burton. **72–73, 74, 75**

Spruce, Richard (1817–1893)
British botanist and explorer who spent 15 years in South America (1849–64) gathering botanical specimens, mapping rivers, and classifying the vocabularies of 21 Amazonian languages. Spruce, a schoolmaster's son, was employed by leading botanists to send plants home to Britain where they were named, classified, and distributed. **108–9**

Stanley, Sir Henry Morton (1841–1904)
Welsh explorer and journalist. Born John Rowlands, he survived a poverty-stricken childhood before sailing as a cabin boy to New Orleans in 1859. He was adopted by a wealthy man who, unfortunately, died without making provision for his young charge, but whose name Stanley took. Stanley fought in the Confederate Army in the American Civil War, and in 1864 enlisted in the US navy. He then embarked on a career as a freelance writer, traveling across parts of the United States, through Asia Minor and Tibet and North Africa. In 1870 the *New York Herald* sent him to central Africa to find David Livingstone. This he accomplished in 1871. In 1874–77 he went on a second expedition to Africa, during which he crossed the continent from east to west, following the course of the Congo (Zaire) River, and establishing its navigability. His work from 1879–84 led to the establishment of the Congo Free State on behalf of Belgium. His expedition of 1887–89 up the Congo to rescue Emin Pasha resulted in a massive loss of life and did not add a great deal to the geographical knowledge of the area. In his later years Stanley married, traveled on lecture tours and, from 1895 to 1900, served as an MP for a London constituency. **78–79, 80–81, 88**

Stark, Dame Freya Madeline (1893–1993)
British explorer and writer, who traveled widely in the Middle East, especially Arabia. Her explorations in the Hadramaut resulted in her famous book *The Southern Gates of Arabia* (1936). *The Valley of the Assassins* (1934) describes her journeys in Persia (Iran). **52, 53**

Stefansson, Vilhjalmur (1879–1962)
Canadian Arctic explorer of Icelandic descent. He studied theology and anthropology at Harvard University, and subsequently spent many years studying various aspects of the Arctic region, including the culture of the Inuit people of northern Canada (1906–12). From 1913 to 1918 he was continuously above the Arctic Circle, living off the land and exploring huge areas of Canada and Alaska. He discovered Borden and Brock Islands. **179**

Stein, Sir Marc Aurel (1852–1943)
British archeologist, explorer, and orientalist who made numerous journeys in the region between the Hindu Kush and the Gobi Desert in central Asia. Born in Hungary, he was employed by the Education Service in India, becoming Principal of Oriental College, Lahore, and registrar of Punjab University (1888–99). He later transferred to the Archeological Survey, and between 1906 and 1942 made explorations in Central Asia and Persia. **61**

Strabo (c. 64 BC–AD 20)
Roman historian and geographer. He traveled widely, collecting material for *Historical Sketches*, most of which have been lost. His *Geographical Sketches*, which survived almost intact, contain geographical and historical information on countries in Europe, Asia, and Africa. **19**

Stuart, John McDouall (1815–66)
Scottish-born explorer of Australia. In 1844–45 he accompanied Charles Sturt during his unsuccessful attempt to cross the continent, and in 1861–62 he led the first European expedition to cross the continent from south to north. **168, 169**

Sturt, Charles (1795–1869)
British explorer of Australia. Born in India and educated in England, he joined the army in 1813 and fought in the Napoleonic War. He went to Australia with his regiment in 1827 and undertook his first exploration in 1828 to trace the Macquarie River. He found the Murray–Darling system, which he explored thoroughly. In 1835 he was made Surveyor-General of South Australia. Convinced that he would find an inland sea, he led an expedition to the edge of the Simpson Desert (1844–46) but was forced to retreat. He retired to England in 1853. **164–65, 166, 167**

Tasman, Abel Janszoon (1603–c. 1659)
Dutch maritime explorer whose voyages added significantly to European knowledge of the Pacific and Indian oceans. Joining the Dutch East India Company in 1632, he captained ships in the East Indies before being sent in search of a trade route across the Pacific to Chile in 1642. On this voyage he discovered Tasmania, New Zealand, Tonga, and the Fiji Islands, and he was sent on a further two expeditions. However, his voyages were regarded as economic failures by the Company, and he left it in disgrace, becoming instead a successful merchant in Batavia. **154–55**

Thesiger, Wilfred Patrick (1910–2003)
British soldier, explorer, and writer who explored in Ethiopia, Sudan, and Arabia in the 1930s and 1940s. He explored the Danakil Desert in 1933–34 and served in the Political Service in Sudan in 1935–40. After serving in the Special Air Service during the Second World War, he followed in the footsteps of Thomas and Philby, twice crossing the "Empty Quarter" of Arabia. His works include *Arabian Sands* (1959) and *The Marsh Arabs* (1964). **52, 53, 88**

Thompson, David (1770–1857)
British-born Canadian fur trader and explorer. He joined the Hudson's Bay Company in 1784, studied surveying, and journeyed to Lake Athabasca and the Mississippi headwaters. In 1807 he established the first trading post on the Columbia River, traveling and charting the length of the river to the Pacific by 1811. He later charted the US–Canada boundary. His remarkably detailed maps were to be used for much of the 19th century. **142–43**

Thomson, Joseph (1858–95)
Scottish geologist, naturalist, and explorer of Africa. He was sent by the Royal Geographical Society to East Central Africa in 1878, taking over command of the expedition after the death of Keith Johnston. He led his party to the north end of Lake Nyasa, and from there to Lake Tanganyika. His attempt to reach the Congo (Zaire) was thwarted by tribal rivalries, but he discovered Lake Rukwa. In 1882–83 he investigated the possibility of a trade route from the Kenyan coast to Lake Victoria. In 1885 he undertook an expedition to Sokoto to arrange trading links, and in 1890, on behalf of the British South Africa Company, he traveled between Lakes Nyasa and Bangweulu and the Zambezi River, concluding treaties giving the company rights over the territory (now Zambia). **82–83**

Thomson, Sir Charles Wyville (1830–82)
Scottish naturalist who became one of the first marine biologists. After studying medicine and teaching botany and zoology, Thomson became increasingly interested in the study of marine invertebrates. In 1868–69 he joined two deep-sea dredging expeditions in the North Sea and found many new invertebrates, as well as some that had been thought to be extinct. In 1872 Thomson led the scientific team aboard HMS *Challenger* on the expedition which was to provide an enormous quantity of data for research in the fields of oceanography and marine biology. **203, 207**

Tinné, Alexandrine (1839–69)
Dutch explorer in northeast Africa. In 1862 she traveled (with her mother and aunt) up the White Nile and into the Bahr el Ghazal region, before returning to Khartoum. Undeterred by the deaths of her mother and aunt she set out, in 1869, from Tripoli, heading for Lake Chad and intending to travel to the upper Nile, but was murdered by Tuareg in the desert. **78, 84**

Urdaneta, André de (1498–1568)
Spanish monk and navigator who in 1565 established a successful sea-route from the Philippines to Mexico. This contributed significantly to the successful colonization and settlement of the Philippines by Spain, and opened up new markets in the East for Peruvian and Mexican products. **152, 153**

Vaca, Álvar Núñez Cabeza de (c. 1490–c. 1560)
Spanish explorer of the area now known as the Gulf region of Texas, whose stories of the legendary golden cities of Cíbola probably inspired the later explorations by Soto and Coronado. He traveled to what is now Tampa Bay, Florida, in 1528 with a Spanish expedition under Pánfilo de Narváez, and went on with three others to explore the land to the west of the Gulf. Living among nomadic Indians and suffering great hardships for eight years, he returned with stories of a new El Dorado lying somewhere beyond the regions he had explored. He spent the next few years in South America, where he was appointed Governor of Río de la Plata, but he was usurped by Domingo Martinez de Irala and deported to Spain in 1545, and subsequently banished to Africa. **122, 123**

Valdivia, Pedro de (c. 1498–1553)
Spanish conqueror and Governor of Chile who founded the cities of Santiago and Concepción. After serving with the Spanish Army in Italy and Flanders, he was sent to South America in 1534 where he fought in the Peruvian civil war alongside Francisco Pizarro in 1538. In 1540, with 150 Spaniards and some Indians, he set off across the coastal desert of northern Chile, defeating a large force of Indians in the Valley of Chile and founding Santiago in 1541. He continued to extend Spanish rule south and was eventually made Governor of Chile. He was killed in 1553 during a campaign against the Araucanian Indians. **98, 99**

Vancouver, George (1757–98)
British navigator and explorer of the Pacific. After accompanying Captain Cook on two of his voyages, Vancouver was made commander of his own expedition in 1791 and ordered to survey the northwest coast of North America and to search for a passage from the Pacific to Hudson Bay. He spent three years making a detailed survey but found no passage to the east. As part of his exploration of the area he circumnavigated

Vancouver Island. His work helped to establish British claims to the area, at Spain's expense. **140, 141**

Varthema, Lodovico de (c. 1468–1517)
Italian adventurer who spent five years traveling through the Middle East and Asia (1502–7). He spent part of this time disguised as a Muslim and became the first known Christian to make a pilgrimage to Mecca and to reach the Spice Islands (Moluccas). Varthema wrote a detailed account of his journey, including observations of the people and cultures he encountered, and this brought him considerable fame during his lifetime. **39, 50**

Velázquez, Diego (1465–1524)
Spanish *conquistador* and first Governor of Cuba (1514–21 and 1523–24). He sailed with Columbus to Hispaniola in 1493 and commanded the expedition that conquered and colonized Cuba (1511–14). He commissioned three expeditions to the Mexican coast, placing Hernán Cortés in charge of the third venture in 1519. Cortés declared himself independent of Velázquez, who then sent Pánfilo Narváez in 1520 and Cristóbel de Olid in 1524 to compel Cortés to return to Cuba, but both were defeated. **96**

Verrazano, Giovanni da (c. 1485–c. 1528)
Italian explorer of the New World. He explored the Atlantic coast of North America in 1524 in the service of France and discovered what is now New York harbor. His journey took him from Cape Fear to Maine, and Verrazano mistakenly believed he had discovered a passage to the East. He was killed on a later expedition to the Caribbean. **120, 121**

Vespucci, Amerigo (1454–1512)
Florentine navigator and explorer who was the first to consider America to be a separate continent, and after whom it came to be named. After a period spent as an agent of the Medici Bank, Vespucci was sent to Seville where he met and became friends with Columbus. He crossed the Atlantic with Alonso de Ojeda in 1499–1500, and made several further expeditions along the coasts of Central and South America in the service of Spain and Portugal. **92, 93**

Walker, Thomas (1715–1794)
American land speculator and public official who rediscovered a route through the Cumberland Mountains (the Cumberland Gap) in 1748. From 1752, when he was elected to Virginia's House of Burgesses, he served as a public official in various posts, his last being as a member of Virginia's House of Delegates in the 1780s. **137**

Wallace, Alfred Russell (1823–1913)
British naturalist who developed a theory of natural selection independently of, but at the same time as, Charles Darwin. In 1848 he set out for the Amazon Basin, where he spent six years collecting specimens with fellow naturalists Henry Bates and Richard Spruce. On the journey back to England he lost his entire collection when his ship sank. This did not, however, deter him from traveling to the Far East, where he spent the years 1854 to 1862 collecting specimens in the Malay (Indonesian) Archipelago. While there, he formulated a theory of natural selection, his writings influencing Darwin who was working on similar theories. Wallace also demonstrated a division between Asian and Australian fauna, which came to be called the "Wallace Line." **62, 108–9**

Wallis, Samuel (1728–95)
British naval officer who captained the *Dolphin* on a voyage across the Pacific in 1767–68, which opened up a hitherto unknown part of the ocean to European exploration. He encountered numerous islands, including Tahiti. He is particularly remembered for the attention he paid to the health and well-being of his crews, managing the whole voyage without a serious outbreak of scurvy. He wrote an account of his voyage on his return to England, and was appointed an extra commissioner of the navy in 1782, which position he held until his death. **156**

Weddell, James (1787–1834)
British mariner. On a whaling voyage in the Southern Ocean Weddell, aided by unusually open ice conditions, discovered, in 1823, what subsequently became known as the Weddell Sea. The most southerly point he reached was 74°15′S 34°17′W, a record unbeaten for almost a century. **186–87**

Whymper, Edward (1840–1911)
British mountaineer. After conquering many previously unscaled mountains in the Alps, including the Matterhorn, Whymper traveled to the Andes in 1879. He succeeded in climbing Chimborazo, Cotopaxi, and many other mountains in Ecuador. His study of the phenomenon of mountain sickness showed that it was related to atmospheric pressure. **112**

Wilkes, Charles (1798–1877)
American naval officer and explorer. He was despatched on a surveying expedition of the south seas by the American Congress in 1836, in the course of which he made several sightings of the Antarctic continent. Wilkes Land is named after him. His subsequent circumnavigation of the world took him north through the Pacific, up the Californian coast, and back to New York, via the Cape of Good Hope. He spent the next 27 years working on a report of his voyage. **188, 189**

Yermak, Timofeyevich (d. 1585)
Cossack leader who, after being driven out of the Volga River area by government forces, led an expedition over the Urals and into western Siberia in 1541. Enlisting the support of the tsar, Yermak managed to occupy Iskir (now Tobolsk) and keep the forces of Kuchum Khan at bay until 1584, when Yermak was drowned during an ambush. Yermak's expedition opened up Siberia for Russian conquest and made him a Russian folk hero. **46–47**

Younghusband, Sir Francis (1863–1942)
British explorer and soldier who led an expedition to Tibet in 1903, which resulted in the Anglo-Tibetan Treaty of 1904. Born in India, Younghusband joined the army in 1882 and traveled extensively in Asia, especially in Tibet and northern India. Through his expeditions he made important contributions to geographical knowledge. **57, 60**

Zheng Ho (1371–1435)
Chinese seafaring explorer. He became a eunuch in order to be allowed to serve in the royal household. When Ch'eng Tsu became emperor in 1403 he revised China's previous policy of isolationism and, over the next 20 years, despatched Zheng Ho on voyages all over the Far East, and as far west as the Persian Gulf and the East African coast. In 1433 Zheng Ho made one further voyage, in which he consolidated his previous discoveries. **33**

Time Chart of Exploration

The expeditions included in this time chart are referred to in the main text.

Asia	Africa	Europe	Rest of the World
	c. **2300 BC** Harkhuf led expeditions up the Nile to Yam (southern Nubia).		
	1501–1479 BC Explorations to Punt took place under Egyptian Queen Hatshepsut.		*c.* **1000 BC** Colonization of Samoa and Tonga by Polynesians from Fiji.
c. **515 BC** Scylax reconnoitered lower reaches of the Indus via the Kabul River.	*c.* **600 BC** Pharaoh Necho II's Phoenician fleet searched for a new route from the Red Sea to the Mediterranean.		
	c. **470 BC** Hanno of Carthage sailed through Strait of Gibraltar to west coast of Africa.	**5th century BC** Himilco voyaged in search of the tin islands (probably the Scilly Isles).	
c. **334–323 BC** Alexander the Great extended his empire from the Mediterranean to the Himalayas.		*c.* **340 BC** Pytheas circumnavigated the British Isles.	
c. **146 BC** Eudoxus sailed from the Red Sea to India.	*c.* **140 BC** Eudoxus sailed from the Black Sea to Morocco in an attempt to circumnavigate Africa from west to east.		
c. **138–116 BC** Chang Chi'en traveled along the Silk Road beyond the Jade Gates, reaching Peshawar.			
25–24 BC Aelius Gallus led expedition in Arabian Desert.	**20 BC** Cornelius Balbus traveled 1000 miles (1600 kilometers) south from Tripoli.		
AD 14–37 Hippalus sailed from the Red Sea to the mouth of the Indus.	**AD 61–63** Pretorian Guards marched up the Nile beyond Merowe.		
		c. **AD 150** Ptolemy published his *Guide to Geography*.	
AD 399–414 Fu-Hsien traveled south of Takla Makan. Returned via Ceylon (Sri Lanka) and Java.			*c.* **AD 300** Polynesians from Samoa and Tonga reached Marquesas Islands.
AD 629–45 Hsüan-Tsang crossed the Pamirs to India.			
		c. **AD 800** Norse occupation of the Shetland Islands, Hebrides, Orkneys, and Faeroes.	*c.* **AD 800** Polynesians reached New Zealand.
		c. **AD 860** Gardar Svarvarsson discovered and circumnavigated Iceland.	
		c. **AD 865** Floki Vilgerdason attempted to settle in Iceland and named the island.	
			AD 986 Norsemen under Bjarni Herjolfsson sighted coast of North America.
			1003 Leif Eiríksson explored coast of Newfoundland and Labrador.
1245–47 Giovanni del Carpini traveled through Poland and Russia to Mongolia.			
1253 William of Rubruck traveled through the Crimea to the Mongol capital in the Karakorams.			
1269 Nicolò and Maffeo Polo returned from their nine-year journey to the court of the Great Khan.			
1271–95 Marco Polo traveled through Asia.			
1325–48 Ibn Battuta traveled from Tangier across North Africa to Palestine and Mecca; then through Asia to India, Sumatra, and China.	**1349–54** Ibn Battuta explored part of the Niger River and visited Timbuktu.		
1405–33 Zheng Ho commanded seven voyages from China to the South China Sea, Indian Ocean, Persian Gulf, and Red Sea.	**1433** Portuguese rounded Cape Bojador.		
	1445 Portuguese rounded Cape Verde.		
	1474 Portuguese crossed Equator.		
	1488 Bartholomeu Dias rounded Cape of Good Hope.		

1491 – 1650

Asia	Africa	Central and South America	North America
		1492 Columbus sailed to the West Indies searching for westward route to the Orient. **1498** Columbus reached the mouth of the Orinoco River. **1499–1501** Vespucci explored the northern coast of South America. **1499** Pinzón sailed along the coast of Guyana and northward. **1499** Vespucci reached Gulf of Venezuela and mouth of Amazon. **1500** Cabral blown off course to Brazil, which he claimed for Portugal.	**1497** John Cabot was the first recorded European since the Norsemen to see Newfoundland.
1497–99 Da Gama discovered the sea route from Europe to the East via the Cape of Good Hope to Calicut in India.	**1498** Da Gama sailed up East African coast to Mombasa *en route* to India.		
1502–8 Varthema was first Christian to visit the holy city of Mecca, and first European to reach the Moluccas (Spice Islands). **1511** Albuquerque captured the city of Malacca, advancing Portuguese influence in the East Indies.			**1500–2** Gaspar and Miguel Corte Real explored coasts of Labrador and Newfoundland.
		1513 Balboa crossed the Isthmus of Panama. **1520** Magellan sailed into the Pacific by way of the Strait of Magellan. **1519–21** Cortés and his *conquistadores* conquered Aztecs in Mexico.	**1513** Ponce de León discovered Florida. **1524** Verazzano explored coast from South Carolina to Newfoundland. **1525** Gomez explored coast from Florida to southern Newfoundland. **1525** Ayllón attempted to establish a colony in South Carolina. **1527** Rut sailed from Newfoundland coast to Santo Domingo. **1528–36** Narváez traveled in Florida; Vaca eventually reached Mexico overland. **1534** Cartier explored Gulf of St Lawrence. **1535–36** Cartier traveled up St Lawrence River to site of modern Montreal. **1539–40** Ulloa explored Gulf of California. **1539–42** Soto reached the Mississippi from Florida. **1540–42** Coronado's expedition reached central Kansas and the Grand Canyon. **1542–43** Cabrillo extended exploration of west coast north to Monterey Bay.
		1532–35 Pizarro and his *conquistadores* decimated the Inca Empire. **1535–37** Almagro crossed the Andes to become first European to reach Chile. **1539** Benalcázar, Quesada, and Federmann met at Bogotá in Colombia. **1539** Fray Marcos and Esteban explored northward from Mexico. **1540–42** Orellana traveled down the Amazon from the Napo River to the sea. **1541–46** Valdivia founded the city of Santiago in Chile, and explored south of the Río Bío-Bío. **1549** Jesuits began to arrive in Brazil.	
1549 Xavier sailed to Japan. **1553–54** Chancellor traveled overland to Moscow. **1557** Jenkinson traveled down the Volga to the Caspian Sea, and east to Bukhara. **1561–64** Jenkinson traveled down the western shore of the Caspian Sea.			
1581–82 Newbery was the first Englishman to travel down the Euphrates. **1581–85** Yermak and his Cossacks took control of Siberian capital of Iskir (Tobolsk). **1587** Cossacks moved north down the Ob River and along the Arctic coast. **1598** Anthony and Robert Sherley traveled to Qazvin in Persia. **1601** Lancaster commanded first East India Company voyage to establish an English trading post on Java. **1601** Ricci established Jesuit mission in Peking. **1603–7** Goes became first European since Marco Polo to reach China from west.		**1595–96** Raleigh searched unsuccessfully for gold along the Orinoco River.	**1576–78** Frobisher made three voyages to Baffin Island. **1584** Raleigh unsuccessfully tried to establish colony of Virginia. **1596–1605** Oñate established colony in New Mexico. **1602–3** Vizcaíno mapped west coast to about 42°N. **1604–7** Champlain mapped coast from Cape Breton Island to Cape Cod. **1608** John Smith explored Chesapeake Bay in Virginia. **1608** Champlain traveled up St Lawrence and Richelieu rivers to Lake Champlain. **1609** Hudson explored Hudson River. **1611** Brûlé was the first Frenchman to visit Lake Huron, and then Lake Superior (1621).
	1613 Paez saw Lake Tana, the source of the Blue Nile in Ethiopia.	**1616** Le Maire and Schouten sailed through Le Maire Strait and named Cape Horn. **1617** Raleigh made last voyage to Guyana in search of El Dorado.	**1616** Baffin and Bylot discovered Smith, Jones, and Lancaster Sounds.
1626 Andrade traveled into western Tibet, establishing a mission at Tsaparang. **1631** Azevedo journeyed from Tsaparang to Leh and opened Rotang Pass. **1639** Cossacks reached Sea of Okhotsk. **1643–46** Poyarkov explored the Amur River. **1648** Dezhnev sailed around the Chukchi Peninsula, through what was to become the Bering Strait.	**1628** Lobo followed the Blue Nile from Lake Tana to the Tissiat Falls.		**1634–35** Nicollet traveled from Lake Huron to Lake Michigan.

Pacific/Australia/New Zealand	Arctic	Antarctic	Oceanography
1513 First European sighting of the Pacific, by Balboa in Panama. **1519–21** Magellan discovered strait into the Pacific, north of Tierra del Fuego, pioneering a westward route to the East Indies.			
	1553 Willoughby and Chancellor searched for the Northeast Passage. **1556** Borough reached the Kara Sea.		
1565 Urdaneta made first European west–east crossing of the Pacific. **1567–69** Mendaña discovered Solomons. **1577–80** Drake completed the first British circumnavigation.	**1576–78** Frobisher made three voyages to Baffin Island.		
1595–96 Mendaña and Quiros discovered the Marquesas Islands.	**1585–87** Davis made three attempts to find a Northwest Passage. Reached 72°N. **1596–97** Barents and his crew were first Europeans to spend winter in Arctic.		
1605–6 Torres sailed between New Guinea and Australia's Cape York peninsula, proving New Guinea to be an island.			
1615–17 Le Maire and Schouten pioneered new route into Pacific south of Cape Horn.	**1610** Hudson entered Hudson Bay in search of Northwest Passage. **1615** Bylot explored northern Hudson Bay. **1616** Baffin and Bylot searched northern Baffin Bay and discovered Smith, Jones, and Lancaster Sounds.		
1642 Tasman sailed to Van Diemen's Land (Tasmania) and anchored off New Zealand's South Island.			

1651 – 1859

Asia	Africa	Central and South America	North America
1661 Grueber and Orville reached Lhasa from China, and then crossed into Nepal.			**1659–60** Groseilliers and Radisson explored Lake Michigan and Lake Superior. **1665–85** Father Allouez traveled in the Great Lakes region as a missionary. **1670** Lederer reached the Blue Ridge Mountains. **1673** Jolliet and Marquette made the first journey down the Mississippi to the Arkansas River and back to Lake Michigan. **1679–82** La Salle sailed down the Mississippi to the Gulf of Mexico. Took possession of Louisiana for France.
1714–16 Desideri traversed Tibet from Ladakh to Lhasa. **1728** Bering sailed through strait between Asia and America without sighting land. **1733–42** Great Northern Expedition mapped northern coast of Siberia, from Archangel to Kolyma River. **1741** Bering confirmed Asia and North America to be separate landmasses.		**1686** Jesuit Father Fritz began exploration of length of Amazon River. **1735–53** La Condamine led French Equatorial Expedition and followed whole course of Amazon. **1740–44** Anson sailed round South America, during his circumnavigation of the world. **1765** Byron journeyed to the Falkland Islands and parts of Tierra del Fuego.	**1738–43** La Vérendrye and his sons traveled between Lake Superior and Lake Winnipeg. **1748** Walker of Virginia rediscovered Cumberland Gap in the Appalachians.
1761–67 Niebuhr took part in one of the first scientific expeditions to explore Arabia. **1774** Bogle crossed the Brahmaputra to Shigatse and Tasilhumpo.	**1770** Bruce followed Blue Nile from its source to the sea at Cairo.		**1770–72** Hearne followed the Coppermine River to the Arctic Ocean. **1774** Pérez surveyed coast north of California. **1775** Hezeta discovered mouth of the Columbia River on west coast. **1775** Bodega y Quadra landed on Alaskan coast. **1778** Cook attempted to find Northwest Passage from Pacific coast of Alaska. **1789** Mackenzie followed the Mackenzie River to the Arctic Ocean. **1792–95** Vancouver charted coastline north of Vancouver Island. **1792–93** Mackenzie completed first crossing of North America.
	1777–79 Gordon discovered the Orange River and explored South African coast. **1790** Houghton traveled from Gambia River eastward to the Niger River. **1796** Park led an expedition to the Niger River.	**1789–94** Malaspina charted coast of South America.	
1802 Great Trigonometrical Survey of India established to map the subcontinent including mountains to the north.	**1805** Park led an expedition from Timbuktu down the Niger River.	**1799–1803** Humboldt traveled in the northern Andes and upper Amazon. **1803** Humboldt traveled in Mexico, crossing from Acapulco to Veracruz.	**1804–6** Lewis and Clark's transcontinental journey crossed the Rockies. **1806–7** Pike discovered Pikes Peak. **1807–11** Thompson completed his outstanding surveys of western America by following the length of the Columbia River.
1811 Manning became the first Englishman to enter Lhasa. **1812** Moorcroft and Hearsey crossed the Himalayas to explore the interior of Tibet. **1812–15** Burckhardt's journey around the Red Sea included visit to Petra and Mecca. **1819** Sadlier made first European east–west crossing of Arabia from Hasa to Medina. **1819–25** Moorcroft traveled through the Himalayas and central Asia to Bukhara.	**1812–17** Burckhardt traveled extensively in northeast Africa. **1816** Tuckey ascended the Congo (Zaire) River.	**1812–24** Waterton, a naturalist, wandered in the Guianas. **1817–20** Spix, a zoologist, and Martius, a botanist, traveled in Brazil.	**1817–20** Long surveyed area between Platte and Canadian rivers. **1824** Bridger discovered Great Salt Lake.
1829 Humboldt crossed Altai Mountains. **1838** Wood reached source of the Oxus.	**1825–27** Clapperton and Lander crossed Niger to Kano and Sokoto. **1825–26** Laing reached Timbuktu. **1827–28** Caillié became the first European to visit Timbuktu and survive to tell the tale. **1830** Richard and John Lander sailed down the Niger from Bussa, mapping its course.	**1831–36** Fitzroy in the *Beagle*, with Darwin as naturalist, charted South American coast.	**1826–27** Smith reached California overland via Great Salt Lake. **1833–34** Back traveled down Great Fish River.
1844–46 Huc and Gabet reached Lhasa from Peking.			**1842** Frémont's reconnaissance of Oregon Trail helped to establish US claims to Oregon.
1848 Wallin penetrated the Nejd from Wadi Sihan to Hail, Tabuk, and Tayma. **1851** Semenov explored Tien Shan. **1854–62** Naturalist Wallace traveled in the Malay (Indonesian) Archipelago. **1850s** Schlagintweit brothers became first Europeans to cross Kunlun Range between Tibet and Xinjiang.	**1848–49** Rebmann and Krapf saw Mount Kilimanjaro and Mount Kenya. **1849** Livingstone and Oswell crossed the Kalahari Desert to Lake Ngami. **1850–52** Galton and Andersson explored southwestern Africa. **1850–55** Barth explored the Sahara. **1853–56** Livingstone made first west–east crossing of Africa, via the Zambezi River. **1857–58** Burton and Speke discovered Lake Tanganyika and Lake Victoria. **1858–63** Livingstone attempted to navigate the Zambezi River. **1859–61** Duveyrier explored the Sahara.	**1848** Wallace and Bates, naturalists, traveled up the Amazon to Manaus. Wallace went on up the Negro and across to the Orinoco.	

Pacific/Australia/New Zealand	Arctic	Antarctic	Oceanography
			1662 In its *Directions for Seamen bound for Voyages* the Royal Society recommended certain scientific instruments. **1667** Hooke invented a depth sounder. **1671** Boyle advocated the systematic exploration of the oceans.
1721–23 Roggeveen searched for great Southern Continent. Discovered Easter Island.	**1728** Bering sailed through strait between America and Asia.		**1706–8** Marsigli made study of Mediterranean coast of France, the results of which were later published in *Histoire Physique de la Mer*, the first oceanographic treatise.
1741 Bering and Chirikov explored North Pacific. **1766** Wallis discovered Tahiti. **1767–69** Carteret discovered Pitcairn Island. **1767** Bougainville became the first Frenchman to sail around the world. **1769–71** Cook circumnavigated New Zealand and charted much of its coastline. Claimed New South Wales for Britain. **1772–75** Cook explored southern Pacific. **1778** Cook landed on Hawaii. **1785–88** La Pérouse tried to relocate the Solomon Islands. **1788** First fleet arrived in Botany Bay, Australia.	**1741** Bering crossed Bering Strait to Alaska. **1771–72** Hearne descended Coppermine River to Arctic Ocean. **1778** Cook searched for the Northwest Passage, surveying the Pacific coast of North America. **1789** Mackenzie descended Mackenzie River to Arctic Ocean.	**1773–75** Cook became the first European to cross the Antarctic Circle and circumnavigate the continent. Discovered South Georgia.	**1775** Franklin used a thermometer to locate and chart the Gulf Stream. **1780** Six invented thermometer for use under water.
1814–37 Marsden made many journeys into the interior of New Zealand. **1817–18** Oxley investigated Macquarie River, New South Wales. **1824** Hume traveled from Sydney to Melbourne. **1827** Dumont d'Urville continued charting of New Zealand coast. **1828–29** Sturt reached Darling River. **1830** Sturt and Macley descended Murrumbidgee and Murray rivers to the coast. **1837–39** Grey explored northwest coast of Western Australia. **1839–41** Eyre traveled along southern coast of Australia from Adelaide to Albany. **1844–45** Leichhardt traveled from Moreton Bay (Brisbane) to near Darwin. **1844–45** Sturt and Stuart explored interior of Australia. **1846–48** Heaphy, Brunner, and Ekehu explored western coast of South Island, NZ. **1847** Colenso reached Lake Taupo from Napier, North Island, NZ.	**1806** Scoresby and his son reached latitude of 81° off east coast of Greenland. **1818** Ross entered Lancaster Sound and mistakenly reported it blocked by mountains. **1819–20** Parry sailed through Lancaster Sound. **1819–22** Franklin explored northern coastline of America, traveling overland from Great Slave Lake. **1829–33** John Ross explored Prince Regent Inlet. James Clark Ross reached the Magnetic North Pole. **1845–48** Franklin and 137 crew members died searching for Northwest Passage. **1848–59** Forty expeditions despatched in search for Franklin and his men. **1850–53** McClure discovered possible route of Northwest Passage but was unable to sail through. **1857–59** McClintock found remains of Franklin's expedition on King William Island, and also discovered possible route through Northwest Passage.	**1819–21** Bellingshausen crossed the Antarctic Circle and sighted Antarctica. **1820** Bransfield discovered northwest Graham Land. **1821–22** Powell and Palmer discovered and charted the South Orkneys. **1823** Weddell crossed Antarctic Circle, sailed in Weddell Sea and reached 74°15'S. **1830–32** Biscoe circumnavigated Antarctica. **1840** Dumont d'Urville claimed Adélie Land for France. **1838–42** Wilkes led US South Seas Surveying and Exploring Expedition. **1839–45** Ross's three Antarctic voyages got further south than any previous expedition. **1844–45** Scientific studies by Moore led to important magnetic observations.	**1813** Scoresby Jnr attempted to take deep-sea temperature readings. **1815–18** Russian ship *Rurick* took soundings in deep water during world voyage. **1818** Ross took salinity measurements during search for the Northwest Passage. **1831–36** Darwin, in *Beagle*, studied structure of islands and the origins of coral reefs. **1837–42** Dumont d'Urville, in *Astrolabe*, took deep-sea temperature readings. **1838–42** Wilkes led US South Seas Surveying and Exploring Expedition. **1840** Divers used Siebe's hard-hat suits and pumped air. **1854–55** Maury published first bathymetrical charts of the North Atlantic and his *Physical Geography of the Sea*. **1856–57** Berryman and Dayman surveyed route of transatlantic telegraph cable.

Asia	Africa	Central and South America	North America
1862 Palgrave made the first European west–east crossing of the Arabian peninsula.	**1860** Speke and Grant reached Lake Victoria and discovered its outlet, the Ripon Falls.		
1864–67 Nain Singh plotted the exact position of Lhasa.	**1863** Tinné traveled down the Nile and penetrated the Bahr el Ghazal.		
	1864 Baker discovered Lake Albert.		
1866–67 French Mekong River expedition attempted to find navigable route to China.	**1865–67** Rohlfs crossed the Sahara from the Mediterranean to the Gulf of Guinea.		
1868 Shaw crossed the Aksai Chin. Became first Englishman to enter Yarkand.	**1867–73** Livingstone explored for sources of the Nile around Lake Tanganyika and the headwaters of the Congo (Zaire) River.		
1868–70 Hayward explored valleys between the Kunlun and Karakoram mountains.	**1869–71** Schweinfurth studied Bahr el Ghazal and Nile–Congo (Zaire) divide.		
1870–85 Przhevalsky made four attempts to enter Tibet and surveyed mountains to the north.	**1869–74** Nachtigal established the route between the Nile and Lake Chad.		
1872 Elias made solo crossing of the Gobi Desert and Mongolia.	**1873–75** Cameron crossed Africa from east to west.		
	1874–77 Stanley crossed Africa east–west, descending Congo (Zaire) River.		
	1874 Rohlfs and Schweinfurth explored Libyan Desert.		
1878–82 Kishen Singh sent to Tibet to survey the route to Chinese Turkestan. Reached the western end of the Gobi Desert.	**1878** Rohlfs led scientific exploration of the Libyan Desert, reaching the Oases of Kufru. 1	**1879** Whymper climbed in the Ecuadorean Andes, reaching summits of Chimborazo and Cotopaxi mountains.	
1878–79 Wilfred and Anne Blunt traveled through the Middle East.	**1878–80** Thomson explored unknown land between Lake Nyasa and Lake Tanganyika.		
1880 Kintup followed the Tsangpo to establish link with the Brahmaputra.	**1882–83** Thomson made geological survey of the Rift Valley.		
	1883 Foucauld explored southern Morocco.		
1885–86 Elias crossed the Pamirs.	**1887–89** Stanley led Emin Pasha Relief Expedition.		
1887–91 Younghusband crossed the Gobi Desert, pioneering a new route from Peking to Kashgar via the Muztag Pass.	**1887–90** Binger explored region contained in the great bend of the Niger River.		
1893–97 Hedin explored the Takla Makan Desert, unearthing buried cities along the old Silk Route.	**1893–95** Mary Kingsley made zoological and anthropological studies in West Africa.		
1897–1927 Stein carried out archeological investigations in the Takla Makan Desert and central Asia.	**1899** Mackinder made first ascent of Mount Kenya.		
1906–8 Hedin explored southern Tibet around Lake Manasarowar.			
		1908–11 Bingham, an archeologist, searched for lost Inca cities, and discovered Machu Picchu and Espíritu Pampa.	
1918 Philby crossed from central Arabia to the northern part of the "Empty Quarter."			
		1925 Fawcett and two companions disappeared in Amazon jungle.	
1930 Thomas crossed the "Empty Quarter" from south to north.			
1946–48 Thesiger made double crossing of the "Empty Quarter."			
1953 First ascent of Everest made by Hillary and Tenzing Norgay.		**1950** Snow followed Amazon from supposed source to sea.	

Pacific/Australia/New Zealand	Arctic	Antarctic	Oceanography
1860 Burke and Wills almost crossed Australia from Melbourne to the north coast. **1860–62** Stuart crossed Australia from Adelaide via Alice Springs to Darwin. **1863** Barrington explored Southern Alps, South Island, NZ.			**1867** Diving suit developed based on pressure-regulating valve devised by Rouquayrol and Denayrouze. **1868–70** HMS *Lightning* and HMS *Porcupine* dredged in North Atlantic.
	1875–76 British Arctic Expedition under Nares reached 83°N. **1878–79** Nordenskjöld successfully navigated Northeast Passage. **1888** Nansen crossed south Greenland from east to west.	**1872–76** HMS *Challenger* became the first steam vessel to cross the Antarctic Circle as part of her circumnavigation of the world.	**1872–76** HMS *Challenger* expedition under Nares covered 68,890 miles (110,870 km). **1875–1915** Prince Albert I of Monaco voyaged in his yacht, collecting marine specimens and taking soundings. **1889** Haeckel's Plankton Expedition in the Atlantic looked at comparative distribution of this key organism.
1885–96 Douglas recorded the chief ranges and glaciers of the Southern Alps in New Zealand.			
	1891–1909 Peary's six Greenland expeditions delimited its northern extent. **1893–96** Nansen got to within 230 miles (370 km) of Pole on foot. **1897** Andrée disappeared trying to fly a hot-air balloon to the North Pole.	**1892–94** Norwegian whaler Larsen penetrated Weddell Sea. **1894** Norwegian expedition landed on Cape Adare, the first on Victoria Land. **1897–99** Gerlache de Goméry's *Belgica* trapped in the ice for 12 months. **1898** Borchgrevink established the first winter camp on Antarctica at Cape Adare.	**1893–95** Nansen led *Fram* expedition to determine currents beneath Arctic pack-ice.
	1903–6 Amundsen in *Gjøa* became first to navigate the Northwest Passage **1906–18** Stefansson lived with and studied the Canadian Inuit of northern Canada. **1909** Peary reached the North Pole on April 6.	**1901–3** Drygalski discovered extinct volcano, Gaussberg, on Wilhelm II Land. **1901–4** Scott led British National Antarctic Expedition. Shackleton attempted to reach the South Pole but turned back at 82°17′S. **1901–4** Nordenskjöld and Larsen traveled by sledge along Larsen Ice Shelf to 66°S. **1907–9** Shackleton's expedition came to within 100 miles (160 km) of the South Pole. Mawson reached the Magnetic South Pole. **1908–10** Charcot charted Graham Land and nearby islands. **1910–12** Amundsen's expedition reached the South Pole on December 14, 1911. **1910–12** Scott's expedition reached the South Pole on January 17, 1912. **1911–12** Filchner discovered Luitpold Coast and Filchner Ice Shelf. **1911–14** Mawson led Australasian Antarctic Expedition. **1911–12** Japanese party sledged to 80°S. **1916** Shackleton led British Imperial Trans-Antarctic Expedition.	**1902** International Commission for the Exploration of the Sea (ICES) established fishery research in the Atlantic and Baltic. **1903** Prince Albert I of Monaco published his 24-sheet *General Bathymetric Chart of the Oceans*, based on 18,400 soundings.
	1926 Nobile, Ellsworth and Amundsen flew in a dirigible balloon over the North Pole. **1926** Byrd and Bennett flew over the North Pole.		**1925–27** *Discovery* voyages.
		1929 Byrd made the first flight over the South Pole on November 29. **1929–31** Mawson led joint British-Australian-New Zealand Expedition. **1933–35** Byrd established a major base on the Ross Ice Shelf. **1935** Ellsworth flew across Antarctica.	**1930** Beebe's two-man bathysphere reached a depth of 3031 feet (924 meters). **1933–34** *Mahabiss* used primitive echo-sounder in Red Sea and Indian Ocean.
			1943 Cousteau and Gagnan invented the aqualung.

1955 – 2007

Arctic and Antarctic	Oceanography	Space
1955–58 Fuchs and Hillary led British Commonwealth Trans-Antarctic Expedition.	**1958** US nuclear submarine *Nautilus* took sonic readings beneath the North Pole. **1960** Piccard and Walsh in USS *Trieste* reached 35,840 feet (10,924 meters).	**1957** First artificial satellite, Sputnik I, launched by USSR on October 4. **1958** First successful US artificial satellite, Explorer, launched. Its instruments detected Earth's Van Allen belts. **1959** First successful lunar probes, Luna 2 and Luna 3, launched by USSR. Images transmitted to Earth showing 70 percent of the far side of the Moon for the first time. **1961** Yuri Gagarin of USSR became first man to orbit Earth, in Vostok 1. **1962** John Glenn became first American to orbit the Earth. **1962** First successful planetary probe, Mariner 2, sent to Venus by USA.
1968–69 British Trans-Arctic Expedition crossed from Alaska to Svalbard.		**1964** US probe, Ranger 7, obtained first close-range pictures of the Moon. **1965** First successful Mars probe, USA's Mariner 4, provided close-range pictures that altered all existing ideas about Mars. **1966** An automatic probe, USSR's Luna 9, made first soft landing on the Moon, while Luna 10 became first lunar orbiter. Shortly followed by more sophisticated US Surveyor, which sent back high-quality, close-range pictures of the Moon's surface. **1967** First soft landing of an unmanned probe on Venus made by USSR's Venera 7. **1968** First manned flight around the Moon made by Americans Borman, Lovell, and Anders, in Apollo 8. **1969** First manned landing on the Moon made by Americans Armstrong and Aldrin, in Apollo 11. **1969** Improved pictures of Mars sent by US probes Mariners 6 and 7. **1970** Soviet Venera 7 capsule reached surface of Venus to confirm earlier findings on temperature (797°F/475°C) and establish that atmospheric pressure over 90 times that of Earth. **1971** First capsule landed on Mars from Soviet capsule Mars 2, but contact then lost. **1971** Mariner 9 put into orbit around Mars; sent back thousands of pictures until mid-1972.
	1972–75 Manned submersibles used to investigate Mid-Atlantic Ridge.	**1972** Apollo program ended with the Apollo 17 mission. **1973** First successful probe to Jupiter, USA's Pioneer 10, sent back information on planet from close range. **1973–74** Three successive crews manned US space station Skylab. **1974** First pictures of Venus from close range taken by USA's Mariner 10. **1974** Mariner 10 became first probe to reach Jupiter, and made three flybys of the planet. **1974** Second successful Jupiter probe, Pioneer 11, reached the planet. **1975** First pictures received from surface of Venus from Soviet probes Veneras 9 and 10. Venera motherships became first to orbit the planet. **1976** First successful landings on Mars made by US Vikings 1 and 2. Orbiter motherships provided spectacular imaging survey of planet.
1978 Uemara made solo journey to North Pole. **1981–82** Fiennes's Transglobe expedition circumnavigated the world via both Poles.		**1978** Several probes sent to Venus: Veneras 11 and 12 by USSR and two Pioneers by USA. Further information about the planet obtained, but no more pictures from the surface. **1979** Voyagers 1 and 2 passed close to Jupiter; active volcanoes discovered on Io, one of its four largest moons. **1980–81** Voyagers 1 and 2 flew by Saturn and sent pictures that changed image of planet. **1981** First flight of USA's Space Shuttle.
1986 Steger's expedition was first unsupported party to reach the North Pole since Peary.	**1985–86** Ballard explored the wreck of the *Titanic* in 12,500 feet (3810 meters) of water.	**1984–85** Probes to Halley's Comet launched by USSR, Japan, and Europe. **1986** Europe's Giotto flew through coma of Halley's Comet. **1986** Voyager 2 made flyby of Uranus. **1989** Galileo launched by USA toward Jupiter. **1989** Voyager 2 reached Neptune and its major satellite Triton. **1989** USA's Magellan probe and USSR's Veneras provided more data on Venus. **1990** Hubble Space Telescope launched. **1990** Magellan probe went into orbit around Venus. **1990** USA's Ulysees probe launched with long-term aim of flying over the Sun's poles. **1991** Galileo passed close by asteroid Gaspra on way to Jupiter. **1993** First servicing mission made to Hubble Space Telescope.
	1995 Autonomous Benthic Explorer (ABE), developed by Woods Hole Oceanographic Institution, tested in deep ocean for first time. Used to measure extent of lava flows on ocean floor in northwest Pacific.	**1995** Galileo probe reached Jupiter and became first spacecraft to orbit the planet. **1996** NEAR craft launched on mission to asteroid Eros. **1996** Details on Jupiter's satellites obtained from Galileo. Mars Global Surveyor launched. **1997** US Pathfinder probe landed on Mars. Mars Global Surveyor orbiter embarked on mission to return thousands of images of almost every part of planet. **1997** Cassini mission to Saturn launched. **1998** Japan launched Mars probe, Nozomi. **1998** USA launched Lunar Prospector to conduct orbital chemical survey of Moon.
	1999 Deployment of Autonomous Benthic Explorer (ABE) in east Pacific leads to new discoveries of hypothermal vents.	**1999** Stardust probe to Comet Wild 2 launched. US Mars Climate Orbiter and Mars Polar Lander lost. **2001** NEAR Shoemaker asteroid orbiter landed on Eros. **2001** Borrelly's Comet passed by Deep Space 1. **2002** US orbiter Mars Odyssey began survey of planet. **2003** Europe's Mars Express and two US rovers (*Spirit* and *Opportunity*) launched. **2003** Smart 1 launched to Moon, using ion drive. **2003** Galileo probe deliberately launched into Jupiter. **2004** US rovers *Spirit* and *Opportunity* arrived on Mars. **2004** European Space Agency (ESA) orbited Smart 1 round Moon. **2004** USA launched Messenger on mission to orbit Mercury. **2005** Cassini became first spacecraft to orbit Saturn. European Huygens probe landed on atmospheric moon, Titan. **2005** European Space Agency (ESA) launched Venus Express, which went into orbit round planet five months later. **2005** USA's Deep Impact spacecraft sent projectile into comet Tempel 1. **2006** First Pluto explorer, New Horizons, launched by USA. **2007** Phoenix Mars Mission (first of NASA's Scout program) launched.

Index

PICTURE ACKNOWLEDGEMENTS

AKG LONDON 5, 10 top, 48, 88 top, 92, 97 bottom right, 99 top, 105 bottom left, 105 top left, 106 left, 106 right, 107, 150 right, 150 left, 151, /ALTE NATIONALGALERIE, BERLIN 106 right, /UNIVERSITETETS OLDSAKSAMLING, OSLO 22 top left; **BRYAN & CHERRY ALEXANDER** 23, 119, /PAUL DRUMMOND 216 bottom left; **ANCIENT ART AND ARCHITECTURE COLLECTION** 21; **HEATHER ANGEL** 2; **AUSTRALIAN GEOGRAPHIC** /PETER MEREDITH 214; **BIBLIOTHÈQUE NATIONALE DE FRANCE** 95 top; **BODLEIAN LIBRARY, OXFORD** (MS POCOCK 375, fols 3v-4r) 25 top; **BRIDGEMAN ART LIBRARY** /BIBLIOTHÈQUE NATIONALE DE FRANCE 6, 27 bottom, 30 bottom, /BONHAMS, LONDON 171 bottom, /BRITISH LIBRARY, LONDON 1, 67 top, 70 top, 102 top, 154, 174, /BRITISH MUSEUM, LONDON 128 left, /CHRISTIE'S, LONDON 77, /CROWN ESTATE/INSTITUTE OF DIRECTORS, LONDON 152 bottom, /DOWN HOUSE, DOWNE, KENT 110 left, /THE FINE ART SOCIETY, London 51 bottom, /MITCHELL LIBRARY, STATE LIBRARY OF NEW SOUTH WALES 168 top, /MUSEO E GALLERIE NAZIONALI DI CAPODIMONTE 15, 176, /MUSEO NACIONAL DE HISTORIA, MEXICO 97 top left, /NATIONAL LIBRARY OF AUSTRALIA, CANBERRA 155, 168 bottom, /NATIONAL MARITIME MUSEUM, LONDON 35 top, 158 top, /NATIONAL MUSEUM OF INDIA, NEW DELHI 44 top, /NOVOSTI 47, /PRIVATE COLLECTION 35 bottom, 123, /ROYAL COLLEGE OF SURGEONS, LONDON 111 bottom right, /ROYAL GEOGRAPHICAL SOCIETY, LONDON 8 /9, 59 top, 72 bottom, 73 top, 76 top right, 87, 164, 178 /179, /SCOTT POLAR RESEARCH INSTITUTE, CAMBRIDGE 192 top right, /VICTORIA & ALBERT MUSEUM 33 top left; **BRITISH LIBRARY** 24 /25, 29, 44 bottom (WD316), 54 bottom (WD350), 55 (WD349), 70 bottom, 101 top left, 131 bottom; **BRITISH MUSEUM,** 39, /DEPARTMENT OF ETHNOGRAPHY 101 bottom right; **TRUSTEES OF THE CHESTER BEATTY LIBRARY, DUBLIN** 41 left; **BRUCE COLEMAN LTD** /ERWIN AND PEGGY BAUER 142, /JEFF FOOTT PRODUCTIONS 125 bottom, /LUIZ CLAUDIO MARIGO 105 right, /DR NORMAN MYERS 83, /HANS REINHARD 141, /CARL ROESSLER 200, /NANCY SEFTON 200, NICHOLAS DE VORE 149 top, /GUNTER ZIESLER 212 top; **CORBIS** 118, 120 center left,

122 center, 128 right, 132 top right, 132 bottom, 135 top, 136 bottom, 140 top, 143 top left, 145 bottom right, 145 top right, 145 center right, 178 top, 218 left; **DORKA** 17 top, 22 top right, 25 bottom, 28, 30 top right, 30 top left, 111 top left, 111 top right, 120 bottom left, 120 right, 120 top left, 126 right, 126 left, 130, 132 top left, 136 top, 162 bottom; **MARY EVANS PICTURE LIBRARY** 19 right, 181 bottom, 208 right; **MIKE FARR** 219 bottom; **WERNER FORMAN ARCHIVE** 11; **FUJITA ART MUSEUM** 17 bottom; **RICHARD GREENHILL**/SEVERIN ARCHIVE 27 top; **ROBERT HARDING PICTURE LIBRARY** 10 bottom, 14, 38, 57 top, 63 top, 86 bottom, 88 /89, 89 top, 113 right, 115, 124, 149 bottom, 165 top, 208 left, 223 left, 223 right; **HARVARD COLLEGE LIBRARY** 202; **WALLY HERBERT** 182 top; **MICHAEL HOLFORD** 13 bottom, 40, 139 bottom, 143 bottom, 161 top, /COLLECTION OF MRS RIENITS 161 bottom; **HULTON DEUTSCH COLLECTION** 4, 41 right, 57 bottom, 67 bottom, 68, 69 top, 75 bottom left, 75 bottom right, 76 left, 78, 79 bottom, 79 top, 80, 81 top, 93 right, 112 left, 171 top, 178 center, 180 top, 205; **HUTCHISON LIBRARY** /SARAH ERRINGTON 85, /BRIAN MOSER 60 bottom; **IMPACT** /COLIN JONES 52 top; **DET KONGELIGE BIBLIOTHEK K BENHAVN** 99 bottom; **DAVID MALIN IMAGES**/AKIRA FUJII 231 bottom left; **MANSELL COLLECTION** 66, 183, 187; **MARGARET MEE AMAZON TRUST**/ROYAL BOTANIC GARDENS 114 bottom; **DR ANITA McCONNELL** 201 bottom right, 201 top right; **MIRROR SYNDICATION INTERNATIONAL** /COLLECTION BRITISH EMBASSY, MEXICO (COURTESY MISS M L A STRICKLAND). © BPCC/ALDUS 96; **JOHN MURRAY (PUBLISHERS) LTD** 53; **MUSEO DE AMERICA, MADRID** 95 bottom; **NASA** 222 top, 224 top, 224 bottom, 225 top, 226 top, 227 bottom, 227 center right, 230 bottom; **NASA**/ESA/UNIVERSITY OF ARIZONA 229 center right; **NASA**/GODDARD SPACE FLIGHT CENTER 210; **NASA**/HUBBLE HERITAGE TEAM (Space Telescope Science Institute /Association of Universities for Research in Astronomy)/R G FRENCH (Wellesley College)/J CUZZI and J LISSAUER (NASA/Ames Research Center)/L DONES (Southwest Research Institute, Boulder, Colorado) 229 top left; **NASA**/JET PROPULSION LIBRARY 226 bottom, 227 top left, 227 center right, 228 top left, 228 bottom left, 228 bottom right, 229 top right, 229 bottom right, 230 top left; **NASA**/JET PROPULSION LIBRARY/CALTECH 229 bottom

left, 231 bottom right; **NASA**/JOHNSON SPACE CENTER 225 center, 225 bottom **NATURAL HISTORY MUSEUM, LONDON** 63 bottom, 110 top right, 110 bottom right; **NATIONAL ARCHIVES OF CANADA** 198 /199; **NATIONAL GALLERY OF ART** /PAUL MELLON COLLECTION, © 1995 BOARD OF TRUSTEES 135 bottom; **NATIONAL LIBRARY OF AUSTRALIA** 166, /REX NAN KIVELL COLLECTION 157, 162 top; **NATIONAL MARITIME MUSEUM** 49 top, 100, 158 bottom, 159 left; **NATIONAL PORTRAIT GALLERY** 72 top, 101 top right; **NATIONAL TRUST PHOTOGRAPHIC LIBRARY** /JOHN HAMMOND 43; **PETER NEWARK'S AMERICAN PICTURES** 125 top, 127 bottom, 140 bottom, 145 top left; **JOHN NOBLE**/WILDERNESS PHOTOGRAPHY 216 top, 216 bottom right; **NOVOSTI (LONDON)** 46, 49 bottom; **POPPERFOTO** 188 bottom; **REED INTERNATIONAL BOOKS LTD** 19 left, 33 top right, 69 bottom, 73 right, 76 bottom right, 82, 84 top, 104, 112 right, 113 left, 129 top, 165 bottom, 170, 189, 192 top right, 193, 201 bottom center right, 206 right; **ROGER-VIOLLET /N D ROGER-VIOLLET** 188 top; **ROYAL BOTANIC GARDENS** 86 top; **ROYAL GEOGRAPHICAL SOCIETY PICTURE LIBRARY** 18, 33 bottom, 51 top, 52, 54 top, 59 center, 59 bottom, 60 top, 71, 75 top, 84 bottom, 89 bottom, 97 top right, 108, 114 top, 127 top, 139 bottom left, 139 top right, 175 bottom, 175 top, 180 bottom, 181 top, 182 /183, 186 /187, 186, 194 top left, 194 top right, 195, 197 center, 197 top, 197 bottom, 201 left, 206 top, 207, 215 bottom, 215 top left, 215 top right, 221 bottom, 221 right; **SCIENCE PHOTO LIBRARY** 203 right, 204, /INSTITUTE OF OCEANOGRAPHIC SCIENCES 218 right; **SCIENCE & SOCIETY PICTURE LIBRARY, SCIENCE MUSEUM** 93 left, 203 left; **SCOTT POLAR RESEARCH INSTITUTE** 178 bottom, 190, 191 bottom, 191 top, 192 bottom, 194 bottom, 196; **DOUG SCOTT** 220 /221; **GEOFF SOMERS /P BREI EHAGEN** 217; **SOUTH AMERICAN PICTURES** /TONY MORRISON 102 bottom, 103; **STILL PICTURES** /KLAUS ANDREWS 222 bottom, /NIGEL DICKINSON 212 bottom; **TRIP** /HELENE ROGERS 13 top, /ERIC SMITH 167; **UNIVERSITY OF WASHINGTON** 213; **UNIVERSITETETS OLDSAKSAMLING OSLO** 22 bottom; **US NAVY** 209 bottom, 209 top; **BRADFORD WASHBURN, BOSTON MUSEUM OF SCIENCE** 220 left; **THE TRUSTEE OF THE WELLCOME TRUST** 81 bottom; **WHITBY MUSEUM** 175 center.